AMERICANS FROM SWEDEN

When William Penn landed at New Castle, Delaware, in 1682, he found a fully organized community that was almost entirely Swedish. It had farmhouses, roads, mills, churches, schools and a local government, the work of an industrious people whose descendants have had much to do with the building of America.

Americans from Sweden is the first book to tell in one volume the complete story of the Swedes in America. In graphic language it examines why, when and how they settled here, their geographical distribution, their special talents, their sufferings and adventures as settlers, and the general importance of their contribution to our country.

The book is divided into four sections which take up in turn a historical summary, an account of the religious disputes which loomed so large in the early days of Swedish immigration, an analysis of professional achievement and social organization, and finally an evaluation of their characteristics as individuals. All this is carefully, though unobtrusively, documented.

AMERICANS FROM SWEDEN

Adolph B. Benson

Naboth Hedin

The Peoples of America Series

EDITED BY
LOUIS ADAMIC

FOREWORD BY CARL SANDBURG

J. B. LIPPINCOTT COMPANY
Philadelphia 1950 *New York*

To the memory of
Edith Hedin
(*1922–1947*)
Beloved daughter and pupil

FOREWORD

A cyclopedia brimming with facts, a compendium related in every page and paragraph to Americans from a little country isolated on a peninsula of northern Europe, information organized in Chapters—this we have in Adolph B. Benson's and Naboth Hedin's book. Yet it is more than dry fact. It is a long story told by an American university professor and a great reporter, patient with their immensely assembled facts, spare in style, scrupulous as to accuracy, animated by the anxiety of the true historian. In their many years of duty, one as a teacher of Swedish to American youth and the other chief of the American Swedish News Exchange in New York, they naturally acquired a storehouse of knowledge regarding Swedes in America and how they came to be here. In their narrative and expository treatment of this knowledge, they have permitted the lights of enthusiasm and blood-kin understanding to operate.

Who were the First Comers from Sweden to America and why did they come and what were they? What were the later migrations and what underlay them? What are the military, naval and aviation records of the Americans from Sweden—how and when did they fight for the American flag and what the extent of their sacrifices? These we are told and it is a shining tale with many a saga. In religion, politics, literature, the fine arts, industry, invention, business, law, medicine we meet galleries and galaxies of names and what they stand for, from Hasselquist to Lawson, from Bendix to Bergman, with never a lack of Olsons, Johnsons and Petersons. The data of Swedish-blooded scientists, industrialists and inventors, would have made a book by itself—restless, inquiring spirits, in the forefront among the makers of what is progressively modern in modern life.

The closing chapter on what is distinctive and notable in Swedish character is the authors' personal commentary and analysis, written out of wide and intimate knowledge, mentioning the negative and accentuating the positive. The present writer would speak thanks to them in behalf of Swedes who will highly value their work and the many non-Swedish Americans who through this book will gain new insights and understandings of a breed tracing back to a little homeland that from its rocky peninsula in the north looks with troubled eyes on the continent to the south of it.

CARL SANDBURG

INTRODUCTION

Of the Scandinavian groups in the United States, the Swedish is the oldest and largest. Since 1638, when a colony called New Sweden was founded on the South River, later renamed the Delaware, the Swedes have helped populate and develop America. Though politically the colony was soon lost, first to the Dutch and then to the English, the Swedish population remained, and throughout the eighteenth century individual Swedes continued to settle both in New York and Philadelphia. Religious and intellectual contacts were also maintained. When William Penn landed at New Castle, Delaware, in 1682, he found a fully organized community that was almost entirely Swedish. It had farmhouses, roads, mills, churches, schools, and a local government. "He did found the city of Philadelphia and some other places," writes Dr. Amandus Johnson, chief historian of New Sweden, "but not the colony as such—he merely changed its name."

Before the middle of the nineteenth century a new current of Swedish settlers began to flow across the Atlantic. This time it was directed toward the undeveloped farmlands of the Middle West. Between the Civil War and the First World War over a million persons born in Sweden entered the United States and, with the exception of the deep South, outside of Texas, they gradually penetrated practically every part of the Union. In 1940, according to the United States Census, nearly half a million of them were still living and their children of the first generation numbered over 800,000. How many descendants there were of the earlier generations was not recorded, nor how many had some of the blood of the Swedish colonists.

Whether of the early stock or of the more recent immigration, the great majority of the Swedes came to America because they were poor, rather than because they were oppressed, either religiously or politically, or feared foreign domination. The religious discontent of the middle of the nineteenth century was only a contributory cause, and only in two instances, those of the Eric Janson cult and the pioneer Baptists, was legal action taken. Conversely, the latter case led to the establishment of complete religious liberty. During their first years most of the immigrants had to work as day laborers, farm hands or domestics, but as they acquired a rudiment of English, saved a little money, and acquired some manual skill or were educated for higher occupations, they became farmers, mechanics, businessmen, engineers, teachers, ministers, lawyers, doctors, and public officeholders. Some native-born Swedes have been elected legislators, state officials, and even governors. Their sons have been officers in the Army or Navy or Air Force, Congressmen, Senators, diplomats, and Cabinet members. To aviation, engineering, industrial management, education, journalism, literature, and the fine arts they have made outstanding contributions. Politically, there are no more loyal American citizens and to the national composite they have added an element of self-reliance, common sense and stability.

This inflow of Swedish immigrants has now almost entirely ceased. For years the Swedish quota has not been filled, and as long as sufficient employment is offered at home and the country remains free of foreign domination, Swedish emigration to the United States is not likely to resume on any considerable scale.

What made these self-reliant people leave their native soil in the first place? What had been their environment? What contributions, besides the purely physical, have they made to their new homeland? What is likely to be their place in the future amalgamation of American civilization? In 1920 an American historian, Samuel P. Orth, wrote that the Scandinavians had contributed "the rugged commonplace of American life." But isn't that true to some extent of all newcomers? Being unable to speak English when they first arrived, which was not true, for instance, of the Scotch or the Irish, the Swedes were more severely handicapped, but as they proved themselves to be competent and conscientious workers, they gradually earned the respect of their employers, fellow workers and neighbors. Few Swedes have stood in the American bread lines or idled on the W.P.A. payrolls. For their children they have tried to provide the best education within their reach.

To show what opportunities the American system had given an originally poor and uneducated immigrant group, the American Office of War Information produced during the Second World War a documentary film, entitled *Swedes in America*. It showed them at work in the war industries as well as on their farms or in their homes. It portrayed their religious and social life, their churches, clubhouses, colleges and museums. Ingrid Bergman's appearance in the film did not, of course, decrease its appeal. In fact, the film was so convincing about the blessings of American democracy that the British authorities bought a large number of prints to show in their own military camps and to civilians in their newly occupied territories. A more convincing picture could hardly have been made.

How this rise of the Swedes in America has come about, the authors of this volume have tried to describe as objectively as possible. The account cannot be exhaustive—only selective, interpretative, evaluative. References to other nationality groups have been made only in the spirit of friendly rivalry. Many hands and many minds built America. No conscious, minority group glorification has been permitted.

On the other hand the book cannot claim credit for much original research or discovery. Rather have the authors tried to digest the material already available, abundant though scattered. In the bibliography credit has been given to earlier publications, a majority of which are now out of print. In a sense the book is a continuation of *Swedes in America,* a symposium edited and partly written by them for the celebration of the New Sweden Tercentenary in 1938. That, too, is now sold out.

The full history of the Swedish element in the United States is yet to be written. The immigrant Swedes have left only meagre records, being, as a rule, too busy making their living or too poorly educated to write their own story. In the future their accomplishments are likely to stand out in clearer perspective. That they have made an integral contribution to modern America is already certain.

Berlin, Connecticut   A. B. B.
New York, New York   N. H.

ACKNOWLEDGMENTS

The writers feel especially indebted to the following historians: *Dr. Amandus Johnson,* formerly Assistant Professor at the University of Pennsylvania, Founder and Curator-Emeritus of the American Swedish Historical Museum at Philadelphia, who was the first to investigate and establish from original sources the history of the seventeenth-century Swedish colony, *New Sweden,* on the lower Delaware; *Dr. George M. Stephenson,* Professor of American History at the University of Minnesota, who has written a scholarly and readable study of the religious element in Swedish immigration; *Dr. Florence E. Janson,* Professor of Political Science at the Southern Wesleyan University, Macon, Georgia, who has analysed the economic motives back of the Swedish exodus; *Dr. John S. Lindberg,* one-time member of the staff of the League of Nations, who has stressed the causes of social unrest; *Ernest William Olson,* editor and journalist, who has written extensively on the early history of the Swedish settlers in the Middle West, especially in the State of Illinois; and *Nels Hokanson,* a businessman of Evanston, Illinois, who has spent much of his leisure time in original research for his book *Swedish Immigrants in Lincoln's Time,* with emphasis on their participation in the Civil War. The works of other writers have been listed under Bibliography.

Valuable personal assistance has been received from authorities in special fields who have read and suggested improvements in various chapters. Among these *The Rev. B. W. Selin,* editor of *Sändebudet* (*The Messenger*), has read the chapter on "The Methodists"; *Dr. C. G. Carlfelt,* Professor at the Augustana Theological Seminary, Rock Island, Illinois, the chapters on "The Lutherans," the Augustana, Gustavus Adolphus, and Bethany Colleges, and Luther Academy; *Dr. Evald Benjamin Lawson,* President of Upsala College, the information on that institution; *The Rev. C. Geo. Ericson,* business manager of *The Baptist Conference Press,* Chicago, the parts on "The Baptists" and Bethel College and Seminary; *The Rev. Theodore W. Anderson,* President of the Evangelical Mission Covenant Church of America, Chicago, the section on "The Mission Friends"; *The Rev. Algoth Ohlson,* former

President of North Park College, the part on that school; *Dr. Marshall W. S. Swan,* recently Curator of the American Swedish Historical Museum and now of the U.S. Department of State, the chapters on "Colonization and Trade" and "Early Intellectual Contacts"; *Mr. A. M. G. Swenson,* manager of the SMS Ranch, Stamford, Texas, the section on the first Swedes in Texas in the chapter on "The Early Pioneers"; *Mr. Lorimer Moe,* of the New York *Daily News,* the part on Jameston, New York, in the same chapter; and *Mr. Herman G. Nelson* of the *Morning Star,* Rockford, Illinois, has examined the chapter on "How the Swedes Settled in Illinois." *Dr. Nils G. Sahlin,* Curator of The Institute of Swedish Art, Science and Literature, Minneapolis, Minnesota, has read "The Mass Migration of the Swedes" and "Lawyers and Public Officials"; *Mr. Sigfrid Ek* of the Pratt & Whitney Company, East Hartford, Connecticut, has done research on the Swedish employees of that firm; and *Mrs. Hannah Nicholson Benson* of Berlin, Connecticut, has given substantial help in the preparation of the Index.

Finally, the authors wish to thank Mr. Carl Sandburg for writing the Foreword.

A.B.B.
N.H.

CONTENTS

AMERICANS FROM SWEDEN

PART ONE

HISTORICAL BACKGROUND

═══

I

COLONIZATION AND TRADE

When the Swedes first learned about the existence of America is not known. Being a seafaring people, they must have heard rumors, as Columbus had, of the discovery by Norwegian seafarers, about A.D. 1003, of land west of Greenland, which was so attractive that the Norsemen called it "Vinland (Wineland) the Good." But if so, no record has so far been found. Of the adventures by Swedish traders and marauders to the eastward, in Gårdarike, or "the realm of fortified places," as they then called Russia, their rune-stones have much to tell.

When Columbus discovered the West Indies in 1492, Sweden was ruled, at least nominally, by the same King as Denmark and Norway. In 1513 an ambitious, and able, but crafty and vindictive young monarch, Christian II, inherited the three thrones. His mother was a German princess, Christina of Saxony, and his early youth he had spent in Holland, then as now, a successful trading country. From 1502 until 1512 he had been Viceroy of Norway, residing in the west coast city of Bergen, one of the headquarters of the international business organization known as the Hanseatic League. There he had learned about shipping as well as trade. In 1514 he married Princess Isabella of Burgundy, a granddaughter of Ferdinand and Isabella of Spain, and through her and her relatives he must have heard of the wealth the Spanish Conquistadores were amassing in the New World. But though he drew up plans for similar exploitation to benefit Sweden as well as his other two kingdoms, nothing came of them. Instead, he became involved in a bloody feud with the Swedish nobles, who defeated and deposed him and elected instead one of their own young men, Gustaf Vasa, as King of Sweden. In Denmark, too, Christian gradually aroused so much opposition that he was exiled and, when he returned in 1531 to recover his throne, he was imprisoned and kept confined until his death twenty-eight years later.

But the idea of Scandinavian trade across the Atlantic did not die with him. The income of the Dutch and the English as well as the Portuguese and Spaniards in America did not pass unnoticed in the North. In 1616, or before the Pilgrims landed at Provincetown, the Danes had sent a trading expedition to the Hudson Bay district. (They had previously organized a similar, state-supported trading company in Iceland). Not unreasonably they had assumed that in North America the climate would be the same as in the corresponding latitudes of Europe, but as in this they were mistaken, the venture failed.

By the middle of the sixteenth century the Vasa dynasty had become established in Sweden and under its vigorous leadership the country began an era of expansion. Finland was already part of the Swedish realm, and south of it, at the expense of either Russia or Poland, the Vasa kings acquired one Baltic province after another. Such conquests cost money as well as men, and economically Sweden was then undeveloped. This being the case, the young King, Gustavus Adolphus, a grandson of the original Vasa, who had reached the throne in 1611, eyed with interest the revenues which other European countries, militarily no more powerful than his own, were reaping from foreign exploration and trade, especially in America.

Until then Swedish shipping as well as foreign trade had been pretty much limited to the Baltic. The country's west coast was still in the hands of Denmark, which also governed Norway. In 1613, after a successful bout with the former country, Sweden obtained an outlet to the west—but only against the payment of a large indemnity in minted silver. This outlet was guarded by a fortress, named Elfsborg, situated at the mouth of the Göta River, which drains the lakes of west-central Sweden. To obtain the required silver, practically every inhabitant was specially taxed. But once having obtained control of the fortress (now a relic), the King founded in 1619, a few miles further up the river, a new city which he called Göteborg (Gothenburg). Through it was to flow the main stream of Swedish emigration to America. It is today Sweden's principal seaport and western travel center.

To help lay out and develop the new city the King invited Dutch artisans and merchants. In Gothenburg, as their countrymen were doing about the same time in New Amsterdam, they laid out not only streets but also dug canals, some of which are still open. What the King wanted the Dutch experts to do, besides building up the new city, was to help develop Sweden's foreign trade. The country's most marketable product was then copper, obtained from the mine at Falun, the main source of Sweden's military revenue. In both England and Holland privately managed trading companies with state support had been organized. In 1619, or the year Gothenburg was founded, King Gustavus Adolphus signed a charter for a Swedish company which was to have a monopoly on the sale of Swedish copper in Europe.

Before it had had time to develop much business, there arrived in Sweden, in 1626, an experienced but disappointed Dutch promoter of such enterprises. His name was Willem Usselinx, and he had been the real founder, he said, of the Dutch West India Company, which was then doing such good business in America. Unjustly, he claimed, he had been forced out, and now he sought new employment. As Sweden was then a rising military power, he thought it could use his services. At his suggestion the copper export company was reorganized, and its area of operations enlarged so as to include not only Europe, but Asia, Africa, America, and Magellanica, or Australia. For short, it was to be called *Söderhafskompaniet,* or the South Seas Company.

One of the stated objectives of this company was to aid in the propagation of the Gospel in foreign lands, where the natives, according to a prospectus circulated by Usselinx, "have heretofore been living in abominable, heathenish idolatry and all manner of ungodliness." Such missionary work would give its activities an aura of Christian idealism, then regarded as a requisite for business prestige. Among the pious folk of Sweden it was also a good stock-selling point.

The success of the Spaniards in the exploitation of America was the fact most persistently dangled before prospective Swedish investors. "It is well-nigh incredible," said a stock prospectus, presumably prepared by Usselinx, "what immense treasures, wealth and profits have accrued for the past 130 years and are still accruing to the Spanish nation from Africa, Asia and America—so vast that the receipts from America alone amount annually to 30,000,000 Swedish riksdalers ($20,000,000) and for the most part it is clear gain, both for the king and for his subjects, comprising as it does, gold, silver, quicksilver, pearls, emeralds, amber, cochineal, indigo, skins, sugar, tobacco, all kinds of spices, gum and rare woods, not including some millions of ducats, which (besides other favors) the said king bestows annually upon his servants as wages; upon governors of provinces, bishops, prebendaries, presidents and lords of councils and many other offices, of which some are worth annually 5,000 or 6,000, 8,000 or 10,000 and several 100,000 riksdalers."

In this company not only the King, but his councillors, the higher military officers, and members of the upper nobility agreed to buy stock. The King himself helped promote sales. In his letters to local administrators and other subordinates he would add a word of advice to urge people to buy stock in the South Seas Company. To promote trade, shipping and colonization in America several other minor companies were formed at that time in Sweden, but in no instance, including that of the South Seas Company itself, did either trade or overseas shipping result.

The real reason for Sweden's inability to enter foreign trade or undertake colonization in America was, of course, the war situation in Europe. In 1618 the contest between the Catholic and Protestant states of Germany, which was to last thirty years, had broken out. Since at first the Protestant cause fared badly, and the Danes had failed in their effort to help, the Swedes decided to intervene and thus forestall an attack on their own country and prevent a restoration of the Catholic faith by force of arms. In 1630, with an army of only sixteen thousand men, or hardly more than a modern division, King Gustavus Adolphus landed in Germany; but by joining forces with the German Protestant princes, he assembled a respectable army and won in the fall of 1631 the important battle of Breitenfeld. This made him the leader of the Protestant cause. The German imperial crown itself seemed at times to be within his reach. Under such circumstances his interest in foreign trade and colonial enterprises in America naturally cooled off. On November 6, 1632, at the age of thirty-eight, he was killed in the battle of Lützen, but under the command of his generals the battle was won and the war went on.

As the heir to the throne was his infant daughter, Christina, his real successor was his friend and long-time Chancellor, Count Axel Oxenstierna, whom Cromwell once called "the great man of the Continent," and Cardinal Richelieu, "an inexhaustible source of well-matured counsel." To bring the war to a successful conclusion such a man was needed. But he, too, was constantly hampered by the lack of money with which to pay off the many mercenaries, including six Scotch regiments. As the war began to involve control of Europe as well as the fate of the Reformation, Catholic France gave the Swedes subsidies, or "lend-lease aid," but even that was not sufficient. Sweden was too poor to sustain a long war. In the meantime, such neutral powers as Holland and England, as well as Spain and Portugal, continued to derive ever richer revenue from their overseas colonies, especially those in America.

Then in 1634, or only two years after the Swedish King's death, another dismissed Dutch colonial promoter and administrator appeared in Stockholm looking for a chance to capitalize on his American experience. He was none other than Peter Minuit, the first Governor of New Amsterdam, who in 1626 had bought the entire Manhattan Island from the Indians for blankets, kettles, and trinkets worth sixty guilders, or twenty-four dollars. His ancestry was French-Walloon and Huguenot, hence his name, but he was born, about 1580, at Wesel in the Prussian Rhineland, and at an early age he had entered the Dutch colonial service. Now at fifty-four he had been discharged by the Dutch West India Company. His mistake had been to grant too liberal trading privileges at the lower end of Manhattan to the Dutch landowners further up the North, or Hudson River, the so-called "patroons." Such privileges the stockholders in Holland feared would interfere with their own business monopoly south of Wall Street.

In Sweden, Minuit knew Samuel Blommaert, a Dutch investor in American colonial enterprises, whom Count Oxenstierna had met in Holland and had brought to Stockholm to be his financial adviser. By him Minuit was introduced to Oxenstierna, the *de facto* head of the Swedish Government, and thus had a chance to present his plan for a Swedish trading colony, similar to New Amsterdam, on the South River, as the Delaware was then called. Such a colony, he felt sure, would bring rich profits from trade with the Indians. As Governor of New Amsterdam he had learned to know the opportunities on the South River as well as on the North. It was a plausible scheme, and being in need of revenue the Chancellor gave it his ear.

This time there was action. Several already organized trading companies, including the royally backed "South Seas," were consolidated and refinanced. New capital was subscribed not only by the Oxenstierna family, several members of which sat in the Government Council, but also by Count Per Brahe, representing another powerful family, Admiral Klas Fleming, head of the Swedish Navy, and Peter Spiring, a Dutch merchant and capitalist living in Sweden, who ultimately became a Swedish subject and diplomatic representative. Half the venture capital was subscribed in Holland by friends of Blommaert and Minuit as well as of Spiring, and in Holland Peter Minuit bought the goods to be traded to the Indians for beaver skins and tobacco.

In Sweden, two secondhand but refurbished ships were obtained, a merchant vessel, probably of the contemporary caravel type, called the *Kalmar Nyckel* (*Key to Kalmar,* the name of Sweden's most important stronghold on its southeast border) and the *Fogel Grip* (*Griffon*), a naval vessel, corresponding most closely to a modern light cruiser. It was provided by the Swedish Government as escort to the *Kalmar Nyckel* and had on board a prospective garrison of twenty-three Swedish soldiers under the command of Måns Nilsson Kling, probably a non-commissioned officer. As piracy was then common, both ships were armed. Half of the crews were Dutch and half Swedish. Since none of the Swedes had ever crossed the Atlantic, the navigators of both ships were Dutchmen. To take charge of the stores and the trading with the Indians, another Dutchman, named Hendrick Huygen, was appointed, while as *supercargo* or general manager, Peter Minuit himself went along.

The preparations took a long time and not until late in August 1637 did the two ships leave Stockholm, and then they spent another month sailing around the southern part of the Scandinavian peninsula to reach Gothenburg on the west coast. Final stores were there put on board and about November 20 the ships started to cross the Kattegat, the Skagerrak and next the North Sea, which was then as rough as it often is today. To repair damages sustained in a storm the two ships had to put in at the Dutch port of Texel. Just before New Year's, 1638, they finally left for the English Channel and then headed into the open Atlantic.

As was then customary, they followed the southern route, which brought them to the West Indies before they reached the American mainland. By the end of March 1638, they arrived safely in what is now called the Delaware Bay; and up the South or Delaware River they sailed until they found the mouth of a tributary, known to Minuit as Minquas Kill, which according to the instructions written out in Samuel Blommaert's own hand, was to be their first and preferred goal. Up this river, which in honor of their young Queen, they renamed the Christina (often misspelled Christiana), they proceeded about two miles, reaching what is today the waterfront of Wilmington, Delaware. Among the reeds along the west bank, they found a large, flat-topped boulder, projecting into the water, and there Minuit and his men went ashore.

Since 1938 the spot has been marked by a monument in black, Swedish granite, designed by the Swedish-born sculptor, Carl Milles, and presented as a gift from the school children of Sweden to the state of Delaware. From the trains of the Pennsylvania Railroad, which pass almost hourly between New York and Washington, the monument can be seen across the debris of a defunct ironworks and other water-front cultch. Its base, however, is surrounded by a trim little park guarded by the state night and day against vandals.

After exploring the vicinity to make sure no other white men had arrived during his absence, Peter Minuit made a trade with five Indian chiefs who soon appeared. In the cabin of the *Kalmar Nyckel* a contract was signed by which the Indians sold to Minuit "for value received in merchandise" the land on the west bank of the South River from Bombay Hook, or half-way down to its mouth, as far northward as its confluence with the Schuylkill River, where today sprawls the mighty city of Philadelphia. To the west, the only limit was "where the sun sets." In that direction, the Indians said, Minuit could take as much land as he wished. What the Europeans meant by ownership of land they understood, of course, only vaguely. They sold only what they themselves valued, namely, the right to pass over the land and to hunt and fish. To them land was like the sea. It had no limit and there was plenty of it for everybody.

In the deed, which the Indian chiefs signed with their marks, the buyer was designated as the Swedish Florida Company, the name of the Swedish-Dutch subsidiary of the South Seas Company, formed expressly for the American venture. It was described as being "under the protection of the Great Princess, Virgin, and Elected Queen of the Swedes, Goths and Wends," the formal title of Swedish sovereigns. The Virgin Princess was, of course, Christina, the only daughter of Gustavus Adolphus, then twelve years old. Once the deed was executed, the newcomers took formal possession by hoisting on a pole the Swedish coat of arms, firing salutes and improvising other simple ceremonies. The land they had bought they called New Sweden. Back of the "Rocks," on which they had landed, they built a little stronghold they called Fort Christina, in reality a stockade behind which they could defend themselves and their stores against wild animals as well as human enemies.

As the Dutchmen in the party began their trading with the Indians for return cargoes, the score or so of Swedish soldiers stood guard. When spring came they could see from the color of the grass and the budding leaves that the soil was fertile. With the aid of the crews of the two ships, they then dug up little patches of ground in which they planted the grains they had brought from Sweden, "two barrels of wheat and two of seed-corn," which was really barley. Indian corn or maize they had never seen, or at least did not know how to raise. About trading with the Indians, too, the Swedes knew next to nothing, but they did understand how to till the soil. The weather was warmer than in Sweden and the vegetation richer.

By June the *Kalmar Nyckel* was sufficiently stocked to return to Sweden. With it went Peter Minuit, but at the island of St. Christopher (St. Kitts) in the West Indies, he left the ship to visit the captain of a Dutch vessel. While he was on board a storm tore the Dutch ship from its moorings and blew it to sea. None of those on board was ever heard of again. This was the first serious loss to the new Swedish settlement on the Delaware. It spared Minuit, however, from showing his accounts to his sponsors in Holland and Sweden. Alas for rosy dreams of profit! The total expense of the first trip had been 46,000 florins and the furs could be sold for only 23,849.

But the *Griffon* was still to be heard from. During the early spring of 1638 it had made a trip to the English colony at Jamestown, Virginia, established thirty years earlier, to buy tobacco for a return cargo. But the English Governor refused to sell any because his sovereign claimed title to all of North America from Cape Fear in North Carolina to the Bay of Fundy in Nova Scotia, and to the west as far as the Pacific. The Swedes were therefore trespassers and not allowed to buy anything. The ship had no choice but to return to the Rocks at Fort Christina without merchandise.

Having failed at honest commerce it left the Rocks again in May 1638, "in search of Spanish treasure ships." "About this expedition" writes Amandus Johnson, chief historian of the New Sweden colony, "practically nothing is known," but Christopher Ward, in his book, *The Dutch and the Swedes on the Delaware* (p. 91), seems to take at its face value the declared intention to try a little buccaneering on the side, Spanish treasure ships being considered fair game. For its time, the *Griffon* was a fast ship and well armed. Whatever may have been its mission or adventures, it returned the next winter to the Rocks at Fort Christina, empty. It had on board, however, a Negro boy it had picked up somewhere.

The next spring, or late in April 1639, it left for Sweden, carrying fifteen hundred pelts and some Indian-grown tobacco. Relieved of its escort duties, the *Griffon* traveled fast. Early in June it was back in Sweden—an almost record trip. After that it returned to its naval routine and passed out of history. The *Kalmar Nyckel* had brought back only seven hundred skins; consequently, the balance of the Swedish Florida Company remained in the red.

The most valuable article brought back by the *Kalmar Nyckel* to Sweden was the title to the land. About the qualities of this land, the returning men were enthusiastic. The climate was salubrious, they said, rain abundant, the sunshine invigorating. The woods were full of game and the rivers full of both fish and oysters, some of the latter being over a foot in length. The seed they had planted had sprouted quickly and there was fine promise of a good crop.

The meaning of this the Swedes understood. The next time the *Kalmar Nyckel* set out it had on board, not more soldiers or Dutch traders, but farm hands, farm implements, horses, cattle, foodstuffs, and ammunition, as well as merchandise for barter with the natives. About the prospects of New Sweden as an agricultural community, Admiral Klas Fleming, in particular, had become optimistic. In Sweden he was a landowner as well as head of the Navy. To succeed Minuit as Governor, another Dutchman, already in the Swedish service, Peter Hollender Ridder, was appointed. He was instructed to buy more land from the Indians, which he did and on both sides of the South River. To the north, the Swedish domain was extended in 1640 along the west bank of the South River as far as the falls at Trenton where nearly a hundred and fifty years later George Washington was to make his historic crossing. The next year the southern boundary on the same side of the river was shifted a point below Cape Henlopen, now in the southern part of the State of Delaware. On the east side of the river, Ridder bought in 1641 the shore land from Narraticons Kill, now Raccoon Creek, in southwestern New Jersey, to Cape May at the mouth of the river.

The financial returns of the second round trip, which the *Kalmar Nyckel* made alone, were disappointing too, causing the Dutch stockholders to withdraw. This step the Swedish authorities "found to be expedient, as they are a hindrance," a self-confident dismissal of disappointed business partners. In the fall of 1641 the Dutch investors were paid off in full with eighteen thousand Swedish riksdalers. (How much they had invested in terms of the same currency is not known.) After that the enterprise became wholly Swedish, but as hopes of finding new private capital in Sweden were slim, the Government itself put in enough cash to make it the owner of one-sixth of the capital stock. The company then became a blend of private and public enterprise, examples of which are still to be found in Sweden. In 1641, not only farm workers but artisans, a tailor, a millwright and a blacksmith were sent over. In 1639, on the second voyage, the first clergyman, the Reverend Reorus Torkillus, the first Lutheran pastor in America, had already been on board the *Kalmar Nyckel*. In 1641 a second minister was added, another sign of permanency. His name was Pastor Christopher.

About the beauty of the land and its possibilities Governor Ridder too sent glowing reports. Clearly the American climate and atmosphere had a stimulating effect. In 1641 the *Kalmar Nyckel* was accompanied to America by another vessel, the *Charitas*. More horses, cattle, sheep and goats, as well as more farm tools were brought over and thirty-five additional colonists. That year two new settlements were founded, the first permanent habitations within the borders of present-day Pennsylvania. They were called Upland, now Chester, and Finland, now Marcus Hook, both on the Delaware River itself. Uppland, (spelled with two pp's) is a Swedish province north of Stockholm, and Finland was then a part of Sweden too.

To match the new capitalization, the operating company was once more reorganized, making the colony semi-official. As the next Governor, not a Dutchman but a Swede and a former army officer was appointed, Lieutenant Colonel Johan Björnsson Printz, a veteran of the Thirty Years' War and before that a soldier of fortune in various parts of Europe. Clearly, a new phase was to begin. Colonel Printz was the first definite personality to arrive in America from Sweden. In ability, vigor and picturesqueness he ranked with Peter Stuyvesant, who four years later was to take charge at New Amsterdam. That one should become so famous and the other be left so obscure is a curious twist of history. At fifty-one, Governor Printz was in the prime of his life when he arrived with his family in February 1643. He had a sharp glance, a commanding presence, and like most ex-officers of victorious armies, was inclined to be hot-tempered and pompous. But he was also efficient and full of energy. Nearly seven feet tall and weighing close to four hundred pounds, he was easily the first "Big Swede" in America. Aptly, as usual, the Indians called him "The Big Belly." In accordance with his military training he ruled with an iron hand.

Born in the wooded and stony province of Småland, in south-central Sweden, which later was to furnish more emigrants to the United States than any other, he was descended from a family of clergymen, and in his youth he, too, had studied theology, both in Sweden and at the German universities of Rostock and Greifswald. During a summer vacation spent with some fellow students in the southern German province of Swabia he had been abducted and forced to serve in an Italian regiment. After that he had spent several years as a mercenary, being enrolled successively in the Austrian and Brunswick armies, and then in a Danish regiment, commanded by a Count Rantzau, in the service of France. Militarily this gave him useful experience. In 1625 he had returned to Sweden in time to take part as a cavalry captain in a new war against Poland, and after that in the Thirty Years' War in Germany, during which he was appointed Lieutenant Colonel of the famous Västgöta cavalry regiment.

Suddenly in April 1640, he left his post and returned to Sweden under rather unusual circumstances. Placed in command of the besieged town of Chemnitz, he had judged his position so hopeless that after but a few days of resistance he had surrendered. Then, without reporting to his superiors, he had returned to Stockholm. This so enraged his commander-in-chief, General Johan Banér, another hot-tempered though brilliant officer, that he demanded Printz's arrest and court-martial. In 1641 Printz was arrested and tried, but was acquitted of the main charge, that of cowardice. For leaving Germany without permission, however, he was dismissed from the service. After only a year's retirement in his ancestral parish of Bottnaryd, in Småland, he was recalled to Stockholm, given noble rank and appointed Governor of New Sweden. This was his chance of rehabilitation.

With him in the two ships, *Fama* and the *Swan,* were not only his wife and daughter and two new clergymen, Johan Campanius and Israel Fluviander, but also a number of colonists who were virtually deportees. No professional or hardened criminals were ever sent from Sweden to America, but some of these men had been guilty of petty crimes, such as desertion, vagrancy, poaching, illegal timber cutting, adultery and failure to pay debts. One of the two culprits guilty of adultery had also illegally shot a moose. On board were, furthermore, a few Finns who had tried to clear land for farming in the forests of northern Sweden, but in so doing had followed the old Finnish custom of burning down stands of timber which to the Swedes seemed too valuable. They were, therefore, shipped out of the country as undesirables. In America they could cut down and burn as many trees as they pleased. It was these forest dwellers, whether Swedish or Finnish, and not the Puritans of New England, who were the first to build the famous log cabins in America.

About the fertility and beauty of his new domain Governor Printz, too, waxed eloquent. As a roving soldier he had seen the fairest lands of Europe and not merely the woodlands and stone-infested fields of his native Småland. "A remarkably beautiful country," he wrote to Count Per Brahe on April 12, 1643, when he had seen his first spring in America. "It has all the glories that any human being on earth can ever desire. . . . And this I wish to repeat," he went on, "that such a splendid country as this, endowed with all kinds of wonderful things, I have never seen. Nothing is wanting, except means, diligence and seriousness in the continuation of this work." He found the land well suited to agriculture and he was certain, he wrote, that "in time it would become one of the brightest jewels of the Swedish Crown."

Eagerly and in person he set about directing the development of the colony, as though it had been his private estate. First of all, he directed the reconstruction and reinforcement of Fort Christina, which always remained his principal depot, being near the Rocks, the natural landing place or pier at Wilmington. Between the villages of Upland (Chester) and Finland (Marcus Hook), which had been started by his predecessor, Governor Ridder, he picked a site for a country estate or "suburban" farm for himself which he called Printztorp. On the island of Tinicum further up the South River he decided to build his main home and headquarters which he called Printzhof. (The typical Swedish modesty was not one of his characteristics.) From this island, which has long since been joined to the western shore of the Delaware, he could watch the traffic on the main river, which was not possible from Fort Christina. Here he built a church for the Reverend Campanius, the first Swedish one in America, and to protect his new headquarters a fort which he called New Gothenburg (Nya Göteborg). His first "mansion" of two stories burned down in 1645, but the next one survived until early in the nineteenth century, when it suffered a similar fate. Of neither is there a picture extant. The site is now part of the lawn of the Corinthian Yacht Club and among the shrubbery the original foundation stones have been unearthed, including bricks for the bake ovens brought from Sweden.

Besides providing suitable quarters and protection for himself and his family, Governor Printz began the construction of a number of new villages, six blockhouses and three forts. To control the traffic and trade on the Schuylkill River, a tributary of the Delaware, he built in 1647 at their junction a fort he called New Korsholm. (This was thirty-five years before William Penn arrived to found Philadelphia.) When the Dutch answered with a new fort of their own, Beversreede, situated further up on the east bank of the Schuylkill, where third chapter of his *Knickerbocker's History of New York*.

The pious new name did not suffice to appease Governor Stuyvesant. This time his temper was really aroused, especially as the control of the whole Delaware region was at stake. He obtained reinforcements from Holland and the following summer he again sailed up the South River, this time with seven armed ships and a force of men, variously estimated at from three hundred to seven hundred, or several times the number of white inhabitants in New Sweden. On September 1, 1655, Fort Trinity once more became Fort Casimir. In the excitement, the Swedish commandant, Sven Skute, who previously had been in command of Fort Elfsborg across the river, forgot to stipulate where his men should go after capitulation. Consequently, once they had given up their arms, they were taken on board the Dutch ships as prisoners of war. By his men Skute was after that "regarded as of no more worth than a shoe rag," reports Peter Lindeström, the geographer, who was a fellow officer.

Next came the turn of Fort Christina at Wilmington to which Rising had restored the seat of government. Though considerable provisions, including five barrels of beer, had been taken into the fort, it was in no condition to resist. For several days Rising parleyed with Stuyvesant, using every tactic of delay he could think of. To the last he hoped reinforcements would come from Sweden. On September 15, however, he signed the capitulation papers, after which the Swedes and the Dutch ate a hearty dinner together and finished the beer. There had been no bloodshed, only some raiding of the Swedish farms along the river by Dutch soldiers.

Having gained control of Fort Christina, Governor Stuyvesant became at once suspiciously conciliatory. To Rising he offered the right to remain and help develop the colony under joint Swedish-Dutch jurisdiction. It was not so much English intervention or Swedish retaliation he feared, as an Indian insurrection. Ever since the Kieft massacre in Manhattan the natives had been resentful against the Dutch while they continued to consider the Swedes their friends. Even as he dickered with Rising, Stuyvesant had received news from New Amsterdam that the redskins were restless. A new rebellion might spread to the Delaware.

But Rising was proud and stiff-necked. His Government in Stockholm would avenge the Dutch aggression, he threatened. With his officers and soldiers he preferred, he said, to return to Sweden, which he did after a stopover in London. Official protests were lodged in they had had a small blockhouse since 1633, he built close to it another blockhouse on the same side of the river, all within the limits of present-day Philadelphia. At Kingsessing, now West Philadelphia, he founded another village and, to guard it, built a blockhouse near by which he called New Vasa. On Cobbs Creek near the subsequently built Blue Bell Tavern, he constructed a water-powered grist mill, the first mechanical plant, or "factory," within the confines of modern Pennsylvania. It was situated about two hundred feet above the present Woodland Avenue bridge.

On the New Jersey side he enlarged the Swedish domain by obtaining from the Indians in 1649 title to the land north of Narraticons Kill or Raccoon Creek, as far as Mantas Kill or Mantua Creek, which was as close as he could get to the Dutch fort, Nassau, on Big Timber Creek, another New Jersey tributary to the Delaware. In the southern division of New Sweden on the New Jersey side, he built as early as in 1643 a fort known as New Elfsborg. In some non-Swedish records the name is spelled "Helsenborgh" and today the site is known as Elsenburg Fort Point. It is some seven miles south of Penn's Neck, where the ferry runs from New Jersey to New Castle in Delaware. Even in those days the New Jersey mosquitoes were troublesome and by the Swedish garrison the fort was nicknamed "Myggenborg," or "Mosquito Fort," which gave Washington Irving a peg on which to hang a good deal of humor in his imaginary *Knickerbocker's History*.

One of the purposes of this fort was to observe an English village, established in 1641 on Varkens Kill, now Salem Creek, by the English colony of New Haven, Connecticut. Another aim was to control traffic on the main river. The New Englanders, too, had plans for trade with the Delaware Indians, and to protest against the building of the fort as well as to clarify their business rights on the river, a New Haven fur trader by the name of George Lamberton appeared, in July 1643, before Governor Printz at Fort Christina. The Connecticut colonists had also bought from the Indians some of the land on the west side of the Schuylkill, previously sold by them to Peter Minuit. On the Jersey shore Governor Ridder had likewise bought the land on Salem Creek in 1640, or the year before the New Haven people appeared. This was a typical mix-up over land ownership, based on conflicting Indian deeds. A violent quarrel ensued. Governor Printz, who was more used to command than to argue, lost his temper, had Lamberton arrested, tried and fined for trespassing. When Lamberton returned to New England he complained to Governor Winthrop at Boston, and

between the latter and Printz a long, legalistic and, at times, acri-
monious correspondence ensued. There was no physical action, however,
and in time the dispute died down. In order to be able to sell their
produce, such as corn and tobacco, to the Swedes across the South
River, the English settlers at Salem Creek took an oath of allegiance
to the Swedish Crown and as long as Fort Elfsborg was kept up by
the Swedes, the oath was respected.

The sudden appearance on the South River of the Swedes under
the leadership of their former Governor at New Amsterdam had naturally been observed with growing disapproval by the Dutch. In the
competition for the Indian trade they sensed a serious rival. To his
home office Governor Wilhelmus Kieft, the predecessor of Peter
Stuyvesant, complained that his trade with the natives "had fallen
short fully thirty thousand [florins] because the Swedes, by under-
selling, had depressed the market."

The expansion of New Sweden under Governor Printz increased
their concern. After 1645, when Andreas Hudde replaced Jan Janssen
as commandant at Fort Nassau, situated across the river from present-
day Philadelphia, the relations between the Dutch and the Swedes
became even more tense. This seventeenth century "cold" war was
continued by Governor Stuyvesant after he arrived in 1647. When
his written protests made no apparent impression on Printz, he began action. With a military force and several ships he appeared in
1651 at the mouth of the South River and from the Indians he bought
some of the land on the west side of the river which they had already
sold to the Swedes. As the Dutch forts further up the valley, the Nassau
and Beversreede, had already been neutralized by the Swedish strong-
holds, New Korsholm and New Gothenburg, he decided to abandon
them. Instead, he built on his new land south of the Swedish colony,
a new fort which he called Fort Casimir. It was situated at Sands
Point (now New Castle), Delaware, close to the slip of the ferry to
Penn's Neck in New Jersey. A clearly inscribed stone marks the spot.
As this fort outflanked the Swedish stronghold, New Elfsborg, on the
New Jersey side, the Swedes gave that up. Now it was the Dutch
who had bottled up the Swedes.

Knowing he was weak militarily, Governor Printz had to watch
these proceedings patiently. He had neither the ships nor the men to
match Stuyvesant. His first census after his arrival in 1643 had showed
a male population of only 135 and of these twenty-six died in the
course of the following year and four returned to Sweden. In June 1644,

only 105 adult males were listed. Some of these were English, at least two German, and a few Finnish. As late as 1648, the male population still numbered only around ninety-four, including four Dutchmen, four Germans, at least one Dane and a Negro slave, probably the boy brought back by the *Griffon* in 1638. The Finns were only a dozen or so. To Governor Printz's appeals for more men no attention was paid in Sweden. Obviously he had spread himself too thin. How he had been able to build all those villages and forts with so few men is hard to understand.

In Europe the Swedes had similarly spread themselves too thin. They never had had the men or the means normally required to carry on as many wars as they did. When King Gustavus Adolphus fell in 1632, his German colleagues and brothers-in-arms were asked not to come to Sweden to attend the funeral. Like the Russians of today, the Swedes did not want even their confederates to see how poor they were. Regarding his Chancellor and successor as Regent, Count Axel Oxenstierna, an article in the *Encyclopaedia Britannica* says: "Simple to austerity in his own tastes, he nevertheless recognized the political necessity of impressing his allies and confederates by an almost regal show of dignity; and at the abortive congress of Frankfort-on-Main (March 1634), held for the purpose of uniting all the German Protestants, Oxenstierna appeared in a carriage drawn by six horses, with German princes attending him on foot. But from the first to the last his policy suffered from the slenderness of Sweden's material resources, a cardinal defect which all his craft and tact could not altogether conceal from the vigilance of his enemies. The success of his system postulated an uninterrupted series of triumphs, whereas a single reverse was likely to be fatal to it." Although head of the South Seas Company, he was obviously unable to send the reinforcements Governor Printz asked for in America.

In 1643 while the Thirty Years' War was still under way, a new war broke out between Sweden and Denmark. In this conflict, which Sweden ultimately also won, the New Sweden colony lost another friend, even more important than Peter Minuit. At the naval battle at Femern in the south Baltic, fought in July 1644, a stray Danish bullet killed Admiral Klas Fleming, commander of the Swedish fleet, who was an influential stockholder in New Sweden. In 1649, when the German war was over, still another disaster struck the colony. In July that year a well-stocked ship, *Kattan* (*Tabby Cat*), had finally been sent off from Sweden, but on a reef near Puerto Rico it was

After being raised to the rank of colonel, he calmly resumed his army career. In 1657 he was made commandant of the castle at Jönköping in Småland and the following year he was appointed Governor of the province. At Bottnaryd he built himself another mansion and there in 1668 he died in his bed. In the parish church hangs a contemporary portrait, of which the Swedish Colonial Society in Philadelphia has a copy presented to it by the King of Sweden. It shows a hulk of a man in elegant Renaissance clothes. His glance is sharp, his hair long, and his white cravat overflowing. Somehow he looks a bit too luxurious. Småland was still a poor province.

In Sweden, where the rule of Count Oxenstierna had been replaced more and more by that of the young Queen Christina and her favorites, the return of Governor Printz was not entirely unexpected. The construction of Fort Casimir by Peter Stuyvesant in 1651 had reawakened official interest. Such flagrant disrespect for the authority of Her Royal Majesty was not to be ignored. As one of the victors in the Thirty Years' War Sweden was then a Great Power. The dispatch of a ship with reinforcements had been formally discussed in the presence of the Queen, but nothing was done until 1653. By that time Queen Christina was preparing to abdicate in favor of her cousin, Charles X, and through his influence new vigor was imparted to the Government. The affairs of the colony were transferred from the shoulders of the veteran Chancellor, whom the young Queen had long been anxious to belittle as much as possible, and turned over to the Commercial College or Kommerskollegium, as the Royal Board of Trade was called. (It still exists.) At the head of it was Count Axel Oxenstierna's son, Erik Oxenstierna, also an able man. To assist Printz it had been decided to send a young official of the college, a brilliant but inexperienced economist, a "brain-truster" of the day, by the name of Johan Rising. Tentatively, he was appointed Acting Governor. As a matter of fact his ship, *Örnen* (*Eagle*), had crossed that of Governor Printz at sea. This ship, too, was filled with new settlers.

No sooner had Rising arrived at the mouth of the Delaware in the spring of 1654 than he committed his first major political and military blunder. Without making contact with Acting Governor Papegoja or informing himself about the strength of the Dutch, he attacked and seized Fort Casimir, the apple of Peter Stuyvesant's eye. Since the deed was done on Trinity Sunday, May 23, the stronghold was renamed Fort Trefaldighet, or Fort Trinity. Satirically, and wholly imaginatively, the scene is described by Washington Irving in the wrecked and over a hundred badly needed colonists and members of the crew lost their lives. Only nineteen survived. To make matters worse the French and Spanish residents of the near-by islands, St. Croix and Puerto Rico, plundered the cargo and finally, to cover up traces of their crime, the local authorities ordered the hulk burned. All attempts to recover damages failed. Had this ship arrived, doubling the population of New Sweden, it is not likely that Governor Printz would have had to sit idly by, two years later, when Peter Stuyvesant built his new Fort Casimir at New Castle. The presence of so many colonists on the *Kattan* had been an encouraging sign, though of over a hundred applicants, it had been possible to find room for only about seventy. By this time the news of the favorable American climate and the fertility of soil had spread in Sweden. To get new settlers it was no longer necessary to comb the jails for petty criminals or round up tree-burning Finns.

To make up for the small size of his population, Governor Printz had driven his men too hard. In 1653 they lodged a formal protest against his rule. In eleven articles they accused him of harsh treatment, avarice and brutality, and of enriching himself at the expense of his men, which made it difficult for them "to obtain their sustenance." Evidently the atmosphere in America had already begun to stimulate revolt. Once more Governor Printz lost his temper and, as in the case of Lamberton ten years earlier, he resorted to violence rather than argument. The leader of the opposition, one Anders Jönsson, he ordered arrested and tried for treason. On August 1, 1653, Jönsson was hanged. To be sure, the instructions which Printz had brought from Sweden and which were, in fact, the law of the colony, provided for capital punishment, but only after the hanging was over and the Governor had cooled off, did he make a written reply to the accusations of his people. But it was then too late. Anders Jönsson was not regarded by them as a traitor or any other kind of criminal and his friends continued sullen. Rapidly, from both Dutch pressure and internal discontent, the Governor's position became weaker and weaker. His appeals to Sweden for more men and ships continued unanswered after the *Kattan* had been wrecked. In October 1653, or only a little over two months after Anders Jönsson had been executed, Governor Printz and his wife sailed for home via New Amsterdam, leaving their son-in-law, Lieutenant Johan Papegoja, in temporary command. Printz would soon either return himself, he promised, or send a ship. He did neither.

In Sweden his unauthorized arrival this time was not disapproved.

Holland, but once more Sweden was involved in a war with Poland and after that in one after another with Denmark, so the Dutch were never made to suffer for Stuyvesant's action. Ten years later they themselves were replaced by the English. And having by then won a North European empire that almost circled the Baltic, as well as natural frontiers for Sweden, the new King was content to forget about the unprofitable little colony in far-off America. But, unlike Printz, Johan Rising received no promotion. His surrender had humiliated his country. Never again did Sweden attempt colonization across the Atlantic. All future Swedish settlers in America came as individuals and accepted whatever authority was already established.

To colonial America the Swedes had contributed the first permanent settlements in the Delaware Valley; they had established a small but well-managed colony, free from slavery and based on a friendship with the Indians. They had brought over the first Lutheran ministers, built the first churches, the first flour mills, the first shipyards, the first roads and the first permanent homes; they had introduced farming and logging, built the first log cabins, and made the first detailed map of the region, had taken and recorded astronomical and meteorological observations; had set up the first organized government and had introduced both the court and jury system. The "Instructions" to Governor Printz was the first written law of the territory, in effect its first constitution. By such steps the Swedish colonists had prepared the way for William Penn, who in 1682 landed at New Castle, Delaware, and then proceeded to found, further up the river, the city of Philadelphia.

II

EARLY CULTURAL RELATIONS

Financially, New Sweden was a failure. In return for its investments in ships, men, arms, seeds, household animals, and farm equipment, Old Sweden had received neither the treasures nor the tropical products dangled before it in the Usselinx prospectus. Officially, the loss was written off all the easier because soon after the middle of the seventeenth century Sweden reached a new peak in expansion at home. Sweden had likewise won the two-hundred-year-old contest for leadership in the North, including permanent possession of several former Danish and Norwegian provinces inside its own natural borders, which are still held. Finally, thanks to its participation in the long religious war in Germany, Sweden had become one of the military powers of Europe. To its new rulers, the lost venture across the Atlantic didn't seem to matter much.

The real gainer was, of course, America. To the other little colonies along the Atlantic seaboard had been added another group of hardy settlers. They were few in number, to be sure, but at that time, none of the other colonies was very large either. What the new country needed was people who could make their living from the undeveloped soil. In this respect the Swedes and Finns were preferred stock.

"When the challenge came with Stuyvesant's demand for surrender," writes Christopher Ward, the Wilmington attorney and littérateur, "New Sweden was too weak to resist, and Old Sweden too unconcerned to do more than to protest. On the other hand,—and herein lay the irony of the situation,—as colonizing material, the Swedes and the Finns were of the best quality. Physically vigorous, they withstood hardship. Inured to toil, they subdued the wilderness. Used to rough living, they faced rude conditions with equanimity. Accustomed to agriculture, they developed prosperous farms. Intent on permanent occupation, they struck their roots deep in the soil. Serious of purpose, they were undaunted by obstacles. Self-reliant, they throve individually in spite of neglect. These sturdy peasants were ideal pioneers. Given a measure of protection from external oppression, New Sweden might have survived. Increased in numbers by such a stream of emigrants as flowed to New England, it would have flourished. Undefended, unaugmented, its death was inevitable."

While under Swedish rule the manpower of New Sweden had always been incredibly slight. "With a population of seventy men and a few women and children," continues Mr. Ward, "it pretended to hold both sides of the Delaware Bay and River, from the Capes to the falls [at Trenton], more than 250 miles of coastline with an unlimited hinterland,—a position utterly untenable in the face of any challenge, unless continuously supported and strongly defended by Old Sweden."

It is, therefore, evident that had not Sweden's military prestige in Europe been as high as it was, the colony would have been taken over much earlier either by the Dutch or the English. For years after their easily won occupation, the Dutch officials lived in fear of a Swedish attempt to recapture the colony, especially when the population began to show signs of growth. Every ship coming up the river was closely scrutinized.

One Swedish ship loaded with colonists and supplies the Dutch had obtained without effort in 1654, or a year before the surrender. It was the Gyllene Hajen (Golden Shark) which by mistake was sailed into the mouth of the North River at New Amsterdam instead of the South River or the Delaware, and was there detained, weakening Governor Rising's position at the final showdown in September 1655. In 1645 the ship had originally been bought by the Swedes in Holland, but after a few round trips to New Sweden, it had been left riding idly at anchor in Stockholm, though Governor Printz was pleading for more men and supplies. The Dutch renamed it the Diemen and promptly put it into their own traffic with the West Indies.

In November 1655, two months after New Sweden had surrendered, but before the news had reached Old Sweden, a final ship, the Mercurius, was fitted out and filled up with supplies and colonists, who by that time were easy to obtain—especially Finns. In command was Johan Papegoja, Governor Printz's son-in-law, who had been released as Acting Governor when Johan Rising arrived in 1654. The storekeeper was once more Hendrick Huygen who had made the initial trip on the Kalmar Nyckel with Peter Minuit in 1638. When the ship arrived in front of Fort Casimir in March 1656, more than six months after the capitulation, it was not only ordered to halt, but told either to proceed to New Amsterdam or return to Sweden. Since the passengers numbered over a hundred or almost as many again as the entire previous population of the colony, it was no wonder that the Dutch commander of the fort was apprehensive.

When the ship was detained, Mr. Huygen proceeded overland to New Amsterdam to plead with Governor Stuyvesant and the "High Honorables" of his council for the right of the *Mercurius* and its passengers to remain. He had been surprised, he admitted, to find the South River in their hands, but assured them that his purpose and that of his passengers was to settle down peacefully and obey their authority. But even so, his request was denied.

In the meantime the Swedish colonists on the Delaware had enlisted the aid of their friends, the Indians. Together they boarded the ship riding at anchor before New Amstel, as the new Dutch community around Fort Casimir was then called. Suddenly the ship lifted anchor, hoisted its sails and sailed up the river to Tinicum. Fearing to kill some of the Indians by firing on the ship, thereby causing perhaps another bloody insurrection, the garrison at Fort Casimir did nothing. Without interference, the new colonists and the valuable Swedish supplies were unloaded at Governor Printz's old headquarters, whereupon the ship proceeded empty to New Amsterdam for a return cargo to Europe. The commandant at New Amstel had been officially instructed "to look well after the Swedes," keep them out of the fort so as to forestall surprise moves, like Rising's in 1654, but to do it "with all possible courtesy."

As for their fear of a Swedish-Finnish uprising, writes Ward, "it was, of course, pure funk. There could not have been found in America a more peaceful, law-abiding and obedient group of colonists than these Swedes and Finns on the Delaware." The Dutch themselves were not very strong and in 1664, only nine years later, they were replaced in New Amsterdam as well as on the South River by the English. At the same time by the natural process of repopulation, as well as by occasional individual additions from Sweden, the number of Swedish colonists continued to grow. From time to time single settlers or even groups of them continued to appear. In 1663, a year before the English took over, a mixed body of sixty or more landed at New Amstel. A majority of these too may have been Finns, who, at that time were all Swedish subjects. In 1683, the year after William Penn arrived, 188 families on both sides of the river, comprising 924 persons, were listed as Swedish, and as late as 1754, when many had intermarried with other nationalities, over nine hundred still spoke the language, states Professor Axel Johan Uppvall of the University of Pennsylvania in *Swedes in America*.

Concerning the Swedish population, William Penn wrote in 1683 a memorable paragraph which appears in *The Present State of His Majesty's Isles and Territories in America,* published in London in 1687. "The first planters in these parts were the Dutch," he pointed out, "and soon after them the Swedes and the Finns. The Dutch applied themselves to traffic, the Swedes and the Finns to husbandry. The Dutch have a meeting place for religious worship in New Castle [Fort Casimir] and the Swedes one at Christina [Wilmington], one at Tinicum, and one at Wicaco, within half a mile of this town [Philadelphia]. The Swedes inhabit the freshes of the River Delaware. There is no need of giving any description of them, who are better known in England than here; but they are plain, strong, industrious people, yet have made no great progress in the culture or propagation of fruit trees, as if they desired rather to have enough than plenty or traffic. But I presume the Indians made them the more careless, by furnishing them with the means of profit, to wit, skins and furs for rum, and such strong liquors. They kindly received me, as well as the English, who were few before the people concerned with me came among them. I must needs to commend their respect to authority, and kind behavior to the English. They do not degenerate from the old friendship between both kingdoms. As they are people proper and strong of body, so they have fine children, and almost every house full; rare to find one of them without three or four boys, and as many girls: some six, seven, and eight sons. And I must do them that right, I see few young men more sober and laborious."

The friendly relations the Swedes had maintained with the Indians continued to stand them in good stead after the English had taken over the colony. Thanks to these relations, the Swedes had made better progress than either the Dutch or the English in learning the Indian languages, and were therefore able to serve William Penn as interpreters. Being known to the Indians as *Netappi* or "our friends," they were also able to convince them that the Quakers too were peace-loving and trustworthy. This was the foundation of Penn's success in dealing with the aborigines of Pennsylvania.

Wisely, the Swedish settlers had been officially instructed from the first to treat the Indians justly and to show them "all humanity and respect." Governor Printz was enjoined to see to it that "no violence and no wrong be done to them by the subjects of Her Royal Majesty [Queen Christina]." In 1643 Count Per Brahe, who as over-lord of Småland, was probably the main backer of Johan Printz, wrote him "to keep good friendship with them [the Indians] and allow no harm to be done to them by our people; then you are secure from them and on their account the other neighbors will not dare attack you." Prophetic words! This friendship of the Indians was an additional and important reason why the Swedes in spite of their small number were able to hold their position on the Delaware as long as they did.

On June 8, 1654, or soon after his arrival, as Governor Printz's successor, Johan Rising held a pow-wow with a dozen chiefs at Printzhof on Tinicum Island, distributing among them gifts he had brought from Sweden. The titles to the land bought by Minuit and Ridder, as well as by Printz were then reviewed and affirmed and while under the glow of Swedish hospitality, the Indians promised additional tracts, "as far as the Chesapeake." Rising's own report of the address delivered by one of the sachems has an Old Testament flavor:

"See how good are these friends who have given us these gifts. We shall be as one body and one soul. If in the time of Governor Printz, the Big Belly, we were friendly, we shall now be as a calabash [pipe or bowl] without a crack or crevice and with you we want to make a pact of everlasting friendship. If some one attacks you, even in the middle of the night, we shall come to your aid, and if some one attacks us, though it is in the middle of the night, you must come to our aid."

In addition to keeping on good social terms with the Indians the Swedes had been told to instruct the "wild nations" living close to their territory "in true Christian religion and worship," and "in other ways bring them to civility and good public manners." This was in accordance with the original charter of the South Seas Company.

The first clergyman to undertake this task was Johan Campanius who had arrived with Governor Printz in 1643. In the language of the Lenapi Indians, one of the Algonquin dialects, he wrote out phonetically the questions and answers in Luther's Little or Shorter Catechism which, since the Reformation, every Swedish child has had to learn by heart. After his return to Sweden in 1648 his manuscript was used as instruction material by his successors. In 1656, he made a final version in Stockholm, but it was not printed until 1696, when the Swedish colonists on the Delaware, though no longer Swedish subjects, had asked for Bibles and other religious books, as well as two clergymen. On the title page it was declared to be *Luther's Catechism, Translated into the American-Virginian Language,* which was not quite correct; it was, however, the first book in relation to America to be published in Sweden. Of the original edition of about six hundred copies, five hundred were sent to America with three young clergymen in 1696, but less than twenty are now known to be extant in both countries. In 1938, as part of the New Sweden Tercentenary celebration, a facsimile edition of three thousand copies was printed in Stockholm, but copies of that too are now hard to obtain. In his diary for May 21, 1750, Peter Kalm, the Swedish naturalist, who was then visiting the former colony, wrote that he had seen about a hundred copies of the "Indian Catechism" in the church at Christina, but that as far as was known "only a single Indian had been converted by this means." Reports sent by the clergymen to their bishop in Sweden had been more optimistic. The general attitude of the natives is indicated by a remark one of them is reported to have made after attending a church service: "Why should one man stand up and do all the talking?"

Though the political ties between New and Old Sweden had been severed in 1655, the religious ones were not, and as the Swedish clergymen sent over were university-educated men, intellectual ties were likewise maintained. While they failed to Christianize the Indians, these ministers kept Sweden informed about many developments in America, and served as hosts to visiting Swedish scientists. This cultural contact with America was Sweden's real gain from its attempt at colonization.

When Governor Rising withdrew in 1655 and returned to Sweden, all Swedish clergymen had gone with him, with the exception of the Reverend Lars Karlsson Lock, or Laurentius Carolus Lockenius, as he Latinized his name. He had arrived in 1648 and remained until his death in 1688. According to contemporary records and reports by his Dutch colleagues, "he did not lead a Christian life," but as he was the only ordained minister who knew Swedish or who was even a Lutheran, his alleged aberrations, irregularities and peccadilloes had to be forgiven. Christopher Ward cites the details.

While the Reverend Mr. Lock did what work he could around Fort Christina, or Wilmington, the Swedes living further up the river turned into a church or meetinghouse an old blockhouse they had erected at Wicaco, originally a separate village on the banks of the

Delaware, but now swamped by the Philadelphia waterfront, and to preach in it they invited in 1677 a Dutch minister, Jacob Fabritius, from New York. Even after he became blind five years later, he continued to preach until 1691, when he died. Fearing to be left without any clergymen, the Swedes had several times applied to Sweden for pastors as well as books, but whether their letters were lost or just neglected, they received no answers. Next they tried the Lutheran Consistory at Amsterdam, but a letter sent there in 1691 likewise remained without reply. Through the Swedish diplomatic representative in London, William Penn next tried to obtain for them at least some religious books, but he, too, was unsuccessful. They then appointed lay readers and continued to use what old hymn books and homilies they had.

Then they were suddenly visited by Andrew Printz, a nephew of the former Governor, who had come to the West Indies in an English vessel. On his return to Sweden in 1691, he met in Stockholm Johan Thelin, the postmaster at Gothenburg. Coming from the west coast and being, in addition, a religious man himself, Thelin took an interest in the plight of the Swedes in America as described to him by young Printz. A year later, on November 16, 1692, he addressed, in duplicate, a letter to his American "Hon. Friends and Countrymen" in which he told of having met Printz in Stockholm the year before and also of the efforts by William Penn to get books for them, but which "for some cause or other had not been carried into effect." He also wrote he knew personally in Gothenburg "an elderly woman who says she has a brother living among you, Peter Gunnarson Rambo, through whom this letter may be received." (Ormond Rambo, Jr. a Philadelphia banker and until his death in September, 1949, President of the American Swedish Historical Museum, was a direct descendant of this Rambo who arrived in New Sweden in 1640. His genealogy, supported at every point by documentary evidence, was supposed to be the longest in Pennsylvania.)

In response to Thelin's request for information, which came on May 23, 1693, as to what books and ministers were needed, the Swedes on the Delaware sent their reply on May 31, or only eight days later. It was signed by thirty Swedish residents of the district. When it reached Sweden is not known, but for three years it remained unanswered. On this subject Johan Campanius Holm, a grandson of the preacher, wrote, however, in 1702: "As soon as the letter arrived in Stockholm, His Majesty, Charles XI, of glorious memory, desiring to promote the preservation of our holy religion among the small number of settlers in America, wrote on the subject to the late Dr. Olaus Suebelius, Archbishop of Uppsala." This royal letter, dated February 18, 1696, has been preserved. The correspondence is reported in *The Annals of the Swedes on the Delaware,* by the Rev. Jehu Curtis Clay. (Philadelphia, 1835, 4th ed. Chicago, 1938)

The King's letter enclosed the original request from America, which, the Reverend Mr. Clay says had by then been "copied by many persons and drew tears from many who heard its contents." To the Archbishop the King recommended the selection of such "good and learned pastors as they desire to have" and the payment of the necessary funds for their (travel) expenses. The King, likewise, ordered the Archbishop to "procure the Bibles, homilies, common prayers and hymn books, catechisms, primers and spiritual treatises which are desired." It was to meet this demand that the Indian Catechism as translated by Johan Campanius fifty years earlier was finally printed.

The actual composer of the "America letter" of May 31, 1693, which was to assure the perpetuation of the Swedish parishes on the Delaware for another hundred years and lead to the construction of the five "Old Swedes" churches on the Delaware which are still in use, was a lay reader at Fort Christina, Charles Christopher Springer, from whom many present-day Americans claim descent. He had been well educated in Sweden and had not come to the Delaware as a colonist, but as a refugee from Virginia after the Swedish regime was over. While visiting the Swedish Ambassador in London, who was a relative, he had been kidnapped from a post chaise as he was returning at night to his residence, and then forcibly placed on board an English vessel bound for Virginia. There he was sold as an indentured servant for five years. When he had regained his freedom by working that long, he made his way to the Delaware region and there joined his countrymen. Besides serving them as lay reader, he was for many years a justice of the peace, being the best educated person in the community.

The letter he wrote to Postmaster Thelin is the oldest known "America letter" sent to Sweden and one of the most effective—a little masterpiece of composition. After meeting Thelin's request for information about the needs of the parishes in America and promising to pay in full for whatever Bibles, hymn books, homilies and tracts that might be sent, it asked for two clergymen "who are well learned in the Holy Scriptures, and who will be able to defend them and us against all false opponents." Probably with the late Pastor Lock's shortcomings in mind, the writer then specified that the clergymen should be "men of good moral lives and characters; so they may instruct our youth by their example and lead them into a pious and virtuous way of life." Financially, the letter added, the parishes on the Delaware were well able to support two such ministers and provide them with land for parsonages.

"As to what concerns our situation in this country," the letter then continued, "we are for the most part husbandmen. We plough and sow and till the ground; and as to our meat and drink, we live according to the old Swedish customs. This country is very rich and fruitful, and here grow all sorts of grain in great plenty, so that we are richly supplied with meat and drink; and we send out yearly to our neighbors on this continent and the neighboring islands, bread, grain, flour, and oil. We have here also all sorts of beasts, fowls and fishes. Our wives and daughters employ themselves in spinning wool and flax, and many of them in weaving; so we have great reason to thank the Almighty for his manifold mercies and benefits. God grant that we may also have good shepherds to feed us with his Holy Word and sacraments. We likewise live in peace and friendship with one another; and the Indians have not molested us for many years.

"Further, since this country has ceased to be under the government of Sweden, we are bound to acknowledge and declare, for the sake of truth, that we have been well and kindly treated, as well by the Dutch, as by His Majesty, the King of England, our gracious sovereign: on the other hand, we, the Swedes, have been and still are, true and faithful to him in words and deeds. We have always had at our head good and gracious magistrates; and we live with one another in peace and amity."

In response to this letter and the King's endorsement, the Archbishop then selected three young divinity students at Uppsala, Andreas Rudman, Erik Björck and Jonas Aurén, the last one to be sent only temporarily as an observer. Whenever one of the other two should decide to return to Sweden, the King promised that his career in the state church would be continued. After being ordained in the Uppsala Cathedral, the three left Sweden via England, with their shipment of books, on August 4, 1696, but did not arrive in America until Midsummer Day, June 24, 1697. On the Delaware they were joyfully received and at once it was decided to build not only parsonages but also new churches of a more permanent type than the wooden structures or mere log huts that so far had been used for divine services.

At Wilmington the site was changed from that on the river front at Cranehook, now obliterated, to a hillock a few rods back from the site of Fort Christina, where a cemetery had already been laid out. (It is now separated from the Rocks, or landing place, by a railroad embankment.) The church, completed in 1699, was built of a bluish stone quarried in the hills further inland, and was ready for dedication on June 4 of that year. As on that date it happened to be Trinity Sunday, the church was called the Trinity, just as Fort Casimir had been in 1654, a name it still bears. It is now the oldest Protestant church still in use in America. Of this church the Reverend Erik Björck became the first pastor, a post he held until he returned to Sweden in 1711.

As a site for the Philadelphia church, the scattered parishioners agreed on one near the former blockhouse at Wicaco, in which the Dutch clergyman, Jacob Fabritius, had preached for fourteen years. Though only a few minutes' walk from Independence Square, it is now engulfed in a waterfront slum. Built of brick, this church, called Gloria Dei, was ready for dedication the First Sunday after Trinity in 1700. It is the oldest church building now standing in Pennsylvania and since 1943 it has been an American official national monument under the jurisdiction of the Department of the Interior. It is used daily, however, for its original purposes and, since it is supposed to be lucky to be married in such a quaint old edifice, weddings are frequent. Like the original Holy Trinity in Wilmington, it is surrounded, in the old Swedish style, by a cemetery, in which many of the original settlers and their families are buried. The site was donated by the largest landowners in the Wicaco district, the three Swenson brothers, Sven, Ole and Andreas, from whom William Penn's agent, William Markham, who became his first Governor of Pennsylvania, bought some of the land for the city of Philadelphia including what is now Independence Square, with Independence Hall, the "cradle of American Liberty," in its center. In the new church Andreas Rudman preached until 1702. He later became rector of Christ Episcopal Church in Philadelphia and while holding that office died in 1708. His remains were buried, however, under the chancel of the Gloria Dei.

Other "Old Swedes" churches in the district and their dates of construction are: St. James, on Woodland Avenue and 69th Street in West Philadelphia, once Kingsessing, built in 1762 (this was originally a daughter church of Gloria Dei, but much larger); Christ Church, originally built in 1760 in Upper Merion, now Bridgeport, Pennsylvania, a few miles up the Schuylkill River, also an off-shoot of Gloria Dei;

and, finally, Trinity Church at Swedesboro (originally Sveaborg) in New Jersey, built in 1784. It replaced a log church built about 1704.

To serve such parishes the Swedish state church sent successively during the next 130 years, about thirty clergymen. Some returned after a few years to continue their careers in Sweden; others, like Lars Lock, remained until their death. This was true of the last one, the Reverend Nicholas, or Nils Collin, who arrived in 1770. He lived until 1831, or only a few years before the new immigration to the Middle West began. He was well acquainted with both George Washington and Benjamin Franklin and for many years was a member and finally an officer of the American Philosophical Society of Philadelphia, founded by Franklin. Almost until the end of his life he continued to preach in Swedish as well as in English and sometimes in Dutch. On June 25, 1789, after American independence had been established, jurisdiction over the "Old Swedes" churches was transferred by the Archbishop of Sweden, the Right Reverend Uno von Troil, to the American Protestant Episcopal Church, which still exercises it. At that time there was no general Lutheran denomination in the United States. Christ Church of Upper Merion is supposed to be an exception, being nominally, it is claimed, still a part of the Church of Sweden, but, at best, this is a formality.

In addition to holding church services for the former Swedish colonists and their families which, by frequent intermarriages, included more and more members of other nationalities, the Swedish clergymen kept up various forms of contact with Sweden. It was an era of curiosity and discovery in natural history and besides reporting on their church activities, the ministers were encouraged to send accounts of their observations as to "fishes, birds, and other animals, as well as trees, bushes and other useful things," just as the civil administrators of the colony had done.

Peter Lindeström, a military engineer, who had come with Governor Rising in 1654 and returned with him the following year, wrote a journal which he called *Geographica Americana,* in which he described the lower Delaware Valley, adding an original map he drew of the region. (In an English translation by Dr. Amandus Johnson, it was published for the first time in Philadelphia in 1925.) Governor Rising himself kept a diary in which he described Indian customs as well as "wild life in New Sweden and its wonderfully fine forests and useful trees and bushes." The tradition was kept up by the Reverend Andreas Hesselius, a brother of Gustaf Hesselius, the pioneer American artist, who came with him in May 1712. After some delay Andreas Hesselius became pastor of Holy Trinity in Wilmington, but in 1724 he returned to Sweden. In his journal he describes not only birds, fishes and plants, but also skunks, snakes, and muskrats.

In 1702, a second book about America, following the Indian Catechism, was printed in Stockholm. It was called *A Short Description of the Province of New Sweden,* edited by Johan Campanius Holm, a grandson of the Reverend Johan Campanius who had translated the catechism for the Indians. It consisted of selections from his grandfather's American papers. Subsequent reports by the Swedish clergymen in America, particularly one by the Reverend Andreas Sandel, M.A., dated July 28, 1714, were collected by their Bishop, Jesper Svedberg, father of Emanuel Swedenborg, the scientist and religious seer, and published, in part, in Stockholm in 1732 under the title of *America Illuminata.* In the editing he had the help of another son and namesake, whom he had sent to New Sweden to teach in one of the early Swedish parish schools. At home the young man's conduct had caused his father some concern, but after eight years abroad, including a term in the British Navy, he returned, settled down, got married and became a respected citizen. All present-day members of the noble Swedenborg family are his descendants. He was probably the first problem child to be sent from Sweden to America, but not all the subsequent ones have turned out so well.

While as a rule the letters and "relations" sent back by the Swedish clergymen to their superiors in Sweden concern parish affairs, they also threw light on the contemporary political and social conditions in America as well as on natural phenomena. When the French and Indian Wars began about the middle of the eighteenth century to decide the control of North America, the Swedish press printed translations of articles describing the situation as seen by the French as well as the British. Consequently, it is fair to say that at least the educated people in Sweden were kept fairly well informed about developments in America.

Around the middle of the eighteenth century two other important books by Swedish eyewitnesses were published in Stockholm. Almost immediately one of these received international attention, being translated in fairly rapid succession into German, Dutch, French, and English. It was *Travels in North America, 1748-51,* by Peter Kalm, a Swedish-Finnish naturalist, who had been a pupil of Carl Linnaeus, the noted Swedish botanist, at the University of Uppsala. In a more detailed and scientific manner than that of any previous publication in any language it described American natural phenomena, including such subjects as the climate, medical herbs, Indian corn, northern lights, maple sugar, spruce beer, rattlesnakes, birch bark canoes, ticks, grasshoppers, wild pigeons, tree worms, walnuts, mulberry trees, and sea temperatures. At the suggestion of Linnaeus, Kalm had been sent to America by the newly founded Swedish Academy of Science, which now awards the Nobel Prizes in Science, to look for new plants, as well as dyestuffs, which might be of benefit to agriculture in Sweden and Finland. Some of the specimens he brought back are still on display in Uppsala, including a sprig of poison ivy, and while none of his discoveries turned out to be of much practical use, his book was a great success. Reviews, comments and quotations appeared in almost all languages, as they occasionally still do. In Sweden the first volume was published in 1753, the second in 1756, and a third in 1761. The manuscript for a fourth was lost in a fire in Helsingfors in 1827. The author died in 1779. The German version, which first made it available to a world-wide audience, was also published in three parts from 1754 to 1764; and the first English version in 1770-1771. In America Kalm had traveled as far west as the Great Lakes and from there northward into Canada. His description of Niagara Falls, when published by Benjamin Franklin in English (1750), at once became popular. It was the first effective piece of publicity for the falls. He also recorded many firsthand observations of Indian life and in his book predicted the probability of ultimate American independence —as far as known, the first one to do so.

The other book, which has also been published in English, was called *A Description of the Swedish Parishes on the Delaware,* but it included many other topics of a more general interest. In Sweden it appeared in 1759. Its author was the Reverend Israel Acrelius, a young academician, who from 1748 to 1756 had served as pastor of the Holy Trinity Church in Wilmington. Before being sent to America he had received at the University of Uppsala a degree in the liberal arts as well as in theology. His interests were, therefore, wider than his church work, and except for parts of the second volume of Kalm's travelogue (1756), his book gave for the first time in Swedish an account of the history, agriculture, commerce, system of government, education, and religion in the English colonies. It was the first general book about America to be published in Sweden—the forerunner of so many.

"We now have reason to boast," wrote Lars Salvius, editor of the

Stockholm *Journal of Learning* (*Lärda Tidningar*), in 1759, "that in Sweden we now have the best, the most reliable, and the most up-to-date information about this distant part of the world." Politically Acrelius was inclined to be conservative. Of many of the new ideas brewing in America he disapproved as dangerous to established religion, and as regards the recurring conflicts between the Quakers and the English authorities, he favored the latter.

Through the books by Kalm and Acrelius the Swedish public became acquainted for the first time with a distinctly American personality, that of Benjamin Franklin. In Sweden his name still looms large. Only those of George Washington and Abraham Lincoln, among the presidents, and Thomas A. Edison and Henry Ford, among the inventors and industrialists, are as widely known. It was, of course, through his experiments with electricity that Benjamin Franklin first became famous in Sweden; his repute as a sage and political guide came later.

When Kalm arrived in Philadelphia in 1748 he had with him letters of introduction to Franklin from mutual friends in London and in his diary he wrote for September 15 that year: "It was easy for me to get acquainted. Mr. Benjamin Franklin, to whom Pennsylvania is indebted for its welfare and the learned world for many discoveries in electricity, was the first one who took notice of me and introduced me to many of his friends. He gave me all the necessary information and showed me numerous favors." Conversely, this pupil of Linnaeus was probably one of the first foreign scientists Franklin had ever met. To what extent Franklin's fame was spread in Europe by Kalm's writings has not yet been established, but at least it is safe to say that they helped. When as an unofficial American political agent Franklin first arrived in Paris during the War of Independence, he quickly became acquainted with the Swedish official representative, a noted poet as well as a diplomat, Count Gustaf Philip Creutz. Being also the personal ambassador of the Swedish King, Gustaf III, the latter enjoyed special favor at the French court.

Copies of several of Franklin's publications with autographed dedications to Kalm have been preserved in the University library at Uppsala. Between the two a personal correspondence is supposed to have continued after Kalm's return to Sweden, but if so, the letters were probably lost in the Helsingfors fire in 1827.

Since Franklin was not a churchman, Acrelius did not have the same opportunities as Kalm to make his personal acquaintance, but he, too, referred to him with admiration, paying special attention to his educational ideas. His plan for a practical "English" school, as opposed to the classical or "Latin" type, he described and commended. The addition by Acrelius of "instruction in Christianity" as one of the fundamentals of education, though Franklin himself had not mentioned the subject, may be attributed to professional zeal. In the Swedish school system of today, traces of Franklin's influence are still to be found; subsequent visitors to America described them further. During the coming decades of political turmoil in Sweden the figure of Franklin stood out as a beacon and guide to the contenders for liberty and political rights. "He was undoubtedly one of the greatest men of our age," L. M. Philipson, editor of the "radical" *Patriot* (August 1793), wrote after his death. "To all those who have a tender sentiment for human happiness and honor, his memory will always remain dear, his merits worshipped and his virtues extolled as priceless ideals."

Of the Swedish eighteenth century intellectuals who, conversely, exercised an influence in America, the following stand out: Emanuel Swedenborg, (1688–1772), Carl von Linné (Linnaeus) (1707–78) and Jöns Jakob Berzelius (1779–1848).

In the case of Swedenborg this influence was felt more during the nineteenth century than the eighteenth, when a special denomination, the New Church or the Church of the New Jerusalem, was organized to popularize his doctrines. Among prominent Americans who are known to have been students of Swedenborg the late Professor David F. Swenson enumerates in *Swedes in America:* Ralph Waldo Emerson, Charles A. Dana, Albert Brisbane, Horace Greeley, George W. Curtis, John Greenleaf Whittier, Nathaniel Hawthorne, Thomas Wentworth Higginson, William Ellery Channing, James Freeman Clark, James Russell Lowell, Theodore Parker and Walt Whitman. The most recent and probably the most readable biography of Swedenborg, written by Signe Toksvig, was published in 1948 by the Yale University Press.

The knowledge of Linnaeus in America was also considerable. His *Systema Naturae,* first published in 1735, under which plants have ever since been classified, became at once widely known. In the world of vegetation it created order. Linnaeus named and classified 780 American species. In honor of his pupil, Peter Kalm, he named the American mountain laurel, *Kalmia latifolia,* and the sheep laurel, *Kalmia angustifolia.* (Many plants are named for another pupil of Linnaeus, Carl Peter Thunberg, who was the first to study and report on the flora of Japan. A monument of him is still to be found in Tokio.)

The gardenia is named for Alexander Garden, an American botanist (1730–91), the dahlia for Anders Dahl, a pupil of Linnaeus, and the forsythia for William Forsyth, an Englishman, who brought back the first specimens from China. John Bartram (1699–1777), a famous botanist of Philadelphia, was a student of Linnaeus and so was Dr. James Gates Percival (1795–1856), a poet, linguist and geologist, of Connecticut. Few foreign scientists have had more societies, streets or parks named in their honor than Linnaeus, or even statues erected. By his contemporaries he was called "The King of Flowers," and his domain was world-wide.

Berzelius was a pioneer chemist who discovered or isolated a number of elements, cerium (1803) selenium (1817) silicon (1823) zirconium (1824) and thorium (1828). He also perfected the system of chemical nomenclature initiated by Lavoisier, which is still in general use. Various chemical societies and chemistry buildings such as Berzelius Hall at Yale University, are named in his honor. Karl Wilhelm Scheele (1742–86) was another pioneer Swedish chemist, originally a druggist. Anders Celsius (1701–44), a Swedish astronomer, improved De Lisle's centigrade temperature scale, which is more logical than that of Fahrenheit and is now used in all laboratories. Since the eighteenth century the exchange of ideas between Sweden and America has never ceased.

III

"A State Creates Itself"

Among the signers of the Declaration of Independence was at least one descendant of the original Swedish colonists, John Morton (1724–1777) of Pennsylvania, while John Hanson (1715–1783) of Maryland, who was not a signer, was elected in 1781 "President of The United States in Congress Assembled," the first to serve the full term of one year after the adoption of the Articles of Confederation. In the establishment of the new Republic both played dramatic and sometimes decisive roles. Since their ancestors had then lived in the country for three generations, they were as American as Washington or Franklin. That was also true of the men of Swedish descent who fought under Washington, in the Revolutionary land forces. Some of their names had, in fact, been so Anglicized that it is sometimes difficult to identify their origin. Several were of mixed ancestry. Like the non-Swedish names on the tombstones around the "Old Swedes" churches on the Delaware, they indicate the frequent intermarriages with other nationalities.

In regard to President Franklin Delano Roosevelt, for instance, Arnold Mulder writes in *Americans From Holland:* "In simple fact he was hardly more Dutch than English or even Swedish. If his paternal forebear, instead of the maternal ancestor, had been a Swede, and a Swedish name had been handed down to him, the admixture of Dutch blood would long since have been forgotten."

In the case of John Morton, however, there can be no doubt as to his Swedish descent. His great-grandfather, Morton Mortenson, had been one of the passengers on *Örnen* when it left Gothenburg with Governor Rising on February 2, 1654. In May of the same year, when the ship reached the Delaware, he must have seen the Swedes capture Fort Casimir at Sands Point (now New Castle). The house in which his great-grandson, John Morton, was born is still standing. "It is to be found on the north side of Darby Creek, Delaware County,

Pennsylvania, about half a mile north of the Essington railroad station," writes Colonel Henry D. Paxson. Since 1938 it has been renovated and preserved as a public monument.

Though John Morton's early education had been slight, he became a fluent orator in both English and Swedish, adds Colonel Paxson. At first he worked as a surveyor, but gradually became a public officeholder. For nineteen years he represented Chester County in the Pennsylvania Assembly and during two terms he was Speaker. At various times he held such other offices as High Sheriff and Justice of the Peace. Finally he became an Associate Justice of the Pennsylvania Supreme Court. He was also a member from Pennsylvania of the Stamp Act Congress of 1765, and of the Continental Congresses of 1774, 1775, and 1776. As chairman of the Pennsylvania delegation the last-named year, he voted at the critical moment with James Wilson and Benjamin Franklin for independence while Thomas Willing and Charles Humphreys were opposed. On July 4, 1776, both John Dickinson and Robert Morris were absent, and when the decisive session opened John Morton was ill. When he heard that there was a deadlock, six states being in favor of making the break from England and six opposed, with the final decision left to his own state, he rose from his sick bed and took his seat. As the Pennsylvania delegation was also evenly divided, two against two, it was Morton's vote which decided in favor of separation from England. It was his last public appearance. Less than a year later he died, the first of the signers to pass away. On his marble monument in St. Paul's churchyard in Chester, Pennsylvania, are inscribed the facts cited above; on the north side appears the following: "John Morton, being censured by his friends for his boldness in giving his casting vote for the Declaration of Independence, his prophetic spirit dictated from his deathbed the following message to them: 'Tell them they shall live to see the hour when they shall acknowledge it to have been the most glorious service I ever rendered to my country.'"

John Hanson, whose grandfather had moved from New Sweden to Maryland, was educated abroad. For a score of years, with some interruptions, he represented his native Charles County in the Maryland House of Delegates. In 1769 he was one of the signers of the Non-Importation Act. In 1773 he moved to Frederick County and until his death in 1783 he continued to hold public offices, such as County Treasurer, member of the commission to appoint officers, reorganize troops, and encourage enlistment in the Maryland militia, as well as member of the Provincial Committee of Correspondence, a sort of underground movement among the colonists. Three times he was elected a representative from Maryland to Continental Congresses. On March 1, 1781, he signed the Articles of Confederation, which preceded the Constitution, and as Maryland was the last state to act, the Articles then went into effect. On November 5, 1781, he was elected "President of the United States in Congress Assembled." In that capacity it became his duty to welcome General Washington on his first visit to Congress, November 28, 1781, and to express the official felicitations of the country on the victorious conclusion of the war. The British had just surrendered at Yorktown. To attempt to construe from this, however, as has been done in certain quarters, that John Hanson was the first President of the United States, is, of course, a bit far-fetched. He was never elected to any such office.

Of the temporary union under the Articles of Confederation, he was, however, the chief executive for one year. As such he had a Cabinet consisting of a Secretary of State (Robert R. Livingston), a Secretary of War (General Benjamin Lincoln) and a Secretary of Finance (Robert Morris). The current United States National Seal was ordered by him and he also issued the first Thanksgiving Proclamation, fixing the last Thursday in November as a national day of prayer and expressions of gratitude, as had already been done by the Pilgrims at Plymouth. During his term of office a Postmaster General was appointed and a national postal service begun.

His most important contribution, however, had been made when as a member of the Continental Congress from Maryland he led the fight to vest title to the *western lands,* i.e., those west of the original thirteen colonies, in the new national Government instead of dividing them, as had been begun, among the individual original thirteen states. This was the genesis of all the new states west of the Alleghenies. If this fight had been lost there might never have been more than thirteen states. It was his victory in this contest in October 1780 and the subsequent ratification by Maryland of the Articles of Confederation, which clinched their adoption, that led to his election, in November 1781 as president for a year of the new "Inseparable Union."

Like John Morton, Hanson sacrificed his health to his public service and only a year after his retirement as "President of the United States in Congress Assembled," he died at his home in Maryland at the age of sixty-eight. When the state of Maryland placed its marble statue of him in the national Capitol in Washington, D.C., in 1903, it was said at the dedication that his "name will be associated forever with laying the cornerstone of our great nation"—a phrase quoted by Colonel Frank W. Melvin of Philadelphia in his essay on Hanson.

Since the Swedish colonists had been the first settlers on both sides of the Delaware and on the Pennsylvania side as far north as Trenton, it has been surmised that they were among the farmers who rowed General Washington and his men across the rapids for his surprise attack on the English and their Hessian mercenaries on Christmas Eve, 1776. But if so, it has not been established by documentary proof. In his *History of Western Maryland* (Vol. I., p. 540), J. Thomas Scharf, however, writes: "The Swedes along the Delaware were subjected to great hardships and untold suffering by the English troops for their loyalty to the Revolutionary cause. They fought in large numbers in the ranks and they furnished some of the most brilliant officers and leaders in the struggle."

By that time, practically all contacts with Sweden had been allowed to lapse, and because so many Swedish names had been changed in spelling or otherwise corrupted, they are often hard to identify. *Kyn* had become Keen; *Hvijler,* Wheeler; *Stidden,* Stidham; *Stålkofta,* Stalcop; *Bonde,* Boon; *Höök,* Hawk or Hook; *Fysk,* Fiske; *Symonsson,* Simmons; *Tomasson,* Thompson; just as in more recent times *Solberg* has become Solbert; *Steffansson,* Stephenson; *Bengtson,* Benson; *Berggren,* Bergen; *Johansson,* Johnson; *Nyberg,* Newberry; *Larsson,* Lassen, or Lawson, or even Larcom; *Nygren,* Newbranch; *Sjöberg,* Seaburg; *Sjöstrand,* Seashore; *Sjöholm,* Seaholm; *Strömberg,* Stomburg; *Fredberg,* Freeburg; *Stenberg* first Stoneburg and then Stonebury, and so forth. Occasionally entirely new names of English origin (but hardly ever Irish, the best-known exception being Charlie McCarthy, whose Swedish name was "Kalle," and seldom Scotch) were adopted. Sometimes it was done to conceal the bearer's national origin or his personal identity, but most often to avoid confusion as well as misspelling. Future research may establish a Swedish ancestry for quite a number of the men who fought in the War of Independence, whether as officers or privates. Conversely, none of the names of deserters, so frequently published in the colonial newspapers, appear to be of Swedish origin.

Since contacts between the descendants of the Swedish colonists and their relatives in Sweden had become increasingly rare, the American Revolution was observed in Sweden from a political rather than a personal point of view. Sweden was then an ally of France, and for decades had been deeply influenced by French customs and manners. All educated Swedes were expected to speak French. The idealized descriptions of American life by the French *Enlightenment* writers had, in fact, pre-conditioned public opinion in Sweden to favor the revolutionists. In elegant Alexandrines, poets like Bengt Lidner wrote odes in their honor.

At first the King himself, the brilliant and ambitious, but erratic and theatrical, Gustavus III, was carried away by the general sentiment. In France he had many close acquaintances, including Louis XVI and Marie Antoinette, and on October 18, 1776, when news of the Declaration of Independence had finally reached Stockholm, he wrote a letter, in French, to the beautiful and talented Countess de Boufflers. In it he confessed his great interest in the news and added that if he had not been what he was, i.e., a ruling monarch, he would have liked to go to America himself in order to be able to observe, first-hand, the various stages by which "a state, so to speak, creates itself." He then predicted that some day America might rule Europe, "putting her to tribute as for two hundred years Europe has exacted tribute from America." From the American move for independence he sensed, he wrote, the possibility of a general war in Europe. "However that may be," he concluded, "I cannot but admire their (the American revolutionists) courage and applaud their audacity."

Later on, as his own subjects became more and more restive, inspired, he thought, at least partly, by the American example, he saw more clearly the possible effect on all kings, including himself. Two years later, on August 19, 1778, when France had decided to intervene in behalf of the American colonists, he wrote to his Ambassador in Paris, Count Gustaf Philip Creutz, "I cannot admit that it is just to support rebels against their king. The example will have too many consequences, especially in an era when attempts are made to break down all safeguards of authority, no matter what they may be." It was only with regret, he wrote, that as an ally of France he had to adjust himself to the decision.

In the French forces at the time many Swedish officers held temporary commissions. Their purpose was to get practical experience in order to gain more rapid promotion at home. Among them were some of the most aristocratic young men of the country, future admirals and generals, as well as diplomats and cabinet ministers. In honor of the Swedish King, a French regiment was called "The Royal Swedish," and while this particular regiment was not sent to America, about ninety Swedish officers did take part, on the American side, in the War for Independence. For them it was an ideal opportunity. In her reply to the Swedish King, written over a year after his, the Countess de Boufflers observed wryly that the motive of her nephew, the young Marquis de Lafayette, had been to win military renown rather than to help what she called "the insurgents." She herself remained royalist and pro-British.

About half of the Swedish officers, enrolled with the French in the War of Independence, fought in America or in American waters; the rest on naval vessels in other parts of the world or wherever they could inflict the greatest damage. The majority were naval officers—the most needed and the most difficult to obtain. Since they were with the French in practically every case, whether they fought on land or sea, it was a common American belief until quite recently that they were French. Consequently, their own country rarely received credit for their services. Most of them were of noble birth and being both aristocrats and royalists, they were not ideologically revolutionists. And yet at least one of them gained noble Swedish rank because of his acts of bravery in America. On their return, several were promoted in rank. At the same time, though they admired France, they were not inspired by any special aversion to England. In their letters home, written as a rule in French, they seldom expressed enthusiasm for the American cause, even though they supported the current vogue of liberty which was part of the "enlightenment" philosophy. Personally, General Washington gained their undeviating respect and admiration.

With such mixed motives the most ambitious of the young Swedish officers flocked to Paris to enlist for the war in America. As might be expected, they took their duties seriously and not only fought and bled but in some instances died for American independence. Some of those who returned had lost both their health and property, so that often the Swedish Government, through Ambassador Creutz, had to intervene in their behalf. For their participation most of the survivors received French decorations and two were elected members of the American Society of the Cincinnati. Of this their King did not approve, ordering them to resign from this organization of "former subjects who had rebelled against their legitimate sovereign. . . . While their success has legalized their enterprise," he added "it cannot justify it."

Among the Swedish officers who fought on land none attained a rank higher than that of colonel and among those in the naval forces none above *lieutenant de vaisseau*, since no foreigner could command a French ship, no matter what his competence might be. At critical moments, however, Swedish officers did take command. On the whole they were an able, colorful, if mixed group of men. Some were descendants of mercenaries of various nationalities who had fought in the Swedish armies during the Thirty Years' War and therefore bore names difficult to identify as Swedish, such as Feif, Fock, Hohenhausen, Nauckhoff, Rosen von Rosenstein, Schützercrantz, and Zachaud. And yet thanks to their military services, some of their forebears had held noble rank. In other cases, the names were unmistakably Swedish, such as Otto Henrik Nordenskjöld, who aided in the capture of Granada; Magnus Daniel Palmquist, who took part in the landing operations at Yorktown; Karl Gustaf Tornquist, who left a journal in which he describes the operations of Count de Grasse in which he participated; and Adolph Fredrik Pettersen (Peterson), a Swedish university graduate, who because of his record in America was ennobled and given the more glamorous sounding name of Rosensvärd. At Pensacola, Florida, he was seriously wounded. Of all the Swedish participants he was probably the most valiant. When he died in Sweden in 1799 he had the rank of rear admiral.

Baron von Stedingk, who refused to obey the King's order to resign from the Society of the Cincinnati, to which he had been elected in Rhode Island, was born in Pomerania, then a Swedish province, and before going to America had been a colonel in the French Army. Under Count d'Estaing, he participated in several of the engagements in the West-Indies, and at the siege of Savannah he commanded a division. While leading it in the assault on that city, October 9, 1779, he was severely wounded and because of his injuries he had to return to Europe. His plan to recruit an entire regiment of Swedes for service in America came, however, to naught. As late as in 1813 he was in command, under Crown Prince Carl Johan, the former French Marshal Bernadotte, of the Swedish forces in Germany which took part in the coalition against Napoleon. After the Battle of Nations at Leipzig he was one of the signers for Sweden of the 1814 peace treaty with France. He survived most of the other Swedish participants in the war for American independence. In 1790 he was appointed Swedish Ambassador to Russia, and when he died in 1837 at the age of ninety, he held the rank of a Swedish field marshal.

Of all the Swedish officers who took part in the American War of Independence, Count Hans Axel von Fersen (1755-1810) personally was the most romantic, as socially he was the most favored and professionally the most prominent. To the French Commander-in-Chief, Count de Rochambeau, he was an adjutant and often served as his liaison officer with General Washington. After receiving a military education in Sweden, completed in Germany, Italy, and France, he had been sent to Paris to prepare for a diplomatic career. Introduced at court he soon attracted the attention of the young Queen, Marie Antoinette, and it was to escape an embarrassing emotional dilemma that he enlisted in 1779 in the French forces going to America. Ambassador Creutz has described the young Queen's excitement as she watched him defile with his regiment in its final review. In 1780 he landed in Rhode Island, and as a staff officer remained there a year. His gallantry among the ladies at Newport is still a topic of local gossip. Late in September 1780, he was present at the first meeting between Washington and Rochambeau at Hartford (or Wethersfield), Connecticut, and having been sent ahead to advise Washington of the approach of the French General, probably because he spoke English, he was beyond much doubt the first officer in the French expeditionary corps to make the personal acquaintance of the American Commander-in-Chief. During the war he was entrusted by Rochambeau and Washington with several missions of responsibility. When differences of opinion arose he sometimes served as a mediator. At Yorktown he distinguished himself in the field and was one of the officers present when Cornwallis surrendered. His picture appears in the famous painting of the scene by John Trumbull in the Capitol at Washington.

Some of the letters he wrote in French to his father while he was in America have been published. They are frank and not always complimentary to the people he was fighting for. Professionally he did his work well, however, and at the end of the war he was elected, like Curt von Stedingk, a member of the Society of the Cincinnati, a rare honor for foreigners. Unlike Stedingk, however, he probably obeyed the King's order to resign.

Once the independence of the former colonies had been won, the practical-minded King Gustavus III lost no time recognizing the new Government. As early as in the spring of 1782, or before the British had signed the preliminary peace treaty in London, he instructed Ambassador Creutz to negotiate through Benjamin Franklin in Paris a treaty of trade and friendship with the new Republic. The treaty was signed April 3, 1783, five months before peace was formally concluded on September 3 that year at Versailles. Personally Creutz had remained consistently pro-American, and his relations with Franklin had always been the most cordial. What he told Franklin privately about the King's attitude is not known, but on December 5, 1782, Franklin sent a letter to the American Secretary of State, Robert R. Livingston, about the King's desires for a trade treaty in which he said: "His [Creutz's] commission has some polite expressions in it, to wit: 'that His Majesty thought it for the good of his subjects to enter into a treaty of amity and commerce with the people of the United States of America, who had established their independence, so justly merited by their courage and constancy,' or words to that effect." Thanks to the King's personal initiative, however, Sweden became the first neutral country to recognize the new Republic.

Besides its moral value, the treaty gave official sanction to commercial relations that already had been established. During the war, supplies from Sweden, whether sent via France or direct to America, had been of considerable assistance to the revolutionists. Swedish iron, for instance, was regularly sold in Providence, Rhode Island, and, despite the attempted British blockade, a number of Swedish vessels were able to unload their cargoes in American ports.

These trade relations were continued after 1783 and occasionally Swedish visitors as well as former sailors remained in America. As no immigration records were kept, it is only by accident that such settlers can be traced. Some proved themselves to be men of ability and became quite prominent.

Among the early settlers, for instance, was Colonel John Christian Senf, who was born in Sweden about 1754, and probably educated there. He must have emigrated before or during the Revolution, for he served during that conflict as a captain of engineers in the South Carolina Line of the Continental Army. He was a "strongminded but somewhat autocratic and eccentric genius," who "practically single-handed designed and built the Santee Canal [South Carolina], one of the earliest in the United States [1793-1800]." He had probably had some experience in the construction of canals in Sweden. He died in 1806 as chief engineer of the state of South Carolina.

Then there was Adolph Ulric Wertmüller, a painter, who arrived in Philadelphia on a Swedish brig in 1794, and his friend, Henrik Gahn, who came on the same boat, hoping to make a fortune in this country. Gahn established a mercantile business in New York, became a very enthusiastic American citizen (1796), married an American girl, was appointed Swedish Consul in 1797, and for many years befriended the occasional Swedish visitors who passed through or stayed in New York.

Another early Swede was John Asplund, who after deserting from the British Merchant Marine, some time before 1785, settled in North Carolina and there came in contact with American Baptists, was converted, given a license to preach, and eventually was ordained a Baptist minister in Southampton County, Virginia.

John Erik Lindmark, born near Stockholm in 1792, came to America in the beginning of the nineteenth century, enlisted in the United States Navy as a sailmaker, was honorably discharged in 1818 and after becoming a prosperous merchant in New York, published in 1832 the first two pieces of fiction known to have been written by a Swedish American. In 1857 he devised a sincere if fantastic plan for a League of Nations. During the Civil War he sent plans of ironclad ships to the Secretary of the Navy, only to have them rejected. Probably through the Reverend Olof Gustaf Hedström he was converted to Methodism. He lived until 1868. His great-grandson, John Lindmark, became a well-known bookseller in Poughkeepsie, New York.

A hundred years earlier there had arrived at New Orleans one of the most glamorous leaders of mass emigration who ever came to America—Carl Fredrik Arensburg, a former officer under Charles XII, born in 1693 in Swedish Pomerania. In 1721, or after the King's death, he was appointed by the French *Compagnie des Indes* to head a group of about three hundred Germans selected to settle in French Louisiana. For over forty years he served them as a judge and civic leader in the so-called "German Coast" settlement on the Mississippi River, about thirty miles above New Orleans. A great lover of liberty, he fought Spanish domination and in consequence once came near losing his life. At the age of eighty-four he died in 1777.

King Gustavus III's apprehensions as to the political effect of the American Revolution turned out to be only too well founded. In 1772 he had put through, by surprise action, a change in the constitution by which he arrogated to himself almost autocratic powers. In 1789, when another war with Russia had failed to allay the discontent and some of his own officers had conspired against him, he staged another "direct action" procedure by which his dictatorship became practically absolute. Then the French Revolution, of which the American example was clearly recognized in Sweden as one of the causes, disturbed him still more. "The events in France are horrible," the conservative Bishop Olof Wallquist of Växjö wrote to him on August 17,

1789. "All this is the result of the attention paid to Franklin, Raynal and Linguet." In March 1792, while attending a masquerade party at the Stockholm Opera House the King was assassinated by some of his rebellious officers, an event which is the historical basis for the plot of Verdi's opera, *The Masked Ball.*

After that the repression of agitators for more political liberty became even more severe. In 1792 a translation of Thomas Paine's *The Rights of Man* was published by the radicals in Stockholm with a dedication to George Washington. It was intended to be an antidote to Edmund Burke's *Reflections on the Revolution in France,* for like Burke, many moderate Swedes who had favored American independence could not approve of the French Revolution, especially after the violence had begun. "That may not be the way to conduct a revolution," the Swedish radicals replied in effect, "but see how the Americans did it." The same year a single issue of *The Patriot,* a title which then implied radicalism, was confiscated because it contained a translation of the American Constitution. In June 1794, the reproduction, even in part, of either the American or the French Constitution was explicitly forbidden.

But the political ferment continued to work. In 1809, after losing Finland to Russia, Sweden had a full-fledged revolution of its own by which its King, Gustaf IV, the incompetent and unbalanced son of Gustavus III, was deposed in favor of his childless uncle, Charles XIII, and a French Marshal, Jean Baptiste Bernadotte, elected the latter's heir to the throne. Probably because of the excesses committed during the French Revolution, no strong republican sentiment developed in Sweden. The new Constitution resembled, however, both the French and the American. The principal leader in the Swedish upheaval had been Georg Adlersparre, a newspaper editor and publicist, who had been brought up on the French Enlightenment doctrines. For years he had also advocated American political ideas and institutions. As early as 1796 he had published an account of the prison reforms in Philadelphia.

In the new Constitution the King was given powers corresponding to those of the American President, except that his office was hereditary, and in recent years Sweden has gone further than the United States in democratic reform, so that the Prime Minister whose term of office is dependent on the parliamentary majority, as in Great Britain, has become the chief executive rather than the King. In 1865, in direct and conscious imitation of the American system, as described by De Tocqueville, the Four Estates in the Swedish Riksdag were abolished in favor of a First Chamber, or Senate, and a Second Chamber or House of Representatives. This change took power from the nobility, the clergy, as well as the owners of large estates, and gave it to the middle-class businessmen and farmers. In recent years under this more democratic parliamentary system, organized labor has gained political control.

Throughout the early decades of the nineteenth century many changes, both political and social, were advocated in Sweden on the basis of American experience. Several books about America by French, German, as well as English writers were also published. As early as 1783 a Swedish nobleman, Baron Samuel Gustaf Hermelin who, on the recommendation of Franklin, had been sent to America in 1782 to investigate economic and political conditions, including mineral resources, published a report of his findings. While he was in America Hermelin was elected a member of the American Philosophical Society in Philadelphia, as well as of the American Academy of Arts and Sciences in Boston. In his pocket he carried credentials as the first Swedish Minister to the United States, just as in a commission signed on September 17, 1782, by John Hanson, "President of the United States in Congress Assembled," Benjamin Franklin had been designated the first American Minister to Sweden, but as Franklin never went to Stockholm and no one else was appointed at that time, Hermelin's credentials lapsed. He therefore returned home as a private citizen and after that had a distinguished career in the development of the mineral resources of northern Sweden.

A third study tour under official auspices, similar to those of Hermelin and Peter Kalm, was undertaken in 1818–20 by a young naval officer of noble descent, Baron Axel Klinkowström. It was to cover shipyards, as well as steamboats and other forms of engineering novelties. Robert Fulton had by then made his country famous for his steam-propelled warship, the *Fulton,* which weighed only thirty-eight tons, as he had by the *Clermont,* which furnished the first steamship passenger service, plying between New York and Albany, the route that was soon to be used by so many Swedish pioneers headed for the Middle West.

In his book, *Letters About the United States,* which has never been translated, Klinkowström described not only naval construction and the new use of steam, but also the American military establishment, the political institutions and social advances, such as the Philadelphia prison reforms, which had already attracted attention in Sweden. The new Government he declared a success, tending to promote first of all, he wrote, the happiness of the people, an aim that so far had not been considered in Sweden or in any other European country as the business of the Government. To President Monroe, to whom he was introduced in Washington, he reported he had said that "the time was near when Europeans would travel in America less for the purpose of introducing their own ideas than to gather information about things that were either imperfectly known or wholly new to Europe."

His two volumes of *Letters* were published in Stockholm in 1824. To the English charges that had been spread in Sweden during and after the War of 1812 that the Americans were egotistic and mercenary he took vigorous exception. In Brooklyn he had been a neighbor, he wrote, of a General Swift whose home life he described as idyllic. "How can one still place faith," he asked, "in the statements of certain travelers who are eager to belittle these progressive people by calling them hard-hearted and insensible to the sufferings of others?" Having been brought up himself on the French Enlightenment writers, he was inclined to see all things American in the most favorable light.

The new type of popular newspaper, such as the Stockholm afternoon organ, *Aftonbladet,* which began to appear in 1830, reflected the contemporary American "Era of Good Feeling." America was identified as the new land of hope for the common people. When social or political reforms were demanded, it was usually the American example that was cited. Lars Johan Hierta, editor of *Aftonbladet,* was not only a brilliant journalist, one of the greatest in Sweden of all time, but also a legislator and political leader. By the new Constitution of 1809 the press had been granted full freedom to print anything it wanted, short of criminal libel, and the new popular papers made the most of it. By stressing the United States as the home of everything that was promising for the world's downtrodden, the Swedish radical press thus laid the foundation for the direct emigration propaganda that was to begin in earnest in the 1840s. In *Aftonbladet* appeared the first "America letters" of Gustaf Unonius, that were to be so influential in making his countrymen follow him to the Middle West.

Educational travel by young businessmen, heretofore limited as a rule to England and the European continent, began at this time to include the United States and Canada. Thus in 1834 Karl D. Arfwedson, heir to a successful retail store in Stockholm, wrote a book in English covering a trip to North America. It was called *The United States and Canada, 1832, 1833, 1834.* In 1835 it was also published in Swedish. The same year two other American travel books appeared in Stockholm: *A Tour of North America,* by Kurt Augustus Gosselman, another Swedish naval officer with a flair for writing, who had previously written descriptions of his experiences in both South and Central America; and *Sketches from Social Life in the United States of America,* a Swedish translation from a German book by C. von Hauswolf.

From America as well as England, Sweden began to receive in the 1820s not only political but also moral and religious impulses which helped prepare the way for the coming emigration. Professor George M. Stephenson of the University of Minnesota, has called the effect of this influence a "Second Reformation."

Since the adoption of the First Reformation in the sixteenth century, Sweden had been uniformly and solidly Lutheran. Every child, as soon as born, had to be baptized by a clergyman of the established church and thus enrolled as a member of that body. To preserve this religious unity private prayer meetings, known as conventicles, were forbidden in 1726, as they had been in England by the Conventicle Law of 1664, but whereas in England the ban was lifted by the Toleration Act of 1689, the Swedish law, though indifferently enforced, was not repealed until 1858, and for the next ten years prayer meetings in private houses were declared illegal during the hours when the regular church services were held. The growing agitation against this law, which was kept on the statute books as long as the state clergy constituted a special Estate in the Swedish Riksdag, was to have a certain influence on the earliest emigration to America, a country hailed as a land of complete religious liberty.

The first Methodists in Sweden were English workmen employed by Samuel Owen, a pupil of James Watt, who had been invited to Stockholm in 1806 as a specialist in the construction of the new steam engines. (He built the first power units for Swedish steamboats.) Like his namesake, Robert Owen, he was an advocate of temperance and other forms of social reform as well as a supporter of the Methodist Church. For his workmen he built a little Methodist chapel and as its pastors he brought ministers from England. In 1830 he invited a handsome, twenty-six-year-old Scotchman with curly black locks and heavy eyebrows, by the name of George Scott, born in Edinburgh, where he had preached for a couple of years before coming to Stockholm. He had not only spiritual zeal but also a dynamic personality and on both religious reform in Sweden and the further stimulation of emigration to America he was to exercise a wide-spread influence.

He was, in addition, an agent of the British Bible Society and as such distributed both Bibles and revivalist tracts. Within a year he learned enough Swedish to be able to preach in that language and thereby widened his field.

Shrewdly he did not attack either the state church or the tenets of Lutheranism, but as the country was unmistakably suffering from an excessive consumption of a home-distilled potato brandy, known as *brännvin,* he launched, with the approval of not only his employer, Mr. Owen, but also that of the King, the former Marshal Bernadotte, a vigorous temperance campaign. Ever since his arrival in Sweden as heir to the throne in 1810, the King had felt concern about the drinking habits of his future subjects. A certain amount of temperance agitation had been under way in Sweden before Mr. Scott arrived; as early as 1826 a request had been sent to the newly constituted American Temperance Society for copies of its constitution and by-laws as well as other publications, a request recently recovered in its files, and with the aid of a Swedish temperance advocate, Colonel C. von Forsell, Scott prepared a booklet entitled, *Information about the Recently Organized American Temperance Societies.* This was his first salvo against rum.

The second round was even hotter stuff,—a reprint in Swedish of the famous *Six Sermons on Temperance* by the Reverend Lyman Beecher, father of Henry Ward Beecher, pastor of the Plymouth Congregational Church in Brooklyn, and of Harriet Beecher Stowe, author of *Uncle Tom's Cabin.* These sermons, like those delivered by the Reverend Mr. Scott himself, struck a new note in moral earnestness and religious fervor. Gradually people who were interested in religious as well as social reforms, came from all parts of Sweden to hear him. His contribution to the moral rejuvenation of Sweden that took place during the subsequent decades of the nineteenth century was considerable.

By 1834 the campaign against excessive drinking had progressed so far that Crown Prince Oscar, who like his father had been born in France, presided over a large temperance rally in Stockholm and after that proclaimed himself the royal protector of all such activities. He also allowed himself to be elected Honorary President of the first Swedish Temperance Society. Being under his auspices the campaign against drink could hardly be squelched. He also made a study of other American social reforms which as King he later did much to introduce in Sweden, such as a more humane treatment of criminals.

In 1836 Scott received reinforcement from the United States. It was brought by the Reverend Robert Baird, a young American Presbyterian from Philadelphia, who in the interest of temperance was making a tour of Europe. In Paris he had published a French translation of a book he had written about the budding temperance movement in his own country. When he arrived in Stockholm he was introduced by Scott to the King, and to him he presented a copy of the French version of his book. The King was delighted. Not only was he interested in temperance work, but he always found French easier to read than Swedish. When he had finished the book he sent for Baird and asked for permission to have it translated into Swedish and published at his own expense. This was readily granted and through official channels a copy was sent to every clergyman in the country. For Scott's campaign this was heavy artillery. While it would be unfair to claim that after that all Swedish clergymen became champions of total abstinence, it is safe to say that they dutifully read the publication. Under the name of "The King's Book," as well as "Baird's Book," it was widely discussed, a master stroke of both temperance and, indirectly, immigration propaganda. Before the end of 1836 a young Swedish clergyman from Småland, Peter Wieselgren, organized on the American model a Swedish Temperance Society, and in the course of time International Good Templar Lodges, as well as both Blue and White Ribbon Societies, began to spring up. Since then the Swedish campaign against alcoholism has never ceased. From forty liters per capita in 1830, the consumption of hard liquor had now gone down to approximately (1948) five liters. This agitation against alcohol was the first of the great popular movements which did so much to convert Sweden into a democratic, self-governing country. From it sprang directly the privately managed adult education system which in turn laid the groundwork for both the organized labor and the cooperative movements.

In 1837, after collecting funds in England, Scott was able to build a larger chapel or tabernacle on Haymarket Square in Stockholm, now dominated by the Concert House in which each fall the Nobel Prizes are distributed. In 1840 Baird came back to Sweden and together he and Scott made a preaching tour of the country. From this tour far-reaching consequences were to follow, even though Scott's own career in Sweden was to come to a sudden and surprising end. He was invited by Baird to come to America in 1841 to solicit funds for his work, but when reports of the sombre colors in which he had painted Swedish moral conditions reached Stockholm, there was an outcry against him, especially in the radical press. Politically he was a conservative and a friend of several bishops as well as of the King. Before foreign eyes, it was claimed, he had defamed the country. When he attempted to preach in his Tabernacle in Stockholm on Palm Sunday, March 20, 1842, the sanctuary was invaded by a howling mob which drove him from his pulpit. The press campaign against him became so sharp that he was compelled to return to England. From there he continued, however, to supervise both temperance and Methodist propaganda in Sweden and was able to forward considerable funds received for their support from America. Within Sweden his work was carried on by his friends and followers until complete religious liberty had been obtained. The new free churches were less opposed to emigration than the state church.

By the end of the 1830s the new American literature had also become known in Sweden; first, the works of Washington Irving, though the political satire in his *Knickerbocker's History* was not understood, and, second, those of James Fenimore Cooper, whose Indian stories have continued to be popular reading in Sweden ever since. (*The Last of the Mohicans* has been published twenty-eight times in Swedish translations.) The taste for historical fiction had already been aroused in Sweden by the works of Walter Scott, who had replaced in popularity both French and German authors. In 1835 Henry Wadsworth Longfellow visited Sweden, the first American writer to do so. His stay passed rather unnoticed, and he never met Esaias Tegnér, the national poet, some of whose works he later translated. In 1853 his novel, *Hyperion,* was published in Swedish and both *Evangeline* and *Hiawatha* in 1854-56. New translations of his shorter poems continue to appear in Swedish newspapers and periodicals.

In this way, by books, newspapers, temperance agitation, social reforms, sermons, and popular lectures, the Swedish people became mentally prepared for the great emigration movement to America that was to begin in the 1840s. American political institutions, social progress, engineering advance and new inventions, as well as religious freedom, established the impression of a romantic, rich and happy country. The more personal "America letters" that were to come later clinched the case.

IV

THE EARLY SWEDISH PIONEERS

At the beginning of the nineteenth century, Sweden was a backward agricultural country, with a surplus of landless farm workers. The industrialization which now makes it prosperous had hardly begun and throughout the second half of the century it grew but slowly. "The country is being filled with cottages inhabited by people who have no other wealth than their own labor," wrote Esaias Tegnér, the poet and bishop, in 1833. "The population has increased and the population statistics have become charity rolls." In no other part of Sweden was this more true than in his own diocese in Småland, from which so many of the emigrants were later to come—one-third of the total.

When Henry Wadsworth Longfellow returned from his tour of central Sweden in 1835 he wrote for the July 1837 issue of the *North American Review* an article that was later reprinted in his collected travel papers, *Driftwood*. "Almost primeval simplicity reigns over this northern land," he intoned, "almost primeval solitude and stillness." Ten years later he began his *Evangeline* with these famous lines:

This is the forest primeval. The murmuring pines and the hemlocks,
Bearded with moss, and in garments green, indistinct in the twilight,
Stand like Druids of eld, with voices sad and prophetic,
Stand like harpers hoar, with beards that rest on their bosoms.
Loud from its rocky caverns, the deep-voiced, neighboring ocean
Speaks, and in accents disconsolate answers the wail of the forest.

This atmosphere was supposed to be that of Nova Scotia, a country Longfellow had never seen. Unmistakably, it suggested Sweden, through which the poet had just traveled with his young wife and two of her friends in a horse-drawn coach.

"In 1848," writes Florence E. Janson, "only about eight per cent of Sweden's inhabitants were engaged in industry, while eighty per cent received an income from agriculture. This situation had been more or less the same for over a hundred years. In 1920, on the other hand, it was estimated that 35 per cent of the population were engaged in industry or mining; 15 per cent in transportation or commerce, as contrasted with 44 per cent in agriculture, fisheries or forestry."

Next to agriculture, Sweden's first industry was mining. In the seventeenth and eighteenth centuries both copper and iron were exported practically all over Europe. But the supply of copper, which the organizers of the South Seas Company had hoped to sell in America as well as in Europe and Asia, not to mention Africa and Magellanica or Australia, was soon exhausted. Iron held out better. Not only was hand-wrought Swedish iron sold in America as early as the latter half of the eighteenth century but throughout the early immigration period in the nineteenth century the emigrant ships coming direct from Sweden usually carried iron as their main cargo.

In the twentieth century Sweden's most profitable mineral export has been iron ore from the Lapland mines, but until a railroad had been built through the Arctic wilderness, and the water power converted into electricity, the ore could neither be extracted nor transported. When that had been done, emigration to America had all but ceased.

Another Swedish handicap which delayed industrialization and promoted emigration was the almost total lack of coal. Sweden could not, therefore, equal England's early use of steam. The first steam-powered Swedish industry was the sawmills on the northeast coast, which could utilize their own waste as fuel. And until there was a foreign market for Swedish lumber, which was not the case until England and France had exhausted their own forest resources, the Swedish lumber mills had not enough customers. Now nearly one-half of Sweden's exports originate in the forests and as the lumber products are more and more highly refined they bring higher prices and create more jobs for the Swedes at home.

Though the country still lacks coal as well as gasoline and is greatly handicapped when imports of either are restricted, a great deal of the water power has been turned into electricity. During the main emigration period human muscles and direct water power were the chief sources of energy, whereas by 1949 eighty per cent of all farms had been electrified and it was calculated that in twenty years every house in the country would have at least electric light. Conversely, a technological improvement which stimulated Swedish emigration was the discovery in the nineteenth century of new methods of making steel, particularly the Thomas process, which made use of ordinary coal for smelting, whereas Sweden had only charcoal. This favored England, Germany, Belgium and other coal-producing countries. By the 1830s the Värmland iron masters Selma Lagerlöf writes about had been all but ruined by the new foreign competition and the number of jobs they could provide for Swedish workers correspondingly reduced.

An even deeper economic cause of the emigration wave was the shortage of arable land, which was made worse by defective distribution. (A series of poor harvests in the late 1860s aggravated matters still more.) Throughout the country the young people "who had no other wealth than their own labor," found it increasingly difficult to obtain a patch of land and a modest log cabin in which to raise a family. The large estates were usually held by members of the nobility, or other men with inherited or accumulated wealth. Most of the farms were owned by an only slightly less conservative class known as *bönder,* or peasant proprietors (farmers). They, too, had sometimes kept their land in the same family for centuries. (In the first volume of her *Jerusalem,* Selma Lagerlöf describes supremely well those living in Dalarna, or Dalecarlia.) For ordinary farm laborers, the situation was bleak indeed. They were, in truth, a "landless proletariat." Since there were few industries, and in many districts none at all, the choice was reduced to hiring out to the owners of large estates as *torpare,* or crofters, receiving the use of a modest cabin and a bit of land, usually a clearing in the forest, in return for so many days of labor each week on the owner's estate, or as *statare,* or farm workers, living in special barracks or small houses on the main estate itself and receiving most of their pay *in natura,* that is, part of their own produce from the land of their employers. Or they could hire out to the *bönder* as household help or as seasonal workers. The choice was not alluring. In each case the pay was low and the hours of work incredibly long. If occasionally grain prices went up, that did not benefit the hired hands, whose remuneration had been fixed in advance. This system has long since been broken up and now as an aid to repopulation not only land and housing on easy credit terms, but money for household equipment is loaned to newlyweds by the Government.

When the news of rich land in the Middle West to be had either for a dollar or two per acre, usually $1.25, or free from the Federal Government under the Homestead Act of 1862, reached these landless, dispirited, but usually hardy and often ambitious people the effect was bound to be electric. Gradually the more and more frequent "America letters," brought about an almost country-wide "America fever" which no counter-propaganda could allay. In certain districts of Småland, for instance, there was a mass exodus, which included even farmowners. Appeals to family sentiment, patriotism, fear of unimagined hardships, and, finally, the prospect of interment in alien soil, were powerless.

To this state of mind the religious unrest that was then sweeping Sweden, as it did almost all of Europe, contributed its share. The long, intellectually impressive, but usually unemotional and impersonal sermons preached from a majority of the pulpits of the Lutheran state church, were no match for the warmer, simpler, more dynamic, if often rambling and sometimes illiterate, discourses of the unordained colporteurs, or lay preachers, whether Baptists, Methodists, or Mission Friends. The dignified, slow hymns, usually of German origin, that were sung in the parish churches, could not compete with the lilting revivalist tunes from the West, sung at private prayer meetings or in the roadside Mission Houses that were gradually built in almost every parish, and especially in the new industrial communities.

The new temperance agitation, which likewise had originated in England or America, helped idealize American moral and religious conditions. While not opposed in principle to temperance and usually practicing considerable moderation in the use of liquor themselves, the state clergy disliked temperance lectures delivered outside their own churches as entering wedges of opposition, or separatism. Nearly all the early Lutheran ministers who came to America about the middle of the nineteenth century to serve the Swedish immigrants in their new communities had fallen into bad grace with the church authorities at home because they had indulged in talks on temperance. Such unauthorized and irregular activities were regarded as signs of disaffection, if not downright disloyalty. Whenever induced by his pro-temperance parishioners to speak on the problem of alcohol a certain elderly rector of a country church in Småland, personally known to one of the authors of this book, never failed to make an equally strong appeal for moderation in the use of food. . . . "It is just as wicked to eat too much as to drink too much," he would solemnly declare every time, but since overeating was hardly a public menace in that poverty-ridden province, the temperance advocates, who were inspired by American ideals of total abstinence, would groan.

A further cause of discontent among the young Swedish workers, especially in the final years of the nineteenth century, was the compulsory military service, then unknown in America. It was less the service itself that drove them out of the country than the excessively harsh discipline imposed by haughty young upper-class officers whose model was Prussia. The fact that most of these martinets were the sons of the nobility or of other owners of large estates added to the social discontent.

This sentiment became especially strong in 1890 when the term of compulsory training was extended to ninety days. By contrast, the young men of Sweden have recently trained for the national defense without excessive grumbling for from 270 to 450 days and during the two world wars from two to three years. By that time they had been made to feel more deeply that it was their own country, and they were therefore more disposed to defend it.

Until the first decades of the twentieth century there were also irksome political disabilities which helped promote emigration. While owners of large estates or other kinds of property, whether real or personal, enjoyed plural votes, the landless workers had no vote at all. In many respects social class distinctions were at that time more marked in Sweden than in the United States. "There is no need in America to bow and scrape before gentlemen," was a potent remark tending to stimulate emigration. Now the difference is slight, if any.

"I cannot give the exact reason for emigrating," a Swedish-born coal miner in Pennsylvania who had emigrated as late as 1886 replied to a questionnaire sent by an official Swedish commission appointed in 1905 to ascertain the causes of emigration. (*Emigrantutredningen.*) "The problem of bread was probably the main one; class differences and the question of personal worth. I felt as if I were useless, both to the community and myself. My word was worth nothing, even when it concerned my own soul. I have otherwise nothing to complain about Mother Svea [Sweden]. From her I inherited at least good moral principles."

Prior to 1840 it was forbidden by law to leave Sweden permanently except by special Government permission and temporarily only against an adequate guarantee of return. This law, to be sure, was poorly enforced but in 1840 it was wholly repealed as too harsh and contrary to the spirit of the times. This gave a new fillip to emigration. Gustaf Unonius and his friends, who settled in Wisconsin in 1841, were the first to take advantage of the new law.

The earliest nineteenth century Swedish settlers in the United States were not, however, disaffected farm youths, but in most cases former sailors who either had been shipwrecked or had deserted in some American port, then a fairly common practice, and more venial than now.

One of the earlier runaway sailors, and the first Swede to accumulate a personal fortune in America, was a native of Småland, a tall, handsome youth with agreeable manners as well as a gift for business. His name was Svante Magnus Svensson (later spelled Swenson), born in 1816 in the parish of Barkaryd, not far from Bottnaryd, the birthplace of Governor Printz.

When eighteen years old he was employed as a clerk in a grocery store in Eksjö, a near-by town, and one day in a fit of anger his employer boxed his ear. At this young Swenson was so outraged that he walked out of the store and never returned. Instead he went to sea, and for two years he sailed before the mast on British as well as Swedish ships. He thus learned a fair amount of English. In 1836 he decided to stay ashore in the United States and two years later he was sent by an employer in Baltimore on a commercial mission to the Republic of Texas, which had just declared itself independent of Mexico. Though the ship was wrecked on the coast near Galveston, he managed to save his life, and to salvage some of the merchandise, which he began to sell from a base at Richmond.

Being twenty-two years old and in good health, as well as endowed with that indomitable spirit which is supposed to be the heritage of all natives of Småland, he made his way up the Gulf of Galveston to Columbus, then the capital, where he found employment in the store of a Mr. Adrian. Here his home training stood him in good stead. Before long he was a partner in the business. The young republic was in a state of economic expansion, and driving a pair of spirited horses hitched to a handsomely painted wagon, a former ambulance or hearse loaded with merchandise, Swenson would circulate about the countryside, taking orders from the owners of various plantations. One of his customers was a wealthy physician from Tennessee, Dr. Edward Long, who owned a large ranch called Finckley, near Richmond in Fort Bend County, southwest of Houston. He was so impressed with the ingratiating manners and business ability of the young Swede that he asked him to become manager of his estate. This he did while continuing his retail business and when Dr. Long died a few years later he married, first the widow, Mrs. Jeanette Long, and in 1853, after her death, the latter's cousin, Miss Cora B. McCready of Tennessee, by whom he had four children. By marrying Mrs. Long he also became owner of the plantation, including the slaves. But before 1849, when Texas became a member of the North American union, he had sold both the plantation and the slaves and moved to Austin, a town which he had been tipped off, probably by Sam Houston, was to be the new capital of the state. In advance he had invested in land at the new seat, and when it was actually occupied as such, he had built not only a hotel, but a large general store, the first in the city. At Go-Valley, to the south of Austin, he then developed for himself and his family a country estate. But he never again employed any slaves. Like almost all Swedes he found the system repugnant. Early he had become a friend of Sam Houston, President of the Republic of Texas and later United States Senator and, finally, Governor of the state. For several years he was his business agent.

When the Civil War broke out Swenson's anti-slavery sentiments were so well known in Austin that he decided to move to Mexico, leaving his family at Go-Valley. When the war was over, he settled in New Orleans where he soon built up a large business as a cotton exporter. During the wartime embargo he had been able to buy up cotton at low prices and when the war was over he sold it at a good profit, especially in Europe where supplies had run low.

The cotton business, conducted under the name of the Swenson Mercantile Company, grew so fast that in 1867 he decided to move the main office to New York, where he also organized a private bank, first known as Swenson & Perkins and then as S. M. Swenson & Sons, a name the firm still retains. Of the National City Bank of New York, his oldest son, Eric P. Swenson, became a director and as such served until his death in 1945. From 1921 to 1929 he was Chairman of the Board. Its founder, James Alexander Stillman, was a native of Brownsville, Texas. When the senior Swenson died in Brooklyn in 1896, he left a large estate now managed by his grandsons.

In Texas Mr. Swenson had been an early stockholder in the Buffalo Bayou and Colorado Gulf Railroad which helped open up the western parts of the state. In the development of the sulphur business at Freeport, Texas, his oldest son, Eric P. Swenson, was active, but after his death the family interest was sold.

Prior to the Civil War Swenson became a large landowner in western Texas by accepting as payment for goods at his store in Austin the land script issued by the new Republic of Texas to the men who had fought in its war of independence from Mexico. Records have been found to show that he once owned land in twenty-six different counties in Texas, mostly in the lower Panhandle section. Until the 1880s this was barren, unfenced land over which stray herds and wild animals roamed. At first it was not even taxed, but when the state began to assess it, the Swenson sons decided to develop it into a cattle ranch and then into farmland. Over a thousand homesteads have been sold, and yet there are some three hundred thousand acres left. Not only fencing, but full blooded, registered stock, Herefords, were introduced in Texas by the SMS ranch, and so was scientific feeding. So well established are the standards of this firm that its cattle are sold by mail, sight unseen, to farmers in the Middle West for the final feeding.

As late as in 1927 the general manager of the ranch, A. J. Swenson, a nephew of the founder, visited relatives in Småland where in 1864 he had been born. Like his uncle he was tall, well dressed, suave in manner and picturesque in speech. With his grayish goatee, bushy eyebrows and ruddy complexion he suggested a Kentucky colonel or Uncle Sam. His soft Southern accent was a delightful blend of Småland and Texas. When a fellow passenger on his return trip on board the M.S. *Gripsholm,* whom he had asked to visit him, replied that he would if invited, he said, "In Texas you don't need an invitation; you just come in and hang up your hat." For some years his two sons W. G. and A. M. G. Swenson, both graduates of the University of Texas, have been the managers of the ranch. A former football star, A. M. G. Swenson is a member of the Board of Regents of the University. In their office at Stamford, Texas, hangs a framed letter from Sam Houston to the founder of the firm.

Around the city of Austin, S. M. Swenson gradually organized a permanent Swedish community. Since, in the 1840s, there was a great shortage of farm workers in Texas and slave labor was repugnant to him, Swenson began to encourage immigration from his native Småland—first of all his own relatives and neighbors. As early as 1844, when he was still manager of the Long property in Fort Bend County, he was joined by his uncle, Svante Palm, a former journalist and clerk of the Göta Court of Appeals in Jönköping, whose newspaper articles had irritated the authorities. He was the first educated Swede to arrive in Texas and in 1846 when Texas had been annexed to the United States, he became postmaster at La Grange.

Svante Palm was also a collector of books and on his death in 1897 he had a library of about thirty thousand volumes of which he gave 10,500, in addition to newspapers and pamphlets, to the University of Texas. Since the University library at that time contained only about seventeen thousand volumes, "the gift" in the words of its librarian (1947), E. W. Winkler, "was a tremendous one, not so much because of the Scandinavian material, as by the more immediately useful English sections." Palm's interest included both literature and science. (The University library has since then acquired a Scandinavian collection of over three thousand additional volumes.)

In temperament Palm was an idealist rather than a businessman, but while his nephew was absent in Mexico during the Civil War he acted as his representative in Austin. In 1884 he was appointed the first Consul for Sweden and Norway in Texas and was subsequently decorated by the King of the two countries.

In 1847 S. M. Swenson returned to Sweden to induce land workers as well as members of his family to move to Texas. His letters had so far attracted only his gifted but somewhat eccentric uncle. When Swenson came back in the fall of 1847, he was accompanied, however, only by his sister, Anna; the first Swedish-born woman to enter Texas. The next year his missionary work began to bear fruit. From Barkaryd and its vicinity arrived a group of twenty-five persons including Swenson's own mother and her two other brothers, Anders and Gustaf Palm. The latter was a trained watchmaker who soon set himself up in business. Mrs. Swenson, the first mother to be brought over to America by a former Swedish immigrant, didn't get accustomed to the frontier country and in a few months returned to her home in Småland.

The other members of the group were young farm hands. After landing in Boston, they took another boat for New York and then boarded the schooner, *Stephen F. Austin,* named, like the capital, in honor of the leading Texas pioneer. It was bound for Galveston. In Texas there was not then a single mile of railroad and from Galveston the Swedish immigrant party continued its journey by still another boat up the Buffalo bayou to Houston where it was met by Swenson and conducted to the Long plantation. The young farm hands had brought with them some of their home tools and farm implements including their double-barreled, muzzle-loading shotguns for defense against the Indians, and also a two-horse farm wagon, which they had thought they might need. At first they worked on the Long estate, but later hired out to other plantation owners in the vicinity and then acquired land of their own. Their descendants, as well as those of other Swedish country youths who came later, are now well-to-do owners of fine farms in the fertile, black-soil belt of central Texas, principally in Travis and Williamson counties, in which the loam is rated the best in the state. Some of them still speak the original country dialect of Småland, which blends well with that of Texas.

Encouraged by the quality of the workers he had obtained, Swenson repeated his visit to Sweden in 1849, by which time he had sold his plantation and moved to Austin. When he returned early the following year, he had with him a party of fifty young men, or twice the number of the year before. By that time the letters of the first contingent had had their effect. (Furthermore, Swenson had offered to advance travel costs as well as to act as a personal guide.) He was the first American emigration promoter in Sweden.

On the farms around Austin as well as in the new city itself, Swenson had no trouble in finding work for the newcomers and as soon as they had saved some of their earnings and reimbursed him for their travel expenses, they began to buy land. Once farmowners, they wrote other "America letters" themselves. They also began to advance money to Swenson to cover the travel expenses for additional farm hands whom they wanted to employ.

This system worked so well that when Swenson returned from his voluntary exile in Mexico, after the Civil War, he organized a special agency to promote emigration from Småland to Texas. His chief agent in Sweden was one of his own brothers. From prospective employers in Texas, Swenson obtained the money to cover the travel expenses of the young workers they wanted. This money he then forwarded to his brother in Barkaryd. But, before a ticket was bought, each prospective emigrant had to sign a contract obliging him to work for the farmer who had advanced the money for a certain period, or until the loan had been paid off—a system of "indentured servants" that had long been used in several of the Southeastern states to bring workers from England and other countries. At first, the required labor period averaged about two years, but as wages went up, it was reduced, at times, to as low as three months. But even so some of the new farm hands disappeared, claiming they had been ill-treated. A majority of them, however, kept their agreements and in time became farmowners themselves. About ninety per cent of the early Swedish settlers in Texas are supposed to have been enabled to come to America that way. In 1885 the import of "contract labor" was ended by a Federal law which is still in force. The main objection had been to the mass-importation of Oriental workers who were prepared to work for low wages.

During the Civil War practically all Swedish emigration to Texas was temporarily halted. In 1870, only 364 Swedes of the first or second generation were reported in the United States Census to be living in the state. The main reason Swenson's system failed to attract a greater number of Swedish immigrants to Texas, or the South in general, was the climate. While the land was fertile beyond the wildest dreams of the Smålanders, the temperatures were higher than they liked. Those who remained in Texas are now, however, among the most enthusiastic state boosters alive. The 1920 Census showed that 4,536 inhabitants of Texas had been born in Sweden. The 1940 figure was 3,646, with 7,900 listed as of the second generation with one or both parents born in Sweden. How many there were of the later generations did not appear. In Texas the Swedes still have their own churches and social organizations as well as a Swedish language weekly, *Texas Posten,* published at Austin. Few Swedish American communities are more homogeneously "Smålandish."

The early diversion of the main Swedish immigrant stream to the Middle West was favored by many circumstances. From a Swedish point of view the climate was ideal, land was cheap as well as fertile, and the social system more attractive than that of the South. Before the railroads had been built the water route to the Middle West, via the Erie Canal and the Great Lakes, proved to be more convenient and less expensive than ship travel to Texas or the South in general.

The earliest propaganda in Sweden for settling in the Middle West was made by a university graduate from Uppsala, who, in a material sense, made as great a failure in Wisconsin as S. M. Swenson made a success in Texas. His name was Gustaf Unonius and he was beyond question the best educated Swede who had so far set foot in America. Born of Swedish parents in Helsingfors, the capital of Finland, in 1810, the year after the country had been seized from Sweden by Russia, he had been brought the same year to Stockholm. There his father, Israel Unonius, who was a lawyer, obtained a minor Government position as collector of customs at Grisslehamn, a small port in the outer skerries. The son's earliest education was military, possibly due to family hopes of a *revanche* against Russia, but once he had reached Karlberg, the West Point of Sweden, he decided he did not want to be an officer. Instead he entered the University of Uppsala, where, like his father, he studied law. But though he obtained a degree in the subject, he never practiced. In 1834 a cholera epidemic struck Sweden, and while working as a volunteer in an emergency hospital, he decided he would rather be a doctor and at the university he then became a medical student. But he never practiced medicine either. His real profession, he next concluded, was that of an author. To make his living while he expressed himself in literature he took a position in the office of the local provincial Governor. But publishers remained obdurate and to make matters worse he fell in love and got married. On his meagre salary, his bride, born Charlotta Margareta Öhrström, found it difficult to keep house.

Having literary ambitions, Unonius read as many of the new books as he could lay his hands on. Among them was *Democracy in America,* by Count Alexis de Tocqueville, which the *Encyclopaedia Britannica* calls "the first reasoned account of democratic government in America." In Stockholm it appeared in a Swedish translation in 1839, only four years after its first publication in Paris. The author, a young French lawyer, had gone to America to study the penal system and had ended by describing the whole Government. On Unonius and, through him, on the subsequent Swedish emigration movement to the Middle West it was to have deep effect; for in order to relieve their economic distress, Unonius and his bride decided to emigrate, then an unheard of thing for a young couple with good social connections and a Government job to do. The law repealing the old-time restrictions against leaving the country without a bond had been passed and Unonius and his party were the first Swedes to take advantage of the new freedom.

"I can, I thought," he wrote many years later in his memoirs, "take such a step. I have heard about America. Its rich soil and its industrial possibilities invite just at present thousands of Europeans who in their homeland have been thwarted in their hopes, in one way or another, by economic circumstances or by a precarious livelihood. Work in any industry that is honorable is no disgrace in America. There every workman has the same rights of citizenship as the nobles. Conventional judgments, class interests, narrow-mindedness do not hang on your coat tails, nor trample on your heels."

On a Swedish sailing vessel, bound from the near-by Baltic port of Gävle, in northeastern Sweden, to New York with a cargo of iron, Unonius booked passage for himself, his bride of a few months, their faithful maid of all work, Christina, the first Swedish housemaid brought to America since the days of Governor Printz, their hound dog, Fille, and three young university friends, Ivar Hagberg, Carl Groth, a relative of Unonius, and William Polman, who had studied enough of medicine in Sweden to become a frontier doctor in America. (Ultimately he studied more medicine in New York and obtained his degree.) The fares were $26 a person, not including food. (Hagberg settled for a while in Cleveland, Ohio, and then returned to Sweden. Groth became a businessman in New Orleans but otherwise remained unknown to fame.) Early in the morning on May 11, 1841, after a gay farewell party, the group set off from Uppsala. As far as the first stagecoach station, it was accompanied by a string of horse-drawn vehicles filled with hilarious friends, singing farewell songs and making speeches at every stop. It was such a romantic venture. . . . What might lie ahead no one sensed, nor gave much thought. Food and bedding for the trip had been bought ahead. That some of the former turned out to have been adulterated, was only the first disappointment.

When the group left Sweden the exact goal in America was still undetermined. Some of the members had heard of the Middle West and in New York they expected to learn more. That they lacked the manual skills, as well as the physical stamina to survive on the raw frontier they had never considered. They were still young and it was to be a thrilling experience.

"We were surprised," Unonius wrote later in his memoirs, "to find that in New York most people knew less about Illinois or Iowa than we did." (The Bethel Ship mission under Hedström had not then been established.) In New York they did encounter, however, a fellow countryman by the name of Brodell, who was returning to Sweden after having spent a few years in Illinois. He may have been another roaming ex-sailor, but nothing definite is known about him. He advised Unonius and his friends to try their luck in northern Illinois which he called "one of the most wonderful regions in the world, with extensive, fruitful, easily cultivated plains. . . . If an immigrant desires to engage in agriculture," he went on, "he can choose from a great surplus of vacant land." In addition, there were many other opportunities to earn a living, he had continued. "We decided to go," wrote Unonius.

If they had stuck to that purpose, their fate might have been different. Even if they knew nothing about frontier farming, they were intelligent, able-bodied, well-educated men, for whom there soon would have been opened opportunities in the new country, other than those in agriculture. Unonius himself was versed both in law and medicine; he knew something about military science, he could write and he had had experience in civil administration. On the frontier, such talents were scarce, and in time he would have been sure to find use for at least some of them. But on the boat trip westward from New York he and his party ran into other European emigrants who had heard bad reports about Illinois. The best land, they had been told, had already been bought up by New England and New York speculators and was therefore held at unreasonably high prices. Wisconsin, which had not yet become a state, they claimed, was the real land of opportunity. And as a majority of these new friends debarked at Milwaukee, the Swedes decided to get off too. At the height of the summer season, the scenery did look attractive. It recalled the best parts of Sweden. That the soil might be harder to cultivate than that of Illinois, the young university people didn't foresee, nor that the winter climate might be more severe.

At the hotel in Milwaukee, the Milwaukee House, they ran into a Norwegian maid who understood their language. She introduced them to the only Swede then living in the city. He was a guest, in fact, at the Milwaukee House itself. His name was Olof Gottfrid Lange, a native of Gothenburg, born in 1811, a year later than Unonius, and at an early age he had gone to sea. On board British vessels, he had learned, like S. M. Swenson, to speak English. He had attended school in New York as early as 1824 and in 1838 he had set out for the Great Lakes. In Chicago he had been the first Swedish resident and had worked there in a drug store. (Later he opened one of his own.) At Fort Dearborn he had taught English to immigrants from Norway, and now he was engaged in real estate promotion in Milwaukee. When he heard of Unonius' desire to buy land, he would, of course, be most pleased to serve as a guide.

As a site for a future colony, which they hopefully and nostalgically named New Uppsala, Unonius and his friends selected, with the aid of Lange, an attractive spot on a little lake near Delafield, on the road to Madison, about thirty miles west of Milwaukee, known as Pine Lake. The land was owned by a Mr. Delafield by whom Lange was employed. If the summer foliage looked attractive, that of the autumn appeared even better. In an oak grove overlooking the lake, the Swedes selected a site for their first log cabin, as they would have picked one for a summer cottage in Sweden. In the pond there would, of course, be fish, while game, they were assured, was abundant in the woods all about. What more could a group of young university people desire? On the spot, Unonius bought from Mr. Delafield, 160 acres, or a quarter section. That the soil was not particularly fertile or that it would be hard to cultivate, he did not realize, nor that the winter might be colder than in Sweden. Resolutely he and his companions began to clear the ground and with the aid of neighbors they soon built a little log hut.

By November 11, exactly six months after they had left Uppsala it was finished. Since the walls had not been chinked, it was still drafty and cold, however. Only primitive, rough-hewn furniture was available and the first Christmas was a dreary one. A brave attempt was made, nevertheless, to celebrate it in the traditional Swedish manner.

Since Unonius was not able to earn his living by the labor of his hands and his travel funds were shrinking, he once more turned to writing. This time his words received attention. The letters he sent to Lars Johan Hierta, the alert editor of *Aftonbladet,* the new popular afternoon newspaper of Stockholm, were read throughout the country and in many instances reprinted by other papers. Thousands of Swedish people were hungry for firsthand information about America and while keeping silent about some of his personal problems, Unonius didn't spare either details or colors. His excitement about the new country was reflected in his words. Consciously, he wrote later, he had not intended to promote emigration. From such activities he had, in truth, nothing to gain.

The following spring, however, he was besieged by a motley collection of newly arrived countrymen, romantic souls who sought a new Paradise, decadent noblemen who wanted a new start, hopeful capitalists who desired quick profits, a young clergyman who had left Sweden under a cloud, and others who had even more serious reasons for leaving their native land. The situation suggested a comic opera. A Baron von Thott from Skåne bought land, but finding no crofters to cultivate it, he soon disappeared. A retired businessman from Norrköping, A. Wadman, withdrew to more congenial surroundings in Milwaukee. The Reverend Peter W. Böckman, a prototype of Gösta Berling, tried to hold religious services as a means of earning a livelihood, but finding little response returned to Sweden where, a few years later, he died. But the Unonius letters in *Aftonbladet* also attracted serious-minded Swedish farm workers who were better able to cope with the frontier hardships.

Unonius himself then tried still another profession, that of a clergyman, and as his affiliation he chose the American Protestant Episcopal Church. As such he built the first Swedish church in Chicago, but finding the Lutheran sentiment of his countrymen too strong, he returned to Sweden in 1859, a bitterly disappointed man. After failing to be accepted as a minister in the Swedish state church, he wrote a book about his seventeen years in America, a valuable firsthand record of pioneer life in the Middle West, and the only lasting achievement of his life. It has now been translated. In 1863 he obtained his father's old position as collector of customs at Grisslehamn, which he kept until 1888, and in 1902, at the age of ninety-two, he died at the home of a married daughter whose husband owned a large estate near Uppsala. To the end of his life he used to say, writes Professor Stephenson, that he had made two great mistakes in life; one was that he had ever gone to America and, the second, that he had left it.

The most romantic of the young Swedish immigrants who knocked on the hospitable log cabin door at Pine Lake was a runaway couple from Stockholm, as gently bred as Unonius and his wife, and even more unsuited to frontier life. They were a former lieutenant of the ultra-fashionable Royal Svea Artillery Regiment in Stockholm, Johan Carl Fredrik Polycarpus von Schneidau, and his bride, the former Carolina Elizabeth Jakobsson, daughter of Abraham Jakobsson, a Jewish merchant in Stockholm, who was not a member of the same social circles as her husband. Von Schneidau's father was also an army officer as well as owner of a large country estate in Östergötland, and he himself had been a close friend of the Swedish Crown Prince, Oscar, the only son of the former French Marshal, Jean Baptiste Bernadotte. In origin the Von Schneidau family was Austrian, but had settled in Sweden during the Thirty Years' War. In the military and social Stockholm circles at that time, marriage to a girl who was not a member of the state church of Sweden and who was the daughter of a Jewish businessman was considered an unpardonable *mésalliance*. On May 4, 1842, Lieutenant von Schneidau and Fröken Jakobsson were nevertheless married in Copenhagen and then decided to try life in America. He was then thirty years old and she thirty-two.

Whether they had known Unonius in Sweden or had merely read his letters in *Aftonbladet* is not clear. But in the fall of 1842, they appeared at Pine Lake and, like all other unassorted visitors from Sweden, were cordially received. The bride, however, wept bitter tears, Unonius reports, when she learned she and her husband had to share quarters with so many strangers. She had expected something more spacious as well as gracious, something like a gentleman's country house in Sweden. But, like Mrs. Unonius, who had been just as carefully reared, she gradually accepted things as they were and lived bravely on. For $200 her husband bought another quarter section of land, or 160 acres, on which they then built their own little log cabin. It had but one window, one foot square, and the open fireplace was an inadequate source of heat. One winter morning, early in 1843, they found their first-born child, a boy, frozen to death in his crib. (Before Unonius and his wife finally quit Wisconsin for Chicago in 1849, they had buried at Pine Lake four of their own children.)

The next summer the Von Schneidaus built themselves a larger cabin, containing two rooms and an attic. Unfortunately, the husband had injured his foot while on board the ship and was unable to perform heavy physical labor. As their funds, too, began to run low, Mrs. von Schneidau, probably inspired by inherited talents, opened a little store in one of the two rooms, a single table sufficing to display her wares. The scene is described by no less a celebrity than Margaret Fuller, the famous Concord feminist and author, in her book, *Summer on the Lakes, in 1843,* published in Boston in 1844. In 1843, together with her friend, Miss Sara Freeman Clarke of Boston, she had visited Pine Lake.

"Everything that belonged to the house," wrote Miss Fuller, "though rude, was neatly arranged; the invalid [husband], confined to an uneasy, wooden chair, looked as elegant as if he had been dressed by the valet of a duke. He was of northern blood with clear, full blue eyes, calm features,—a tempering in his aspect of a soldier and man of the world; he formed a great but pleasing contrast to his wife, whose glowing complexion and dark mellow eyes bespoke an origin in some climate more familiar with the sun.

"Seeing the album full of drawings and verses which bespoke the circle of elegant and affectionate intercourse they had left behind, we could not but see that the young wife sometimes must need a sister; her husband, a male companion, and that both must miss the electricity which sparkles from the chain of congenial minds"—a passage quoted by Dr. Victor Oscar Freeburg in *The American Swedish Monthly,* November, 1941.

This album is now preserved by a great-granddaughter of the Von Schneidaus' living in New Jersey. Some of the verses as well as the drawings are signed by the Crown Prince of Sweden who, as Oscar I, succeeded his father in 1845.

Miss Fuller did more than describe the plight of the Von Schneidaus. Through friends in Chicago she helped them move there in November 1844. In the new city the Lieutenant was able to get medical care which soon restored his agility. He then began to teach not only Swedish gymnastics, but fencing and dancing. His class in Ling exercises for women was the first in Chicago and the abbreviated costumes worn by his pupils are said to have shocked the moral sensibilities of the frontier town. In 1848 he became a daguerreotype photographer, then a new profession, and thanks to the good social connections established for him by Miss Fuller, he soon did a flourishing business, enabling him to buy a house of his own. In 1850 he made a trip to New York to take a picture of Jenny Lind, the great celebrity of the day. He also told her about his little daughter, Paulina, and for her the famous singer snipped off one of the gold buttons on her dress, which explains why the daguerreotype taken by Von Schneidau and so often reproduced, shows a button missing. This trinket is likewise treasured by the great-granddaughter in New Jersey.

In 1850 the Von Schneidau family was visited in Chicago by Fredrika Bremer, the famous Swedish novelist, who found their circumstances comfortable. The next year Von Schneidau not only received a gold medal from the Chicago Mechanics Institute, but by his old friend, Crown Prince Oscar, who by then had become King of both Norway and Sweden, he was appointed the first Consul for those two countries in Chicago. Being an educated man with good manners and a friend of the city's leading families as well as of the local officials, he was able to be of considerable assistance to the Swedish immigrants who had begun to pour through the city. Such help they needed especially during the recurring cholera epidemics.

By Chicago's first Mayor, William Butler Ogden, elected in 1837, and other Chicago capitalists, Von Schneidau was employed as a prospector for copper mines in the Lake Superior region and in 1848 did some of the advance survey work on the Chicago and Galena Railroad, the first westward line, now a part of the Illinois Central; and by Edwin A. Sheldon, another wealthy Chicago businessman, his daughter Paulina was practically adopted. In her behalf Mr. Sheldon made early investments which turned out to be profitable, so that though her mother died in 1855 and her father four years later, she received the best education obtainable including enrollment in a private school for girls in New York. In 1867 she was married to Eugene Murray Jerome, a New York lawyer, who was a brother of a schoolmate. By degrees their children became scattered in places as far apart as Glen Ridge, New Jersey, Albany, New York, Williamstown, Massachusetts, Los Angeles, California, and New York City, and while their grandchildren continue to treasure some of the momentoes brought from Stockholm by the original runaway couple, they have lost all personal contacts with Sweden.

While traveling through the Middle West in 1850, Fredrika Bremer, the Swedish novelist whose intimate pictures of American family life, published in Stockholm in 1853–54 and in New York in 1853 as *Homes of the New World,* were to help stimulate emigration to America still further, visited the Pine Lake colony and with the self-same Captain Lange as her guide. "The little Swedish colony at Pine Lake," she wrote, "although scattered, still contains half a dozen families who live as farmers in the neighborhood. . . . Almost all of them live in log cabins and appear to have scant means. The most prosperous is a black-smith—who has built himself a lovely frame house in the woods. Bergvall is also prosperous. In Sweden he had been a member of the gentry, but here he is a practical farmer and has obtained several acres of good land which he works with much industry and perseverance. He seems well and has retained his happy, optimistic Swedish nature." Another member of the original colony who had managed to hold on was B. Peterson, a shoemaker. (In 1948 a single granddaughter of one of the original settlers was still living at Pine Lake.)

From a rowboat on the lake Miss Bremer viewed the site of the original log houses. "Here on a high promontory, covered with gleam-ing masses of leaves," she wrote, "the New Uppsala was to be built. That was what Unonius and his friends planned when they first came into the wilderness and were delighted with its beauty. Alas! the wild soil would not support Old Uppsala's sons. I saw the deserted houses where he [Unonius] and Von Schneidau in vain fought poverty and tried to live."

If Unonius and Von Schneidau failed as pioneers themselves, their letters caused a number of better qualified Swedes to emigrate. The departure of the very first group of Swedes to settle in Iowa, for instance, was directly attributable to letters written by Von Schneidau to his father, whose estate was situated at Kisa, in Kinda County, the hilly southwestern corner of Östergötland, close to Småland. In 1845, when he was fifty-four years old, a millwright of that town and inventor of sorts by the name of Peter Cassel, whose Scottish ancestor Peter Castle had come to Sweden in 1596 to become an equerry of Charles IX, the father of Gustavus Adolphus, organized among his neighbors an emigration party of twenty-five persons. Though he had had but little formal schooling, he had learned to read and write and for years he had absorbed avidly everything he could find to read about America. The letters to Major Von Schneidau from his son in Wisconsin, when copied and circulated about the neighborhood, were the final stimulant. Cassel was a man of natural ability and mental vigor. At one time he had been manager of a large estate in Östergötland and later he manu-factured a hand-driven threshing machine designed by himself. (Before he died in Iowa in 1857 he had become a licensed Methodist preacher.)

Once he had become settled in Iowa, where his party founded in 1845 the first colony, New Sweden, he began writing enthusiastic "America letters" himself,—clear, detailed and readable. They were not only cir-culated by hand but were reproduced in newspapers all over the country. Finally they were collected and reprinted in a 48-page booklet. On the early emigration from southern Östergötland and northern Småland, they were to have a decisive effect.

Paying fares of $20 each, the members of Cassel's party sailed in the spring of 1845 from Gothenburg, probably the first emigrant group to leave from that port. In addition to the people from Kisa, some of whom comprised entire families, ten other Swedes went on board, including four men, probably former sailors, who had already been in America. Among the rest were a few Swedish noblemen, presumably also headed for the Unonius colony at Pine Lake in Wisconsin. In New York Cassel encountered, however, a congenial countryman by the name of Pehr Dahlberg, who had already explored the Middle West and now awaited another ship bringing his wife and seven children. After a perilous journey in a leaky sailing vessel from Stockholm, requiring the use of pumps almost the whole way, the Dahlberg family finally arrived in New York, August 12, 1845. It was Dahlberg who induced Peter Cassel and his friends to set out for Iowa instead of Pine Lake, Wisconsin, which by that time had already been abandoned by the Von Schneidau family. (What became of the four Swedish sailors and the noblemen is not known.) In Sweden, Dahlberg had been first a cobbler, then a cabinetmaker and finally an occasional evangelist. In the United States, he was to be the real Swedish pioneer in the most fertile region beyond the Mississippi, that of Iowa. Though not a farmer himself, the fact that he had come from the almost equally fertile southern Swedish province of Skåne probably helped him rec-ognize the quality of the soil. Born in 1802, he was, like Cassel, a middle-aged man when he decided to bring his family to America. In 1827 he had married Inga (Ingeborg) Nilsdotter of Brantvik, also in Skåne, but in 1836 they had moved to Stockholm, where during the winter months Dahlberg worked as a cabinetmaker instead of a cobbler while each summer he went to sea. In Stockholm he and his wife became acquainted with the Reverend C. O. Rosenius, a liberal-minded Swedish clergyman, who was a friend of George Scott, the Scotch Methodist preacher and the Reverend Robert Baird, the American Presbyterian, who had been the first to carry the American temperance message to Sweden. (After Scott had been forced to leave Stockholm in 1842, Rosenius carried on much of his work and became the founder of a left wing movement in the state church, which, in time, helped liberalize the whole body.) Through the discourses of Scott and Baird, the Dahlbergs became more and more interested in America and, finally, on April 25, 1843, Dahlberg left for America alone, promising either to return or to send for his family. He chose the latter. In the meantime he had roamed as far west as Wisconsin, Illinois, and Iowa, and from firsthand observation he was able to convince Peter Cassel and his friends that Iowa had better prospects as a farming country than Wisconsin, which he could not know was destined to become America's "Dairyland."

Dahlberg had also learned how to travel and, unlike Unonius and his group in 1841, he did not take his family and the Cassel party over the Hudson River, Erie Canal and Great Lakes route, but by railroad to Philadelphia, then a new means of communication, and from there by various canals across the Alleghenies to Pittsburgh. Over some stretches the barges had to be carried overland on rails. From Pittsburgh they took a river boat down the Ohio as far as the Mississippi at Cairo and then proceeded up that river as far as Burlington, Iowa, where they headed inland.

In Iowa they found the nearest available Government land on Bush Creek, about forty miles west of Burlington and a few miles from Rome, in Jefferson County. There they built their first cabins or sod huts, the earliest Swedish settlement in this rich farm belt, and like the colonists on the Delaware in 1638, they called it New Sweden. It is still a small community, but, unlike the Delaware colony, it retains at least the original name. In 1848, or three years later, the first Swedish Lutheran church services in the Middle West were begun there by a friend of the Dahlbergs from Stockholm, a lay preacher, by the name of Magnus Fredrik Hokanson, who in 1853 was formally ordained a minister of the Swedish American Lutheran Church. For some years he had five congregations under his care. In his youth, he had been a cobbler like Dahlberg, and by that trade he was able to support himself when the church revenue was insufficient. He was a devout man of the evangelistic type who had found the state church in Sweden too conservative.

The following year the "America letters" sent back to Sweden by

Peter Cassel caused two additional groups to leave the neighborhood
of Kisa for New Sweden, but through different circumstances both
failed to reach their goal. Instead, members of each of the two parties
laid foundations for two other, widely separated communities which
still exist and flourish much better than New Sweden. They are Madrid,
Iowa, originally called Swede Point, and Jamestown, New York, the
largest and most homogeneous Swedish settlement in the Empire State.

The first of these two groups, consisting of forty-two persons, including women and children, sailed in May 1846, from Gothenburg on
the Swedish brig *Augusta* bound for New York with a cargo of iron.
Their crossing required nine weeks. By that time the Reverend Olof
Gustaf Hedström, a Swedish Methodist minister employed by the
American Methodist Church, had begun his long and fruitful work
as a missionary among Scandinavian sailors and immigrants in the
port of New York, using as a chapel and rescue mission a demasted
schooner, called the Bethel Ship, which was tied to a pier near the
Battery in lower Manhattan. By him the group was advised to avoid
the trip by canal boats across Pennsylvania used by Cassel and to
take, instead, the Hudson River and Erie Canal route as far as Buffalo
and then the lake steamers as far as Toledo on Lake Erie. From there
they could cross the state of Ohio by other canal barges as far as Cincinnati and then follow the same course as the Peter Cassel party to
Iowa.

But once in Iowa, they got lost. They had been advised by Cassel
to disembark at Keokuk and then proceed along the west shore of the
Mississippi northward as far as the mouth of the "smaller" or Skunk
River and then follow that river westward until they reached Jefferson
County and New Sweden. Instead, they mistook the Des Moines River
itself for "the smaller river" and followed that westward for about 200
miles, until they had reached Boone County northwest of Des Moines
in what was practically the center of the state. This was then open
Indian country with only a few white settlers. By the end of September
1846 they had identified their position, and by recrossing half the
state they finally reached their destination. Four families, however,
liked the unpopulated region they had struck by accident so well that
they decided to remain permanently.

In surviving the first winter 1846–47, they were aided by a former
American soldier by the name of Charles W. Gaston, who while in
the army had fought Indians west of Des Moines. He too had liked the
country so much that when discharged he returned there in January

1846 to live as a trapper and hunter. During the following spring he had cleared some of the land and then raised a crop which demonstrated the fertility of the soil. Ultimately he married one of the Swedish girls, Anna Catharina Dalander. On April 21, 1848, her sister, Ulla Dalander, was married at Fairfield, Iowa, to Carl Johan Cassel, a son of Peter Cassel, probably the first Swedish wedding west of the Mississippi. The next year they too settled at Swede Point. After being surveyed, or "platted," the settlement became known also as Madrid and when the Milwaukee railroad was put through in 1881 the latter name was permanently adopted as more dignified. The community remained, however, largely Swedish. Throughout the state many modern farms were gradually developed from the unbroken prairies by new settlers arriving from Sweden. The couple in Grant Wood's famous painting "Modern Gothic" represent the type. Carl Sandburg has fixed their profile a bit more tenderly in his short poem, "Illinois Farmer."

The second group, which likewise set out from the neighborhood of Kisa in May 1846, for New Sweden, Iowa, was similarly diverted from its goal and founded, instead, a permanent settlement at Sugar Grove, in northern Pennsylvania, which in the course of time was extended to the near-by Jamestown in New York. This they developed into one of America's leading furniture centers. How they got there is an odd saga of immigration. The second group was larger than the first, seventy-five persons including children. In May 1846, it sailed from Gothenburg on the Swedish schooner, *Virginia,* also bound for New York with a cargo of iron. The fare was 90 kronor or about $20 per person, not including either food or bedding. For eight weeks and five days the ship was out of sight of land. At sea two of the women and three children died and were buried at sea, while one child, a boy, was born and survived. The ship was overcrowded and gradually the hygienic conditions became deplorable.

On August 5, 1846, the ship finally reached New York, which was then in the throes of one of its usual August hot weather spells, and after but two days' rest and a consultation with the Reverend O. G. Hedström, the group set out for Iowa, taking the Hudson River and Erie Canal route for Buffalo. From there its members intended to travel by a lake steamer to Chicago and then proceed either by canal and river boats or on foot across northern Illinois to New Sweden across the Mississippi. But they never got beyond Buffalo. While changing boats in Albany most of the travel-weary and inexperienced countrypeople from

Sweden were robbed of their funds. Their fares had been prepaid as far as Buffalo, but while being towed by mule or horse power along the Erie Canal they had to subsist on the wild plums and other fruit they could pick along the banks.

By the time the group reached Buffalo it had been reduced in various ways to sixty persons and of these only fifteen had enough money to proceed further. The rest were stranded on the windy waterfront. Their combined cash resources added up to twenty-five cents and with this sum they bought bread and sausages which they consumed together as their last common meal. None of them could speak a word of English and in the city they knew no one. "Like a flock of frightened sheep, we stood there helpless on the shore," a survivor recalled many years later. To make matters worse, a heavy rain began to fall. Longingly they watched the lake steamer depart for the Middle West with their more fortunate friends on board.

At this point a veritable *deus ex machina* intervention occurred. Looking wet and dejected in their country clothes which they had worn since they left Sweden, they attracted the attention of a young man passing by. A native of Sweden himself, he had caught the familiar intonation of their voices. How he happened to be in Buffalo or what he was doing there has not been recorded, and beyond the fact that his last name was Svedberg and that his native town was Gävle, the port from which Unonius had sailed, nothing is known of him. His first act was to fetch a friend, another young Swede, by the name of Haglund, a native of Stockholm. (Both names suggest a social status above that of ordinary farmers or day laborers, whose names usually ended in "son.") Whatever their origin or occupation, they proved themselves Good Samaritans. Before nightfall they found an empty house in which their disconsolate countryfolk could at least get shelter from the rain. Over the first week-end they also procured enough food to keep the hungry strangers alive. Next they found an English-speaking Norwegian boy, who probably hailed from the near-by Norwegian settlement at Lockport, founded in 1825, and with him as an interpreter and guide the men set out on Monday morning to find employment.

Since it was the end of August and the harvest season still under way, six of the men soon found farm work in the village of Hamburg, now a suburb of Buffalo, at fifty cents a day. Before hiring them, the farmers felt of their muscles as if they had been dumb animals and inspected their hands to see if they were used to manual labor. Quickly the newcomers proved their capacity as harvesters and before long every man in the party found at least temporary jobs of the same nature, while some of the women got work as laundresses, housemaids, or cooks. The rest took care of the children. For two years the Swedes remained in Buffalo without being able to earn enough money to pay their fares further west. In August 1848, six or seven families did reach Andover, Illinois, where they had been invited by two Swedish immigrants, Hans Hurtig and Samuel Samuelsson, whose acquaintance they made when the latter passed through Buffalo on their way West. As an inducement to settle in Andover they were offered free transportation by horse and wagon from Chicago.

The rest never reached the Middle West. Their decision to move, instead, a hundred miles or so southward to the high country around Lake Chautauqua on either side of the New York–Pennsylvania border, came about by pure chance. No Swedish advance agent had scouted that country.

When the plight of the stranded Swedes became known in Buffalo, some of the charitable women of the city took an interest in their fate. Among them was a Mrs. Bovet, who, though married to a Frenchman, was herself of Swedish origin. She was also one of the directors of an orphanage known as the Bethesda, which had a day nursery, and there some of the children were cared for while their mothers were at work. Among the children were two sisters, Louise, aged nine, and Sara Sophia, later renamed Josephine, aged seven, daughters of Germund Johnson, one of the immigrant farmers, and his wife Catherine. That they were unusually attractive children may be assumed from what follows.

One day in the fall of 1847, or a year later, there arrived in Buffalo a gentleman farmer from Warren, in the hill country of northern Pennsylvania, by the name of Thomas Struthers. He had land business with a real estate agent in Buffalo by the name of Coyet, which, like Bovet indicates, a French origin. By him Struthers was introduced to Mrs. Bovet who, in turn, took him to see the Swedish children at the Bethesda nursery. He was so impressed by the beauty of the two Johnson girls that he immediately obtained permission from the parents to take the older one with him to his home in Warren and also to find a similar shelter in the neighborhood for the younger girl, so they could play together. This he did in the house of another gentleman farmer, Robert Falconer, at Sugar Grove, not far from Warren, and at once Mrs. Eliza Falconer drove the ninety miles by horse and buggy to Buffalo to fetch the child. To the Falconers the girl was indentured by a contract signed January 4, 1848, until she was eighteen. The text of this curious document has been preserved. It constituted a sort of temporary adoption.

Before long the Johnsons had begun to miss their children so keenly that one day they started to walk the ninety miles to Sugar Grove and Warren to see them. There they not only found the children well cared for, but Mr. Falconer offered them permanent employment with housing for the rest of their family. While Mrs. Johnson remained in Sugar Grove, her husband walked the ninety miles back to Buffalo. On an ox cart, which he drove on foot and thus walked the ninety miles for the third time, he brought the other children and the family baggage. After working for the Falconer family for about a year, he bought land for a farm and then began to urge his friends in Buffalo to give up all thoughts of the middle west and join him, instead, in northern Pennsylvania.

To check up on his favorable reports on the hill country around Lake Chautauqua, which he declared more beautiful than either Östergötland or Småland, they sent Frederick J. Johnson, who had been a leader among them in Sweden, and Samuel Dahl, who had accompanied him on a scouting trip to Andover, Illinois, from which they had returned disappointed. The land was too flat, they thought, to please the people from the highlands in southern Sweden. (The first newcomers from Sweden in the Middle West often concluded that because the prairies were treeless, the soil must be poor.) They also reported that the drinking water was unsatisfactory. In the richly wooded hills in southwestern New York and central Pennsylvania they felt more at home. There spring water was abundant. On their advice, the main caravan of Swedish settlers set out from Buffalo by ox teams, arriving in Sugar Grove on October 13, 1848. The first winter the men worked as wood choppers, walking as far as Dunkirk, New York, to get jobs at fifty cents a day. Somehow they managed to acquire land and by the next spring they started farming. The donor of the first site for a Swedish church in Sugar Grove was Germund Johnson. In Jamestown, New York, his two daughters grew up and got married and lived until old age. Even late in life, photographs show them to have been unusually attractive women.

As more immigrants continued to arrive in Chandlers Valley and most of them were skilled woodworkers from the highlands of Småland, they moved more and more often from the Pennsylvania farms to the little town of Jamestown across the New York border where both hard lumber and water power were available. Gradually they built up a furniture industry, rivaled only by that of Grand Rapids, Michigan. The chairs used by the Supreme Court Justices in Washington were made in Jamestown, by a manufacturer of Swedish descent.

Jamestown had been founded in 1809 and named for himself by James Prendergast, the son of a neighborhood farmer. At a rapids in the river he had built himself a log cabin, then a sawmill, and finally a little village grew up. The first post office was opened in 1816, but when the Swedes began to arrive in 1848 Jamestown was still a small community. Now it has about fifty thousand inhabitants of whom roughly seventy per cent are of Swedish descent. At first, farming and lumbering were the main occupations. Not until the Swedes began to make furniture did the place develop industrially. Gradually wood has been replaced more and more by metal, and a variety of other goods such as tools, builders' hardware, washing machines, and motor car radiators are made. The hollow metal doors now used in practically all New York City office buildings were first produced in Jamestown by the Dahlstrom Metallic Door Company, while other concerns made metal window sash and ornamental bronze doors for banks and vaults. Another veteran furniture maker of Jamestown is Charles L. Eckman. In the Chandlers Valley district, across the Pennsylvania line, some of the farms continued to be owned by Swedish settlers and their descendants, but when the industries of Jamestown provided better-paid work, a majority of the Swedes settled there. In time they built some of the largest Swedish churches in the country and until the Second World War supported a weekly Swedish-language newspaper. In local political affairs they dominate the city, usually preferring their own countrymen as mayors, fire chiefs and police commissioners. Thanks to its industries Jamestown has become a prosperous, conservative community which until the New Deal era could be depended on to vote the straight Republican ticket. In 1948, President Truman too carried the city.

By the middle of the nineteenth century small groups of Swedish immigrants had settled in as widely separated places as Texas, Illinois, Wisconsin, and western New York, as well as in New York City and Philadelphia. In 1850 the United States Census listed 48 as living in Texas, 1,123 in Illinois, 88 in Wisconsin, 231 in Iowa, 753 in New York state including the city, and 133 in Pennsylvania. During the decade before the Civil War the Swedes began to concentrate more and more in Chicago and northern Illinois. How this came about will be told in the next chapter.

HOW THE SWEDES SETTLED IN ILLINOIS:
THE BISHOP HILL COLONY

Who the first Swedes were to settle in Illinois is not known. Since some of the descendants of the Swedish colonists on the Delaware must have followed the ever westward-moving frontier, it would be surprising if some of them did not reach the upper Mississippi Valley. In the first decades of the nineteenth century several Swedish sailors are known to have worked their way up the river from New Orleans. Some remained; others returned to Sweden. The earliest known native-born Swede to settle permanently in Illinois was a businessman and politician by the name of Raphael Widén. Except that he was born in Sweden, little is known of his early life. At the age of eight he was taken by his parents to France where he was educated for the Roman Catholic priesthood—in itself an unusual circumstance. How or why or when he came to the United States is not known, either. As early as 1814, however, he was appointed a justice of the peace in St. Clair County. In 1818 he was married at Cahokia, the county seat of St. Clair, to a girl of French extraction. The following year he moved to Kaskaskia in Randolph County, where he continued to serve as a justice of the peace. In 1820 he was elected a member of the Illinois State Legislature and was re-elected several times. In 1826 he became President of the State Senate. Like most Swedes he was a strong opponent of slavery and in 1824 he helped pass a law banishing the system from Illinois. On April 30, 1825, when General Lafayette visited Kaskaskia, Widén, then listed as a local businessman, was one of the guests at a reception, a natural consequence of his French education as well as his political prominence. In 1833 he fell victim to one of the recurring cholera epidemics. As far as is known, he had kept up no contacts with Sweden or with other Swedish settlers, nor did he promote Swedish immigration to Illinois.

The first fully identified Swedish-born farmer in Illinois was

Christian Benson, born in Gothenburg in 1805. His father was captain of a lumber schooner on Lake Vänern, the largest in Sweden, which has its outlet at Gothenburg. Like so many of the boys born in that seafaring town, Christian went to sea early—some records say at the age of thirteen. In 1819, when he was but fourteen, he arrived in New York and after that served as a sailor on various American vessels, some going as far as China. Then he met a girl from Providence, Rhode Island, Miss Maria Brotherson, whose ancestry was Scotch. To see more of her he quit the sea and for ten years, beginning in 1825, was employed as a pilot on a freight line between New York and Providence owned by Commodore Vanderbilt. In 1827 he was married to Miss Brotherson and in 1835, after a shipwreck, she persuaded him to quit navigation in favor of farming. This he took up in Whiteside County, Illinois, not far from the present city of Rock Island, now a Swedish center of church and college life. In 1846 he was joined there by a brother and in 1849 both took part in the gold rush to California, going by different routes. The brother did not arrive in California and was never heard from again. Christian, on the other hand, reached the gold fields, but found no gold. Instead, he established an inn or rest house for other gold seekers at the junction of the Overland trail and the route from Sacramento to San Francisco, a point known to this day as Benson's Crossing. Later Benson returned to his Illinois farm, where he died in 1885 at the age of eighty. He was a devoted adherent to the Republican Party. Except for his brother, he is not known to have induced any of his countrymen to settle in Illinois.

This was done, however, by Gustaf Flack, another Swedish ex-sailor, who prior to 1843 was a farmer at Victoria, Illinois, which subsequently was to become an important Swedish community. Flack was a native of Alfta, a parish in the northern Swedish province of Hälsingland, from which a few years later came a majority of the members of the religious-communistic colony at Bishop Hill in Henry County. It was letters from Flack, circulated about his native countryside, which originally had attracted the attention of Eric Janson and his religious adepts to northwestern Illinois, then a pioneer country. Flack is supposed to have reached Victoria via New Orleans, but exactly when is not known, probably in the late 1830s. After 1843 he kept a store near the Clark Street landing in Chicago and in 1846, the very year the first Bishop Hill colonists arrived in Illinois, he returned to Sweden, only to die on the way from the port of Gävle to his birthplace at Alfta.

At Andover, destined to be another center of early Swedish settlements in Illinois, the first known Swedish resident was Sven Nilsson, also a former sailor. He had lived there since 1840 and in 1849 he married "Stigs-Lena," one of the women who had come to Bishop Hill with Eric Janson. Where he was born or how he happened to go west is not known. As he lived in almost complete seclusion until his death in the late 1870s he could hardly have had much influence on immigration.

The same cannot be said of Captain P. W. Wirström, another former Swedish-born seafarer, who like Captain Lange forsook the oceans for the Great Lakes and then became a real estate agent and promoter of Swedish settlements in Illinois. He had been born at Vaxholm, near Stockholm in 1816, and in 1846, when the Bishop Hill colonists began to arrive, he was a sailor on one of the boats that carried them across the Great Lakes to Chicago. Being able to speak their language, he became well acquainted with them and gave them considerable assistance. For a while he even joined their colony, less for religious reasons than because he had fallen in love with one of its young women members, Johanna Sofia Lundquist, whose father, J. E. Lundquist, before casting his lot with Janson, had been a well-to-do paper manufacturer at Forssa in Hälsingland. In 1846 both father and daughter were members of one of the first groups of Eric Jansonists to arrive at Bishop Hill. Before marrying Captain Wirström in 1847, Miss Lundquist had quit the colony, probably because at first Eric Janson prohibited matrimony, and to support herself she took a position at Andover as a domestic in the home of an American family. After a brief stay at Andover, Mr. and Mrs. Wirström moved to New Orleans where he had been appointed manager of a slave plantation. Of this he soon tired, being, like Widén and most other Swedes, opposed to the slave system, and in 1849 he returned with his wife to Andover. The next year he set out alone for California to dig gold but, like Christian Benson, he found none and set up, instead, a hotel or boarding house for other gold seekers. He soon returned to Illinois and next became a land agent. As such he met incoming Swedish immigrant ships in New York to induce his countrymen to buy land in Illinois. In 1854 he returned in poor health to Bishop Hill where he died, February 25, 1855.

The most potent agents in directing the early Swedish immigrants to Illinois were, however, two Methodist ministers of Swedish birth, the brothers Olof Gustaf and Jonas J. Hedström, the first stationed in New York as an American Methodist missionary to Scandinavian sailors and immigrants, and the other working at Victoria, Illinois, as a blacksmith on weekdays and devoting his evenings and week-ends to spreading the Gospel. Both were born in Nottebäck parish in southern Småland, their father being a corporal in the Swedish Army and living in a modest log cabin, the rent of which was part of his pay. There were six children, four sons and two daughters; Olof Gustaf, the oldest, was born in 1803 and when but twelve years old was apprenticed to a local tailor. After his confirmation two years later he moved to the adjoining province of Blekinge, where Sweden's chief naval base, Karlskrona, is situated. Though he never enlisted in the navy, he became acquainted with the naval personnel and in 1825, when he was twenty-two years old, he was invited to take part in a trip to New York on board an over-age, wooden Swedish man-of-war, named *af Chapman,* which together with several other aged vessels had been sold more or less surreptitiously by the Swedish Government to the Spanish rebels in South America, who were then waging their war of independence from Spain. The deal was made through a private banking firm in Stockholm, Michaelson & Benedicks, and after delivering the ships to their new owners in New York the crews were to be paid off and then left free to find their own way back. Hedström's position has been described as secretary to the Captain, C. B. Nordenskiöld, but since he had practically no education and was, on the other hand, well trained as a tailor, he most likely served as valet to the officers.

After being paid off in New York, Hedström was promptly robbed on the waterfront of every penny, an experience that prepared him singularly well for his future lifework. In New York he knew no one, could not speak a word of English, but being a native of Småland, he soon found a way to earn his living. Walking along Lewis Street at the upper end of South Street near Corlears Hook, he espied the sign of a tailor, Samuel W. Townsend, listed in the New York City directory for 1831–32 as doing a clothing business at No. 133. Quickly he proved his skill with the needle and "goose" iron and before long he had a permanent position. He was over six feet tall, had bushy, black hair and a ruddy, typically Swedish complexion. His diligence won him the special favor of his employer, who not only made him his partner but also introduced him to his niece, Miss Caroline Pinckney, who in turn conducted him to the near-by Willett Street Methodist Episcopal Church on Manhattan's East Side, over which now arches the Williamsburg Bridge. There, to use his own words, he was "soundly and gloriously converted." He also fell in love with Miss Pinckney and on June 11, 1829, they were married. With her he enrolled in the Sunday school of the church and there he learned to read and speak English and after that was gradually advanced from class leader to exhorter and then to preacher. By 1835 he had mastered the English language well enough to be sent to the western foothills of the Catskills as a circuit rider. What he lacked in linguistic polish, he more than made up in religious fervor and force of delivery. For the next ten years he preached in Charlottesville, Jefferson, Windham, Durham, and Prattsville—all in New York state.

While employed by the American Methodist Church, he did not forget his family in Sweden and in 1832 he recrossed the ocean for the express purpose of converting his aged father, in which he was successful. At that time the Methodist denomination was all but unknown in Sweden and completely so in the backwoods of southern Småland. "Compared with the happy land of America"—it was the era of "Good Feeling"—Hedström wrote in his diary, "Sweden is under bondage." When he again returned to Sweden during the American Civil War to restore his health, he received from the Swedish clergy a much warmer reception than he had in 1832. Though not ordained a Lutheran minister, he was invited to speak from some of the state church pulpits.

On his return trip to America in 1832 he brought back with him to New York two of his younger brothers, including Jonas J., who was then twenty years old and by trade a blacksmith. During a storm at sea, "when we were in grave danger and while I was giving an exhortation," to quote Olof Hedström's diary once more, Brother Jonas embraced the Methodist faith and after his arrival in New York he too prepared to become a Methodist class leader, exhorter, and preacher. Like his older brother he also fell in love with an American-born girl, Miss Diantha Shornberger, who was of Dutch Colonial ancestry and living in the Catskills region of New York, where Olof Gustaf Hedström then preached. Her people were farmers and in 1837 they joined the general migration westward to take up new land in Knox County of western Illinois. Before long Jonas Hedström followed and in 1838 he and Miss Shornberger were married. To support his family, he continued working as a blacksmith, first in Farmington, Fulton County, and then at Victoria, Knox County, where he built himself a house destined to be a haven for many a tired and discouraged Swedish immigrant.

In the meantime the movement of Swedish people to the United States began to gather momentum. Most of them entered through the port of New York, where at first there was no one who spoke their language to receive them. As late as 1835 the Swedish population in the city had numbered less than a hundred and in 1836 their first organization, The Swedish Society, which still exists, was formed for charitable purposes, but no religious services were provided. Since Olof Gustaf Hedström's own arrival in 1825, the moral conditions on the waterfront had not improved. In 1832 an educated Swede by the name of Peter Bergner arrived as mate on a Swedish vessel. He had once held a commission in the Jämtland Light Infantry (Jämtland's Fältjägare) which, curiously enough, was also the regiment in which a much more famous Swede, Captain John Ericsson, inventor of the *Monitor,* who arrived in 1839, had once held a commission. Whether the two had been previously acquainted is not known; nor why Bergner had quit the Swedish Army for the sea. His pictures show him to have been a heavy-set man with a full beard and a fine military bearing.

During his early life in America he worked as a stevedore and ship's carpenter on the New York waterfront and, according to his own statements in later years, his life was far from exemplary. Then one day a cotton bale fell on his leg, breaking a bone. In the hospital he was visited by an American missionary worker, Captain R. Gelston, who, finding Bergner asleep, left on his pillow a tract entitled, "Conversations with an Infidel." When Bergner woke up he read the pamphlet and from this reading resulted a spiritual awakening that lasted to the end of his life. When he had recovered the use of his leg, he too became a part-time missionary, paying special attention to the sailors and immigrants from Sweden and the other Scandinavian countries. His first religious meeting was held on board a German vessel tied up to Pier 11 at the foot of Liberty Street on the North River. Besides Bergner, only four sailors were present, and, having had a military education, Bergner did not venture to preach a sermon. Instead, he read one by Martin Luther.

By degrees the attendance grew, and to get larger quarters and the services of a professionally qualified leader, Bergner appealed to the Reverend David Terry, Secretary of the Missionary Society of the American Methodist Episcopal Church. To him he pictured the plight of the newly arrived Swedish immigrants as well as the sailors who were only too often victimized by the loose waterfront population. Both groups, he urged, needed the services of a clergyman familiar with their language as well as with the problems confronting them in the United States. The Reverend Mr. Terry recognized the need and set about to collect funds among his friends for a religious meeting place and information center for the Swedes. The fact that services had already been held on board a ship moored to a pier in the North River may have suggested the idea of converting a demasted vessel into a missionary chapel. Early in 1845, a condemned brig, the former *Henry Leed,* was bought by the Methodist Asbury Society of New York and after being reconstructed as a meeting place it was renamed the *John Wesley* and moored to Pier 11.

To manage this mission in behalf of the American Methodist Church, the Reverend Olof Gustaf Hedström was then summoned from the Catskills. On the church's clerical roster he was the only one who could speak Swedish. At first he was hesitant. In Sweden his education had been most meagre and after twenty years in the United States, during which he had spoken only English, he felt no longer fluent in his native tongue. "It is dark as a pocket," he sighed, but after a conference with Bergner and Terry at the former's home on the eve of the Methodist Conference on May 14, 1845, he finally declared: "If the Bishop appoints me, I'll come to the ship. I believe it is of the Lord." The next day he was appointed and on May 25, 1845, he preached his first sermon in Swedish on the Bethel Ship to an audience of about fifty. Under his management the ship soon became a beehive of activities and its influence radiated rapidly not only to the Midwestern states, or wherever the incoming immigrants settled, but also back to Sweden, where the Methodist faith was spread by his former assistants and converts.

When the original ship was outgrown, the New York Methodist Church bought and equipped another and larger one. For thirty years, from 1845 to 1875, the Bethel Ships served as a welcome meeting place for the incoming Swedish immigrants. On its North River Mission the New York Conference of the American Methodist Church spent over $60,000, not including the cost of the two ships. In 1847 alone over three thousand immigrants and sailors were aided with advice, books and money. In 1850 more than fifteen thousand Bibles or New Testaments were distributed as gifts from the American Bible Society. Financial support was also received from Swedes living in New York, such as Captain John Ericsson who contributed to a variety of religious activities, though not a church member himself. In 1851 Jenny Lind, the singer, visited the ship, knelt in prayer with Hedström and before leaving donated $475, of which $200 was to be spent for Bibles and the rest given to the poor.

After Hedström's retirement in 1875 the second Bethel Ship was towed over to the Brooklyn waterfront where, at the foot of Harrison Street, it was used for a few years as a mission for Danish and Norwegian immigrants rather than Swedish. Next it served as a mission for canal workers in New Jersey. In 1890 it was finally dismantled; the equipment sold at auction.

In a non-religious sense, it was as a guidepost to the fertile acres of western Illinois that the Bethel Mission in New York rendered its most effective service. When Olof Gustaf Hedström saw how the number of immigrants from Sweden increased and how eagerly they inquired about land in the Middle West, he wrote to his brother, Jonas, in Victoria, Illinois, to prepare himself to preach to the future Swedish settlers in their own language. This he did, and on December 15, 1846, he delivered his first sermon in Swedish in an abandoned log cabin at Victoria to an audience of five persons. This was the first Swedish Methodist service held in the Middle West. A permanent Swedish Methodist congregation was also organized.

When Olof Gustaf Hedström met the incoming immigrant ships, he was consulted on temporal as well as spiritual matters, and most of all on the problem of finding the best land for the least money. Having learned from his brother of the rich acres in western Illinois, he naturally advised them to head for that region and, when they arrived, to get in touch with his brother, who would help them not only with religious counsel but also in the acquisition of land. Thus between these two brothers, one in New York and the other in Illinois, was set up a kind of shuttle service which helped direct a large number of the early Swedish immigrants to some of the best farmland in the country—a veritable land of Goshen. In comparison, for instance, with the early English Pilgrims, who happened to strike the anything but fertile acres of Plymouth County in Massachusetts, the Swedish pioneers were indeed fortunate.

In the fall of 1845 Mr. Hedström received at the Bethel Ship in New York an unusual visitor, whose errand in America was to have far-reaching consequences. His name was Olof Olsson, and together with his wife, two children and two associates, he had arrived the day before on the Swedish brig *Neptune,* carrying a cargo of iron from Gävle to New York. He was a tall, gaunt, heavy-set farmer with a voluminous set of whiskers, a man of resolution and executive ability.

With his two friends he had come, he said, to look for a large tract of land suitable for a sizable religious colony, the followers of a new religious leader in the northern Swedish province of Hälsingland, from which so far almost no immigrants had arrived in the United States. (Originally the name of this leader was Erik Jansson, but in America he adopted the form of Eric Janson.) Popularly his followers became known as Eric Jansonites—a new type of pietists or "Devotionalists," also known in Sweden as *läsare* or "readers," meaning that they read the Scriptures and other religious books themselves and made their own interpretations, independent of the official state church. Though during the preceding two or three years there had been a good deal of publicity in Sweden about Eric Janson and his cult, it is not at all certain that in New York Hedström had ever heard of it.

In any event it is probable that Olof Olsson explained the situation approximately as follows: While Olsson himself had come from Hälsingland, in northern Sweden, whereas Hedström had been born in Småland, at the other end of the country, the two provinces were similar in being heavily wooded and both had so far remained relatively isolated from the rest of the country. The Hälsingland people, even more than those from Småland, were known for their independence of spirit and their lively temper, which at times might take rather strong emotional expressions, especially under the influence of either religion or liquor. Several religious revivals had taken place in Hälsingland, leaving the people in a state of doubt or spiritual ferment. In 1840, for instance, they heard sermons by George Scott, the British Methodist missionary and his American Presbyterian colleague, the Reverend Robert Baird of Philadelphia.

On their annual trips to Stockholm to sell smoked salmon, which they had learned to cure as a side line to farming, Olof Olsson and his older brother, Jonas, whose name was later to loom large in the annals of western Illinois, had attended the services conducted by Scott at his Methodist chapel on Haymarket Square.

In January 1843, they had been unexpectedly visited in their home at Söderala, Hälsingland, by a stranger from the more southerly province of Uppland, near Stockholm, who said his name was Erik Jansson. He was a self-educated farmer with a taste for religious controversy, a seeker after new truths and new interpretations of the Scriptures. He had been born, he said, on December 19, 1808, at Biskopskulla (Bishop Hill), a farm near Uppsala, the old university center. He was therefore thirty-five years old. Though there were then no public schools, at least for farm youths in northern Sweden, he had early learned to read and when being prepared for his first communion at the age of fifteen had shown unusual ability in grasping the elements of the Lutheran theology. Voraciously he then read such religious books as were available in the neighborhood, chiefly sermons by Luther, Johann Arndt, and other Germans, as well as by Swedish pietistic theologians such as Anders Nohrborg. Biblical quotations and theological phrases literally poured from his lips. In 1830 he had passed through a religious crisis and at the same time he had been miraculously cured, he thought, of a physical malady. After that he had read devotional literature even more assiduously and had gradually come to the conclusion that only in the Bible was the way to salvation indicated and that, consequently, all other religious books were either superfluous or downright harmful. His second conclusion was that belief in God, through Christ, led not only to forgiveness of sin but to a complete obliteration of it.

These were heady doctrines for an emotionally starved population, writes Professor Stephenson, and as Janson supported them with copious biblical quotations, he began to draw considerable crowds at private prayer meetings. He was a good debater with a prodigious memory. After being married in 1838, he had bought a farm of his own and for a while he ceased his preaching, but continued his reading. In October 1840, he attended the annual cattle fair at Uppsala and the drinking scenes he witnessed so shocked him that he resumed his revivalist preaching, warning his countrymen, like a second John the Baptist, "to flee the wrath to come." Many of the state clergy, he declared, were too indifferent to heavy drinking and loose living, even if they did not condone or personally indulge in such acts.

By January 1843, he felt ready for an expansion of his activities. Ostensibly to sell flour, but really to find a new missionary field, he then made a trip northward to Hälsingland where he was directed to the home of the Olsson brothers. They found him personally congenial and his religious views in accord with their own. As a speaker at their private prayer meetings he repeated his successes in Uppland.

The following year he bought a farm himself in Hälsingland and in April 1844, he moved there with his family. As his audiences grew in numbers, he became more and more sensational, as well as openly defiant of the church authorities. On June 11, 1844, he staged on the shore of a lake a demonstration of his religious beliefs by the public burning of religious books collected in large numbers by his overwrought followers. This was a violation of Swedish law and for his act he was put in jail. On his promise to abstain from further vandalism, and to stay out of the district, he was soon released. This promise he did not keep. In October of the same year there was another bonfire, and in December a third. Each time Janson was locked up and several of his followers fined. These court actions caused national publicity and gradually the whole country became aroused. During the winter of 1844-45 Janson spent four months in jail, but in April 1845, he was once more released after a petition had been presented in his behalf to the King. For fifteen weeks he remained in seclusion and after that decided to ask for a public trial at Delsbo, where he felt public sentiment was back of him. This was granted, but though the court decided to acquit him, public excitement had reached such a pitch that for his own safety the authorities thought it wiser to place him in temporary protective custody in the city jail at Gävle. While on the way there he was rescued by his followers and then kept in hiding until he was able to make his way secretly to Norway. In January 1846, he set out from Christiania (now Oslo) via Copenhagen, Hamburg, and Liverpool, for New York, where he arrived early the following summer accompanied by his wife, two children and three of his disciples. To prepare the way Olof Olsson and his family had been sent ahead the fall before.

During the summer of 1844 several court actions were instituted against followers of Janson for holding prayer meetings in their homes. Both Jonas and Olof Olsson were among those incarcerated and fined for reading the Scriptures aloud in their own houses and fined extra for doing it on Sundays while divine services were being held in the state churches. One excess led to another and gradually the whole region worked itself into a state of semi-hysteria. Finally mob violence broke out and several of Janson's followers, including his wife, were subjected to personal indignities. A little more tact and patience on the part of the authorities might have caused the popular excitement to run its course, but the persecution also increased the pretensions of Janson until he finally proclaimed himself a special representative of God, Whose will was revealed to him directly. On his followers he thereby exercised an even stronger, almost hypnotic influence.

Once the law had been invoked, it had to be enforced and under pressure no repeal was possible. As usual under such circumstances, Janson's followers grew in number until they represented several provinces and included substantial farmers and industrialists, as well as landless people. As a cure for social ills emigration to America was then much in the Swedish mind, and during his days in jail or in hiding, Janson developed a scheme of mass departure to a New Canaan across the sea where he and his friends could hold as many private meetings as they wished, and might add to their fellowship from other nationalities than the Swedish. To finance such an enterprise, all believers were told to sell their belongings, including farms and cattle as well as personal property, and turn the proceeds into a common fund from which the travel expenses of all, rich and poor, as well as the cost of new farmland in America, were to be paid. Like the early Christians, the Janson followers were to "have all things in common," at least until established in the New Jerusalem they hoped to find in the West. While some adherents could pay very little or nothing, others were relatively wealthy. One farmer from Dalecarlia, known as *guld-gubben,* paid into the fund over 24,000 riksdalers, nominally the current equivalent of $6,400, and in purchasing power at that time considerably more.

As an advance agent to scout for land Olof Olsson had thus arrived in New York and to the Reverend Olof Gustaf Hedström, always a sympathetic soul, he confided his project. What was more natural than that Hedström would once more recommend western Illinois and consultation with his brother Jonas in Victoria? He and Mrs. Hedström even offered to care for Mrs. Olsson and the two children while the men folk went west.

The letters of Gustaf Flack, which had been copied and circulated in the Jansonite regions in Hälsingland, had already attracted the attention of Olsson and his fellow scouts to the so-far untilled prairies of northwestern Illinois, but before these made up their minds, they decided to explore not only in Illinois and Iowa, but also in Wisconsin and Minnesota. Not until Eric Janson himself and his family arrived at Victoria in July 1846, was any property actually bought. On August 1, 1846, title was taken in the name of Olsson to sixty acres of new land near Red Oak Grove of Henry County, Illinois, the price being $250. On August 21 a complete farm of 156 acres with buildings and livestock was acquired for $1,100. At this farm both the Janson and the Olsson families lived while they prepared for the arrival of their followers from Sweden. On September 26, 1846, 480 acres of Government land was bought at the prevailing price of $1.25 per acre. These purchases included Hoopal Grove, a shallow, wooded valley, which is today the attractive center of Bishop Hill, a name Janson made up by translating literally that of his birthplace, Biskopskulla, in Sweden. Whatever the merits of their theology, in buying land the Jansonites showed superb judgment.

Of economic theory they were completely innocent. The *Communist Manifesto* of Marx and Engels had not then been published and the main purpose of the Swedish venture was to achieve religious liberty in combination with economic independence. The communistic arrangement was only a temporary expedient. Of the Brook Farm, the Oneida Community, the Shaker colonies, and the other sixty or more American experiments in communal ownership, they had probably never heard. Their only guide was the Bible. For the time being all property was held by four trustees, appointed by Janson, including himself, and by him empowered to act in his absence. Except Janson, all were former residents of a single parish, Söderala, which had been the home of the two Olssons. The property was therefore in the hands of a very close corporation.

In the fall of 1846 the first contingent of the new settlers began to arrive. Some had started in the spring, but to find places for so many on the few Swedish ships, carrying cargoes of iron to New York, was not easy. One ship was wrecked soon after leaving the port of Söderhamn in eastern Sweden, another required five months to reach America, some of the time being spent waiting for repairs in a British port, a third was lost without a trace, a fourth was wrecked on the coast of Labrador and on several cholera broke out. Since none of the ships were equipped to carry passengers, the hygienic conditions on board became unspeakable. Almost all were overcrowded. Below decks double-decker bunks were installed, each berth being seven feet wide and giving space for five persons to sleep on straw pallets. When seasickness, to say nothing of cholera, broke out, the sanitary conditions became worse.

Each boatload of passengers was under the temporal as well as spiritual care of a leader in whom absolute power was vested. To maintain morale on board, frequent religious services were held, including almost constant prayer meetings with Scripture readings. As to the remarkable self-control exercised by these Swedish pilgrims many contemporary testimonies have been published. (See Chapter on Methodists for the effect on Victor Witting and Peter Newberg, future Swedish Methodist leaders in America.) "We had a pleasant voyage, and I was not in the least affected by seasickness," one Anders Jönsson wrote from Bishop Hill to Sweden on February 9, 1847. "My words are inadequate to describe with what joy we are now permitted daily to draw water from the well of life and how we have come to a veritable land of Canaan, flowing with milk and honey, which the Lord has prepared for his people"—a passage quoted by Professor Stephenson.

Naturally such "America letters," reflecting the eloquence of Eric Janson, were intended to bring more participants to Bishop Hill; in February 1847, came a new party of twenty-one men and one woman, which must have included the above Anders Jönsson; in June 1847, about four hundred more. Between 1847 and 1854 nine different groups, adding up to almost 1,500 persons, arrived from Sweden—or about one-fourth of the inhabitants of Henry County, in which the first white men had settled only eleven years earlier. In population Bishop Hill soon became several times larger than the New Sweden colony, established in 1638 by official Swedish authority on the lower Delaware. Such numbers testified to the power exercised by Eric Janson. In 1864 when he was no longer alive, the membership had shrunk to 655 of whom 172 were minors.

At first the newcomers were sheltered in tents, and religious services were held under canvas. As the weather grew colder, dugouts had to be excavated in the sides of the ravine or gully running through the central grove. These were about eighteen feet wide and from twenty-five to thirty feet long. At the rear end in the hillside was a fireplace and along the side walls were installed double-decker bunks of rough boards or planks on which from forty to fifty persons were expected to sleep. The ceilings were made of rough hewn logs or wooden rails covered with sod or earth. The front walls were made of wood, in the center of which was a crude door, flanked by two small windows. During the winter many died from pneumonia, malaria, or dysentery. No doctors, or drug stores were within reach; no experienced neighbors to consult. The nearest grist mill was twenty-eight miles away and to keep starvation at bay, the hand mill on which corn was ground had to be kept in motion night and day. The corn mush had to be boiled from ten to twelve hours. Finally certain fast days had to be imposed. Every morning at five a prayer meeting was held, lasting two hours. By spring, no boards were left for coffins and many who died the first winter had to be buried in shrouds and in mass graves. The mounds were not marked and to keep up morale funeral services had to be omitted. Those who survived such an ordeal must have been hardy folk.

In the spring of 1847 farming began. To "bust" the virgin sod thirty-six-inch plows pulled by eight yokes of oxen were used. Later smaller plows were pulled by three yokes of oxen and land already broken was cultivated by horse power. In subsequent years more and better implements were acquired and the yield per acre correspondingly increased. By 1855 the colony owned 586 head of cattle, 109 horses or mules, over a thousand hogs, besides geese, chickens and turkeys. To make linen cloth as well as rugs for sale, flax was planted, a crop well known in Sweden, and by their hard work the farmers, born and raised on the frostbitten acres of northern Sweden, gradually made the Illinois prairie bloom and bear fruit. Broom corn was one of their first "cash crops." The blue-flowering flax fields, alternating with the golden wheat fields, must have been a sight for their weary eyes.

Gradually the grain they raised, whether rye, barley or wheat, provided a better diet than they had ever enjoyed in Sweden. Step by step more land was bought so that by 1856 the community owned 8,500 acres, of which 3,250 had been put under cultivation. In 1859 the assets were appraised at $770,000. (To offset the financial crisis of 1857 some money had then to be borrowed against a mortgage.) Some of this accumulated wealth had been brought from Sweden, but most of it had been wrung from the soil. In 1851, for instance, 28,322 yards of linen cloth were woven from flax grown on the colony land, and 3,237 yards of carpets produced from the community's own materials. As they had been accustomed to do in Sweden, the members made their own clothing from the soil up, spun their wool, wove their own cloth, tanned their own leather, made their own shoes, and built their own houses either from lumber they milled themselves or from hand-made bricks produced in their own yards. After a hundred years their buildings are still among the sturdiest in the neighborhood. The colonists not only laid out and paved new roads, but when the first railroad was put through the region by the Chicago, Burlington and Quincy Company, they did much of the grading under contract. In the new town of Galva (a corruption of Gävle) they invested money in city lots and otherwise helped build up a new business center.

In every human Eden there is, however, a snake and Bishop Hill was no exception. Many of the colonists found Eric Janson's regime too autocratic in an economic sense, and the love of private ownership was always strong in the breast of almost every Swede. They also began to tire of his social and religious rules, particularly his requirement, during the first two years, under what he claimed to be divine authority, that celibacy be observed by everyone, even married couples. Back of this was the inescapable fact that no material provisions were at hand for the care of children. In June 1848, when the ban against matrimony was lifted by virtue of a new revelation, mass weddings took place. On Sunday, July 23, 1848, for instance, the records show, twenty-four couples were married in the community church and on July 30 sixteen more. In the month of September there were seven. In some cases Janson himself decided who should marry whom.

Certain outside influences were also at work. In the new country opportunities for earning money and for investment in private enterprise were plentiful. There were also religious rivalries. At first both Olof Olsson and Eric Janson and their respective families and companions had been hospitably received by Jonas Hedström in his home at Victoria. Janson and his family lived for a while in the very log hut in which Hedström later held his first church service in Swedish. When the colonists began to arrive, Hedström visited them at Bishop Hill and seeing their misery, he brought them what aid he could, and also warned Janson in regard to the sanitary conditions and the lack of adequate medical care, even threatening to have him put in jail. The Janson partisans accused him of religious proselyting, but to this the Methodists replied that Hedström acted only as a Good Samaritan. The fact remains that in the fall of 1848 about 250 members of the colony left Bishop Hill en masse and then settled in the vicinity of Victoria and Galesburg, many of them joining Hedström's Swedish Methodist church. In 1864, a Methodist congregation was organized at Bishop Hill itself and today a church of this denomination is the only one in the village.

In the summer of 1849 the cholera struck the colony; some visiting immigrants from Norway had caught the infection on a canal boat from Chicago to Peru. Among the hard working and tired-out colonists, it spread rapidly. To check it, those who seemed well were sent off to a farm near La Grange, now Orion, Illinois, but there they were even more helpless. They had brought the contagion with them and no means to fight it. In a few weeks seventy of them died, while the fatalities at Bishop Hill were kept down to forty-four. (The site of the cholera-stricken farm near Orion is now marked by a stone monument.) To save his own wife and children from the plague, Janson hurried them off to a fishing camp on Rock Island, the island in the middle of the Mississippi River from which the city gets its name and on which the great Government arsenal was built prior to the Civil War. But it was too late. Not only Mrs. Janson but two of the children died from the pest and were buried on the island in unmarked graves.

Within a year Janson found himself a new spouse, Mrs. Sophia Pollock-Gabrielson, who had accompanied him from New York in 1846. Born in Gothenburg, Sweden, she had arrived in New York when but fifteen years old. There she had first married a sailor, who soon disappeared at sea. Her second husband was an American schoolteacher by the name of Pollock, who did his best to educate her. When she quit him to accompany Eric Janson to Illinois in 1846, he is supposed to have died of a broken heart. In one of the mass weddings at Bishop Hill, in July 1848, she married one of the Swedish-born colonists by the name of Lars Gabrielson. The following year he fell a victim to the cholera, which left her free to marry Eric Janson. Being the only member of the colony who could read, speak, and write English, at least after a fashion, she had been appointed by Janson as the teacher in a school in English which he had started for the purpose of train-ing missionaries for his doctrines among the American population in general, as well as of educating the children born to the colonists at Bishop Hill. Early he understood that in the future English was the language they must know best of all.

The school plans for future missionaries came to naught because of Janson's death at the hands of an assassin in 1850, but some of the Swedish-born boys taught by Mrs. Gabrielson became Union officers in the Civil War. Indirectly the murder of the prophet was the result of his autocratic rule over the personal affairs of his followers. Among the latter was his niece, Charlotte Janson, who in one of the summer mass weddings of 1848 was married to a Swedish-born veteran of the Mexican War bearing the apparently assumed name of John Root. In the war he had learned the rough-and-ready manners of the military camps and had become what is known as "trigger-happy." As a con-dition for the marriage he had promised Janson that he would not attempt to remove his wife from the colony. This promise he did not keep, but each time he tried to take her and their son, born October 25, 1849, from Janson's control, he was blocked by Janson and his colonists. His threats of violence finally made Janson move temporarily to St. Louis, taking with him his niece and her child. During their absence, on April 1, 1850, Root again appeared at the colony with a group of friends demanding his wife and son and threatening to use force, if necessary, only to find them gone. On Saturday, May 11, Janson re-turned from St. Louis. On Monday, May 13, he had to appear in court at Cambridge, Illinois, where, as a leader of the colony, he was the defendant in a lawsuit. During the noon recess Root suddenly appeared in the courtroom and by firing two revolver shots point-blank at Janson killed him instantly.

For several days the faithful colonists refused to believe that their leader was dead, expecting an immediate resurrection, but gradually they had to accept the fact and arrange a funeral. Today a marble monument marks his grave at Bishop Hill. That he was a dynamic personality who might have accomplished important results had he lived is certain. His influence over his followers was very deep and the value of his contribution to the early development of western Illinois cannot be questioned. That he had many faults is evident, but it is also true that many of the charges leveled against him by his contemporaries were unfounded. Like Brigham Young, who had abandoned Illinois for Utah only four years before the arrival of Janson, he had the qualities of a true pioneer and frontier executive.

After two years of court delays Root was finally convicted of manslaughter and sentenced to three years in the penitentiary. After his release he subsisted for some years in extreme poverty in Chicago.

The death of Janson caused a crisis in the affairs of the colony. No sooner had the cholera epidemic been overcome than the California gold fever set in. Rumors of easy riches to be had for the digging were too alluring for the hardy Swedish pioneers to resist. Having walked from Chicago, they did not hesitate to walk to Council Bluffs on the other side of the Mississippi, from which many of the caravans for California set out. Land for some of the present-day farms owned by descendants of Swedish pioneers in western Illinois was originally purchased with the gold or other earnings in California. Having crossed the mountains and the great desert on foot, they usually came back, if they had been at all successful, by boat via Panama and New Orleans. Some of them continued by boat to Philadelphia to get their gold minted.

Among the Bishop Hill colonists who set out for California was Jonas Olsson, brother of Olof Olsson, the first Swedish religious scout in America, both Janson's original sponsors in Hälsingland. On April 25, 1850, eight of the Jansonites met at Fort Kearney and on August 12 the same year they reached the gold fields at Placerville, California, 2,512 miles from Bishop Hill, but as far as known the whole venture was a failure. When the news of Janson's death reached Olsson in California, he hurried back via Central America to take over his rule at Bishop Hill. His closest rival on the Board of Trustees was one Olof Johnson, who had helped develop the town of Galva. Johnson was less conservative than Olsson, and with the funds of the colony he made investments which in the panic in 1857 turned out to be worthless. New land had been bought, expensive buildings erected, railroad construction contracts signed, new stock and new machinery acquired. For a few years, as more and more willing workers arrived from Sweden, the colony was quite prosperous. The buildings erected were the largest in the United States west of Chicago. When Janson died the colony debts amounted to only $8,000, but in December 1857, the trustees authorized a loan of over $50,000 against a first mortgage on the property, and in 1858 another $40,000 was borrowed from a New York banker. In 1860 the colony's debts added up to $112,000, but since the value of the property had been appraised in 1859 at $770,000 the financial situation was still good.

In 1853 the colony had been incorporated under the laws of Illinois, the charter giving almost unlimited power to the seven trustees. In theory, all earnings of the members were to be placed in a common treasury, but as the country developed and not only wages but business opportunities outside the colony improved, rumors of more and more Ananiases and Sapphiras began to spread. Furthermore, most members complained that they had been kept in complete ignorance of the business ventures of the trustees, which included banking, publishing, dealings in produce, both wholesale and retail, tradings in stocks and bonds, city real estate, coal mining and other operations that were bewildering to simple-minded Swedish farm folk. In 1860 Olof Johnson was deposed as a trustee and lawsuits were begun, which in costs and lawyers' fees ate up considerable portions of the hard-earned assets. In 1870 there was a final division of the property. The debts then were close to $400,000 and the court costs, including lawyers' fees, added up to $57,000 which, at least according to Swedish standards, seemed enormous. Even so, each member of the colony in good standing received an impressive allotment. The value of the apartments in the common dormitories was fixed and while some families took their shares in the form of titles to certain parcels of land, others took some of theirs in the form of housing.

In 1890, the population of Bishop Hill was 3,329 and in 1900, 6,114. At the celebration of its seventieth anniversary in 1916 over three thousand persons, chiefly descendants of the original settlers, attended. In many communities throughout the nation, several had achieved prominent positions. To the Civil War, the colony contributed an entire company of volunteers. Of the original 107 men and twenty-two officers who had enlisted, two officers and thirteen men were killed in action. The very first native-born Swede to be appointed a cadet at West Point was Eric Bergland, a son of Andrew Berglund, one of the original trustees of Bishop Hill. Jonas W. Olson, a son of Olof Olsson, who had been the first scout, was the first Swede to be admitted to the bar in Illinois. He was also elected a member of the State Legislature and during both Cleveland administrations served as postmaster at Galva. John Root, a son of the man who shot Janson, also became a lawyer and for many years served as master in chancery for Henry County. In 1916 he was President of the Bishop Hill Old Settlers Association. Eric Johnson, a son of the founder and an officer in the Civil War, became a writer, newspaper publisher, and successively, legislator in several states: Nebraska, Texas, and California. Other descendants of the Bishop Hill colonists had become manufacturers, businessmen and teachers, including college and university professors. They stemmed from a vigorous stock and their influence has spread far and wide.

Today Bishop Hill is an unusually attractive country town. The buildings around the central oak grove with its conventional Civil War monument in granite are more impressive than the average in the neighborhood. In 1928 the main dormitory, which looked like a college hall, burned down, but a majority of the other original two- and three-story houses are still intact, including the impressive "steeple" building which looks like a court house.

In 1850 the Illinois residents born in Sweden numbered only 1,123, a majority being members of the Bishop Hill colony. During the ensuing decades several other farming communities with a relatively large proportion of Swedish-born inhabitants grew up in the vicinity —at Victoria, Galesburg, Knoxville, Monmouth, Moline, and Rock Island.

Since its earliest days Chicago has always been a Swedish stronghold. To its development the chief contributions of the Swedes have been those of builders, whether as architects, contractors or carpenters. In 1840, when the first Swedes began to arrive, the city had only 4,470 inhabitants. As early as 1838 Olof Gottfrid Lange had settled there and a few years later Gustaf Flack. In 1920, 58,836 of its 2,701,000 inhabitants were natives of Sweden, making Chicago the third largest Swedish city in the world. In 1940 they numbered 46,258, while their children born in America added up to 63,940.

For the state of Illinois the corresponding figures in 1940 were, respectively, 79,906 and 130,540. In 1920 the Swedish residents of Illinois of the first and second generation constituted 3.3 per cent of the total population; in 1940 the percentage had gone down to 2.67. Numerically Illinois was for many years the strongest Swedish state in the Union, gradually replaced by Minnesota where in 1940 the percentage of Swedes of the first and second generation was 8.2 per cent.

Between the Swedish residents of the two states there is a certain good-natured rivalry. While as a "Swedish" state Minnesota has passed Illinois, Chicago still outranks Minneapolis. The situation is illustrated by a remark made by a Swedish resident of Chicago in regard to the annual Sweden Day celebrated in the Twin Cities each June. "By drawing on the whole state," he sniffed, "they claim they attract from thirty to forty thousand visitors to a picnic in Minnehaha Park. In Chicago we have every Sunday all summer long at least six different picnics, each one with a larger attendance than that."

THE SWEDES IN THE CIVIL WAR

The American Civil War was the first national event in which the Swedish pioneers took part. On their assimilation as American citizens it had deep effect. Though their native country had by then enjoyed almost half a century of unbroken peace, many of them had had military training, and suddenly this became a valuable asset. Even those who had been too young to be conscripted, were prime military material, being, as a rule, hardy farmers, accustomed to life in the open, and trained from childhood to obey and to feel responsible for themselves, their animals and their fellow workers. From the beginning they took the war seriously. In the state of Illinois, for instance, more Swedes in proportion to their numbers volunteered than the rest of the population—one out of five, regardless of sex or age, as compared to one out of seven for the state as a whole. In his book, *The Swedish Element in Illinois* (Chicago, 1917) Ernst W. Olson has told their story.

To the Swedes the issue seemed fundamentally a moral one. About the fine constitutional or political points, such as states' rights, or the Missouri Compromise, they were largely ignorant or indifferent. In their former country the federal system had never existed and while many of them had arrived in time to become voters in 1860, they had had little political experience. In Sweden the party system had not by then been developed so as to reach the common people, and most of the emigrants had been too poor to be allowed to vote anyway. In the United States they found a different atmosphere. Everyone talked politics and defended his own party. In the slavery debates, particularly those of Lincoln and Douglas, the Swedes took a keen interest. In the 1860 election the Republican Party owed much to the well-nigh solid Swedish vote, especially in Illinois. Among the Swedes Lincoln had many friends and some party workers. In Rockford, for instance, eighty of them are supposed to have marched to polls in a body, led by their minister, to vote for Lincoln.

By the time the hostilities broke out in 1861, the Swedes were relatively well prepared. Those who had had military experience in Sweden, had already begun to train their fellow countrymen, and those who had been officers in the Swedish Army became suddenly preferred stock. Some of them rose quickly to high commands; others had to be content with low ranks while serving as expert technicians, usually in the artillery or the engineering corps. As the struggle continued many additional Swedish officers came to America for the purpose of gaining practical experience, as others had already done in the Mexican War and before that in the War for Independence. Some of the newcomers were at once entrusted with important commands. Even the ordinary manual skills of the Swedes were put to good use for such purposes as constructing shelters, repairing equipment, shoeing horses, and driving supply wagons. Throughout one winter a company of Swedish volunteers from Illinois operated a lumber mill in the hills of eastern Tennessee.

One of the first Swedish immigrant communities to organize a military unit was Bishop Hill, the religious-communistic colony in Henry County, founded in 1846 by Eric Janson. One of its first officers was his own son, Eric Johnson, born in Sweden in 1838. His maternal grandfather had been a soldier in Sweden's last war with Russia (1808–09), and in his youth Eric Janson himself had done his military service as a conscript. Having already been elected an officer in the Bishop Hill company, Eric Johnson was commissioned, at the age of twenty-three, a lieutenant in the Illinois Volunteers, when the company was incorporated in the state troops in the fall of 1861. After taking part in the critical Battle of Shiloh, or Pittsburg Landing, in western Tennessee the following spring, he was promoted to captain, but during the subsequent siege of Corinth he contracted typhoid fever and, in September 1862, was permanently mustered out of the service.

His subsequent career exemplified the new spirit of the Swedish veterans, especially those who had served as officers. Having learned the rudiments of English at the Bishop Hill village school, conducted by his future stepmother, Mrs. Sophia Pollock-Gabrielson, Eric Johnson first became a newspaper editor and publisher at Galva, the city nearest his home town, and then entered politics. From his father he had inherited a gift for leadership as well as the ability to express himself in words. In 1871, only nine years after he had left the battlefront, he was appointed a journal clerk of the Illinois State Legislature. Between 1883 and 1885 he served as a Government clerk in Washington and in 1888, after having resumed his newspaper publishing at Holdrege, Nebraska, he was elected a member of that state's legislative assembly. After various publishing ventures, both in English and Swedish, including a *History of the Swedes in Illinois,* in collaboration with Carl Fredrick Peterson, a Swedish journalist, and an attempt at real estate promotion in Texas, he moved in 1907 to Clearwater, California, and as late as 1913 he became an assistant clerk of the California State Legislature. He died in California in 1919 at the age of eighty-one. Of his father there are no photographs extant, but those of Eric Johnson show a remarkably attractive appearance from which it may be concluded that his father could not have been as repulsive as his enemies alleged.

The man who had drilled the Bishop Hill company for a year before the hostilities began was a veteran of the Swedish Army by the name of Eric Forsse. Born in 1819 at Falun, in Dalarna, a province with long military traditions, he had been a mature, full-bearded man, and head of a family when he arrived in Bishop Hill in 1850. Before leaving Sweden with his wife and five children, he had served twelve years as a private and probably also as a non-commissioned officer in the Dal Regiment of his native province. His practical knowledge of drill formations, the use of firearms and trench construction, was therefore considerable.

What had attracted the Forsse family to Bishop Hill is not certain. They had not arrived by the usual route through New York and Chicago or as members of an organized party of Janson converts, but on a Swedish sailing vessel via New Orleans. They then proceeded up the Mississippi to St. Louis where they were attacked by the cholera, a persistent affliction of the mid-nineteenth century immigrants. After recovery the family lived, successively, in Galesburg, Knoxville and Moline before joining the Bishop Hill settlement in the fall of 1851. What work Forsse did in the colony is not known; probably the usual farm chores. But when rumors of armed conflict became rife, his military experience came to use. He was then forty years old. Foresightedly he drilled the Bishop Hill boys and did it so well that they won a flag in an open competition with other volunteers in the state and, on September 16, 1861, they were accepted in the first official call for armed men as a company in the newly formed Fifty-sixth Regiment of Illinois Infantry Volunteers. Before the end of the month they entrained at Galva for further drilling at Camp Buteau near Princeton,

Illinois, where a Colonel Winslow was in command.

The first enlistment was for only three months and the common illusion that the war would be short, if dramatic and violent, was shared by the Swedes. Their state of mind as well as that of the military discipline at the time is shown by an episode in which the Bishop Hill company became involved. Few of the newly organized regiments by then had their full quotas and "raiding" for recruits was a common practice. The inducements were, as a rule, cash bonuses, offers of better fellowship, promises of more exciting and immediate war experiences, or all of these in conjunction.

In St. Louis a special regiment of sharpshooters was then being formed and to get sufficient enrollment, scouts were sent to the various camps on either side of the upper Mississippi, farm boys being known for their skill with rifles. At Camp Buteau the daily drill without rifles, which were not yet available, had become more and more tedious, especially to the Bishop Hill boys who had already marched and countermarched for a year. Furthermore, the regiment was only six companies strong and since recruiting was obviously slow, the prospects for real and early action became daily more and more dim. For their propaganda the smooth-tongued scouts from St. Louis found fertile ground at Camp Buteau and a secret deal was made for the wholesale transfer of the entire regiment to the new rifle corps. To bring the men down to St. Louis a river steamer, the *Musselman,* was quietly sent up the Mississippi and Illinois rivers and when Colonel Winslow awoke on the morning of October 23, 1861, he found the camp empty. Having observed the mysterious vessel, which was now gone, he suspected wholesale desertion, but when he tried to send out an alarm by telegraph, he found the wires cut. By a messenger to another telegraph station he managed to inform the state authorities at Springfield and at once they dispatched a battery of light artillery to Acton, further down the Illinois River, to intercept the fugitives. When the *Musselman* floated into sight, a warning shot was first fired across its bows, but when no attention was paid, a ball was sent crashing through the prow. That stopped the boat.

Shamefaced the young soldiers confessed their plan, giving the excuse that they had only wanted to face the enemy at once. Ordered ashore they were locked up in the Acton State Penitentiary for the night and the next day were taken to Camp Butler, near Springfield, to stand military trial on charges of desertion in time of war. There was no firing squad, however. Men who wanted to fight were what President

Lincoln had asked for, and wiser counsel prevailed. All were acquitted or rather given a Scotch verdict. As further recruiting seemed hopeless, the Fifty-sixth Regiment was, however, disbanded. The entire personnel, minus Colonel Winslow, was sent to Camp Douglas, near Chicago, and there merged with the Fifty-seventh Illinois Infantry Volunteers, of which Colonel Silas D. Baldwin was in command. On December 26, 1861, the day after Christmas, the enlarged regiment was mustered into the Union Army with Eric Forsse still in charge of Company D, made up of the Bishop Hill boys.

In the war it made a fine record. Early in 1862 it participated in the siege of Fort Donelson in western Tennessee where General Grant first used the words "unconditional surrender" which was to play such a fateful role in the Second World War. In the Battle of Shiloh or Pittsburg Landing on the Tennessee River on Sunday, April 6, 1862, the Fifty-seventh lost 187 men and officers in dead, wounded, or missing. After it was over, Eric Forsse was advanced to major, his Swedish military experience having proven its worth, and First Lieutenant Eric Johnson, son of the Bishop Hill founder, was promoted to succeed him. Next, the regiment took part in the siege of Corinth, Mississippi; in General Sherman's campaign in Tennessee; in the Battles of Atlanta and Resaca; and, finally, in the famous "March to the Sea." On December 21, 1864, when the regiment had all but completed its three-year enlistment, Savannah was reached. Near that city on the Savannah River the final clash with the Confederates took place January 24, 1865. On May 24, 1865 the regiment, including Company D, took part in the victory parade at Washington, D.C., and on July 14, it was disbanded.

On several occasions Eric Forsse had commanded the whole regiment, but being a foreigner and unaccustomed to English he was never promoted beyond the rank of major. At the Battle of Allatoona Pass he had had charge of an entire brigade, as he did at the Rome Crossroads encounter in Georgia. In October 1864, feeling that the war was almost over, he and several of the other older officers resigned their commands and returned to Illinois. Forsse was then forty-five years old and at Bishop Hill he had a wife and five children. With the money he had saved from his army pay and what he received for his share in the Bishop Hill community, he bought a farm near Galva, Illinois, and there, like Cincinnatus of old, he settled down. In 1869, however, he and about fifty other Swedish farmers in the neighborhood, sold out and moved further west to Kansas where they took up new land. In honor of Major Forsse's birthplace the new community was called Falun, a name it still bears. In 1870 Forsse was appointed its first postmaster and as such he served seventeen years. In 1872 he was elected to the Kansas State Legislature, but served for only one term. He was also a township trustee and a justice of the peace. Having been a commander of men in the war, it seemed natural that he should hold public office when it was over. In 1889 he died. His oldest son, Olof, born in Sweden in 1842, grew up to become a replacement in Company D and after taking part in the Georgia campaign, he was mustered out with the regiment in July 1865. At Falun, Kansas, he became a grain dealer and served both as county commissioner and sheriff.

A much more distinguished climax capped the military career of another Bishop Hill officer, that of Eric Bergland, son of Anders Berglund, from Söderala parish in Hälsingland, who had been one of Eric Janson's original co-leaders at the colony in Illinois. Born in Sweden in 1844, Bergland had been brought to the United States with one of the first Eric Janson groups in 1846. He was therefore only seventeen years old when commissioned a second lieutenant in 1861. After the Battle of Shiloh, or practically on his eighteenth birthday, he was promoted to first lieutenant in the same company, and as such served almost all through the war. Toward its end he often acted as company commander. Then, in the fall of 1864, when the regiment was encamped in Georgia, he suddenly received an appointment to West Point, the first ever given a native of Sweden.

When he reached the United States Military Academy on November 16 that year, however, he found that the classes had been under instruction since September 1. As his own formal education had been limited to that of the village school at Bishop Hill, conducted by Mrs. Pollock-Gabrielson, he was told by the Academy Superintendent that he could not hope to catch up in time for the mid-year examinations in January; especially those in mathematics. He was, therefore, given permission to postpone his entry until the following year. In the meantime he was assigned to rather light duties with an engineering corps at Johnson's Island in Ohio, and with the kindly aid of older officers, he was able to continue his preparatory studies. On July 1, 1865, he was formally admitted to West Point and four years later, June 15, 1869, he was graduated at the head of his class.

At first he was commissioned in the artillery, but after serving at various New England posts and on the Canadian border during the Feenian raid in 1870, he was sent to the artillery school at Fort Monroe and after that was transferred to the engineering corps, in which, in 1895, he became a major. In the meantime he had served at various times at West Point as an instructor in mathematics and military engineering and was finally appointed Assistant Professor of ethics and military law. Next he was put in charge of river and harbor improvements in the states of Tennessee, Mississippi, Arkansas, Louisiana, and Texas; and after the disastrous Johnstown flood in Pennsylvania in 1889 he was sent there to construct emergency pontoon bridges. In 1891 he was appointed chief engineer of the Fifth and Sixth Lighthouse districts with headquarters at Baltimore, Maryland. As such he had charge of the construction of lighthouses at Cape Charles, Hog Island, Wolf Trap and other points on the Atlantic coast. On June 5, 1878, he was married in Washington to Miss Lucy Scott Mac-Farland of Kentucky, a cousin of the wife of Rutherford B. Hayes, at that time President of the United States. After thirty-five years of military service, he retired in March 1896, but continued to live in Baltimore until his death on November 3, 1918, when the First World War was being won. He was then seventy-four years old. A career like that could probably have been made only in the United States.

Several other Bishop Hill volunteers became officers in the Civil War and after its close gained public office. One of them was Andrew G. Warner, a native of northern Hälsingland, who had been brought to Illinois in his early youth. Though he lived at Andover and was never a member of the Bishop Hill colony, he took part in the preliminary training under Eric Forsse, and then joined Company D of the Fifty-seventh Regiment. At Shiloh he was wounded in the arm, but refused to be evacuated. In August 1863, he was promoted from sergeant to second lieutenant and in 1864, when the slaves had been freed, he volunteered to command a company in the Sixty-third U.S. Colored Infantry—a dangerous post as the Confederates swore they would shoot on sight any white man caught commanding colored troops. On his return to Andover, just prior to the end of the war, he married Miss Mathilda Johnson, a daughter of Eric Janson, the late leader of the Bishop Hill colony. In 1868 he was elected sheriff at Andover on an independent ticket. The Republicans had refused to nominate him, but he won easily as the Democrats abstained from designating an opponent.

The command of Company D, after Captain Eric Johnson had become ill during the siege of Corinth, was held throughout the rest of the war by Peter M. Wickström, also a native of Sweden, and a member of the Bishop Hill colony. After his return in 1865, he, like Major Forsse, bought a farm near Galva. He was of a studious nature, and after the war became quite liberal in both his political and religious views. Almost alone of the Swedish-born veterans, he joined the Democratic Party, but never held public office. By his more practical Swedish neighbors he was considered a bit of a dreamer.

While the Bishop Hill company was probably the most homogeneously Swedish in the Union armies, other Swedish communities in Iowa, Wisconsin, and Minnesota, as well as in Illinois, furnished predominantly Swedish companies for service in the Civil War. The one organized in Galesburg, Illinois, for instance, became Company C in the Forty-third Regiment of Illinois Volunteers and, like the Bishop Hill group, was sent south early in 1862 to fight in western Tennessee under General Grant. Having been assigned to guarding supplies during the siege of Fort Donelson, its members feared the war would end before they had seen action. Their baptism of fire came, however, only too soon. On Sunday morning, April 6, 1862, while encamped near the church at Shiloh, they were one of the few units ready for action when the Confederates launched their surprise attack before breakfast, forty thousand strong under General Albert Sidney Johnston. Grant had thirty-six thousand, but most of them were not prepared. Many were still asleep. By chance, the Forty-third Illinois had been warned the night before to be ready for inspection at seven o'clock the next morning and thus it happened that while many other regiments broke without resistance, never having had time to fire a shot, the Forty-third, including the Swedes from Galesburg, held its line for several hours and then retired in good order. In less than an hour the next division, commanded by General Sherman, had been put out of the fight, exposing the flank of the Forty-third.

The scene at Shiloh was described by Horace Greeley as follows:

"Some of the [Union] men were dressing, others washing or cooking, a few were eating breakfast, many, especially officers, had not yet risen. Neither officers nor men were aware of the approaching enemy until his magnificent lines of battle poured out of the woods in front of the camps and at double-quick time rushed in upon our bewildered, half-dressed and not yet half-formed men, firing deadly volleys at close range, and then springing upon the coatless, musketless mob with the bayonets. Some fell as they ran; others as they emerged from the tents or strove to buckle on their accoutrements; some tried to surrender, but the rebels could not stop then to take prisoners."

Among the 13,047 Union dead, wounded, or missing were many Swedish boys. The Forty-third Illinois alone lost 206 of the five hundred actually engaged. Among the dead was Captain Olof S. Edwall of Galesburg, Illinois, who had commanded Company C, originally composed of a hundred Swedes and three Germans. His successor was Carl Arosenius, a Swedish-born newspaperman of Galesburg, who kept the command through the rest of the war. Three privates, Lars O. Berglöf, Claes Danielson, and Charles Samuelson, all of Galesburg, were also among the fallen. Several of those wounded, having been left too long without care, died of their injuries.

"Delay counts everything for us," Carl Sandburg, also a native of Galesburg, Illinois, quotes General Grant, in *Storm Over the Land,* as having remarked while on horseback he watched a Confederate attempt to take a hill near Pittsburg Landing, guarded by an Illinois artillery battery commanded by Captain Axel Silversparre as well as by Union gunboats on the river. "Tomorrow we shall attack them with fresh troops and drive them, of course."

During the night, the Union forces rallied and before daybreak re-formed their lines. Early in the morning General Lew Wallace, the future author of *Ben-Hur,* arrived with six thousand men. He had been stationed at Crump's Landing, further down the river, and the Swedes who had guarded the road along the river bank, felt that he could have arrived the afternoon before had he not chosen a round-about way. On Monday morning General Don Carlos Buell also appeared, as General Grant must have known he would, with twenty thousand men and by four o'clock in the afternoon the Confederates had been driven back.

After Shiloh, the Galesburg company took part in the siege of Corinth, and then in the Tennessee campaign. From June 2 to July 4, 1863, it participated in the investment of Vicksburg. Then it was sent to take part in the clean-up campaign in Arkansas, and remained in that state until the end of the war. On November 30, 1865, it was mustered out at Little Rock. After three years and four months of service, only thirty of the original 103 Swedes and Germans were left. Thirty had been discharged for various disabilities and twenty-nine had died from wounds or various diseases. The remaining fourteen were either missing or had been transferred to other units.

In command of the battery that General Grant had watched defend the supply depot at Pittsburg Landing, was a Swedish-born and trained officer, Baron Axel Silversparre, a former lieutenant in the ultra-aristocratic Royal Svea Artillery Regiment of Stockholm, from which twenty years earlier Lieutenant Polycarpus von Schneidau had resigned because of his marriage and then left for Wisconsin. After his career in Stockholm had been broken, Silversparre too had set out for the United States where he arrived early in 1861. As indicated by his title, he likewise was of noble birth. His father, Baron, or *Friherre,* Gustaf Johan Silversparre, was a lieutenant colonel in the even more exclusive Royal Horse Guards, while his mother, the former Sophie Mörner of Morlanda, had been born a countess. Their son had naturally enjoyed the very best social and educational opportunities but unfortunately, together with some other young officers, he had become involved in a night brawl with Stockholm civilians, which led to their court-martial and dismissal from the service. Axel Silversparre was then twenty-six years old. The impending civil war in the United States suggested a way out. In Missouri he first offered his services to General John C. Frémont, the former explorer of California, who, in 1856, had been the first Republican candidate for President, and who, in 1861, was the chief army commander in the West. He put the young officer to work checking up on the artillery park at Camp Girardeau in Missouri and when the guns seemed to be in order he commissioned him to recruit and train men to handle them.

For this purpose Silversparre went north to Illinois where he knew most of his own countrymen were then to be found. On Christmas Day, 1861, he obtained the required authorization from the Governor of Illinois and accompanied by John A. Anderson of Chicago, who knew exactly where the Swedes lived, he visited on a recruiting tour such Swedish centers as Rockford, St. Charles, Batavia, Geneva, Sycamore, De Kalb, Princeton, Galva, Bishop Hill, Andover, Moline, Knoxville, Victoria, and Galesburg, all in Illinois. By that time, however, most of the available young men in these communities were already enrolled in the infantry and on their way south to fight under General Grant, but Silversparre did manage to round up a scratch company for the artillery, half the men being Swedes and the rest made up of ten other nationalities. Early in January they met in Chicago where they elected Silversparre captain. Under his command they began intensive training. On

February 20, 1862, they were mustered in at Camp Douglas as Battery H, First Illinois Light Artillery, of which Colonel Joseph D. Webster was the commanding officer. Early in March the regiment was sent to the Benton barracks near St. Louis where the men received another three weeks' training with four twenty-pound Parrott guns.

By the end of the month the regiment was rushed south by boat and on April 5, 1862, the day before the Battle of Shiloh began, it reached Pittsburg Landing on the Tennessee River. On a little hill overlooking the Landing, Silversparre at once placed his guns in position, protecting them with improvised breastworks, partly made up of sacks of grain. When twitted by his fellow officers for his precautions, he said: "My battery is here to stay and not to run."

When the Confederates made their surprise attack early next morning he was able to fire quick rounds of shrapnel or canister at them almost point-blank and thus protect the Landing where the main supplies were stored. This was the action watched by General Grant. It may have saved him from a rout. By equipping his men with handles for the sponge heads, Silversparre had enabled them to clean the guns' barrels while they were still hot and thus fire them five times as fast as usual. Such tactics General Grant appreciated, and next day when the battle was over, both he and General Sherman congratulated the young Swedish officer. They did not, however, mention his name in their dispatches. There was so much else those two Generals had to report on. Thereafter, however, Silversparre's battery was placed under Sherman's command, and until the end of the war it remained with the Second Division of the Fifteenth Army Corps.

Silversparre's own career came to an early, unexpected, and rather inglorious end. The next fall, on September 16, 1862, he was detached from his battery and ordered to take charge of the artillery park at Fort Pickering, near Memphis, Tennessee, and also to train that winter not only two additional companies of his own division but two more in the division commanded by General Stephen A. Hurlbut. Competent artillery officers had suddenly become well nigh invaluable. The teaching duties imposed on him Silversparre found to be overwhelming. Some of his pupils held ranks much higher than his own and yet did not have the advanced training in mathematics required of an artillery officer. Consequently, he resigned from his teaching post and asked to be assigned to more exciting duties at the front.

While waiting to be reassigned he ran into a band of Confederate guerrillas, or "bushwhackers," and was taken prisoner. After spending nine months in the notorious Libby stockade at Richmond, Virginia, which he found even more tedious than teaching trigonometry at Fort Pickering, he escaped by bribing a guard and, wearing the latter's uniform, he made his way to Wilmington, South Carolina. There he obtained a position as engineer on the Confederate blockade runner, *Cornubia*, but once at sea she was chased by Union gunboats as far as a British base in Bermuda. From there Silversparre gradually made his way back to New York, but by then the war was so nearly over that he never returned to active duty.

Instead, he got in touch with his original commanding officer, General Frémont, and under his direction began to work on plans for an extension of the Union Pacific Railroad across the Rockies. With a Colonel W. W. Adams he also worked on plans for a suspension bridge across the East River in New York, twenty years before the Brooklyn Bridge was built, but for financial reasons both projects had to be deferred.

Late in 1864 Silversparre was engaged by a syndicate of copper companies in Michigan to return to Sweden and recruit workers for their mines. When he came back later the same winter he had with him about a hundred and fifty Swedes, Norwegians and Finns, some of whom brought their families. When they reached Detroit, writes Nels Hokanson in his book *Swedish Immigrants in Lincoln's Time* (New York, 1943, p. 76) a United States Army recruiting officer prevailed on over a score to enlist instead in the Union forces as special workers. The mining companies lost most of the money they had invested to promote immigration.

In 1865 Silversparre became an assistant city engineer in Chicago and after losing his house and most of his instruments in the great fire of 1871, he helped draw plans for the rebuilding of the burned area. In 1880 he moved to Denver, then a new city, and there he not only laid out some of the early streets, but also helped survey the first part of the route for the Denver, Pacific and Rio Grande Railroad which ultimately was to penetrate the Rockies through the Royal Gorge on the way to Salt Lake City, Utah. Next he became a mapmaker for the Government in Washington, but after 1888 he spent most of his time in various Old Soldiers' Homes, and finally, in March 1906, died in one at Danville, Illinois. In 1866 he had married Miss Mary Jane Gunning of Chicago, and they had three children, but in 1884 they were divorced. A son, Servais Zacharias Silversparre, became a lawyer in Denver, and publisher of a mining journal, *Ores and Metals.*

In a worldly sense a much more glorious postwar career was carved out for himself by Charles John Stolbrand, another Swedish-trained artillery man, who not only rose to the rank of brigadier general but after the war became a plantation owner at Beaufort in South Carolina and a Republican office-holder in that arch-Democratic state. When he died in 1894 he was buried with full military honors within sight of the state Capitol at Columbia, South Carolina, which he had once ordered shelled. He had been wont to boast that he had set off the first charge himself with the use of a sun glass.

Socially he was of much humbler origin than Silversparre and his military education was of a practical rather than an academic nature. Born in 1821 in a modest home near the city of Kristianstad in southern Sweden, his original name had been Carl Johan Möller, which may or may not indicate a German ancestry. His early education was scanty, but before enlisting as a private at the age of eighteen in the Royal Vendes Artillery Regiment, stationed at Kristianstad, he had learned enough mathematics to work as an assistant to a surveyor. When enlisting he changed his name from Möller to Stålbrand, a common practice at that time, but in his case there was no need to escape from a confusing patronymic ending in "son." Usually, martial-sounding names like Stålbrand, meaning "fiery steel," had been reserved for members of the nobility. In America he changed the spelling to Stolbrand.

After only four years of service he was promoted to the rank of sergeant, which means that he had taken full advantage of the educational opportunities offered by the regiment, but since he lacked academic training, he could not expect then to become an officer. His only hope for further advancement lay, therefore, in foreign service. The first German-Danish war over Slesvig-Holstein in 1849–50 offered an opportunity and Stolbrand, as he spelled his name in the United States, became a member of the Swedish forces placed in reserve at Flensburg, near the German-Danish border. They were not, however, called upon to take part in the fighting and when Stolbrand returned to Kristianstad he was still a sergeant. But, having seen "foreign service," he carried his chin a little higher and after a tiff with one of his superior officers he resigned from the service. With his recent bride, Carolina Pettersson, daughter of another non-commissioned officer of the same regiment, he then set out for America. In 1851 they arrived in Chicago.

Being better educated than most Swedish immigrants at the time, he was not compelled to earn his living by manual labor. Like most of his fellow natives of the province of Skåne, which was once Danish, he had a natural flair for politics and before long he gained employment as a clerk in the Cook County Recorder's Office. There were at that time only a few Swedes in Chicago, but among them Stolbrand soon became a leader. When the patriotic Svea Society was formed in 1857 he was elected its first president and as such he was re-elected every year until the war began. In the 1860 presidential campaign he took part as a Republican spellbinder among Swedes throughout the state.

When President Lincoln issued his first call for volunteers in the late spring of 1861, Stolbrand was at De Kalb, making abstracts of land titles. At once he quit his clerical work and began to organize a company among the local country youth, many of whom were Swedes, and to train them for the artillery. On October 5, 1861, his group was mustered in as Battery G, Second Illinois Light Artillery, with Stolbrand as captain. Before the end of the year he had been promoted to the rank of major and placed in charge of General John A. Logan's entire artillery force. As such he served through most of the war. During the siege of Vicksburg he had as many as ten batteries under his command. On May 26, 1863, while the siege was still under way, General Logan, the Illinois chief commander, reported: "The admirable manner in which this battery was handled reflects the highest credit on Major Stolbrand, my chief of artillery." Another time he used such complimentary phrases as, "To Major Stolbrand, my chief of artillery, I am indebted for valuable aid." Later that year, when General Logan was promoted to be commander of the Fifteenth Army Corps, he placed Stolbrand, though still only a major, in charge of its entire artillery force.

While stationed at Kingston, Georgia, in May 1864, Stolbrand was captured by the Confederates, as Silversparre had been in western Tennessee in 1863. Officially, General Logan reported the incident on September 4, 1864 as follows: "While examining the surrounding country at my direction, Major C. J. Stolbrand, a gallant and untiring officer, was captured by a squad of the enemy's cavalry." The following October, after spending the summer in the ill-famed military prison camp at Andersonville, Georgia, Stolbrand was back at his command. Some reports have it that twice he had broken out by himself and the second time had succeeded in sneaking through the country at night until he found his own men. Others state that General Logan had had him exchanged for two Confederate generals of infantry—

a version favored in artillery circles.

During the winter of 1864–65, Major Stolbrand was stationed with his brigade at Beaufort, South Carolina, and being, again like nearly all natives of Skåne, real estate-minded, he acquired, presumably at a fair price, a former slave plantation and having then served longer than his term of enlistment required and the war being almost over, he resigned his command as of January 28, 1865. His lack of promotion after three years of strenuous duties at the front may likewise have irked him. He was then forty-four years old and in Chicago he had a family to support.

When General Sherman received the resignation, he merely asked Stolbrand whether on his way home he would deliver some very confidential papers to President Lincoln personally; at least that was the way the General himself related the incident at a political banquet in St. Paul, Minnesota, in 1866. (It was there recorded by Colonel Hans Mattson, another veteran of the Vendes Artillery Regiment, who later included it in his memoirs.) When the President had glanced through the documents sent by Sherman he stuck out his long arm and shaking Stolbrand firmly by the hand he said, "How do you do, General?" "I am no general, Sir, only a major" blurted out Stolbrand, flushing slightly through his red beard. "You are mistaken," declared the Commander-in-Chief. "From now on you are a general."

In a few hours the formal commission was made out at the War Department and, on March 30, 1865, after a rest in Chicago, the new Brigadier General reported back to Major General Sherman for further duty. A month later he was given command of the Second Artillery Brigade, Fourth Division, Seventeenth Army Corps, but by then the war was over. After the victory parade in Washington on May 24, 1865, when President Lincoln was no longer there, Stolbrand was assigned to the command of the artillery in the Fort Leavenworth district of Kansas. There his three regiments, the 14th, 15th, and 32nd, Illinois Volunteers, were mustered out in 1865 and in January 1866, General Stolbrand himself left the service. "A braver man than General Stolbrand could not be found in the entire Army," General Sherman declared at the banquet in St. Paul. In the South his name appears on several Civil War battle monuments. From the King of Sweden he received in 1866 the Royal Order of the Sword, a high military honor.

His career as an estate owner and Republican politician in South Carolina began at once. He was General Secretary of the carpetbagger convention which framed a new constitution for the former secessionist state, and in 1868 an official delegate to the Republican National Convention in Chicago which nominated General Grant. In the subsequent election he was chosen a presidential elector from the same state. For several years after that he served as head of the South Carolina State Penitentiary and during the Benjamin Harrison administration (1888–92) he had charge of all Federal building construction in Charleston. As a plantation owner he also prospered. When he died at the age of seventy-three, three of his children were living in New York, where he had been in the habit of spending his winters, and a married daughter in Atlanta, Georgia. None of them appears to have kept up any contacts with Sweden.

The careers of Silversparre and Stolbrand in the artillery were matched in the infantry by Lieutenant Colonel Oscar Malmborg of the Fifty-fifth Regiment, Illinois Volunteers, another native of Sweden who was possessed of a good Swedish military education. Unlike General Stolbrand, Colonel Malmborg had no flaming red beard, but a photograph of him shows him in a cocky pose with a martial-looking pair of mustaches and wearing around his waist a romantic-looking scarf which was probably red. With one arm akimbo, he strikes the attitude of a true-blue, devil-may-care, professional soldier. One can almost smell powder. He was beyond a doubt a martinet or so he seemed to the undisciplined frontier youths and young Chicago workmen whom in the shortest possible time he had to convert to good, wartime soldiers. The traditional Swedish standards, which he tried to maintain, seemed too harsh to them as volunteers, unsuitable, they felt, to free-born American citizens. He was always upheld, however, by his superior officers who understood better what real warfare required. Repeatedly they called the Fifty-fifth Illinois the best-drilled regiment in the Union Army.

Like Silversparre, Malmborg came of a socially prominent family and like him he had had the benefit of the best Swedish training available, both academic and military. He was a nephew of Lieutenant General Otto August Malmborg, under whose command Stolbrand had served in Denmark. (General Malmborg was later ennobled as Von Malmborg and by that name his descendants in Sweden are still known.) After graduation from the Karlberg Military Academy, the Swedish West Point, Oscar Malmborg was given a commission in the infantry and there he served eight years. He then resigned to take part in the Mexican War, the training ground for so many of the most prominent commanders on both sides in the Civil War. Speaking but little English, he enlisted in the artillery as a private, but saw no action. During the entire twenty-one months of his service he was kept at Fort Brown on the Rio Grande.

Why he did not then return to Sweden to resume his military career is not known. In 1852, when he was a little over thirty years old, he arrived, instead, in Chicago, where he was employed by the Illinois Central Railroad as an immigrant and land agent. His record in Sweden, unlike that of Silversparre, must have been spotless, for in 1858 he was appointed Consul for Sweden and Norway, a post first held by Polycarpus von Schneidau and then by Gustaf Unonius, both of whom likewise had good family connections in Sweden. Before he assumed the office, however, the war, which interested him more, became imminent. He then turned to drilling recruits for the American infantry. Socially he had been highly esteemed in Chicago, too, and when he left for the front his fellow employees of the Illinois Central presented him with a finely ornamented sword.

The Fifty-fifth Illinois had been organized chiefly by David Stuart, a Chicago lawyer of good education and general ability, but with little or no military training. After the Battle of Shiloh, where Malmborg had been his adviser, he was nominated a general by President Lincoln, but when the nomination was not confirmed, he resigned. Whether he had known Malmborg in civil life, is not certain, but it did not take him long to appreciate the latter's military experience. This was shown by the rank of lieutenant colonel he obtained for him at once—a high honor for an unknown foreigner. Immediately it caused jealousy among the company commanders who had helped with the recruiting. If they could not all expect to be "Brigadiers," as General Logan later remarked, they certainly had hoped to become regimental officers. This was especially true of two former Methodist ministers, one of whom, Milton L. Haney, resigned his rank as captain when the company reached the front. Instead, he chose that of regimental chaplain.

"A strict disciplinarian," Colonel Stuart called Malmborg, while the rank and file used other terms, among which "the damned old Swede" was one of the mildest. Malmborg was then forty years old. At one time a cabal headed by the two former Methodist ministers preferred formal charges against him, asking for his court-martial. He was accused of indulging not only in strong drink, but in the use of strong language. What his habits were as to drink was never demonstrated, as the charges were dismissed without trial; but while Malmborg never got over his Swedish accent, the language he was quoted as having used when drilling his men was made up of idiomatic and standard military terms, shocking as they may have seemed to the former Methodist ministers. All other evidence tends to show that Malmborg was, in reality, a first-class military gentleman. At the front his standards of discipline paid off. There the Fifty-fifth soon became known as a model regiment.

"I boldly claim for it," wrote Colonel Stuart to Governor Yates of Illinois, when the charges had been filed against Malmborg, "and it is conceded by the commanding generals that it is the most efficient, the best drilled, best disciplined, best behaved, cleanest, healthiest, and most soldierly regiment in the army. They [the malcontents] would like to get rid of him [Malmborg] and have a slipshod, easy-going time of it. It is this vigilance, this zeal and discipline which has made this regiment in every regard today the best in the army. . . . It would not only be ungenerous, but ungrateful in me to appropriate to myself any share of the credit and honor which so justly belongs to him." While such claims to regimental superiority were also in the best military tradition, the Colonel's personal disclaim of credit was unprecedented. There was no court-martial, as the Brigadier General squashed the charges.

On October 31, 1861, the Fifty-fifth Illinois had been accepted for service and mustered in at Chicago. On December 9 it started south. At the Benton barracks near St. Louis, it was attached to General Sherman's division which was part of the Army of Tennessee under General Grant. In the surprise attack by the Confederates under General Johnston at Shiloh on Sunday morning, April 6, it first saw action, being there brigaded with the Fifty-fourth Ohio, of which Colonel Thomas Kilby Smith was the commander. Holding the extreme left wing of the Union forces, these two regiments with only six hundred men in line claimed to have held off five Confederate regiments, a battery of four guns, and a cavalry unit. Only after the cartridge boxes of even the fallen had been emptied did the men retreat toward Pittsburg Landing, where fresh supplies of ammunition were known to be stored. Among the wounded was Colonel Stuart, which left Malmborg in command of the regiment and when Colonel Smith, who was acting as brigade commander, went in search of a detached group as reinforcement, Malmborg took charge of the whole brigade. During the afternoon he was able, under the supervision of General Grant, to form a new line composed of various scattered units amounting to three thousand men. The morning rout was then checked and the next day the Confederates were driven back.

Next to the Ninth Illinois, the Fifty-fifth had suffered the heaviest casualties: one officer and fifty-one privates had been killed; nine officers and 190 men wounded, but only twenty-six were missing. In its first test, despite the retreat and the feeling against Malmborg, the regiment had held together. In his report, Colonel Stuart, whose wounds were not serious, wrote: "I was under great obligation to Lieutenant-Colonel Malmborg, whose military education and experience were of great importance to me. Comprehending at a glance the purpose and object of every movement of the enemy, he was able to advise me, promptly and intelligently, as to the disposition of my men. He was cool, observant, discreet, and brave and of infinite service to me."

In the second day's battle the Fifty-fifth, operating directly under General Sherman's command, suffered but slight losses. In the subsequent siege of Corinth, whither the Confederates had withdrawn, Colonel Malmborg, who after Colonel Stuart's promotion to brigadier general, had been placed in full command of the regiment, laid out the entrenchments for the Union forces, using techniques he had learned in Sweden. From him both General Grant and General Sherman learned procedures which they later used themselves, especially at Vicksburg. Both went on record giving Malmborg high credit, especially as the enemy quickly gave up resistance. At Vicksburg it was another story, and there the Fifty-fifth under Malmborg often held the most advanced positions, being at times within twenty-five feet of the enemy stockade. Exposing himself recklessly to danger, Malmborg was wounded in both eyes, and so badly that ultimately he became completely blind.

After the victory at Arkansas Post on January 12, 1863, Colonel Thomas Kilby Smith, who was once more the brigade commander, had reported: "I desire to make special mention of Colonel Malmborg, commander of the Fifty-fifth Illinois, whose zeal and unremitting diligence in superintending working parties and in planting batteries, performing at the same time his whole duty to the regiment, demand compliment." After the fall of Vicksburg early in July 1863, Colonel Smith once more reported: "With Colonel Malmborg of the Fifty-fifth Illinois I have been side by side in seven battles; have stood with him literally among heaps of slain. He is always cool, prudent, and of dauntless courage and in the recent engagement, although wounded twice, and, by a strange fatality, first in the right and next in the left eye, displayed those qualities with the ardor and cheer so necessary in a charge."

Within the regiment, however, the intrigues of those who wanted to replace him continued unabated. In the spring of 1864, when the three-year term of enlistment was completed, they obtained as the price of their re-enlistment, the right to elect their own officers. For reasons that can be guessed, only a minority voted, and in the contest for colonel, Malmborg got only twenty-two votes while 164 were cast for the Reverend Milton L. Haney, the chaplain and one of the ring-leaders of the opposition.

The corps commander, Major General John A. Logan, the original "Black Jack," who knew his Illinois men, had other ideas. "I have been accustomed to look upon the Fifty-fifth regiment as the best in the army," he said to the defeated Malmborg. "And how shall I express my astonishment at finding that they are after all only a lot of damned fools? Electing a chaplain, a civilian, as their colonel! Are they pre-pared to go into battle under the command of such a man? Do you suppose the Governor of Illinois and the Adjutant-General will com-mission him?"

As a matter of fact they didn't, but under the circumstances Malm-borg had to be assigned to other duties, first as chief engineer of the Seventeenth Army Corps, then commanded by General Logan, and as his sight grew steadily worse, to inspector of posts along the Missis-sippi, which was probably only make-believe work. On September 20, 1864, he was mustered out of the service for physical disability and then returned to Chicago. On January 1, 1865, he was made a colonel in the First Veteran Army Corps, but even that was too much. He had given his all and was a broken man. On May 31, 1865, he retired on a pension, returned to Sweden, and there spent the remaining fif-teen years of his life in total darkness. In 1880, at the age of sixty, he died at Visby, on the Baltic island of Gotland, a forgotten man. The official history of his regiment, written by his enemies, some of whom he had recommended for promotion, had only sneers for his "alleged engineering ability," writes Ernest W. Olson. Other historians of the war have neglected him too, as they have many other foreigners who fought in the Civil War. As an officer he had been a success; as a politician he had failed.

The fighting spirit and discipline he had infused in the regiment did not die. Under their new officers, some of whom had been in line for promotion on Malmborg's recommendation, the men carried on, and distinguished themselves further at Jonesboro, Kenesaw Mountain, and in the Atlanta campaign. Having taken part in thirty-one engagements by the time the war was over, they had spent 128 days under fire, had lost 108 men in battle and 329 wounded, some of whom died of their injuries. Throughout the war only forty-nine had been reported missing. But no memorial to Colonel Malmborg, who had trained them, was ever erected; his name was not inscribed, like that of General Stolbrand, on any of the battle monuments.

Another Swedish-born veteran of the Mexican War who also took part in the Civil War was Lieutenant Colonel Fabian Brydolf of the Twenty-first Iowa Infantry Volunteers, who lost his right arm in the Battle of Shiloh. Until after the fall of Vicksburg early in July 1864, he was able to continue his command in the field. He was then appointed commander of the Shelburne barracks at Washington, D.C. Born in Hellestad, Östergötland, in 1819, the son of the state church minister, he had become a landscape painter, and after losing his right arm he learned to paint with his left. Originally he had emigrated to the United States as early as 1841, or the same year as Gustaf Unonius. At first he lived in Cleveland, Ohio, and then in various other places until in 1846 he settled in Iowa, where he went as an interpreter for the Peter Cassel group, which also came from Östergötland. In 1847 he enlisted in the Fifteenth U.S. Regiment for service in the Mexican War, during which he took part in several battles. When the Civil War broke out he too organized a company of volunteers which became a part of the Sixth Iowa and it was while leading this company as a captain at Shiloh on April 6, 1862, that he lost his arm. In 1850 he had married Miss Fannie West, who was of English descent. By her he had seven children. In 1897 he died at the age of seventy-eight.

The sentiments inspiring the young Swedish volunteers in the Civil War were expressed with eloquent restraint in a letter which one of them, Paul Esbjörn, the oldest son of the Reverend Lars Paul Esbjörn, founder of the Swedish Lutheran church in the Middle West, wrote to his father after enlisting without his father's knowledge in April 1861. Written by a youth barely twenty years old, it deserves greater attention than it so far has had. Like the five oldest of his brothers and sisters, William Paul Esbjörn had been born in Sweden and with the family had arrived in America on a Swedish immigrant schooner in 1849. At the "Illinois State University" at Springfield, which was in reality an early Lutheran academy and seminary at which his father had been a teacher in the late 1850s, he had been a schoolmate of Abraham Lincoln's son, Robert, who bequeathed to the Library of Congress the Lincoln papers unsealed in 1948.

The letter, dated at Delevan, Tazewell County, Illinois, April 23, 1861, or only a week after Fort Sumter had been fired on, read as follows:

DELEVAN, TAZEWELL CO., ILLINOIS
April 23, 1861

DEAR FATHER:

I embrace this opportunity to inform you that I am well and I hope that these few lines may find you enjoying the same blessing. Under circumstances rather strange I write this letter to you. I have come to the conclusion lately to try to do something for my country and for the poor African race. This is news which I think that a man of your principles would delight to hear and one thing I have to tell you which makes my heart rejoice. I feel my peace made with my God. I think this cause is just and a righteous war and should I meet my death on the battlefield I feel I shall die in a glorious cause.

I do not know yet where we will be ordered, but we will leave in a few days from here so it is no use to write me here but when we get stationed I will then write to you, if I am alive.

Try to forget and forgive all old things and if this is the last letter you ever get, I think you will give up your son freely in this cause. Take my best love and respect to my sisters, brothers, mother and friends.

So nothing more at present, but I desire and hope that we may meet our mother in heaven and may we there make an unbroken family.

Respectfully from your son,
(*Signed*) WILLIAM P. ESBJÖRN

As early as September 1861, Paul Esbjörn fell in the Battle of Lexington, Missouri. In 1852 his own mother, the gently born Amalia Planting-Gyllenbåga, had died of the cholera at Andover, Illinois.

In August 1861 his younger brother, Joseph, though then less than eighteen years old, enlisted in the Second Illinois Light Artillery, the regiment commanded by the Swedish-born Major Stolbrand. He, too, had been a schoolmate of Robert Lincoln at Springfield. In the Union Army he took the name of Osborne, instead of Esbjörn, and used it the rest of his life. After taking part as a private in the siege of Vicksburg, he was assigned in July 1864 to special duties at Major General John A. Logan's headquarters. Later in the same year he was commissioned an officer in a colored regiment and placed on garrison duty at Columbus, Kentucky, as a member of the staff of Major General Edward O. C. Ord. Though then only twenty years old, he was given charge of the whole ordnance depot. Before enlisting he had worked as a printer's devil and after the war he tried various occupations. For some years he worked in Sweden as an immigrant agent for the American Emigrant Company of New York and then for the Chicago, Quincy and Burlington Railroad. After that he became successively a publisher, a church organist, and, finally, an employee of the State Auditor's office in St. Paul, Minnesota. There he died in 1933 at the age of ninety.

As to the total enlistment by the Midwest Swedes in the American Civil War, Ernest W. Olson writes: "The U.S. Census of 1860 recorded a total of 18,625 Swedes then living in the United States. Of these 11,800 were then living in the four [Midwestern] states of Illinois, Iowa, Minnesota and Wisconsin. The immigration from Sweden during the next two years was 2,300. Allowing the previous proportion of two-thirds for these states, we find their combined Swedish population during the enlistment period to have been approximately 13,500. The best estimates of the Swedish enlistments in the four states give a total of 2,250, or exactly one-sixth of the entire Swedish population. Illinois, with a Swedish population in 1860 of 6,470, and approximately 7,000 at the end of 1861, contributed not less than 1,300 Swedish volunteers, indicating that in this state one Swede out of every five volunteered for military service, while out of the whole population only one out of every seven persons enlisted. . . . More than half of the Swedes in Illinois fit for military duty actually served."

In addition to the Swedes who were already in the United States, thousands still in Sweden offered to enlist in the Union cause. On November 12, 1862, United States Consul Epping at Gothenburg reported to Washington that he could enroll both trained artillery men and sailors in great numbers, while his colleague, Consul B. F. Tefft, wrote from Stockholm that he could enlist up to a thousand men a month and ship them to the United States for enlistment, if he only had the ships to carry them. At the American consulate in Stockholm he already had on file, he wrote, over two thousand applications.

Two years later, September 16, 1864, William Widgery Thomas, Jr., of Maine, who had been one of the thirty young consular agents sent to Europe by President Lincoln to promote emigration to the United States, wrote from Gothenburg that many of the Swedish volunteers in the lost Danish War with Prussia and Austria had returned home much embittered by the defeat and that they were flocking to the American consulates to enlist in the Union armies. "We have forwarded over thirty this week," he continued. "Most of them non-commissioned officers who had served three years in the Swedish artillery before volunteering in the Danish war. Their fare was paid from a purse contributed by 'some good friends in America,' including the consul himself. . . . I am very well aware that as consul I have nothing to do with soldiers but no international law can prevent me from paying a soldier's passage from here to Hamburg out of my own pocket."

The offers to enlist finally became so numerous that the Swedish Government issued a general warning against emigration in wartime. In June 1864, the Swedish Minister of Foreign Affairs, Count C. R. L. Manderström, informed the American Legation in Stockholm that his Government could not countenance recruiting by American consular agents in Sweden. Whether such recruiting had ever taken place was not established. As the Confederate states were never recognized by Sweden as an independent, belligerent power, there could be no charge of unneutrality, and at times the Swedish authorities probably looked the other way. In the course of time Mr. Thomas became a long-time American Minister in Stockholm, as well as founder of the New Sweden Colony in Maine.

During the war A. Dudley Mann, a special agent sent by the Confederate states to the Vatican, complained to Pope Pius IX: "It is not only the armies of northern birth which the South is encountering in hostile array, but it is the armies of European creation, who were influenced to emigrate (by circulars from Lincoln & Company to their numerous agents abroad) ostensibly for the purpose of securing higher wages, but in reality to fill up the constantly depleted ranks of the enemy."

That President Lincoln himself favored continued immigration is indisputable. In an address at Cincinnati, delivered in 1861, when he was on his way from Springfield to Washington to assume the Presidency, he said: "Inasmuch as our country is extensive and new, and the countries of Europe are densely populated, if there are any abroad who desire to make this the land of their adoption, it is not in my heart to throw aught in their way to prevent them from coming to the United States."

Throughout the war American agents abroad, including those in Sweden, were instructed to spread information about opportunities to acquire land and otherwise earn a living in the United States. After the Homestead Act had been passed in 1862, offering free Government land to settlers, that was used as the best argument. On September 30, 1863, Consul Tefft in Stockholm reported: "I have taken special pains to give publicity to the liberality of our Government to immigrants. . . . Furnish me with ships or free passage and I could take a quarter of the working population of this country to the United States next spring."

Not only Captain Silversparre but other American agents induced Swedish laborers to come to the United States. As soon as they had learned sufficient English, they could enlist, they were told. Some joined the Union armies at once as civilian workers. From personal statements by one C. A. Freed (originally *Frid?*), Nels Hokanson states that one "Sveysack" (may have been Von Vegesack) brought over one hundred Scandinavian laborers who were put to work behind the Union lines in the vicinity of Chattanooga, Tennessee, at fourteen dollars a month, plus keep. They were blacksmiths, including farriers, wagon repairmen, and bridge builders. For the Northern Army they worked from 1864 to 1865, but were never enrolled as promised. Hokanson surmises that not all worked off their passage money as agreed, either. After the war was over some returned to Sweden, but a majority remained.

In addition to such manpower, whether for fighting or labor, Sweden furnished a number of militarily trained men who became officers in the Northern armies. Some enlisted because of enthusiasm for the Union cause, others to gain military experience. Hokanson lists over forty. Sometimes the two motives were mixed. As unquestionable examples of the first category may be cited Knut Oskar Broady (Brundin), a graduate of Colgate, who was promoted to the rank of colonel and at the end of the war received from Major General Hancock an offer of a permanent appointment as brigadier general if he would remain, and Johan Alexis Edgren, an experienced maritime officer who on enlistment was given at once the rank of lieutenant in the United States Navy and promised promotion if he would continue in the service. Both decided, however, to resume their chosen professions as Baptist ministers and teachers, whether here or in Sweden. Another resignation was that of August Hjalmar Edgren, a younger brother of Johan Alexis, who had held a commission in the Army as a lieutenant and after the war earned in 1874 his Ph.D. degree at Yale. He ultimately closed his American career as a language teacher and Dean at the University of Nebraska.

These men had never been professional soldiers and did not intend to remain in the armed forces. Other Swedish participants in the American Civil War were army officers who, after the war was over, resumed their profession in Sweden and, in some instances, ultimately won high rank, exactly as had some of the Swedish officers who fought in the French forces during the American War for Independence.

Under the date of September 11, 1861, President Lincoln sent to General Winfield Scott, of Mexican War fame, then in command at Washington, the following handwritten note: "This is to introduce Capt. Ernst von Vegesack of Sweden, who wishes to enter our Military service. Feeling grateful for his offer but not being able to decide the questions involved, I have the greatest pleasure in introducing him to you with the remarks that we need all the skill we can get and if you can employ him satisfactorily, I shall be glad. A. Lincoln."

Since Captain von Vegesack had been introduced to the President by the Swedish Minister in Washington, Count von Piper, he must have come with the good wishes, if not the formal approval, of the Swedish authorities. He was then forty-one years old, a man of noble birth, and well educated. He had, to be sure, resigned his commission as captain in the Dal Regiment of which Major Forsse had likewise been a member as a non-commissioned officer, and when he returned to Sweden in August 1863, after having won the Congressional Medal of Honor as well as postwar promotion to brigadier general, he was able to resume his military career in Sweden, rising ultimately to the rank of major general. After his army days were over, he was elected a member of the First Chamber of the Swedish Riksdag. When he died in Stockholm in 1903 at the age of eighty-three, he had become generally recognized as one of the country's Grand Old Men.

General Scott at once offered him a commission as a captain in the Fifty-fifth Ohio Volunteers, but this he declined in favor of a post as major on the staff of Major General John E. Wool in Washington. Early in 1862 he was ordered to conduct reinforcements to Major General J. K. F. Mansfield at Fort Monroe in Virginia, and at Newport News on March 9, 1862; he then became one of the many eyewitnesses of the epochal battle between the U.S. *Monitor,* designed by his countryman, Captain John Ericsson, and the Confederate ironclad, *Merrimac.* To Sweden he sent an account of the battle which proved he had understood at once the significance of what he had seen as regards all future naval warfare.

At that time General McClellan was finally ready to move his Army of the Potomac southward for the Peninsular campaign in Virginia and to be able to take part in that campaign, which might have been decisive, Von Vegesack resigned his commission as major and enlisted instead as a private under McClellan. As such he saw what fighting there was at Yorktown and Williamsburg. In the Battle of Hanover Court House he so distinguished himself that when it was over he was once more commissioned a major in the Northern Armies and appointed a member of the staff of General McClellan himself. After the clash at Gaines Mills, where his troops had covered General Porter's retreat, he was given command with the full rank of colonel of the Twentieth New York Volunteers, made up chiefly of New York City Germans, who as members of their various gymnastic societies, known as *Turnvereins,* had prepared themselves to be physically fit as soldiers. In the Second Battle of Bull Run, which was almost as disastrous to the Union cause as the First, he commanded a brigade and after the bloody September day at Antietam, Colonel William H. Irwin, regular commander of the Third Brigade, wrote in his report: "The Twentieth New York Volunteers, by its position was exposed to the heaviest fire in the line, which it bore with unyielding courage and returned at every opportunity. . . . Colonel Von Vegesack was under fire with his men constantly and his calm courage gave an admirable example to them." At Frederick Center, Maryland, a contemporary print, which must have been based on pure imagination, shows him leading a bayonet charge, carrying the regimental banner on horseback. (He actually did it on foot.) Twice the field had been taken and lost. Nine of his officers and 250 of his men were lost, but once more Washington was saved and this time the Emancipation Proclamation followed.

Later in the fall of 1862, the New York regiment under Von Vegesack took part in the futile Union attack on Fredericksburg on the other side of the Rappahannock and, on May 4, 1863, in the equally futile slaughter of young men at Chancellorsville. There the Twentieth New York lost seven officers and 125 of the 444 men actually in line. Little wonder Colonel von Vegesack felt discouraged. Personally he had done so well that three days later he was relieved of his field command and placed on the staff of the new commander of the Army of the Potomac, Major General George Gordon Meade. In that capacity he took part, the first days of July 1863, in the ultimately decisive Battle of Gettysburg. But by then he had had enough. On August 3, 1863, or only a month later, he resigned his commission as colonel and returned to Sweden. Like so many other European officers who served in the American Civil War, he had gained professional experience that was to influence all future military tactics.

In *Swedish Immigrants in Lincoln's Time* Nels Hokanson lists over forty Civil War officers who had received training in Sweden and who came over after the war started to serve the Union cause. Two bore the name of Rosencrantz: Palle and Fredrick Anton Ulrick. The latter served successively as an adjutant to McCellan, Burnside, Hooker, and Meade; (how he missed Pope is not told). Both had been born in the province of Skåne and both in the year 1825. They may have been relatives. (Neither is to be confused with the American-born Major General W. S. Rosecrans of Ohio who was of Dutch descent.) Like Brigadier General Stolbrand, both had originally been non-commissioned officers in Swedish regiments—Fredrick Anton Ulrick in the Skåne Hussars and Palle in the Skåne Dragoons. By 1850, the first named had become a sergeant-major in a Royal Body Guard Regiment of Stockholm. In 1852, he was advanced to first lieutenant and in 1859 to captain, which means he had also managed to obtain the academic education required for an officer's commission. On April 9, 1865, when the war was over, he was advanced to lieutenant colonel in the United States Army for "gallant and meritorious service during the operations leading to the fall of Richmond and the capture of the insurgent army under General Robert E. Lee."

Less is known about the American record of his namesake, Palle Rosencrantz. By 1844 he had become a second lieutenant in the Skåne Dragoons and in 1849 he volunteered in the Danish Army for the first Slesvig-Holstein war with Prussia. By 1852 he was back at his post in Sweden. In 1853 he once more left the country, this time to enlist in the French Foreign Legion, in which he became a captain in 1855. Next he sailed for the United States and between 1861 and 1863 he was a major in the Fourth New York Regiment of Cavalry, a branch of the service which attracted fewer Swedes than the artillery or infantry. What became of either of the Rosencrantzes after the war was over is not known.

More tragic and more mysterious was the career of another Swedish-trained officer, Lieutenant Colonel Gustaf Bildstein Helleday, which was supposed to be an assumed name, though it was not. Born in Sweden in 1831 he died at Fortress Monroe in Virginia in 1862. On August 25,

1862, the New York *Times* carried the following obituary:

"Col. Helleday, of the Ninety-ninth New York Regiment (Union Coast Guard) died at Fortress Monroe, a day or two since. *The Philadelphia Press* says of him, 'Col. Helleday was one of the most accomplished foreign officers in our service— He was learned in the art of war, brave, generous, and faithful. He was born in Sweden and at the time of his death was about 35 years of age [actually thirty-one].

" 'Early in life he entered the Swedish navy, rising rapidly until, unfortunately, a trouble arose between himself and a fellow officer, which resulted in a duel, a result of which was the death of Col. Helleday's companion. Resigning his commission instantly, he changed his name to "Helleday" and in disguise came to America. When Lieutenant Bartlett commenced raising a regiment, called the Naval Brigade, Helleday enlisted as a private.

" 'When the "Brigade" was transferred from sailors to soldiers at Fortress Monroe, Helleday, on recommendation of President Lincoln, was made a captain, then a major, and, finally, lieutenant-colonel of the Coast Guard. In appreciation of his ability General Thomas J. Wood appointed him commander at Fort Wool, Rip Raps, and the General had only one fault to find with him, which was that he was too anxious to disturb the rebels at Sewall's Point, against the orders of the Government.

" 'With every species of artillery he was familiar and never aimed his gun at an object without striking it, if the piece was true. He has gone to his grave, mourned by many friends and admirers, but, alas, his real name is not known, and his relatives will never know how or where he died.' " As a matter of fact, he was the son of Henrik August Helleday, a Swedish judge and his wife, born Christina von Bildstein, hence his middle name. The reason assigned for his departure from Sweden may be just as imaginary. Relatives are still living in Sweden.

Equally tragic, even more romantic, and better documented was the career of Colonel Ulric Dahlgren, a son of Admiral John A. Dahlgren, inventor of the famous Dahlgren guns, which were widely used in the Civil War. His grandfather, Bernard Ulric Dahlgren, was a native of Sweden who had arrived in the United States soon after the War of Independence and in 1809 became the first Swedish Consul at Philadelphia. His descendants are now among the city's prominent families. In 1864, after Colonel Ulric Dahlgren had led a daring, though unsuccessful, cavalry raid to liberate the Union soldiers in the notorious Libby Prison in Richmond, he became a national hero, comparable to

Colonel Charles A. Lindbergh after his flight to Paris in 1927. When his death was announced the whole country mourned him.

Born in Bucks County, Pennsylvania, Ulric Dahlgren was a student of law when the war broke out. Though only nineteen years old, he proved the mettle of his pasture by enlisting in the Army, whereas he probably could have had a soft berth in the Navy, his father being then Commandant of the Washington Navy Yard and a close personal friend of President Lincoln. After serving for a while as a private in the defense of Alexandria, the Virginia suburb of Washington, he was commissioned as a captain and placed on the staff of General Franz Sigel. In November 1862, just before the Battle of Fredericksburg, he led his company of 150 cavalrymen on an exploratory raid into that town and held it for some time against a numerically superior Confederate force. He then returned with valuable information and a certain number of prisoners.

To his father General Sigel then wrote: "It affords me great pleasure to say that your son, Ulric Dahlgren, on my staff, has retired from Fredericksburg after executing one of the most brilliant and daring expeditions since the breaking out of the war, the particulars of which you will learn from the newspapers and from a copy of the report to me which I enclose to you."

At Chancellorsville the next spring, May 4, 1863, Colonel Dahlgren led a final desperate cavalry charge in a vain attempt to stave off another Union defeat. After that he was transferred to the staff of General Hooker, another new commander of the Army of the Potomac. On the eve of the Battle of Gettysburg, two months later, he took part in a minor engagement during which he received a bullet through a foot, which required the amputation of the leg. While in the hospital, he was promoted to the rank of colonel though less than twenty-two years old. In transmitting the new commission, the Secretary of War, Edwin M. Stanton, wrote, "Enclosed you have a commission for colonel, without having passed through the intermediate grade of major. Your gallant and meritorious service has, I think, entitled you to this distinction though it is a departure from general usage which is only justified by distinguished merit such as yours. I hope you may speedily recover, and it will rejoice me to be the instrument of your further advancement in the service."

The wound was too badly infected to heal, but the loss of a leg did not end his cavalry career. Though invalided, he volunteered early in 1864 to lead the desperate attempt to liberate the war prisoners at the Libby Prison in Richmond as well as those at Belle Isle, Virginia. His final letter to his father, who by then had been placed in command of the South Atlantic fleet, ranks with that of Paul Esbjörn, as a moving American document, worthy to be read in the schools:

"Dear Father:" he wrote,
I have not returned to the fleet because there is a grand raid to be made and I am to have a very important command. If successful, it will be the grandest thing on record; and if it fails, many of us will go up. I may be captured or I may be "tumbled over," but it is an undertaking that if I were not in, I should be ashamed to show my face again. With such an important command, I am afraid to mention it for fear this letter may fall into wrong hands before reaching you. I find that I can stand the service perfectly well without my leg. I think it will be successful, although a desperate undertaking.
Aunt Patty will tell you when you return. I will write you more fully when we return. If we do not return, there will be no better place to "give up the ghost."

Your affectionate Son,
ULRIC DAHLGREN

Caught in a night ambush, he and about a hundred of his men were shot down and immediately killed. After the war was over, his remains were recovered and given a public funeral in Washington. The chief orator was the Reverend Henry Ward Beecher, pastor of the Plymouth Congregational Church in Brooklyn, who delivered himself of one of his characteristic pronouncements. "Dahlgren," he shouted. "The name was strange to English lips and of sound foreign to English ears. But now it is no longer your land from which it came! It is ours! It is American! Our children shall revere it, and as long as our history lasts, 'Dahlgren' shall mean truth, honor, bravery and heroic sacrifice."

Here the question may be asked: Why was Dahlgren less American, if less English, than Beecher, for instance? Who had made the greater sacrifice for the country in which the young colonel and both his parents had been born? President and Mrs. Lincoln, who had grown up in the Middle West, made no such distinctions. On March 28, 1864, Mrs. Lincoln had written to Senator Charles Sumner of Massachusetts: "We have no good news from that brave youth, Colonel Dahlgren. Fears are now entertained that he is certainly killed." On March 4, the President had written to Major General Benjamin Butler of the same state, then stationed at Fort Monroe: "Admiral Dahlgren is here and, of course, very anxious about his son. Please send me at once all you know or can learn about his fate."

The following Thanksgiving Day, in 1864, Admiral Dahlgren was the only guest at the White House dinner. In his diary he wrote for November 28, 1864: "Thanksgiving Day, I dined at the President's and made one of a party of three," a typical Lincoln gesture.

In the United States Navy during the Civil War many officers and sailors of Swedish birth or descent performed services, but the two most prominent were Admiral Dahlgren, inventor of the guns that bear his name, and Captain John Ericsson, whose ship, or "floating battery," the *Monitor,* the first to use a revolving turret, was armed with two of those Dahlgren guns and with them stopped the Confederate ironclad, *Merrimac.* Of the former, President Lincoln was a close associate and from him he must have had some advance information about Ericsson's proposed *Monitor,* as otherwise he would hardly have intervened in favor of constructing it as decisively as he did.

Born in Philadelphia in 1809, the same year as the President, Dahlgren had entered the United States Navy as a midshipman in 1826. After a European study tour lasting from 1843 to 1845, he began to specialize in ordnance, designing both light and heavy artillery. "In at least nine engagements in the Civil War," writes Nels Hokanson, "his guns were a factor in turning the tide of success for the Union."

When the war broke out he was in command of the Washington Navy Yard with the rank of captain. To President Lincoln his name presented no difficulties whatever. "I like to see Dahlgren," Nels Hokanson quotes him in his book as being in the habit of saying to his close friends. "The drive to the Navy Yard is one of my greatest pleasures. When I am depressed, I like to talk to Dahlgren. I learn something of the preparations for defense and I get from him consolation and courage. On the whole, I like to see Dahlgren." To a member of Congress the President wrote on January 28, 1862: "Captain Dahlgren gave me his views in this letter at my request. I have so much confidence in him in naval matters that I enclose it to you as Chairman of the Naval Committee."

The very next month, on February 12, 1862, his Secretary of the Navy, Gideon Welles, who, like Henry Ward Beecher, was a native of Connecticut, made the following entry in his diary: "Had a call from Dahlgren who is very grateful that he is named for admiral. Told him to thank the President, who had made it a specialty—that I did not advise it. Dahlgren, always attentive and much of a courtier, has to a great extent the President's regard and affection." This attitude of his superior, who was obviously jealous, may explain the delay in the confirmation of the appointment; the new commission was not signed until February 7, 1863, or nearly a year afterwards. In July 1863, Admiral Dahlgren replaced Admiral Dupont, for whom the famous circle in Washington is named, as commander of the blockading South Atlantic fleet, composed of over ninety ships. In the fall of 1864 he helped General Sherman take Savannah by shelling it from the sea. In 1866, when Lincoln was no longer in Washington, he was transferred to the command of the South Pacific fleet, but before long he again became Chief of Ordnance and before his death in 1870, he had been appointed once more, and at his own request, head of the Washington Navy Yard, where he had designed most of his guns. Dahlgren Hall, in which the United States naval cadets hold their graduation exercises at Annapolis, is a well-deserved memorial.

During the Civil War Admiral Dahlgren's oldest son, Charles Bunker Dahlgren, was also an officer in the United States Navy. Born in 1839, he was three years older than the heroic young colonel. When the war began he was transferred from the engineering division, in which he had been commissioned an ensign, to the line. When the U.S.S. *San Jancinto* stopped the British naval vessel *Trent* at sea to take off the two Confederate commissioners, Mason and Slidell, who were on their way to negotiate official British recognition of the seceding states, and thereby caused an international incident which all but led to war with the British Empire, Charles B. Dahlgren was the Second Officer under Captain Wilkes. In reply to the British charges of brutality justifying war he testified at the subsequent official inquiry that "as far as it came under my observation, everything was conducted in an orderly and gentlemanly manner." In the subsequent campaign to clear the Mississippi from New Orleans to Vicksburg he served under Admiral David Porter and after the fall of Vicksburg on July 4, 1863, he received generous words of praise from both Porter and Walker. (The late Ulric Dahlgren, who for many years was a professor of biology at Princeton University, was his son.)

Another prominent naval officer of Swedish descent, according to the *Encyclopedia of American Biography* and his own granddaughter, Ida Dudley Dale, was Charles Gideon Dale, "Chief Engineer of the U.S. Navy during the Civil War under Admirals Farragut and Porter." His father had arrived in New York from Sweden in the 1820s and had changed his name from *Otterdahl* to Dale. His family stemmed from the vicinity of Gothenburg.

It was to the United States Navy that the most dramatic and probably the most important contribution was made during the Civil War by an American citizen of Swedish birth, Captain John Ericsson. At first mocked as a "cheesebox on a raft," his *Monitor* revolutionized all naval warfare. Like so many of the Swedish officers in the Civil War, Captain Ericsson had had military training in Sweden and his title of captain, to which he clung proudly all his life, indicated his Swedish army rank. When a mere youth he had worked as a surveyor on the construction of the Göta Canal across Sweden and before arriving in New York in 1839 he had made many notable inventions, including improvements in the screw propeller which for the first time made it workable. He had also competed with George Stephenson for the first steam locomotive and lost only because his hastily constructed engine blew up. Until it did, it had made greater speed than Stephenson's "Rocket." Long before either electric or internal combustion motors had been thought of, he had designed and built by the thousands a hot air or "caloric" engine which is now only a museum piece. As late as the beginning of this century, however, it was used to pump water and furnish other mechanical power for farm buildings and country homes. Early in 1853 he had exhibited in Washington a small war vessel, the *Ericsson,* propelled by hot air. A much larger ship, the *Princeton,* which ultimately blew up and killed many high American officials, including the Secretary of the Navy, was driven by steam, but it used Ericsson's type of propeller.

His scheme for a low, ironclad war vessel, which he called a "floating battery," using for the first time a revolving gun turret, was several years old when the Civil War began. Once he had offered it to Emperor Napoleon III of France, only to have it rejected in a polite note. When the Confederates began to salvage the wooden Union warships and cover them with heavy armor plate, he once more brought out his plans for a "floating battery" and after discussing it with Admiral Dahlgren, who in turn must have informed President Lincoln, he offered it to the American Government. Except for the President's timely intervention, it would in all probability have been once more rejected, particularly as the construction of an old-type ironclad, the *Galena,* built like the *Monitor* by Cornelius S. Bushnell of New Haven, Connecticut, was abandoned. In three months the *Monitor* was completed at a private yard in Greenpoint, Brooklyn. Of the crew, commanded by Lieutenant John L. Worden, a native-born American, two petty officers and at least four sailors were Swedes.

On Saturday, March 8, 1862, the rebuilt Confederate ironclad, *Merrimac,* steamed up Hampton Roads in Virginia, where the line ships of the Union Navy were stationed. (Reports that the *Monitor* was about ready to leave Brooklyn had been printed in the New York newspapers.) At first, the frigate *Cumberland* offered resistance, but was helpless against the heavy armor and guns of the *Merrimac.* In a few minutes it was sunk. The *Congress* then hoisted a white flag. The next day, when the *Merrimac* was expected to return, the *Minnesota* would surely be doomed. News of imminent disaster spread through the nation.

That same Saturday afternoon an emergency meeting of the Cabinet was held in Washington. The situation was summed up by the usually so self-confident Secretary of War, Edwin M. Stanton, as follows: "The *Merrimac* will change the entire character of the war; she will destroy, seriatim, every naval vessel; she will lay all the cities on the seaboard under contribution. I shall immediately recall Burnside; Port Royal must be abandoned. I will notify the Governors and municipal authorities in the North to take instant measures to protect their harbors. I have no doubt that the monster is this minute on her way to Washington and not unlikely we shall have a cannonball from one of her guns in the White House before we leave this room."

The next morning, Sunday, March 9, 1862, the *Merrimac* did return to Hampton Roads and started firing on the helpless *Minnesota,* then thought to be her only obstacle to naval supremacy in America and perhaps the world. Suddenly she was attacked at close range by the insignificant *Monitor*—Captain Ericsson's little David sent against the Southern Goliath. It was probably the most public naval battle ever staged. From the shore and from the decks of numerous vessels thousands of people watched every move and saw the effect of every salvo. New Yorkers, who had seen the little "cheesebox on a raft" towed out of their harbor a few days earlier, had taken trains to Virginia to see the contest as if it had been a prizefight or football game. Many eyewitness accounts of the battle have been printed; that of the Swedish-born Major Ernst von Vegesack, who happened to be on a mission conducting troops to Newport News, is not only as vivid as any, but probably, in a technical sense, more correct than most.

"Last Saturday," he wrote to Sweden, "when the ironclad steamer of the Rebels, *Merrimac,* appeared, I was commanded by General Wool to depart with two Regis. of Inf. and six Squadrons of Cavalry in order to reinforce General Mansfield's A.C. at Newport News and by way of this had occasion, at a distance of some hundred yards, to witness the most interesting fight which has probably ever taken place. I have hardly beheld anything that made a more lugubrious impression on me than this *Merrimac,* which, black and gloomy, slowly kept advancing on the crystal clear surface of the water, proud in her consciousness of spreading death and devastation about herself. The combat you have seen at length described in the newspapers. Painful as it was to see the frigate *Cumberland* gradually sinking in the midst of a heroic defense and finally disappear, taking with her into the deep about 150 men, who dead or wounded in the struggle, could not be brought safely to the shore, the sight of a white flag, hoisted on the frigate *Congress,* as a sign that it wanted to capitulate, was one that arrested more grief than anger because it was not an act of indefensible cowardice. When landing, the commander and crew of the *Cumberland* were greeted with enthusiastic cheers, whereas those of the *Congress* were almost avoided. We held everything to be lost and thought Sunday would bring about not only the loss of the remaining man-of-war, but also driving us from Newport News and maybe Fort Monroe too.

"As a rescuing angel then on Sunday morning Ericsson's iron battery, *Monitor,* appeared, the most curious little thing that was ever afloat on the water; most of all it resembles some joined planks with a tar barrel in the middle. The fight that day between the frigate *Minnesota* and *Monitor,* on one side, and *Merrimac,* on the other, inspired a complete conviction that henceforth entrenchments for coast defense are totally unpractical and that wooden vessels forever have lost their value as Men-of-War. *Merrimac* and *Monitor* will give occasion to a total subversion of the Navies of all nations, and our compatriot, Captain Ericsson, has made himself immortal."

That night both Secretaries Stanton and Welles breathed easier. Washington, Baltimore, Philadelphia, New York, and Boston, had escaped. In the fight Lieutenant Worden, who was immediately promoted to captain, had been slightly injured by flying splinters of steel, but when Captain Dahlgren, Commander of the Washington Navy Yard, offered to replace him, the Secretary of the Navy, Gideon Welles, who had opposed his promotion to admiral, objected on the ground that he was too valuable where he was. The President's judgment as to who best understood naval matters had finally been vindicated.

In a letter, dated January 20, 1862, and addressed to Gustavus Vasa

Fox, Assistant Secretary of the Navy, Captain Ericsson, inventor of the *Monitor,* had explained why he had chosen the name. Fox had had professional naval training, while Welles was a political figure. Despite his first name, that of a famous Swedish King, Mr. Fox had no Swedish ancestry.

"Sir:" wrote Ericsson,

In accordance with your request, I submit for your approbation a name for the floating battery at Green Point. The impregnable and aggressive character of the structure will admonish the leaders of the Southern Rebellion that the batteries on the banks of their rivers will no longer present barriers to the entrance of the Union forces.

The ironclad intruder will thus prove a severe monitor to those leaders. But there are other leaders who will also be startled and admonished by the booming of the guns from the impregnable iron turret. "Downing Street" will hardly view with indifference this last "Yankee notion"; this monitor. To the Lords of Admiralty the new craft will be a monitor suggesting doubts as to the propriety of completing those four steel-clad ships at three and a half million apiece. On these and similar grounds, I propose to name the new battery *Monitor.*

> *Your Obedient Servant*
> J. ERICSSON

Though the Swedes, as a rule, did not approve of slavery, quite a number of them, who had happened to settle in the South, fought on the Confederate side in the war, proving that patriotism and loyalty may be determined by accidents of birth, residence or economic interests. Their story is told by Nels Hokanson.

In the South, Admiral Dahlgren had a brother, Charles G. Dahlgren, who, like him, had been born and brought up in Philadelphia. For him he had named his oldest son. In the war, this Dahlgren became a Confederate general, proving that military ability was common in the family. Originally he had been a bank clerk, employed at the Philadelphia office of the Bank of the United States, against which President Andrew Jackson waged his famous campaign. In 1828, or thereabout, Charles Dahlgren had been sent as a cashier to the branch at Natchez, Mississippi, and when the bank was closed he became a cotton planter and slaveholder in the same state. In this he was financially successful; when the war broke out he was supposed to be worth $750,000, then a larger fortune than it would be now. As late as 1859, Ulric Dahlgren, the future Union war hero, spent part of the year with his uncle in Mississippi. In 1861, when hostilities began, the latter raised a regiment, the Third Mississippi, of which he became the colonel. Jefferson Davis, a fellow citizen of Mississippi, promoted him to the rank of brigadier general. In May 1862, he was appointed commander at Camp Moon in his own state, and his work there was highly praised by General G. T. Beauregard, one of the best Confederate leaders. Later he was put in charge of Camp Fayette in Louisiana. At the siege of Vicksburg, in which so many Swedes took part on the Union side, he first saw action and was wounded. At the head of his regiment he carried on, however, throughout the war. A daguerreotype of him, owned by the Tennessee Historical Society, shows him to have been a handsome man of dignified mien. When the war was over he was ruined. His slaves had been set free and his plantations confiscated. At first he settled in New Orleans, where he fell ill. In 1870 he moved with his family to New York and in December 1888, he died in Brooklyn.

Except to Texas, the prewar Swedish emigration to the South had never been considerable. The 1860 Census listed only about 750 Swedes in the states that later seceded. Miss Ella Lonn of Goucher College, Baltimore, who has made a special study of foreigners in the Confederate forces, has found only twenty-five Swedish names. Nels Hokanson has found more. Many names common in the South, such as Johnson, Nelson or Anderson may or may not be of Swedish origin. Some, like that of the late Senator Claude Swanson of Virginia, who was Secretary of the Navy under President Wilson, may have stemmed from the Swedish colonists on the Delaware, but it may also have been of British or Irish origin. President Johnson, who succeeded Lincoln, was considered to be of Scotch-Irish descent. General Robert Anderson, who as major was in command at Fort Sumter when it was first fired on, was not of Swedish origin. Brigadier General Alfred Ivarson of the Confederate Army was of Danish and not Swedish descent. On the other hand, Brigadier General Roger W. Hanson, who was killed on the Confederate side in the Battle of Murfreesboro on Jan. 2, 1863, was definitely a descendant of the colonial Swedish Hanson family of which John Hanson of Maryland was a member. Like so many Confederate commanders, Roger Hanson had taken part in the Mexican War and when the Civil War broke out he was an officer in the state militia of Kentucky. He chose the Confederate side and in the Battle at Fort Donelson on February 16, 1862, his men held the Confederate right wing. After being included in the "unconditional surrender," demanded by Grant, he was exchanged in October 1862, and then promoted to brigadier general for "conspicuous service on the field of battle."

A noted Confederate colonel who was actually born in Sweden was August Forsberg, leader of the famous and feared "Forsberg's Brigade" of Virginia. Born on January 1, 1831, he was a nephew of Carl D. Forsberg, a war-office councillor in Stockholm. Like Silversparre and Malmborg on the Union side, he had enjoyed a good education in Sweden, being graduated from the Institute of Technology at Stockholm. At the age of twenty-two he was given a commission in the Swedish engineering corps, but in 1855 he emigrated to the United States, settling first at Columbia, South Carolina, and then at Charleston. After enlisting in the Confederate Army he was employed at first as a topographical engineer on the Charleston defense works. Soon he was transferred to more active duties in western Tennessee. After the battle at Fort Donelson on February 16, 1862, he too was cited for bravery and gallant action. Like all the other Confederates who had to surrender "unconditionally," he was taken prisoner, but after having been exchanged the next September, he took part in one of the battles of northern Virginia, after which General G. C. Wharton, commanding the First Virginia Brigade, commended him as follows: "Lieutenant August Forsberg, attached to the Brigade as engineering officer, rendered very efficient service in rallying his men and throughout the day distinguished himself for gallantry and acts of daring." Soon after that the thirty-one-year-old Swedish engineer was promoted to colonel and given charge of the Fifty-first Virginia Regiment. Under his command this regiment became so active that it earned the popular title of Forsberg's Brigade. Altogether Forsberg took part in ninety battles and was wounded three times. When General Lee surrendered at Appomattox, Forsberg was made a prisoner of war, but at the special request of the Swedish Minister in Washington, Count von Piper, who probably knew his family in Sweden, he was soon released. His subsequent fate is unknown.

In the Battle of Shiloh, April 6, 1862, the Confederate artillery was under the command of Major J. H. Hallonquist, a graduate of West Point, who was born of Swedish parents in South Carolina. On January 1, 1861, he resigned his commission in the United States Army and on April 26, 1861, he was placed in charge of a battery at Fort Sumter, which was then in Confederate hands. He was next attached to the Second Battalion of the Alabama Artillery. On July 16, 1862, he was promoted to lieutenant colonel and on October 8, 1864, made chief of artillery of the Confederate Army of Tennessee.

The only prominent Swedish-born Confederate officer who made a career in Sweden after the hostilities in America were over was Carl Jakob Hammarskjöld, who ultimately became head of the Swedish State Railways. Born at Skultuna, in central Sweden, famous for its brassworks, he emigrated in 1850 to North Carolina where his father, Carl Vilhelm Hammarskjöld, formerly manager of the Skultuna plant, had preceded him. In North Carolina the older man had built up the Spring Hill Forge, which he owned and managed until his death in 1860. In the same town his son established his own ironworks and before the war broke out served as the local postmaster. He was also an owner of slaves and favored the secession. When war began he enlisted and having had military training in Sweden, he soon became a Confederate colonel. As early as June 1861, he was wounded and in 1862 he retired from the service. He, too, had friends in Sweden and in 1863 the Swedish Minister in Washington helped him get back there. His railroad career followed.

Some of the Swedish privates in the Southern armies complained, when taken prisoners, that they had been forced by their neighbors to enlist. Others like S. M. Swenson of Texas moved out of the country rather than support the Confederate side. A few of the other Texas Swedes appealed to the local Swedish consulate for help in escaping military service. Several Swedish sailors, captured on Confederate blockade runners, appealed to the Swedish legation in Washington on the ground that they had not known their ships were engaged in illegal traffic. On the Minister's plea, some were released by the Federal authorities. Further study of Swedish records would certainly reveal a variety of facts about the Civil War.

In the American-Spanish War as in the two world wars many American citizens of Swedish descent likewise participated, but as, in most instances, they had been born in the United States or had lived here long enough to be Americanized, they did not enlist or fight as Swedes. Even a partial list of their names and achievements falls outside the scope of this book and yet it is worth mentioning, for instance, that Major Richard Bong, the leading American air ace in the Second World War and a native of Wisconsin, was of partly Swedish descent, his father having been born in Sweden.

VII

THE MASS MIGRATION OF THE SWEDES

At the height of the Civil War, as related in a previous chapter, the American Consul in Stockholm, B. F. Tefft, wrote to the State Department in Washington that if furnished ships or free transportation he could take a quarter of the Swedish working population to the United States—a boast that came close to being justified when the war was over. A new Swedish immigration wave then began and during the next generation it threatened to depopulate the country. The peak came in 1882 when 64,607 persons left for the United States. The next highest number, 54,698, departed in 1888.

The causes for this exodus, unexampled as far as Sweden was concerned, were many, even if the religious reason was no longer valid. Wages were still low as compared with those paid in America, arable land continued scarce and closely held, whereas in the United States it was not only plentiful and cheap, but under the Homestead Act, passed in 1862, was actually given away to people who proved they could live on it. While the War Between the States was under way the impulse to emigrate had been checked and when it was over the pent-up desire was released with increased effect. In the later sixties, moreover, Sweden suffered from a succession of crop failures which virtually confronted many families with a choice between starvation and departure. Furthermore, during the two decades before the American Civil War, the country had been flooded with an ever-increasing number of books, pamphlets, newspaper articles and private letters—all stressing the demand for workers in America and the opportunities for healthy and ambitious young people to become independent. Some of these were written by former emigrants or visitors to the country and some by authors who had never left Sweden.

This new wave continued to flow from New York to the Middle West, reaching into Michigan, Minnesota, Wisconsin, and Indiana, as well as Illinois and Iowa. Everywhere the Swedish settlers proved so successful in creating farms out of the brush- or forest-covered virgin soil and so eager were both private landowners and state governments, not to mention the new railroads, to have their land developed and their waste areas populated that they sent their agents to Sweden to bring over more of them. Such emigrant agents, some of whom were employed by the new steamship companies, American, British, Dutch, French, or German, published in Sweden not only alluring advertisements in the regular newspapers but also special newspapers of their own. Commissions on tickets sold were paid to a multitude of part-time agents, stationed in almost every community. Except in the case of young men liable to military service, there was no law against emigration, and requests for permits to leave the country could not be refused. Moral arguments were not enough and in all justice the state church clergymen whose official duty it was to issue such permits (*utflyttningsbetyg*) could not deny that the economic distress of the applicants was often grave.

The first known Swede to settle in the territory that is now Minnesota was Jacob Fahlström, who was born July 25, 1793, in Stockholm, where his father was a potter. Like so many of the earliest Swedish settlers in the other Midwestern states, he had originally been a sailor. An uncle was a sea captain and on his ship Jacob first set out as a cabin boy when only twelve years old. Some reports have it that his uncle's ship was wrecked on the coast of England and others that he became lost in a London fog and boarded the wrong vessel, and still others that he deserted to escape the strict discipline. A fact seems to be that in London he entered the employ of Lord Thomas Douglas Selkirk (1771–1820) who after becoming controlling owner and managing director of the Hudson Bay Company, obtained in May 1811, the grant of an immense tract in the Red River Valley of central Canada to which he sent Scottish settlers to hunt furs and develop the land. Among them was Jacob Fahlström who in time became an expert woodsman, fur trapper, and canoeist.

After the clash at Fort Douglas, in June 1816, between the staffs of the Hudson Bay and the Northwest Fur Company, Fahlström made his escape southward along the Red River and found refuge with a Chippewa Indian tribe, three miles above the mouth of the St. Louis River. After learning its language and adopting its way of living he was accepted as a member. In 1832 he was married to a Chippewa maiden, Margaret Bungo, and by her he had nine handsome children. To support them he worked in various places as a pioneer farmer and in 1837 took up a claim in Washington County, Minnesota. At one time he lived near Fort Snelling, close to Minneapolis and St. Paul, where he supplied the garrison with firewood and carried its mail on foot or by birch-bark canoe from Fort Crawford further down the Mississippi, near Prairie du Chien in Wisconsin. In 1840 he staked a claim near Afton, Minnesota, where he developed a farm and there he died in 1857. Together with some of her children, Mrs. Fahlström continued to live at the farm until her own death in 1880. During the Civil War a son, Isaac, who was probably a soldier, died in a Washington hospital, and long after the family had scattered, the homestead at Afton continued to be known as the "Fahlström" farm. Having become converted as a Methodist, Fahlström served for some years as an itinerant Methodist missionary among the Indians whose language he spoke and after 1850, when his own countrymen had begun to arrive, he preached to them in Swedish, a language he had not had a chance to use for over forty years. The class records of a former Methodist mission at Kaposia, now part of South St. Paul, show that Mr. and Mrs. Fahlström and three daughters, Nancy, Jane, and Sally, were members.

The list of charter members of the first American Methodist Episcopal Church at St. Paul, formed in 1848, contains the Swedish-sounding name of Joseph Lundbäck, but about him nothing further is known. Equally obscure are the antecedents of Jacob Törnell, who in the 1840s lived in the vicinity of Taylors Falls and Stillwater. To relatives in Sweden he is supposed to have written enthusiastic letters about the St. Croix Valley; other Swedish immigrants who arrived there later found that he had been killed by an Indian in 1847. The United States Census Report of 1850 lists only four persons born in Sweden as living at that time in the Territory of Minnesota, and the entire white population was then only about six thousand. The rest were Indians.

The first log cabin built by Swedes in Minnesota was erected in the fall of 1850 at Hay Lake in Washington County by three young men who had arrived that spring in Illinois from their native Swedish province of Västergötland. During the summer one of them by the name of Carl Fernström made an exploratory tour to the north and came back so enthusiastic about the lakes and forests of Minnesota, which had reminded him of Sweden, that in October that same year he returned with his two friends, Oscar Roos and August Sandahl, all three in their early twenties, and together they made themselves at home on a forty-acre tract on Hay Lake. The winter, however, was probably colder than any they had experienced in Sweden and the next year they sold out their log cabin and land holdings to a fellow countryman by the name of Daniel Nilsson, who settled down there permanently. In 1852 Fernström set out for California to dig gold, Roos moved to Taylors Falls, and Sandahl returned to Sweden. In 1902 the spot of their settlement was marked by a tall granite monument, suitably inscribed.

In 1850 the St. Croix Valley was explored also by another visitor from Illinois whose name was Erik Ulrik Nordberg. In Illinois he had been a member of the Bishop Hill colony. His letters, in turn, brought to Minnesota the first group of Swedish families and they settled permanently the following year at Chisago Lake, about nine miles from their landing place at Taylors Falls on the St. Croix River. Some of them had lived for a while in Illinois, a country they thought too flat and treeless compared with their native Hälsingland in northern Sweden. Some were *läsare* or pietists of the conservative Hedbergian variety who had come on the same ship as Anders and Eric Norelius. Others had arrived direct from Sweden. One family, that of Anders Swenson, had traveled by water the entire way from Motala in the central province of Östergötland, first by the Göta Canal across Sweden to Gothenburg, from there by ship to New Orleans, then on the Mississippi to Illinois, and finally by that river and the St. Croix to Taylors Falls.

After that one settlement led to another. At Chisago Lake, as the inscriptions on tombstones in the cemetery at Center City testify so definitely, most of the later arrivals came from southern Småland. While there never was any organized Swedish community in Minnesota, like those at Bishop Hill in Illinois or Lindsborg, Kansas, families from the same province often settled in the same vicinity, so that to this day the dialects of the older people reveal their place of birth in Sweden. For the same reason, many of the Swedish provincial customs are supposed to have been preserved better in Minnesota than in any other state. On the other hand, the Minnesota Swedes are intensely patriotic, both as Americans and as Minnesotans.

Early in the fall of 1850, when the foliage had begun to tint, a different kind of visitor from Sweden arrived at St. Paul as the guest of Governor Ramsey. She was Fredrika Bremer, Sweden's first and, in the opinion of many, still its most important novelist, the first professional Swedish writer of either sex to explore the United States. When she arrived in New York in 1849 she was already famous as a writer of "intimate" fiction, that is, novels of home and family life. But she was interested in a great variety of subjects and was a keen observer. Her letters from America were filled with shrewd comments on almost all phases of life—art, books, economics, including slavery (which she studied firsthand in the South), food, social manners, domestic life, politics, and the prominent men and women of the day, chiefly the men.

When she set out from Sweden in 1849, at the age of forty-eight, to see life in America for herself—then an unprecedented step for a single female—she was armed with introductions to a number of influential people, chiefly from mutual acquaintances in England. Being an ardent feminist, she was particularly eager to study the part played by women in the New World. That she usually found the men more interesting as individuals did not, however, change her faith in her own sex. Her lasting influence within the feminist movement is indicated by the fact that to this day the leading organization of feminists in Sweden is called Fredrika Bremer Förbundet.

Like both Peter Kalm and Gustaf Unonius, she had been brought up in a fairly well-to-do Swedish family living in Finland. (Kalm was actually born in Sweden.) After the Russians took the country in 1809, the Bremers had moved to Stockholm, as the parents of Unonius had done. That year, when Fredrika was but eight years old, she began to write. In 1828, when she was twenty-seven, her first book *Sketches from Everyday Life* was published. In 1831 her first work of fiction, *The H. Family* appeared in Stockholm, and three years later her second, *The President's Daughters*. When Longfellow returned in 1835 from his Europeaan tour, which had included Sweden, he brought with him for the Harvard Library copies of Miss Bremer's novels, which are still preserved. In 1844 James Russell Lowell reviewed her whole production in the *North American Review*. His sister, Mrs. Mary Lowell Putnam, had then translated, directly from the Swedish, her only dramatic sketch, *The Bondmaid*. Two years earlier, *The Neighbors,* another novel, translated by Mary Howitt into English from the German version, had appeared in London. In the United States, too, Miss Bremer found many readers. For a while she was, in fact, the most popular author of the day. In the Brooklyn *Daily Eagle,* of which he was then the editor, Walt Whitman, wrote: "If I ever have any children, the first book after the New Testament, that shall be their household companion shall be Miss Bremer's novels."

When she came to America in 1849 she was cordially received by the literary and social lions of the day both in New York and Boston; in the South and in the Middle West. It was the era of Webster, Clay, Calhoun, Charles Sumner, Wendell Phillips, William Lloyd Garrison, Stephen A. Douglas ("the Little Giant"), Washington Irving, Emerson, Longfellow, Holmes, Hawthorne, and Lowell. She met them all. Hawthorne called her "the funniest little person one could imagine—a withered briar rose still retaining the freshness of the morning." He also thought her "worthy of being the maiden aunt of the whole human family. . . . There is no better heart than hers and not many sounder heads."

As she traveled she wrote and mailed make-believe letters—intimate, detailed, gossipy—to a "beloved sister, no longer on this earth." When she reread them in 1852, after her return to Stockholm, she felt "reanimated." They brought back, she wrote, so many happy memories of America. When the first volume of these letters was published in May 1853 it was dedicated: "To My American Friends."

Probably no more effective "America letters" have ever been published. In Sweden they made a deep impression. For the first time they pictured the Americans as they were at close range and in intimate personal terms. Furthermore, being published just prior to the outbreak of the Civil War, they helped explain the causes of the conflict. How many young Swedes were thus inspired to enlist in the Union armies can never be known. Being friendly, human, interpretive, they were welcomed in the United States as a counterbalance to such English books as Mrs. Frances Milton Trollope's *The Domestic Manners of the Americans,* published in 1832, and Charles Dickens' *Martin Chuzzlewit,* which had first appeared in 1843–44. Unlike the English authors, Miss Bremer had not felt called upon either to educate her hosts socially, or to make fun of them. When republished in New York in English her letters became an instant success. Within a month the volume of over 1,300 pages had to be reprinted five times. When republished in condensed form as a "Scandinavian Classic" in 1924, they once more became an American best seller.

Once the Civil War was over, her letters helped stimulate Swedish emigration to the United States in general, and to Minnesota in particular.

"What a glorious new Scandinavia might not Minnesota become!" she had rhapsodized in 1850. "Here the Swede would find his clear, romantic lakes, the plains of Skåne, rich in grain, and the valleys of Norrland. Here the Norwegian would find his rapid rivers, his lofty mountains. The Danes might there pasture their flocks and herds and lay out their farms on richer and less misty coasts than those of Denmark." If this was not conscious immigration propaganda, it has been regarded as Minnesota's introduction into Swedish literature.

As a matter of fact, her vision has come true more than she could have imagined. In 1905, when immigration was still unrestricted, the state had a population of 1,997,401 of which 12.5 per cent or 126,223 had been born in Sweden—the largest foreign-born group. Those born in Germany numbered 119,868 and those in Norway 111,611. In 1920, when the population had gone up to 2,387,125, the natives of Sweden had been reduced to 112,117, while the Germans had gone down still further to 74,634 and those born in Norway to 90,188. In 1940 the total population of Minnesota was 2,792,300 of whom only 8.2 per cent, including members of both the first and the second generation with at least one Swedish-born parent, was of Swedish descent. (Compare this with 2.67 per cent in Illinois, a state in which the Swedish element had originally been numerically, if not relatively, larger.) The common impression that Minnesota is a predominantly Swedish or Scandinavian state may therefore be accepted as an unconscious tribute to the strong personal qualities of the people from the North. It recalls the compliment paid during the Civil War, as related in a previous chapter, to a Virginia regiment commanded by a Swedish-born officer, Colonel August Forsberg. It was referred to as Forsberg's Brigade.

By the middle of the century American intellectual life, the public schools, free libraries, lecture lyceums, and institutes, had been described in another book, *A Trip in the United States,* by Per Adam Siljeström, published in 1852—the first one in Swedish about the country to omit from its title the words "North America." Its author was a Stockholm scientist, legislator, and school administrator, who in 1849–50 had made a tour of the United States at Swedish public expense, accompanied by Pehr Erik Bergfalk, a professor of history and a liberal political leader. Siljeström was the man who popularized in Sweden Benjamin Franklin's educational ideas. He had also become acquainted with such living Bostonians as Channing, Emerson, and Parker. He described too the American legislative procedure, the new transportation system by rail, which by then had begun to displace the steamboats and canals described in the 1820s by Klinckowström.

In Sweden Siljeström was a pioneer in the modernization of both the school and library systems, partly on the American model. "The

Americans," he wrote, "are the most practical people in the world; they are also its most inveterate readers." As Jenny Lind had discovered their love of music, and Fredrika Bremer their domesticity and love of literature, so Siljeström described their desire for education. Such books were the best emigration propaganda, especially when backed up by personal letters from relatives or former neighbors.

Prior to the Civil War owners of undeveloped land in the Middle West had contented themselves with sending their agents to meet the incoming Swedish immigrants in New York or Chicago. During the war itself, mineowners in Michigan sent Baron Axel Silversparre, a former artillery officer in the Union Army, to recruit Swedish workers. President Lincoln himself had dispatched thirty special consular agents to Europe, including Sweden, to explain the opportunities for immigrants offered by the Homestead Act of 1862. After the war was over the railroad companies began an even more active campaign to get more settlers to whom they could sell the land they had received free from the Government as subsidies for constructing new lines through relatively uninhabited territories. Several of the states also appointed special "Immigration Commissions" with office staffs and suitable appropriations, whose duty it was to increase the wealth and population of their respective areas by inducing more and more immigrants to settle in them. The fruit of their work was soon reflected in the immigration statistics.

After the sailing vessels had had their day, there was little direct Swedish passenger traffic to New York until 1915 when the Swedish American Line was organized and within ten years after that the new American quota law had reduced immigration to a fraction of what it had been after the First World War was over. Businessmen, tourists, and students then replaced the immigrants as passengers.

In Sweden the new popular newspapers, such as *Aftonbladet* of Stockholm, consistently printed extensive and favorable descriptions of the United States. Editorially, American institutions and laws were stressed as models which Sweden ought to copy. Gradually Methodist and Baptist clergymen-writers with American experience such as Witting, Henschen, Palmquist, and Wiberg returned to emphasize the greater religious liberty in America, while lay journalists like Isidor Kjellberg, who had learned new methods in America, began to belabor the antiquated political system in Sweden, and demand greater suffrage rights. In Chicago, where he arrived in 1869, Kjellberg had been the publisher and editor of a radical, anti-clerical weekly, *Justicia*. In the small

local Swedish circle then dominated by the ministers of various denominations, he soon made too many enemies to continue his paper, but
in Sweden he founded, on his return in 1872, a new truly liberal paper,
called *Östgöten,* which made him both politically influential, and relatively wealthy, proving that the public liked his championship of American ideas. His main argument was that in the United States personal
ability rather than family influence and inherited social position was the
key to success. In the same spirit he lectured widely, particularly before
the newly formed labor organizations. His lectures about America were
published in 1883. When the first great Swedish strike broke out in the
sawmills of Sundsvall in 1879, he went there and in personal harangues
urged the strikers to emigrate rather than accept the terms of the employers.

To promote emigration to America several special Swedish newspapers were published in the late 1860s and early 1870s. The headquarters
of this activity was usually Gothenburg, where in December 1869, the
first issue of a tabloid called *Amerika* appeared. It was followed by *Nya
Werlden* and then by *Tidning för Menige Men. (Newspaper for the
Common People)* which continued to appear from 1872 to January 1874.
In Jönköping, in northern Småland, a paper called *Sverige och Amerika*
appeared during 1871 and 1872, and in Örbero, during 1867 and 1870,
Amerika-Bladet, followed during the summer of 1870 by a monthly
Swedish American Review. The contents of these newspapers were
chiefly "America letters," but also rather lurid descriptions of the privations suffered by the poor people in Sweden. Next, the Methodists and
Baptists, who were influenced by American ideas and to some extent
supported by American funds, began to publish periodicals of their own,
like the Methodist *Nya Sändebudet (The New Messenger)* and the Baptist *Evangelisten,* in which were printed sermons by American revivalists, such as Dwight L. Moody, Theodore L. Cuyler, DeWitt Talmadge,
R. A. Torrey, A. B. Simpson and others, a welcome contrast to the usually dry sermons preached in the state churches, and also "America
letters," as well as biographies and narratives favorable to the United
States.

The earliest and most prominent Swedish-born, official American promoter of immigration from Sweden to the United States, particularly
Minnesota, was Colonel Hans Mattson. Like General Stolbrand, Mattson
was a native of northern Skåne, born in 1832, and like him a veteran of
the Vendes Artillery Regiment at Kristianstad and also a former regimental commander in the Civil War. In 1869, after having been the

Secretary and General Manager of the official Immigration Board in Minnesota, he was elected Secretary of State, the first Swedish-born citizen to reach such high public office in the United States.

Though born on a farm, Mattson had enjoyed a certain amount of secondary education in Sweden, first at a small private school, then from a tutor at home, and finally at the "Latin School" in Kristianstad. During his second year in this school the first conflict over Slesvig-Holstein broke out between Prussia and Denmark and by watching the Swedish troops march off to help the Danes he became so excited that he enlisted in the local Vendes Artillery Regiment. In this regiment Stolbrand was already a sergeant and as such took part in the expedition to Denmark. Mattson's mother, however, prevailed on the regimental surgeon, who was also her family physician, to declare her son unfit for duty, as he was suffering from a cold; and after that was cured he never did go to Denmark. The war, moreover, was settled before any of the Swedes arrived, and none of them saw action.

Mattson, who was then seventeen, remained in the Swedish artillery service for a year and a half, but as he then realized, according to his memoirs, that a son of a farmer would have little chance of promotion in competition with the young sons of the nobility, he resigned and decided instead to emigrate to America. He had wanted, he wrote in his memoirs, to seek his fortune in a land where inherited titles were not prerequisites for success. "At that time," he added "America was not much known in the part of Sweden in which I lived; only a few persons from the whole country had so far emigrated. But what we knew was that America was a new country with a free and independent people; that it had a free form of government and great natural resources. For us [his school chum, Hans Euström, and himself] this was reason enough for us to go there." In May 1851, they set off, first by horse and farm wagon to Hälsingborg, from there by schooner to Gothenburg, and then on the Swedish brig *Ambrosius* for Boston. On board were about 150 other Swedish emigrants.

After a succession of hardships during the next two years, including adventures in Boston, New York, New Hampshire, the Middle West and on ships between New York and Charleston, where he saw slaves lashed like animals on their way to work, which "made me a Republican for life," he became in 1853 a pioneer in Goodhue County, Minnesota, where he helped found the still almost solidly Swedish community of Vasa, so named by Mattson in honor of the famous sixteenth century Swedish monarch. After a few years as a farmowner he moved to Red

Wing to become a real estate agent. Ruined in the panic of 1857, he studied law and entered politics. His first public office was that of County Auditor, to which he was elected by the newly formed Republican Party—a significant first link in the chain of events which was to make Republicans of so many voters of Swedish origin. In the course of time, Mattson helped found, successively, three Swedish-language weeklies, all of which reflected his political views.

When the Civil War began, Mattson not only organized a preponderantly Swedish company of volunteers at Red Wing but he also wrote in *Hemlandet,* a Swedish-language weekly then published in Chicago, a fiery appeal to all his countrymen to enlist. As captain of the all-Scandinavian Company D, Third Minnesota Volunteer Regiment, Mattson left early in Nobember 1861 for Buell's army in Kentucky. After eight months of service he was promoted to the rank of major. During his absence on sick leave in Minnesota in July 1862, his own regiment, as well as the Twelfth Michigan, and a battery of artillery were bluffed by the Confederate cavalry general N. B. Forrest, into surrendering at Murfreesboro, Tennessee.

On his return to the battle area, after reading the shocking news in a local paper, Mattson was given command over the paroled men. They came back to Minnesota in time to help repress the Sioux Indian outbreak. Early in 1863, the officers had been exchanged and the regiment reorganized. After campaigning in Tennessee it joined General Grant's troops in the siege of Vicksburg. When the city had finally surrendered, the Minnesota men were sent to Arkansas, where, after taking Little Rock, they served as occupation troops until the war was over. Though still only a colonel in formal rank, Mattson often had command of a brigade.

When peace had been restored, Mattson returned to his law practice in Red Wing. He was next appointed editor-in-chief of a recently started Swedish-language newspaper in Chicago, *Svenska Amerikanaren,* the first issue of which was dated September 8, 1866. It is still published and after absorbing various other weeklies enjoys the largest circulation in the country. The following spring he resigned and began to work as an immigration promoter for the state of Minnesota. In this role he twice visited Sweden, the first time as an employee of the state and the second time as an agent for the Northern Pacific Railroad, which "had been granted by the government the ownership of several million acres of land along the proposed route." On his first return, in the spring of 1869, he was accompanied by a group of eight hundred such emigrants, and he had already sent ahead "a large party" under the leadership of "my representative, Captain Lindborg, a veteran of the English-Russian [Crimean] and the American wars." These Swedish farm workers were a welcome addition to the small population of the state and as a reward Mattson was elected Secretary of State on the Republican ticket in the fall of the same year.

The purpose of the Minnesota Immigration Board had been defined in the St. Paul *Press* for March 14, 1867 as follows:

"A State Immigration Board composed of Governor Marshall, Colonel Rogers, and Colonel Mattson was formed yesterday, when a general plan for its activities was also outlined. The Board intends to publish in the newspapers of both the Eastern states and Europe information regarding the State of Minnesota. It intends to conclude agreements with the railroad companies to provide immigrants with better accommodations than they have enjoyed heretofore; by the employment of interpreters and by other means it intends to supply them with reliable information regarding the best ways to reach Minnesota from the eastern ports, to give them an idea about the character of every place of importance in the state, and otherwise to render every possible aid within its means."

One of Mattson's first tasks as general manager was to succor the new settlers along the Minnesota River, who the year before had been afflicted with a severe drought. When that was done he was instructed to engage Swedish, Norwegian, and German agents and interpreters to meet "our" immigrants in New York and Quebec and then escort them to Minnesota. Information about jobs and land for sale was also to be provided. Next, he wrote, "agreements were made with newspapers in various languages to publish complete articles, composed by myself and others, regarding the state of Minnesota and its natural resources." Mattson himself also wrote promotion booklets, had them printed in Swedish, Norwegian, and German, and distributed at railroad stations, on ocean vessels, and within the countries in which the above languages were spoken. They were as correct and informative as possible, "And," wrote Mattson, "I have many times, when visiting well-to-do farmers on the western prairies, seen these booklets, carrying my name as author, carefully preserved on the bookshelf with the family Bible, the prayer book, the Lutheran catechism, and a few other souvenirs from the old fatherland."

While working for the state, Mattson also acted, he writes, as a land agent for a railroad passing through Wright, Meeker, Kandiyohi, Swift, and Stevens counties. And whereas when he first visited this region in 1867 only a few families had been scattered here and there, "it is now," he wrote in 1890, "a continuous Scandinavian agricultural district, extending over a hundred miles, dotted with villages and towns —all of which was accomplished, for the greater part, by the efforts of the State Immigration Board in 1867, 1868, and 1869." To attract more Swedish immigrants Colonel Mattson offered to procure free sites for churches, parsonages, and cemeteries.

Even after his first election as Secretary of State in 1869 Colonel Mattson was retained as a member of the State Board of Immigration, but his success as a promoter of new Swedish settlements also attracted the attention of private interests. In the fall of 1870 he received an invitation from Jay Cooke, the Philadelphia financier, who was then promoting the new Northern Pacific Railroad, to spend a week in his "palatial residence in Philadelphia." There he met a group of French and German bankers who were prospective investors in the new railroad. The upshot of the meeting was that Mattson was offered employment by Mr. Cooke at twice the salary he received as Secretary of State. As an agent for the Northern Pacific he was to work in Europe, using Sweden as a base. "My principal duty," he wrote, "was to disseminate in the northern countries knowledge about the natural resources of the Northwest and especially Minnesota. I was also instructed by Mr. Cooke to draw up a general plan for the utilization of the company's land, which I subsequently did, and this plan was then adopted for the guidance of the railroad's land and immigration officials and agents." In May 1871, he once more set out for Sweden, this time accompanied by his wife and children, but before leaving he organized a private banking agency, Mattson & Company, which was to continue his land and immigration business under the management of his partners. As agents for the Cunard Line, this agency originated the plan of selling prepaid tickets by which former immigrants were enabled to pay for the passage of relatives in Europe —a potent immigration stimulant.

Visiting old friends and relatives in Sweden, Mattson traveled all over the country. He also went to Norway, Finland, and Russia. As to the technique he used in spreading information about the natural resources of the American territories through which the new railroad was to pass, his book is silent, but when he returned to Minnesota, in the spring of 1873, he was again "accompanied by a large number of immigrants." After a couple of months, he went back to Sweden via Philadelphia, New York, and Quebec, but before his arrival the financial crash of 1873 had struck and his employer, Mr. Cooke, had been ruined. Mattson himself lost not only his position but once more all his property in Minnesota, as he had in 1857. On his way to Sweden he passed through Holland where he tried in vain to interest Dutch capitalists in investing more money in Minnesota railroads. When Mr. Cooke recovered his financial position, they regretted their caution. In Sweden Mattson took charge of a drainage project and also helped organize a scheme to colonize Manitoba which in time became the foundation of the first Icelandic settlement in the Northwest. In 1876 he returned to Minnesota to begin all over again, only to become a victim of the grasshopper plague. He then re-entered politics and in the fall of 1876 was chosen a Rutherford B. Hayes presidential elector. As a reward for his work in the next campaign (1880) President Garfield appointed him American Consul General in Calcutta. Ever since as a boy he had heard a missionary lecture by Reverend Peter Fjellstedt he had dreamed about India. After his return to Minnesota in 1883, he continued his real estate activities and in the fall of 1886 was once more elected Secretary of State and then re-elected in 1888. The Swedish population of the state, which had been only 3,178 in 1860, had gone up to 20,987 in 1870—a gain that was at least partly due to Mattson's work. By 1890, or only a few years before his death in 1893, he saw it rise to 99,918.

The last official action to bring in Swedish immigrants *en masse* to the United States was made in 1870 by the state of Maine under the direction of William Widgery Thomas, who later in life served for many years as the American Minister in Stockholm. Born in Portland, Maine, in 1839 and graduated in 1860 from Bowdoin College, Thomas had originally been sent to Sweden in 1863 by President Lincoln as one of the thirty special wartime consular agents whose duty it was to induce immigration by making known the offer of free land under the Homestead Act, passed in 1862. In Sweden he married a Swedish wife and learned the Swedish language. After his return to Maine in 1866 he practiced law in Portland and in 1870 was appointed State Commissioner of Immigration. His task was to bring in enough new settlers to stem the decline in population. In 1864 a private Maine corporation had signed up several hundred workers from Sweden, but none of them ever arrived in the state; along the route they had found better jobs elsewhere. In March 1869, the Maine Legislature decided on official action and Mr. Thomas, probably the only Swedish-speaking citizen of the state, was appointed head of the new Immigration Commission. The inducement he was to offer was free land in the very extreme northern forest area of the state, 100 acres of virgin forest land to each family. For nine years, sections of 165 acres each had been offered in vain to native-born settlers.

To obtain his immigrants Mr. Thomas went personally to Sweden and began an advertising campaign which resulted in enough applications to enable him to pick out twenty-two men, eleven women, and eighteen children as the first contingent. With these he sailed early in the summer of 1870 from Gothenburg to Halifax and then escorted the group by boats and horse teams to the wilderness of Aroostook County, the extreme northeastern corner of the United States. This was no fertile prairie ready for the plow, but rugged forest land which had to be cleared tree by tree and foot by foot. Each immigrant family had paid its own fare, lots were drawn for the land allotments, and the first winter wage-paying jobs were offered by the state in wood cutting and road building. A few log cabins had also been built in advance so that in this case there was no need to resort to either tents or dugouts. On the way a nine-year-old girl had died, but during the first year in the woods "there was not a day's sickness of man, woman, or child in New Sweden," Mr. Thomas was able to declare proudly on the tenth anniversary in July 1880. Turnips and winter grains were planted the first summer and fall, and after that the colony became self-sustaining. Before the end of 1870, 114 immigrants had arrived and, besides paying their own fares, they had brought in over $3,000 in cash. Three years later the number of inhabitants was six hundred and in ten years it reached 787. For the first four years, Mr. Thomas lived among them in a log cabin himself, to watch over "his children in the woods."

Being situated in the heart of the famous Aroostook potato district, the colony would undoubtedly have grown faster had there been more free land available, but instead of continuing its policy of colonization the state of Maine turned its forest land over to private lumber companies for exploitation, a policy of "squandering" that Mr. Thomas deeply deplored in his tenth anniversary address in 1880. "Had the state continued to own its land" he said, "Aroostook County alone would today number more than three thousand Swedes." But even so, the population of Maine has never ceased to grow after the Swedes began to arrive, which may be a pure coincidence. In 1910 the number of Maine residents born in Sweden reached an all-time high of 2,247, which twenty years later had gone down to 1,182—not an impressive figure compared with the Swedish-born population in some of the Midwestern states. While about sixty per cent of the former immigrants continued to live in Aroostook County, steadily more of the younger generations left to work in the more diversified industries in other parts of the state or elsewhere in the country. "Actually the sons of the farmers" wrote Professor Helge Nelson in 1943, "usually go to the cities and the New Sweden settlement has thus served as a distributing center for Swedish descendants to the industrial communities of New England." The newcomers in the Maine potato district are apt to be French Canadians, rather than Swedes. "Today New Sweden represents a farming district in stagnation," concluded the noted Swedish geographer. The high wartime price on potatoes brought better prosperity.

By 1900 the Swedish-born population in the United States as a whole had gone up from 3,567 in 1850 to 571,926, or over half a million. The highest peak was reached in 1910, when the number was 683,158. After that a recession set in. In 1930 their number was 594,333, still over half a million, but ten years later it had sunk to 445,070. Since for some years immigration had steadily declined, the figure proved the longevity of the average American born in Sweden. But since the average individual age had also gone up the future mortality rate was certain to be high. Population statistics also show that families of Swedish origin in the United States do not have as many children as, for instance, the Germans, the Norwegians or the Italians in the same areas. Neither do the families of the second generation have as many children, on the average, as their immigrant parents. Professor Nelson explains this by the greater tendency of the second generation to settle in cities. The corresponding phenomena have been observed in Sweden.

In recent years immigration from Sweden has dwindled to very low levels. During the First World War the number dropped to a few thousand annually; in 1918 the figure went as low as 2,298. After the war was over and Sweden suffered from a depression, while the United States enjoyed a boom, there was a revival. In 1924, for instance, the number of Swedish immigrants entering the United States reached a postwar maximum of 18,310. After that the quota law went into effect and then came the great depression. In 1933, when Sweden had recovered more than the United States, only 105 Swedes entered the country, and as late as 1935 only 160. From that time until the outbreak of the Second World War, Sweden enjoyed full employment with increasingly improved wages and social security benefits, and at no time since then has the Swedish immigration quota of 3,313 a year been even approximately filled.

Between the two wars Sweden began to suffer from a serious repopulation crisis itself and since the Second World War it has been a country of immigration rather than the contrary. A Gallup poll, taken in 1948, showed that next to the Americans, the Swedes were the least eager of any nationality to leave their own country—thirteen per cent as compared with four per cent in the United States. France came next with twenty-five per cent; Norway with twenty-eight per cent; Italy twenty-nine per cent, and Holland thirty-three per cent, while in England the percentage went as high as forty-two. As long as Sweden remains free and independent and is allowed to trade in the world at large, it is not likely to have any surplus population for export to any country. Nor, on the whole, is the Swedish element in the United States holding its own in quantity in proportion to inhabitants of other national origins. It is, however, improving in both quality and social status.

PART TWO

RELIGIOUS LIFE

===

VIII

THE SWEDISH BACKGROUND

Like the men of Athens, to quote St. Paul, the Swedes have always been deeply religious, ready to erect altars to new, and sometimes unknown, gods. Their oldest known records of mental life are crude picture-writings on flat ledges, known as *hällristningar,* or rock carvings. Though their date of origin is unknown, they are supposed to have been made during the Bronze Age, or about four thousand years ago, and archeologists believe they indicate a primitive form of sun worship or fertility cult. Later came the worship of the gods of Valhalla to whom the Vikings erected wooden temples. As early as A.D. 830 Christianity was preached in Sweden by a Frankish monk, St. Ansgarius, born near Amiens in Picardy, and in the eleventh century the country was gradually converted to the new faith by English as well as Continental missionaries. Early in the sixteenth century the Reformation of Martin Luther was adopted and to this day, to use the opening words of George M. Stephenson's scholarly volume, *The Religious Aspect of Swedish Immigration:* "Sweden is one of the most intensely Protestant countries in the world."

This attitude the Swedish emigrants carried with them across the Atlantic; among them the Roman Catholic Church has probably made fewer converts than in any other nationality group. On the other hand, they have not all remained Lutherans, but have become members of almost every kind of religious organization found in the United States. It has been said that the history of Sweden is the history of its kings; with equal justice it can be said that the history of the Swedes in America is the history of their churches. Politically, on the other hand, they have not been able to organize and least of all on a national scale. They have, therefore, never been a pressure group.

In Sweden, though the state church is still Lutheran, complete religious freedom now obtains. This was not the case a hundred years ago, when the large-scale emigration to the United States began. While the main cause for this exodus was economic, religious disaffection played a part, especially in the early days. It was, in fact, more potent than either political or social unrest.

Once they had left the country the Swedish emigrants were given little or no attention by the established church in Sweden. The first missionary work among them was done by the American Methodist Church in New York. Not until 1893, for instance, did a Swedish state-church bishop visit them. (In 1948, by contrast, the Archbishop of Uppsala himself attended the Swedish Pioneer Centennial in the Middle West.) Consequently, they were left free to join or organize whatever churches they preferred and this explains the religious anarchy that still prevails among them. In even the smallest of their communities it is not unusual to find two or three little churches of different denominations, each supported at considerable sacrifice.

For the spiritual welfare of the seventeenth century Swedish colonists on the lower Delaware, who had been sent there under semi-official auspices, the Swedish state church took greater responsibility. To them a number of already ordained, well-educated clergymen were sent. Not until after American independence had been won in 1789, was the jurisdiction over the "Old Swedes" churches on the Delaware turned over to the American Protestant Episcopal Church, which still exercises it. By contrast, few state clergymen could be spared for the newly formed little Swedish Lutheran congregations in the Middle West. Those who came were, as a rule, young dissidents, or pietistic zealots, who were considered a good riddance. The early Swedish churches in America of other denominations than the Lutheran never asked for ministers from Sweden since there were none. Rather did they send some of their own American-educated preachers to the mother country as missionaries.

This aloofness of the state church in the nineteenth century was due, partly, to its disapproval of emigration and, partly, to the religious unrest that had disturbed the country for several generations. While there had been no serious attempt at disestablishing the state church, into which every Swede is automatically born a member, the number of lay preachers and religious revivals had become steadily greater. (The Eric Janson revolt was only a minor one though it led to the only mass emigration.) In the United States and England, as well as in various continental countries, particularly Germany, similar disturbances had occurred even earlier, and to a great extent the Swedish "great revival" in the nineteenth century, which Professor Stephenson calls "the second reformation," was inspired by them.

The state church clergy, supported as they were by taxes, were freely criticized as being too formal, too remote from the common people, too ritualistic and, in many instances, too irregular in their own lives, especially as regards temperance, even if Selma Lagerlöf's drunken priest-hero, Gösta Berling, was an exception. Many of the early Lutheran ministers who came to the Middle West on their own initiative had often irritated the church authorities at home by giving lectures on temperance. Any such activity outside the church was regarded with suspicion. After the loss of Finland to Russia in 1809, a feeling of discouragement prevailed throughout Sweden, and all public officials, lay as well as clerical, were subject to attack. The time for moral and religious as well as national regeneration was at hand.

Gradually, the "Second Reformation" contributed much to this social and religious rehabilitation as well as to emigration to America. The temperance movement, directly inspired by that in the United States, led to the adult education movement and that, in turn, laid the groundwork for the political and social reforms that took place during the latter half of the nineteenth century and the first two decades of the twentieth. While a majority of the former Swedish emigrants in America have remained undeviating Republicans, their relatives in Sweden have built up a strong Social-Democratic Party, which, since the First World War, has become more and more powerful—a divergence in development that is explainable by the difference in economic circumstances as well as both social and political environment.

IX

THE METHODISTS

As related in a previous chapter, the first religious work among the nineteenth century Swedish immigrants was done in New York by the Reverend Olof Gustaf Hedström under the auspices of the American Methodist Episcopal Church. Having arrived on board a wooden Swedish warship in 1825, he had become converted to the Methodist faith and for some years served as an American Methodist circuit rider in the Catskills. Appointed head of the newly established Methodist Mission for Swedish immigrants on board the Bethel Ship tied to Pier 11 in the North River, he served from 1845 to 1875, except for a couple of years during the Civil War, when he visited Sweden to recover his health. Besides conducting frequent services in Swedish on board the floating chapel, he met the incoming immigrant ships from Sweden, offering his guidance to the newcomers in both spiritual and material matters. As the work grew in scope, he employed a succession of assistants whom he gradually trained to be Methodist ministers. Some had been sailors and others ministers in the Lutheran state church of Sweden.

On a visit to Sweden in 1833 to convert his own family to the Methodist faith, he had brought back with him his younger brother, Jonas J. Hedström, a blacksmith, whom he helped educate to become a Methodist class leader and exhorter. About five years later Jonas Hedström moved to western Illinois to marry an American girl of Dutch Colonial descent whom he had met in the Catskills while his brother served as a minister in that region. Her family had then moved west to take up new land. While continuing to earn his living as a blacksmith, Jonas Hedström was licensed as a part-time Methodist preacher. Usually he held his services evenings or week-ends, preaching in English. When his brother had been appointed head of the Bethel Ship mission in New York, he urged his brother in Illinois to brush up on his Swedish, as he himself had done, and prepare to serve his incoming countrymen after they arrived in Illinois, where fertile but undeveloped land was available at low prices. This he did and in a log cabin at Victoria, Illinois, he organized in December 1846, the first Swedish Methodist parish in the United States, and, except for the Bethel Ship mission and the Swedish colonial churches on the Delaware, which were older than the Republic, the first of any denomination.

To the new little communities formed by the immigrants he had befriended in New York, Olof Gustaf Hedström began to make visits, holding services and urging them to form permanent Methodist congregations. In June 1851 he made a trip to the new Swedish settlements at Sugar Grove and Chandler's Valley in northern Pennsylvania and the near-by Jamestown, New York, whose origin has been described in an earlier chapter. In the fall of the following year he was authorized by Bishop Waugh of the American Methodist Church to make a similar missionary journey to the Middle West. From his brother's home in Victoria he reported at New Year's, 1854, that he had been absent from New York sixty-one days and had preached fifty-nine times.

On his way west he once more visited the Swedes in northern Pennsylvania and western New York and at Jamestown he then organized the first Swedish Methodist church in that region. In Chicago he founded in the fall of 1852 the first congregation of the same order. To encourage the members in their faith, he made a second preaching tour to the Middle West in 1858.

To the Swedish immigrants who had settled in New England, Hedström made his first visit in the fall of 1853 when he preached to a group of them in a family kitchen in North Bridgewater, Massachusetts, now Brockton, the shoe city, and the next year he was sent as an official delegate to a Methodist missionary convention in Boston. He then preached to his countrymen at Lynn as well as in Boston and in both cities he formed societies that later became permanent congregations. He was the first Methodist minister they had ever heard and in his own words, he "awakened joy among many and consternation among many." Some of the latter, he recorded, planned to "initiate Lutheran worship." In those days all Methodist preachers were inclined to be more vehement than the Lutherans.

Besides Peter Bergner, the former Swedish Army officer and sailor, who had been his original sponsor at the Bethel Ship, Hedström's first assistant in New York was the Reverend Carl Petter Agrelius, who for about twenty years had been a curate in the Swedish state church, but who in 1848 arrived in Boston "with a large party," presumably as its spiritual guide. What became of the group is not known, but Agrelius himself continued to New York, where late in 1848 he joined Hedström after failing to organize a Lutheran congregation of his own. The next year he was sent west to assist Jonas J. Hedström in his work among the Swedes in Illinois and almost until his death in 1881 at the age of eighty-three, he continued as a Methodist preacher among the Norwegians and Danes as well as the Swedes in Minnesota and Wisconsin. Though a graduate of the University of Uppsala and well read, he was relatively ineffective as a public speaker and lacked executive ability. "Enthusiasm was the chief characteristic of Methodist preaching in those days," write the historians, Wallenius and Olson.

After the departure of Agrelius, Hedström engaged a succession of former sailors or immigrants as his aids. The first was a Norwegian by the name of O. P. Petersen, who later became the founder of Methodism in Norway as well as among the Norwegian immigrants in the United States. Similarly fruitful in the Middle West was the subsequent career of Sven B. Newman (Nyman) who had already been a Methodist preacher in the South, where he had arrived as early as in 1842. He came to Hedström in New York in 1851. Born in 1812 in Skåne, he had enjoyed a fair degree of education, and in Sweden he had been a schoolteacher as well as a storekeeper.

In 1854, Hedström received the help of another former curate of the Swedish state church, Jakob Bredberg, whose reasons for emigrating are not known. The following year he was sent to take charge of the church Hedström had founded at Jamestown, New York, and there he remained four years. After that he moved to Chicago to become pastor of the congregation Hedström had organized there. After a few years, during which he edited the first Methodist hymnal in Swedish, he became rector of the St. Ansgarius Protestant Episcopal Church in Chicago founded by Gustaf Unonius. From this post he retired in 1877 and a few years later he died.

Some of the young sailors influenced by Hedström in New York returned to Sweden to propagate the Methodist gospel there and on his own second visit in 1863 he was much more cordially received than he had been thirty years earlier. He was even invited to speak from the pulpit of some of the Lutheran state churches; in the meantime the Second Reformation had been accepted and in 1873 religious liberty was established by permitting dissenters to organize their own churches.

In the Middle West many of the early Swedish Methodist ministers
had been associated in some form or other with the Bishop Hill colony.
Disillusioned by the autocratic and communistic regime of Eric Janson,
they had preferred the Methodism of Jonas J. Hedström, whose work
at Victoria antedated the colony. Among these men were John Brown,
Peter Newberg (Nyberg), Peter Challman (Källman), while Erik
Shogren (Sjögren) was trained by the Hedström brothers in both
New York and Illinois. All were prominent Methodist pioneers among
the Swedes in the Middle West. John Brown, whose name must have
been assumed, was born a Dane, and his real mother tongue was German. Whether he preached in Swedish, Danish, or English, he did it
with a strong German accent. How he had joined the Bishop Hill
colony is not known, but he soon left and under Jonas Hedström's
tutelage became a Methodist. Unlike Agrelius he was a "lively revivalist," who "when he got specially warmed up both by his text
and the summer heat on the prairies, he would throw off his coat and
neckwear, and sometimes his vest, and then go on preaching with
a vim that was overpowering," write the two above-mentioned historians.

In marked contrast to these picturesque and usually self-educated
pioneers were two Swedish intellectuals who came from higher social
stations in Sweden, Victor Witting and William Henschen. Before
becoming Methodist preachers and educators, both had had varied
and romantic careers.

Victor Witting was born in Malmö, in southern Sweden, in 1825,
his father being a Swedish artillery captain and war veteran of Finnish
origin, and his mother the daughter of the city's postmaster. His early
education had been of the best; he was also a voracious reader. In particular, he had early become interested in America from reading
the novels of James Fenimore Cooper. His interest became heightened
when in 1841 he read about the departure of Gustaf Unonius who,
like his father, had been born in Finland. Some day he resolved he
would try the same adventure. He was then sixteen and employed in a
Malmö drug store, an occupation he found prosaic and tedious.

Two years later as a first step toward realizing his ambition he went
to sea as an ordinary sailor, but at the same time he studied navigation and soon had his master's certificate. America was his goal
and in 1846 when the schooner *Ceres* was to leave Söderhamn with
a cargo of iron and the first contingent of Eric Janson's followers on
board as passengers, he signed on as a crew member. On the same
ship Peter Nyberg, whom he had already met on a trip to England

and who like him was destined to play an important role as a Methodist preacher in America, had signed on as the ship's carpenter. The first night out the *Ceres* was wrecked in a violent storm, but by being lodged between two ledges near shore was kept from sinking and all on board were saved. The fortitude shown that night by the Eric Jansonists so impressed both Witting and Newberg that they became converted themselves.

The following year, after having served as a mate, Witting had another chance to accompany another group of the same persuasion, but this time to get on board he had to sign as a steward. He became so popular among the passengers that when they arrived in New York they persuaded him to accompany them to Bishop Hill with his passage paid by them. In Chicago he fell ill with the cholera and when he recovered he worked for a year in a Chicago drug store. In 1848 he finally reached Bishop Hill with a third contingent of the Janson pilgrims and that summer, when the prophet had lifted the ban against matrimony, he was married in one of the mass ceremonies in the community church to one of the colony members whom he presumably had met the year before while crossing the Atlantic.

He soon became disillusioned with the communistic-religious regime of Eric Janson and in 1849 he withdrew with his wife to near-by Galesburg, Illinois, where he once more became a druggist. Next he was struck by the California gold fever and in 1850 with eleven other young Swedes, most of them former sailors, including his old friend Peter Newberg, as well as Peter Challman, and Eric Shogren—all four future Swedish Methodist ministers—he set out over the Santa Fe trail. By April 1852 most of the members of the party were back in Illinois, wiser if poorer. They had saved enough money, however, to come back by boat via Panama.

Being once more destitute and with a wife to support, Witting tried to cultivate medical herbs at Victoria, Illinois, the home of Jonas J. Hedström, with Eric Shogren, his former fellow gold seeker, as an assistant. His experience as a druggist ought to assure success, he thought. To sell his herbs he made a trip in 1854 to New York, but the prices he was able to obtain were so low that he became convinced that he had scored another failure. Discouraged, he once more sought out Olof Gustaf Hedström whom he had met at the Bethel Ship when he first arrived from Sweden and whose brother he had known in Victoria, and by him he was then definitely converted to Methodism. Once back in Illinois he again reverted to his trade as a druggist, this time at Peoria, where other Swedes had begun to settle. Among them he organized, first, a Methodist Sunday school and then prayer meetings. His ability as a speaker at the latter attracted the attention of Henry Sumner, a local Methodist elder, and he persuaded him to become a full-time preacher. After being ordained he was placed, in 1855, in charge of the Swedish Methodist church, dating from 1854, at Andover, Illinois, where, in 1850, the Reverend Lars Paul Esbjörn had organized the first Swedish Lutheran congregation. Four years later he was transferred to Rockford, Illinois, and there in 1862 he began to publish *Sändebudet,* the first Swedish Methodist denominational weekly, now the oldest Swedish periodical in America that is still published. Witting had a special gift for translating the stirring Wesleyan hymns from English into Swedish and to this day wherever Swedish Methodists gather anywhere in the world they sing these hymns in his words.

Being himself an educated man, Witting understood better than a majority of his colleagues the importance of having specially trained men as ministers. In his addresses as well as in his editorials in *Sändebudet,* he began to urge the need for a Swedish Methodist theological training school and in 1866 he was designated to collect funds for such a purpose. The very next year, however, he was sent to Sweden to take charge of the new Methodist school for the training of missionaries. He also helped organize the first Swedish Conference in 1876. The next year he was back in the United States and until his death in 1906 at the age of eighty-one in Quincy, Massachusetts, he continued his preaching and his editorial work both in the Middle West and New England. His memoirs, *Sailor, Emigrant, and Missionary,* were published in 1902 at Worcester, Massachusetts.

An even better educated Swede who for many years bore the main burden of educational work among the Swedish Methodists in America was the Reverend William Henschen, who was born in 1842 at the old university town of Uppsala. In many respects his career resembled that of Gustaf Unonius. His father, like the elder Unonius, was a lawyer, and in time he became not only a noted judge, but also a member of the Swedish Riksdag. His mother had been born a member of an old noble family, Munck af Rosenschiöld, one of the more distinguished in Sweden. His early education had been provided in his own home at Uppsala by private tutors and so rapid was his progress that at the age of sixteen, or three years earlier than the average, he was ready to enter the university. He then spoke Latin and several modern languages. In 1862, when he was but twenty years old, he had finished his work for his Ph.D. degree which was awarded the next year. Despite his training as a linguist he then decided, like Unonius, to become a physician, and, first at Uppsala and then at a German university, he studied medicine. But, again like Unonius, he never practiced. The preparation period he found too long and like his prototype he had fallen in love and decided to get married. This he did in June 1868, his bride being the beautiful and euphoniously named, Hilda Johanna Maria Liljebjörn, daughter of a Swedish army captain. Ultimately she bore him eleven children, six of whom survived both parents. To support himself as well as his growing family, the twenty-six-year-old Henschen then became a language teacher at junior colleges or *läroverk,* first at Lund and then at Hälsingborg, in southern Sweden. Small-town life he found, as Unonius had done at Uppsala thirty years before, unbearably dull, and to break the tedium and make money for his wife and child he decided to emigrate to America. In 1863 Unonius had published the second volume of his American memoirs beginning with pioneering in Wisconsin, and taking warning from his descriptions of the northern winter climate, Henschen decided to settle in Florida where he had read that as early as the sixteenth century Ponce de Leon and his Spaniards had hoped to find the Fountain of Youth. The Civil War was then over and a new South emerging. Together with a few congenial friends, as Unonius had done in 1841, Henschen set out in 1869, but left behind him his wife and newly born daughter, promising to send for them as soon as he had become established.

Near Sanford, in central Florida, Henschen and his friends took up claims under the Homestead Act and began to plant orange trees, then a relatively new enterprise. The settlement they called, as Unonius and his friends had done in Wisconsin, New Uppsala, for their university town in Sweden. But orange trees take time to bear fruit, and in the meantime the Swedish immigrants, though well educated, had to earn their living as carpenters, blacksmiths, shoe cobblers or tailors, or at whatever jobs they could find.

Within a year, or as soon as he had built his first shack, Henschen sent for his family, but he soon decided that being an orange planter was not as romantic or as rewarding as he had hoped. Tropical diseases were then more prevalent in Florida than they are now, and fearing for the health of his children, he pulled up stakes and moved to Brooklyn, New York, just as Unonius had given up farm life at Pine Lake in Wisconsin and had moved to Chicago in 1849 to serve as an Episcopal minister. At that time Henschen had not had any theological education and for two years he supported himself and his growing family by editing *Nordstjernan* (*The North Star*), a newly started Swedish language weekly, of which George P. Johansen is now the publisher and Edgar Swenson the editor.

In the course of his newspaper work he became acquainted with Albert Ericson, the young pastor of the Immanuel Swedish Methodist Episcopal Church on Dean Street in Brooklyn, which was a direct outgrowth of Hedström's Bethel Ship mission on the North River, and the oldest Swedish church of any denomination in the city. Born in Stockholm, the son of the rector of the rather fashionable Katarina Church, Ericson had also received a good education, but in 1857 at the age of seventeen, he had decided to emigrate to America. His first year he had spent at the Bishop Hill colony, about which he had read in the Swedish press, but which was then, because of the 1857 panic and general depression in America, in a state of financial difficulties. Moving to Andover, Illinois, where Witting had become the pastor in 1855, Ericson joined the Swedish Methodist Church and because of his natural ability as a speaker and his command of Swedish, he was soon ordained a minister. At the age of twenty-four he was made editor of *Sändebudet,* the weekly founded in 1862 by Witting.

Through Ericson's influence, Henschen decided in 1874 to join the Brooklyn church, and one summer while Ericson was in Sweden on a vacation he substituted for him in the pulpit. His learning and eloquence soon attracted attention and the following year he was appointed not only editor of *Sändebudet,* then published in Chicago, but also Professor of Swedish at the newly founded Swedish Methodist theological seminary which Witting had planned. At first he was virtually the only teacher and had to give almost all the courses. By 1883 he had had enough of this work and decided to accept a call as pastor of the Swedish Methodist church at Jamestown, New York, which Hedström had founded in 1852. But even there he resumed his journalism, editing a local Swedish newspaper called *Folkets Röst* (*The People's Voice*). The double task broke down his health. To recuperate he returned to Florida, where his brother and other former fellow colonists had by then gained secure positions as orange growers. Once more the sunshine worked its magic and in 1885 Henschen was able to return to Sweden to succeed Witting as head of the Methodist seminary for the training of preachers. It had been established in 1873 at Örebro, in central Sweden, but in 1883 it had been moved to Uppsala.

In Sweden, Henschen edited Methodist publications, while he also taught and preached and in general helped build up the young denomination. But after twenty years in the United States he had become too Americanized to remain in Sweden. No longer could he feel at home in Uppsala. In 1889 he returned to Chicago where for twenty-two years he continued his work as editor of *Sändebudet,* preacher, and teacher at the Swedish Methodist seminary at Evanston, Illinois. (From 1898 to 1902 he was pastor at Galva, Illinois.) As might be expected from such a classicist, his editorials were models of simplicity and clarity. As an educator he had an influence on his denomination that was outstanding. In 1913 he became the first Swedish American to receive an Honorary Doctor's degree from the university at Uppsala. After retiring in 1911, he lived at Chesterton, Indiana, and in 1925, at the age of eighty-two, he died in Chicago in the home of his son, Henry S. Henschen, then a banker and Swedish Vice Consul. Unlike Unonius and Witting, he never wrote his memoirs. Professor Stephenson thinks a full-length biography is in order.

For some years the theological training school organized by the Swedish Methodists in the United States led an ambulatory existence until, in 1881, when it was invited to Evanston, Illinois, as a long-term tenant of Northwestern University. In 1883 the Reverend Albert Ericson was appointed President and Professor as a successor to Henschen, and for twenty-five years he remained at the head of the school. Another able teacher for about forty years after 1889 was the late Reverend C. G. Wallenius, who died in 1947.

As the Swedish Methodists were the first in the field in the United States, so they were the first to become wholly merged with their American parent organization. As soon as a majority of their members spoke English more readily than Swedish, there was no longer any need, it was judged, for a separate organization. In 1942 the last conference of the Swedish division was absorbed by the English-speaking body of the same area. As late as 1930 there had been, however, about two hundred and fifty Swedish Methodist congregations in the country, served by over two hundred clergymen. The approximate membership was twenty thousand. The two hundred and thirty churches and the various charitable institutions founded and built up by the Swedish Methodists in the course of a century were then valued at nearly $5,000,000. The publishing house and the ministerial training school at Chicago have also been taken over by the mother church, but *Sändebudet* is still published in both languages.

In Sweden, the Methodist Church had in 1946 a membership of 12,666, likewise not an impressive figure, but the theological seminary and the denominational publishing business are still maintained. The work in Sweden as well as in several adjoining countries, is under the personal supervision of a Swedish-born bishop, Theodore Arvidson, whose seat is in Stockholm. Step by step, more and more official recognition, such as the right to perform marriages, has been granted by the Swedish authorities to Methodist clergymen.

X

THE EPISCOPALIANS

Almost simultaneously with the first American Methodist missionary work in behalf of the incoming Swedish immigrants in New York, a similar step was taken by the American Protestant Episcopal Church in the Middle West. It was done through Gustaf Unonius, who had arrived in Wisconsin in 1841. Since there was not at that time any nationally organized Lutheran denomination in the United States and the jurisdiction over the original "Old Swedes" churches on the Delaware had been turned over fifty years earlier to the American Episcopal Church, this seemed a logical move. In its form of government the Lutheran state church of Sweden had likewise maintained the episcopal system and had retained unbroken the apostolic succession, though on that point less emphasis has always been laid in Sweden than in England. In doctrine, too, the Espiscopalians were the closest to the Lutherans.

At least so argued the Reverend J. Lloyd Breck, an Episcopal missionary in Wisconsin when he called on the newly established little Swedish colony at Pine Lake, about thirty miles west of Milwaukee, and so he persuaded Gustaf Unonius and his friends. While none of them had so far shown any special interest in denominational matters, beyond the routine observances required by the state church in Sweden, they were not averse, in their new situation on the open frontier, to participating in the informal talks of their clerical visitor. He was probably the first educated man they had met and, conversely, he must have been intrigued by the high degree of culture shown by the newly arrived group. They became his close friends.

For the young Swedes and a few Norwegian pioneers who had previously settled in the neighborhood, the Reverend Mr. Breck began to hold church services and in the administration of Holy Communion Gustaf Unonius assisted him with a translation of the ritual.

The next summer when, in response to Unonius' letters in the Swedish press, more Swedes had arrived at Pine Lake, he agreed with the Episcopal Church authorities that something should be done for their spiritual welfare. "I thought it more than doubtful," he wrote in his memoirs, "that ministers from Sweden would ever come." Since he was ill prepared to earn his living and that of his family as a frontier farmer, but had a good university education in both medicine and law, he was readily enough persuaded in 1843 by his friend, the Reverend Mr. Breck, and other Episcopal clergymen in the neighborhood to enter their near-by seminary at Nashotah and there prepare himself for the ministry in the American Protestant Episcopal Church. In 1845 he was ordained and after serving for a few months as a missionary in the state he was given that same year his first charge at Manitowoc. In taking this step, Unonius did not feel he was deserting the church of Sweden, even though the Swedish Archbishop, Carl Fredrik af Wingård, whom he consulted, had warned him to the contrary.

In 1848 Unonius was invited to visit his friends Mr. and Mrs. Polycarpus von Schneidau in Chicago, whom he had received hospitably when they arrived at Pine Lake as a newlywed, runaway couple from Sweden in 1843. In Chicago they had become well established by 1848, and by that time the main Swedish immigrant stream had begun to pour through the city. Many were poor and bewildered; outbreaks of cholera and other epidemics were frequent. His hosts and their well-to-do Chicago friends had done what they could, but the need of a clerical adviser who spoke their own language was only too evident, as it had been in New York a few years earlier. There was not then a single Swedish clergyman in the city. The pioneer Lutheran pastor, Lars Paul Esbjörn, did not arrive until 1849, and then settled in Andover.

Here was a real opportunity for Christian service, thought Unonius, and the following year he obtained his transfer from Wisconsin to the Chicago district and on March 5, 1849, in the home of the Von Schneidaus the first Scandinavian congregation of the American Protestant Episcopal Church was organized. There were thirty-four charter members, including some Norwegians. In honor of the first Christian missionary to the North, it was called the *St. Ansgarius*. In order to be admitted Mrs. Von Schneidau, who until then had adhered to her ancestral Jewish faith, was baptized and confirmed.

At once Unonius began to collect funds for a church building. In this he was hampered, writes Professor Stephenson, by the fact that the year before Chicago had been visited by a certain "Gustaf Smith" who claimed to be a Swedish Lutheran clergyman, but who after collecting

about $600 for church building, had absconded from the city. Remember-
ing that the "Old Swedes" churches on the Delaware had been taken
over by the American Protestant Episcopal Church in 1789, Unonious
and his friend Von Schneidau, the former Swedish army officer, made
a trip east to appeal for aid in building a new Swedish Episcopal church
in Chicago. In this they were at least partially successful and with about
$4,000 contributed from all sources, they started a church building at
the corner of Franklin and Indiana streets in Chicago. It was the first
Scandinavian church in a city which now has over a hundred.

When the funds ran too low for its completion, Unonius and Von
Schneidau once more went east, this time to appeal to Jenny Lind, the
singer, who under the management of P. T. Barnum, had made her
sensational American debut in New York in the fall of 1850. Her contributions to charities had been widely heralded by her astute manager
and to the appeals of former countrymen, particularly the men of the
cloth, she was especially responsive, regardless of their denominational
affiliations. To Olof Gustaf Hedström's American Methodist mission at
the Bethel Ship, she had already contributed $475. For Von Schneidau
who was then a successful daguerreotype photographer, she posed for
her picture, which turned out very well, and to Unonious she gave
$1,500 for the completion of his church. With this sum not only the
church but an adjoining parsonage was finished. Later Miss Lind gave
an additional $1,000 for a silver communion service and though the
church was destroyed in the great Chicago fire of October 7, 1871, the
communion service was saved and is still in use. A new church building
was completed for the early Christmas morning service in 1872, only a
little more than a year later.

Though Unonius, who was an able and energetic man, traveled about
and preached persistently in the new Swedish communities in the Middle
West, he was not able to form any more parishes of what he termed
"The National Church of Sweden." His Chicago church reached its peak
in membership in his time with 195 in 1852, writes Professor Stephenson. By that time not only Esbjörn but a few other young ministers
ordained in the Lutheran state church in Sweden had arrived in the
Middle West and to their appeals to their countrymen to adhere to the
Evangelical Lutheran faith of their ancestors, most of the newly arrived
immigrants responded better than to Unonius' pleas for a church of
which most of them had never heard. To the finer points of doctrine
they were largely indifferent or at least unresponsive. Whatever may
have been their attitude toward the Swedish state church before they

left, they felt a special, inner pull at the mention of the word Lutheran.

Disappointed, Unonius returned to Sweden in 1858 and there failed to be admitted to the state church as a clergyman. Had he remained in the United States, he would surely have had a useful or even brilliant career. Instead, he wrote his memoirs which are a lasting memorial to his life.

After Unonius had left, the work was carried on by a number of less able men, and ultimately half a dozen Swedish Episcopal congregations were founded in such places as Minneapolis and St. Paul in Minnesota and Galesburg and Englewood in Illinois. Others were formed in New York, Providence and Boston. Some of them still exist, but they never have had any large memberships, and being affiliated with their American Episcopal mother church in their respective dioceses, they never had any need of a national, denominational organization of their own.

For several decades after the departure of Unonius, sporadic attempts were made by various Episcopal authorities, such as Bishop Henry Benjamin Whipple of Minnesota, (elected in 1859) to affiliate the young Swedish Lutheran churches with their own, but without success. "The claim that the American Protestant Episcopal Church was much like the Lutheran state church of Sweden," writes Professor Stephenson, "found little response among the early Swedish immigrants, at least some of whom had left their native country because they felt hampered in their religious life by that very church."

In 1866 Bishop Henry John Whitehouse of Illinois visited Sweden itself for the purpose of knitting more closely the bonds between his own church and the Swedish Lutherans in America, but he was able to obtain only an official ruling according to which departing emigrants were to be advised that if there was not already a Swedish Lutheran church in the community in which they settled, they should join the American Protestant Episcopal in preference to any other. But even that guarded recommendation was protested by the clergymen of the Augustana Swedish Lutheran church as unfair. It was then dropped.

When the language handicap had been overcome, a considerable number of former Swedish immigrants have individually joined the Protestant Episcopal Church, especially in communities in which their children had been baptized, trained in the Sunday schools, and confirmed by clergymen of that denomination. The plan to organize special Episcopal churches for the Swedes in America was only a temporary step, but even so it cannot be said to have been a success, logical as it seemed at first to Gustaf Unonius and his friends.

XI

The Lutherans

Under the banner of the Augustana Synod, the largest organization of former Swedish immigrants and their descendants in America, whether religious or secular, the Lutherans have so far preserved both their identity and their autonomy better than either the Methodists or the Episcopalians. When they arrived in the United States there were neither missionaries of their own faith to receive them, nor a general Lutheran denomination to help them organize churches in their new settlements, and since like all other Swedish immigrants they were left strictly alone by the state church in Sweden, they had to shift pretty much for themselves, which made them independent and self-reliant.

On the other hand, they had certain important advantages: Since they stemmed directly from the established Lutheran Church of their own country, they could draw from this body not only members who already regarded themselves as Lutherans, but also a certain number of well-educated and in most instances unusually competent ministers—whereas other denominations had both to win converts and to educate their clergymen.

At first they made attempts to affiliate with their co-religionists of other national origins, as, for instance, in the Synod of Northern Illinois in 1851, but such attempts stranded on two obstacles: doctrinal and national. As Lutherans the Swedes were fervent supporters of the Augsburg Confession, the basic doctrinal charter, and in that respect they felt more orthodox than their neighbors whether of German or older American origin. Politically, they had no interest in German nationalism and on similar grounds were wrecked their attempts to merge with the Norwegians with whom they had at least shared a common king.

The pioneer Swedish Lutheran pastor in the Middle West was the Reverend Lars Paul Esbjörn, who arrived in New York on September 6, 1849, as the spiritual guide of a group of immigrants from northern Sweden, where he himself had been born. Like the ship that had brought the Unonius party eight years earlier, it had sailed from the port of Gäfle with a cargo of Swedish iron. Esbjörn was then forty-one years old and since 1831 he had been a minister in the Swedish state church. Besides his spiritual charges, numbering 147 souls, he was accompanied by his wife, the gently born Amalia Planting-Gyllenbåga, and five minor children. A sixth had died on board and another succumbed at Detroit.

His fellow passengers were religious dissenters or *läsare* from the province of Hälsingland from which a majority of the followers of Eric Janson had come some three years earlier. The members of the new group were, however, ardent Lutherans, who had rebelled against the lack of spiritual fervor in the established church. Coming from the same district as most of the adherents of Eric Janson, they had undoubtedly been influenced in their decision to emigrate by the "America letters" of the latter as well as by those of other Swedish settlers in Illinois towns like Andover, Galesburg, Princeton, Victoria, and Moline. All such letters had told the same story of complete religious liberty and rich, if undeveloped, land at prices ranging from $1.25 to $2.00 an acre. Like the Bishop Hill colonists, they had undertaken their trip in a body, but without any kind of economic communism. For their spiritual comfort they had invited the Reverend Mr. Esbjörn to be their guide.

Though a minister in the state church, Esbjörn had become known as a pietistic or *läsare* preacher. Part of his expenses were defrayed by the Mission Society of Stockholm.

He had been born in 1808 in the parish of Delsbo, known for the vigor and occasional excesses of its inhabitants. His father was a country tailor, Esbjörn Paulsson, whose first name he had adopted as his last. (As a volunteer in the Civil War, one of his own sons, in turn, was to change it to Osborne.) At the age of seven Esbjörn had become an orphan, but even then he had shown such signs of unusual intelligence that a former woman servant in his family had determined to have him educated for the ministry. At the cost of heroic sacrifices, both by herself and him, her purpose was achieved though his real bent was in the direction of mathematics and the natural sciences. He was offered a post in the army engineering corps, but took a degree in theology at the University of Uppsala in 1831 and was immediately ordained in the Uppsala Cathedral. His first post was that of curate in the parish of Öster-Våhla, near Uppsala, to which he was to return as rector in 1863 after thirteen years of teaching and preaching in the United States. There he died in 1870 at the age of sixty-two.

From 1835 until his emigration in 1849 he was the chaplain of an industrial plant at Oslättsfors in the province of Gästrikland, which adjoins Hälsingland. There he married Miss Planting-Gyllenbåga. To support her and their increasing number of children, he also taught school at the near-by town of Hille. For a man of his ability and intelligence this was a slower rate of promotion than he had a right to expect. Repeatedly he failed to be elected to better paid posts. His recent Swedish biographer, the Reverend Sam Rönnegård, thinks it was his anti-liquor stand rather than his revivalism which offended the church electorate, dominated as it often was by big property owners who enjoyed plural votes. When the Reverend George Scott, the British Methodist, and the Reverend Robert Baird, the American Presbyterian, spoke at a giant temperance and evangelistic mass meeting in the city of Hudiksvall during their revivalist tour of Sweden in 1840, Esbjörn served as its general secretary, another sign of independence, if not unorthodoxy.

When his party arrived in New York in the fall of 1849 no definite place of settlement had been selected, but before disembarking it was approached by land agents from Illinois. Among them was Captain P. W. Wirström who represented the New England owners of much undeveloped land in Illinois. From them stemmed such typical New England place names as Andover and Cambridge. Wirström had by that time been married to a former member of the Bishop Hill colony and he and his wife were living in Andover. To induce the newcomers to buy land in his town, he offered them, free of charge, a ten-acre lot as the site of a future church. That scored, and for Andover a majority of them and their pastor set out.

Before leaving New York, Esbjörn called on Olof Gustaf Hedström, the Methodist pastor of the Bethel Ship mission in the North River, and by him he was given the opportunity to preach twice before his own countrymen, as well as to give a lecture on temperance. The chance of being supported in his work among the newly arrived Swedes in the Middle West by the American Methodist Church was also held out to him, but as that would involve adhesion to that denomination, he declined, hard pressed for funds as he was. He also called on the Reverend Robert Baird, the Presbyterian, and by him he was advised to apply to the American Board of Home Missions in Boston, a Congregationalist and Presbyterian body, for temporary support. This he did, only to be refused because he did not represent any recognized American church body. Otherwise the denominational lines were not drawn so tight in those days as later.

When he arrived at Andover, Illinois, in the fall of 1849 with his frail wife and four children, he was unquestionably in difficult financial circumstances. By that time several of the earliest Swedish settlers in the neighborhood had been induced by Jonas Hedström, a brother of Olof Gustaf Hedström in New York, to move to his own town of Victoria, where in 1846 he had organized the first Swedish Methodist church in the Middle West. Esbjörn was able, nevertheless, to form on March 18, 1850, the first Swedish Lutheran congregation, consisting of ten members, including his wife and himself. Five days later thirty new members were enrolled and the average attendance during the ensuing year varied between fifty and seventy.

In 1848, or two years earlier, Swedish Lutheran services had been begun at New Sweden, Iowa, by Magnus F. Hokanson, a lay reader, who later was ordained, but since no congregation was organized and no records kept, the church at Andover has a certain priority as the first Swedish Lutheran congregation in the Middle West.

Like the Hedström brothers in New York and Illinois and Unonius in and about Chicago, Esbjörn next visited the budding Swedish communities in the vicinity, urging them to form Lutheran congregations. In Galesburg, the birthplace of Carl Sandburg, he met President Blanchard of Knox College and through his intervention was able to get, after all, a grant of $300 from the American Home Missionary Society in Boston and without any denominational stipulations. "I have preached here [at Andover]," he reported to this Society in 1851, "and at Galesburg and sometimes at Henderson, Berlin, Rock Island and Moline. A small church will soon be organized at Henderson and branches of our Andover church have been established at Berlin and Moline." At Andover, he further reported, he had helped organize among the Swedes a society to promote temperance—a cause ever close to his heart.

To collect funds for new church buildings, he made a trip east in 1851—as the Episcopalians, Unonius and Von Schneidau, had done the year before. In Boston, he was able to make a personal appeal to Jenny Lind, the opera star, and from her he obtained $1,500, matching the sum she had already donated to the new Swedish Episcopal church in Chicago. During his eleven-week trip he collected altogether $2,200 which was to be divided between Andover and Moline with a few hundred dollars left for New Sweden, Iowa. With its share of this money and contributions from Swedish pioneer farmers in the neighborhood, the first Swedish Lutheran church was then built at Andover. At the Swedish Lutheran Centennial celebration in 1948 it was officially renamed The Jenny Lind Chapel. Near by, another much larger church had long since been erected.

In 1851 the newly organized Swedish Lutheran congregations joined with American, German and Norwegian Lutherans in forming The Evangelical Lutheran Synod of Northern Illinois, the organization meeting being held September 18 at Cedarville, near Freeport. From the outset it was rent by doctrinal disputes regarding the validity of the Augsburg Confession, which the new Synod finally held, officially, to be only "mainly correct." With this qualification, the Scandinavian members were never satisfied and in 1860, on the eve of the Civil War, they withdrew, and on June 5 that year they formed at Jefferson Prairie, Wisconsin, a new synod of their own, which they called *Augustana,* the Latin word for the Augsburg Confession, which was accepted without reservations. The charter adherents were thirty-six Swedish congregations with 3,747 communicants, and thirteen Norwegian with 1,220. In 1869 the Norwegians withdrew and formed a synod of their own.

The first President of the new Augustana Synod was not, however, Esbjörn, but the eight years younger, Reverend Tuve Nilsson Hasselquist, who in 1852, at the age of thirty-six, had arrived from Skåne in southern Sweden to become pastor of the new church Esbjörn had founded the year before at Galesburg, Illinois. He had been recommended to the post by his nephew, a young farm hand by the name of Ola Nilsson from Önnestad, who with other farm youths had arrived at Galesburg in 1851. Hasselquist had been born in 1816 at Hasslaröd in the same province and from that place he had derived his name which was to loom so large in the annals of Swedish American Lutherans. After graduating from the junior college at Kristianstad, he had received his university training at Lund, of which he was probably the first graduate to emigrate. Like Esbjörn he earned his passage across the Atlantic by acting as pastor for a group of about sixty emigrants.

In Sweden he had served five different parishes as a curate but, again like Esbjörn, he had committed the indiscretion of giving lectures outside the church on temperance. Just before starting for America he had married the talented Eva Cervin, who, like her husband, had musical tastes. (Their home in Galesburg was supposed to be the first Swedish house in the United States to have a piano.) He was also a good writer; in Galesburg he founded *Hemlandet,* the first Swedish-language newspaper of any kind in America. He was likewise a popular preacher and a good singer. Before leaving Sweden he had taken the precaution to obtain a guarantee that his service in America would be credited to his record should he decide to return. As a matter of fact, he found life in the virgin country of the Middle West so engrossing that he remained until his death in 1891 at the age of seventy-five. For thirty years he dominated the Augustana Synod.

Hasselquist was favored by a robust constitution, abounding physical energy and a certain *bonhomie* which suited the temperament of his pioneer parishioners. While he could be formal, he was not overawed by vestments nor did he depend on them for effect. When after the Civil War more and more Swedish immigrants settled throughout the upper Mississippi Valley, he sometimes had to travel long distances to reach them, whether on horseback or on foot, sleeping in farm houses, log cabins, sod houses and even in the haystacks in the open fields. When he first became President of Augustana College at Paxton, Illinois, he taught not only theology, but fifteen other subjects, edited *Augustana,* the denominational weekly, and, furthermore preached regularly as a parish minister in the town. If Esbjörn had planted the seed of Swedish Lutheranism in the Middle West, Hasselquist tended it indefatigably.

In January 1853, after a stagecoach ride on primitive roads across the state of Illinois, from Moline to Chicago, Hasselquist helped organize in the latter city, its first Swedish Lutheran church, of which there are now over forty. The new church, named the Immanuel, invited as its first pastor another graduate of Lund University, the Reverend Erland Carlsson, who was destined to be one of Augustana's "Founding Fathers." Born at Elghult in southern Småland, he had been ordained in 1849 in the cathedral at Växjö, one of the episcopal seats of the province. After that he had four years of pastoral experience in his native district, including Lessebo, the oldest paper mill in Sweden. Like his two predecessors he had, however, indulged in giving temperance lectures which earned him the disfavor of the consistory at Växjö. For the Chicago church he had been recommended, moreover, not by the bishop of his diocese, but by Peter Wieselgren, a spiritually awakened minister of the state church, who was the organizer of the first Swedish Temperance Society, and Peter Fjellstedt, another leader of the growing evangelistic wing of the state church. Like both Esbjörn and Hasselquist, Carlsson earned his passage across the Atlantic by acting as religious counsellor to a group of about 175 emigrants who, on June 4, 1853, left Kalmar, on Småland's east coast, for New York

on board the Swedish ship *Gauthiod*. Like Hasselquist he had obtained
formal leave of absence, with guarantee of service credit for his work
in America and for six years instead of three, but he too never returned to Sweden. As pastor of the Immanuel Church in Chicago
he remained for almost twenty-two critical years. To the constantly
larger stream of Swedish immigrants, passing through or settling in
the city, he was ever a friend and counsellor, his Chicago home being
popularly known as a "miniature Castle Garden."

He was especially active during the cholera epidemics which frequently ravaged the tired and hungry immigrants. In 1884 he helped
found Chicago's Augustana Hospital, now one of the most important
in the city. At first the patients were cared for in his own house, which
he later sold, with a fairly large lot, to the Illinois Conference of his
church as a hospital site. Being a native of Småland, he was endowed
with a certain amount of business acumen, rare among clergymen of
any denomination, and for nine years he was manager of the Swedish
Lutheran Publishing Society, whose offices were fitted into the basement of his church. In 1875 he was transferred to less onerous duties
as pastor of the original Swedish Lutheran church at Andover, Illinois,
and while preaching there he likewise served as manager of the local
Swedish orphanage, which he cleared of debt. In 1887 he retired to his
farm near Lindsborg, Kansas, where, in 1893, he died.

In Chicago he was reputed to have made judicious real estate investments, which was his privilege. Of him one writer, C. F. Peterson,
says: "He was the most energetic, the most tireless and the most successful promoter of the Swedish Lutheran Church in America." From
1881 to 1888 he was President of the Synod. When his original church
was destroyed in the great October fire in 1871, some of his parishioners
thought the congregation would be justified in going through bankruptcy proceedings in order to escape liability for a mortgage on the
empty, smoking lot, but Pastor Carlsson would have none of it. Professor Stephenson calls him "a man of affairs and a business manager,"
endowed with the practical "Martha" qualities, which Hasselquist as
well as several other clergymen lacked. For his own church he drew
up a constitution which was so clear and so practical that it was widely
copied. At the annual Synodal conventions, when other ministers had
floundered in words, sometimes passing mutually conflicting resolu-
tions, Carlsson usually edited the final minutes, making them logical
and consistent. "Ecclesiastical organizations owe more to men of that
type," writes Stephenson, "than they usually acknowledge." While a

pastor in Chicago, he prepared a practical guide for immigrants, exposing the chicaneries and tricks to which the newcomers were so often exposed. Having a mind like that he almost certainly would have been even more successful as a lawyer than he was as a minister. He was fonder of rituals than most of his colleagues and at services wore the vestments of the state church clergy in Sweden; they made him look more familiar to the newly arrived immigrants and helped win their confidence.

The fourth patriarch of the early Swedish Lutherans and the first one to be educated in the United States was Eric Norelius, the pioneer pastor in Minnesota. As early as in the fall of 1850, when he was but seventeen years old, he had arrived in New York on another iron-laden Swedish immigrant vessel, the *Oden,* from Gävle, with a group of about one hundred conservative *läsare* from the northern provinces on board. They were followers of the Reverend Fredrik Gabriel Hedberg, a Swedish-speaking minister in Finland, who was of the ultra-conservative, pietistic type. Among the passengers was also Eric's older brother, Anders, aged twenty, who first became a Baptist minister at Moline, Illinois, then a volunteer in the Civil War, and after that a public officeholder, first in Minnesota and then Iowa. For eighteen years he was postmaster at Kiron, in the latter state.

The younger brother was also a versatile man. In Sweden he had had a smattering of secondary education. On arriving in New York he met Olof Gustaf Hedström, the immigrant missionary, probably the first Methodist he had ever encountered. At the Bethel Ship he heard him preach and in his diary he states he was not favorably impressed by Hedström's dramatic manner of delivery, which must have seemed strange to a *läsare* of the quiet, Hedberg variety, nor did he enjoy, coming from the north of Sweden, Hedström's Småland accent. Finally he objected, in his youthful wisdom, to the Methodist "perfectionist" doctrine, proclaimed by Hedström. It clashed with the traditional Lutheran concept of sanctification.

When he arrived with his fellow immigrants in Andover, Illinois, after a difficult trip via the Erie Canal, the lake boats as far as Chicago, and then by canal boats and finally on foot, Norelius looked up the newly established pastor, Lars Paul Esbjörn, whom, as a fellow native of Hälsingland brought up in the same school of theology as himself, he found more congenial. By Esbjörn he was advised to enter the newly founded "Capital University" at Columbus, Ohio, which was less a university than a Lutheran denominational academy and seminary, owned by the Ohio Synod which was made up, for the most part, of Germans. Here by superhuman physical labor, he was able to support himself while studying for four years and in 1855 he became a member of the first group of four Swedish young men to be ordained in the United States as Lutheran ministers. Thereupon he headed for Minnesota, into which territory the Swedish immigrants had by then just begun to pour. There he formed at Vasa, on September 3, 1855, the first Swedish Lutheran church. Like Hasselquist at Galesburg, he also founded a Swedish-language weekly newspaper, *Minnesota Posten,* which in 1859 was merged in Chicago with *Hemlandet.* Finally, he organized a little academy or training school which in time became Gustavus Adolphus College of St. Peter, Minnesota. At this college many leaders of Swedish origin, governors, preachers, teachers, and public administrators, have been trained.

During two periods Norelius was President of the Augustana Synod; from 1874 to 1881, and again from 1899 to 1911. At the celebration of its fiftieth anniversary in 1910, he and two laymen, G. Peters and John Erlander, one completely blind and the other totally deaf, were the only participants who had been present at the founding in 1860. Though he was then seventy-seven years old, Norelius was able to make a moving address. "He seemed like a venerable prophet of old," wrote a guest from Sweden. His most enduring work was perhaps his historical writing, which, in addition to his memoirs, included a two-volume *History of the Swedish Lutheran Congregations and the Swedes in America,* published in Swedish in 1890 and 1916, respectively. Unlike his memoirs, they have not so far been translated, but being written by an eyewitness and participant in many of the events they describe they are a primary source of Swedish American history. In 1916 he died at Vasa, Minnesota, at the age of eighty-three.

In the early days the demand for educated and otherwise properly qualified ministers to serve the increasing number of Swedish Lutheran congregations in the United States, could never be wholly met. Unonius may have been wrong in his conclusion that "ministers from Sweden would never come" but, in truth, the state church authorities did very little to supply the need. Rather was it individual, far-sighted and liberally inclined clergymen like Wieselgren and Fjellstedt, writes Professor Stephenson, who advised their young friends in the church to emigrate, especially those who had made themselves objectionable as pietistic or *läsare* preachers or as temperance lecturers.

One of these was the Reverend Jonas Swensson, whose brief career in America was to have important consequences. Born in Våthult, Småland, in 1828, the son of a farmer-blacksmith, he had managed by much overwork, hard study and extreme physical privations, which ultimately ruined his health, to graduate in 1851 from the theological department at the University of Uppsala. Until 1856 he served as curate at the country parish of Södra Unnaryd, near his birthplace in Småland, and there he soon won a reputation as an earnest and eloquent pulpit orator. Among those who had walked long distances to hear him preach were some of the settlers at Jamestown, New York, and Sugar Grove, Pennsylvania, and one day in May 1855, he read in the pietistic Swedish weekly, *Väktaren* (*The Watchman*) that the Swedish immigrants of those towns had decided to ask him to become their minister. The news had been conveyed in a private letter from the Reverend Erland Carlsson in Chicago to a friend in Sweden. By midsummer Swensson did get a formal call, sent through the Reverend Peter Fjellstedt, who had originally recommended Erland Carlsson himself.

On May 20, 1856, Swensson sailed from Gothenburg for New York on the schooner *Minona*. He was accompanied by his young wife whom he had married at Unnaryd the preceding March, as well as by her younger sister, Hanna Swensson, who ultimately settled in Lindsborg, Kansas. On July 5, after a journey of seven weeks, they arrived after having seen from the deck of their boat the Fourth of July fireworks on shore. Like most Swedish newcomers, they were met by the Reverend Olof Gustaf Hedström, the Methodist missionary. "We attended a Methodist religious service on board the Bethel Ship," Swensson wrote in his diary for July 6, 1856. "We felt quite ill at ease. I feel deeply the difficulties with sects and the lack of discipline in this country."

When he and his wife arrived in Jamestown on July 9, they were invited to be the guests of the Reverend Jacob Bredberg, another former curate of the state church of Sweden, who was then pastor of the Swedish Methodist church in Jamestown, founded in 1852 by the Reverend Olof Gustaf Hedström. "We were well off," Swensson noted briefly in his diary.

After only two years at Jamestown and Sugar Grove, Swensson moved west to become successor of Esbjörn at Andover, Illinois. There he preached for fifteen years, or until 1873, when he died at the age of forty-five. His health had been so undermined by his early privations that he was never able to cope with all his burdens.

In addition to Swensson's pastoral work and his earnest, reverberating preaching, his greatest contribution to America was his son, the even more able and equally eloquent Reverend Carl Aaron Swensson, clergyman, college president, public school official, state legislator, and Republican spellbinder. At Lindsborg, Kansas, he founded Bethany College and started the annual singing of Händel's *Messiah,* which has become a widely publicized event in the musical life of the Middle West. His was perhaps the most dynamic personality so far produced by the Swedes in America. Unfortunately he, too, wore himself out and died before he reached fifty.

A certain number of individual Swedes had settled in Kansas while it was still a territory and only potentially a state without slavery. The financial panic of 1857 caused many Swedish farmers in western Illinois to hope for better luck further west, particularly in Kansas, then boomed by land agents as a new Eldorado. Among the disappointed California gold seekers who had crossed Kansas via the Santa Fe trail were also a number of Swedes who in the early 'fifties returned there to take up land. When the Kansas Territory was set off from that of Missouri in 1854, the new Governor launched a vigorous publicity campaign to attract new settlers. One of his pamphlets reached William Shannon, an Irish farmer living near Galesburg, Illinois. With his Swedish hired man, John A. Johnson, who had been born in the province of Östergötland, Shannon set out in 1855 for the new Eden across the Mississippi and Missouri rivers. On the Blue River, a Kansas tributary to the latter, in Pottawatomie County, they found land to their liking. The next year they were joined by Johnson's older married brother, Nils P. Johnson, who in a month's time drove a prairie schooner, pulled by two yoke of oxen, from Galesburg to Kansas, along the trail used only ten years before by the Mormons in their flight to Utah. In the wagon he had, besides household goods, his young wife and their infant child. In the open country, twenty miles from the nearest settlement, the Johnson brothers then built their first sod hut and started farming. In this they were very successful and in 1859 were able to send to Sweden for their mother and three brothers. The next year the mother died; probably the first Swedish-born person to be buried in the soil of Kansas. In her honor the first Swedish Lutheran congregation in Kansas, organized in 1863 by a visiting Lutheran minister, was named Mariadal (Mary's Valley) a name it still bears. Gradually this Swedish settlement extended over large parts of the Blue River region. An article about it, published in *Hemlandet* promptly brought more Swedish settlers from western Illinois and in time the Johnson brothers, who had much land to sell, became quite wealthy. The younger one lived until 1893 and the older one until 1910. In their wills both left large bequests to various educational and charitable institutions, probably the first Swedish Americans to do so.

Prior to the Civil War several other Swedish settlements were begun in Kansas, such as those of Axtell in the valley of the Vermilion River, a tributary of the Blue, and at Lawrence on the Kansas River, where a Swedish blacksmith, Anders Palm, born in Skåne, was the first in the state to make iron plows. At Fort Riley, the first Swede, L. O. Jäderborg, arrived in 1858. After taking part in the Civil War as a farrier and driver for the Second Kansas Cavalry, he founded a prosperous community at Enterprise.

When the Civil War was over, the most famous, if not the most important Swedish community, that of Lindsborg, was founded under Lutheran auspices in the Smoky River Valley. It was the last of the religious Swedish mass-settlements in the Middle West. As early as February 15, 1864, a Swedish-born farmer, Anders Bengtson Carlgren, had arrived in the valley and decided to file a claim some distance north of Lindsborg, where his first shelter had been a hollow tree trunk. In 1866 seventeen former railroad construction hands, also born in Sweden, took up under the Homestead Act their permitted 160 acres each, near Lindsborg, but they did not organize a town. This was done in Chicago by another group of more or less recently arrived Swedes, who, under the leadership of one Sven August Lindell, formed in April 1868, a stock company they called "The First Swedish Agricultural Company," the purpose of which was to acquire a large tract of land somewhere in the West for an exclusively Swedish and Lutheran community. Obviously the example of Bishop Hill continued to haunt the minds of Eric Janson's countrymen. Since the Swedes were known to be successful pioneers, offers of land at various prices came from many quarters, chiefly from the new railroads, which had obtained land as subsidies from the Government in return for the construction of new lines. As developers the Swedes were good prospects. The final choice was a tract of 13,160 acres in northern McPherson and southern Salina counties in the Smoky River Valley of central Kansas. The price was $29,629.84 or about $2.25 per acre, or a dollar more than the most fertile land in western Illinois had cost only twenty years earlier. Of the purchase price $5,925 was paid in cash; the rest was to be paid in five annual instalments, plus accrued interest. In honor of the principal founders, who besides Lindell, were S. P. Lindgren, the company's treasurer, and Daniel Lindahl, a member of the land purchasing committee, the new settlement was called Lindsborg.

The first problem was to get settlers who could pay for their allotments and then turn them into productive farms. The statutes of the company specified that "every one received as a member of the company shall be a believing Christian, adhere to the doctrines of the Evangelical Lutheran Church, be industrious and thrifty, and exert himself in the upbuilding of the company." All stockholders' meetings were opened with prayers.

By chance some of the stockholders in The First Swedish Agricultural Company of Chicago, had friends and relatives in the western Swedish province of Värmland, which so far had been but little touched by emigration. The *läsare* or pietist movement, however, had begun to make inroads and at the end of 1860 several successive crop failures, due to droughts, had made the population even poorer than usual.

For many emigration was the only solution, and as leader of the first Värmland exodus for America a young pietistic pastor of the state church by the name of Olof Olsson was chosen. By his evangelistic activities he too had earned the displeasure of his bishop. Born at Karlskoga in Värmland, he was in 1868 only twenty-seven years old. Since his parents, like those of Jonas Swensson, were poor, he had obtained his education at great sacrifice, first at the local *läroverk* or junior college at Karlstad, and then at the new Fjellstedt school at Uppsala, founded by Peter Fjellstedt to educate gifted but impecunious youths for the priesthood. Olsson's first ambition was to become a foreign missionary and to prepare himself for such a career he attended for a while the University of Leipzig, but he soon returned to Sweden deeply disillusioned with German university life. In 1863, he was ordained at Uppsala. He then returned to Värmland, where, like Jonas Swensson in Småland, he soon became known as an able and persuasive preacher. In 1868 he was visited by Eric Norelius, the pioneer Lutheran pastor in Minnesota, and from him he learned about the religious freedom in America.

This disposed him to accept the leadership of the new emigrant group headed for Kansas and in the middle of the summer of 1869 he arrived at Lindsborg with his bride, his parents, several other relatives, and eighty other families, or altogether about 250 persons including children—a valuable addition to the population of the young state. At Lindsborg, which had not then even been laid out, they encountered very much the same hardships as those which had beset the Eric Jansonists at Bishop Hill in Illinois some twenty years earlier. As there were no houses and few trees, they had to construct sod houses or dugouts, a novel experience for the natives of the heavily wooded province of Värmland. With daily prayers and Scripture readings they went to work with the same spirit and faith in the Lord as their countrymen from Hälsingland at Bishop Hill in Illinois. The climate was milder than that of Värmland and somehow they managed to survive. By Christmas, 1870, they had completed a little stone church—now a sacred memento.

As stipulated in the company charter, only true believers in the Lutheran doctrines were to be admitted to the community, as well as the church, and even the minister's wife had to pass a test before the elders. Soon human nature revealed its usual traits, as it had at Bishop Hill. "Dissension, jealousy, and quarrels disrupted the congregation," writes Professor Stephenson, "and many old friends turned against the pastor." But even if a spiritual Utopia had not been reached, Olsson was happy in the free air of central Kansas, where he could preach according to his own ideas and to his heart's content. For such freedom, living in a one-room cabin, where snakes sometimes dangled from the ceiling, was not, he thought, too high a price to pay.

Being by far the best educated man in the district, Olsson was soon called to perform public service. He became the first Superintendent of Schools in McPherson County and later a representative in the Kansas State Legislature. Following the example of Hasselquist at Galesburg and Norelius at Vasa in Minnesota, he likewise started a little publication he called *Kyrklig Tidskrift* (*Church Periodical*). In many respects he proved himself ahead of his times or at least ahead of some of his parishioners. But like both Esbjörn and Hasselquist he was too well educated to be spared as pastor of a frontier village, and in 1875 he was made Professor of Theology at the Augustana College and Seminary which had just been moved to Rock Island, Illinois. In 1891 he was appointed President of both the college and the seminary, a post he held until his death in 1900, but he was never elected President of the Synod itself. On his students, who were to be its future pastors, he left, however, a deep impression. By many Olsson was considered the last of the great pioneers. Professor Stephen-

son, who had known him personally since his own student days at
Augustana College, calls him "a noble, lovable man in whom there
was no deceit." At Rock Island Olsson introduced the singing of
Händel's *Messiah,* which he had heard at Albert Hall in London. At
Lindsborg, his successor, Carl A. Swensson, and his young wife, both
of whom had been his students at Augustana, trained the people to
sing it every year, which at Easter time they still do.

As the annual number of Swedish immigrants arriving in the United
States began to swell, reaching an all-time peak of 64,607 in 1882, the
number of Swedish Lutheran churches grew in proportion, especially
as the more recent arrivals had been less and less induced to emigrate
because of religious motives. In Sweden too religious freedom was gradually established and in 1868 the final traces of the law against private
prayer meetings were repealed.

In 1947 the Augustana Synod included 1,175 congregations, served
by 989 ministers. It had 1,299 church buildings, including chapels and
parish houses. The adult membership was 306,786, plus 105,954 children
enrolled in the Sunday schools. (Its colleges and humanitarian institutions are described in other chapters.)

The Swedish language organ of the Synod is the *Augustana,* a weekly,
edited for thirty years, from 1909 to 1939 by the Rev. L. G. Abrahamson, a
native of Sweden, who died in 1946 at the age of ninety. The present
editor is Dr. A. T. Lundholm. The English language weekly is *The
Lutheran Companion,* edited by Dr. E. E. Ryden, a brother of the late
Professor George H. Ryden of the University of Delaware. *The Augusta
Quarterly* is edited by Dr. Oscar N. Olson. The Synod has its own printing and publishing plant at Rock Island, Ill., the Augustana Book Concern, which employs over a hundred people. The General Manager is
Mr. Birger Swenson.

From 1870 to 1918, the Augustana Synod was a member of the
General Council of Lutheran churches in America, but in the latter
year, in order to preserve its identity, it did not join the United Lutheran Church of America. For this there were special reasons connected with the First World War which seemed important at the
time. In 1930, however, it joined the National Lutheran Conference
and in 1947 it sent delegates to the International Conference of Lutheran churches in thirty countries, held at Lund, Sweden, where an
agreement was reached to form a "world-wide Lutheran body, a free
association for common objectives" with permanent headquarters at
Geneva, Switzerland. The Augustana Synod also sent representatives

to the ecumenical meeting at Amsterdam in 1948.

In 1947 the Reverend Petrus Olof Emanuel Bersell of Minneapolis, the son of a former Professor of Greek at Augustana College, was re-elected to a fourth, four-year term as President. Born at Rock Island, Illinois, in 1882, his education has been wholly American. In 1947 he was authorized by the Synod's annual convention to wear, as a symbol of his high office, a pectoral cross, like those worn by bishops, abbots and canons. On the other hand, no episcopal form of government like those of the American Protestant Episcopal Church, the Church of England, and the state Church of Sweden, has ever been adopted. The term "daughter church," sometimes poetically applied in Sweden to "The Augustana Evangelical Lutheran Church," the title officially adopted in 1948, Professor Stephenson thinks unjustified. In fact, there has never been any organic connection. "Sister church" is the more realistic term used in recent years.

XII

The Baptists

In the free-for-all competition for the church affiliation of the Swedish settlers in America, the Baptists, like the Methodists, Episcopalians and Lutherans, entered early. Their historians can point to the fact that as far back as the latter half of the seventeenth century, a Swede by the name of Robert Nordin was ordained a Baptist minister in London and then left for America where, in Prince George County, Virginia, he organized a Baptist congregation and served as its pastor until his death in 1725. Another Baptist minister by the name of Richard Nordin came to Virginia in 1727, but soon returned to England. He may have been a son of Robert Nordin.

Later in the eighteenth century John Asplund, who was born in Sweden, came to America from London, where he had worked as a bookkeeper. He had crossed the Atlantic as a sailor on a British vessel, but had deserted in an American port. His conversion to the Baptist faith took place in North Carolina. First he joined the church at Ballard's Bridge and after having been ordained in Southampton County, Virginia became its minister. In 1785 he made a European tour, in which he included England, Denmark, and Finland, as well as his native Sweden. On his return he prepared a *Baptist Register,* visiting between 1791 and 1794 all the Baptist churches in the United States —sometimes on foot. It is now a rare historical item. After the book had been published, he did not resume his preaching, but entered the real estate business in Maryland, in which he was not successful. In 1807, during a fishing trip in a canoe on Fishing Creek in Virginia, he was drowned.

In Asplund's *Register,* the late Professor Emanuel Schmidt, a Baptist editor, historian and college president, who was also born in Sweden, found nineteen names of American Baptist ministers which seemed to be of Swedish origin and they had all appeared, moreover, in the parish records of the "Old Swedes," or Gloria Dei Church in Philadelphia, built in 1699–1700. From this coincidence Schmidt felt justified in concluding that at least that many of the early American Baptist clergymen were descendants of the Swedish colonists on the Delaware.

In Sweden itself the Baptists got a foothold much later. Prior to 1858, Swedish law required every child born in the country to be baptized as soon as possible and in any case within ten days. If the child's parents or guardians did not do their duty, the civil authorities were required to intervene and, if necessary, use force. Furthermore, if a child had not been baptized, it could not be confirmed or admitted to the Holy Communion, and no one who had not partaken of the Lord's Supper within the past year could be legally married, which recalls Mrs. Day's apprehensiveness in *Life With Father* about the legitimacy of her children since her husband had not been baptized. Furthermore, if a person had not attended Holy Communion within a reasonable time, he or she could not take the oath to tell the truth in court and without such an oath no testimony had any validity. Attendance at Holy Communion was also required for holding certain public offices and anyone who was found to be disseminating doctrines contrary to the pure Evangelical Lutheran teachings of the state church could be banished from the country.

All these obstacles the early Baptist missionaries encountered in Sweden. The first Baptist victim of the banishment law as well as the last one of any denomination, was a Swedish-born sailor, by the name of Fredrik O. Nilsson, who, after being imperiled at sea, had been converted in New York. His exile from his native land in 1851 caused international reverberations and ultimately helped repeal the law, proving once more the adage that the best way to get rid of an unpopular measure is to enforce it. Before going to sea in 1827, when he was eighteen years old, Nilsson had been a farmer and a cobbler and after serving on various Swedish vessels throughout the world, he joined the crew of an American ship running between New York and Charleston, South Carolina. In a severe storm off Cape Hatteras, he was wont to relate, he had been close to death, and when he next arrived in New York he received spiritual comfort from the Reverend Henry Chase, a Methodist pastor of that city. Like his contemporary countrymen, Peter Bergner and Olof Gustaf Hedström, who enjoyed Methodist support, he then worked among the Scandinavian sailors and immigrants on the New York waterfront as a distributor of tracts for the New York Tract Society.

In 1839 he returned to Sweden and there became a lay missionary without any denominational affiliation. In the course of his work he became acquainted with the Reverend George Scott, the British Methodist pastor in Stockholm, and by him he was advised to lay special stress on temperance, as Scott himself had done. In 1842 Nilsson was engaged by the Seamen's Friends Society of New York to work among the sailors of all nationalities in the port of Gothenburg and thanks to his friendship with George Scott, who in 1842 had been forced to leave the country, he was also retained by the British Bible Society to distribute its publication, as Scott himself had previously been.

In Gothenburg, Nilsson made the acquaintance of Captain Gustavus W. Schröder, another ex-sailor and a native of the city, who in 1844 had been converted to the Baptist faith in New Orleans. On Schröder's next visit to New York he had been baptized by total immersion in the East River and become a member of the Baptist Seamen's Bethel, near Chatham Square, later known as the First Baptist Mariners' Church. After the Civil War, Schröder played an important role in Sweden as an American emigrant agent, his house in Gothenburg being the headquarters of both emigration promoters and religious revivalists.

On August 1, 1847, Nilsson was baptized by total immersion in the River Elbe by the Reverend J. G. Oncken, the Baptist pioneer in Germany and pastor of the church at Hamburg. After that Nilsson began to work as a Baptist missionary in Sweden and in 1849 he was ordained in the same Hamburg church. Previously his Swedish converts had been baptized more or less privately by the Baptist minister in Denmark, the Reverend A. P. Förster. No sooner had Nilsson begun to perform the ceremony himself than he fell afoul of the law. He had not been licensed to administer such a sacrament.

The unwonted spectacle of adult baptism by total immersion out of doors soon attracted an extraordinary amount of public attention and to escape further notoriety, Nilsson performed the ceremony secretly at night, which made the public curiosity even greater. After the state church had officially warned the Swedish people against such heresies, the Baptist converts were subjected to social ostracism and business discrimination. In the fall of 1849 Nilsson was formally declared an apostate by the church consistory at Gothenburg and when he continued to preach, nevertheless, he was seized by a mob on New Year's Day, 1850, as he was conducting a service in a private house at Berghem, a suburb of Gothenburg, and delivered to the civil authorities. At his trial he was released from custody but was sentenced to exile for two years. When this verdict had been confirmed by the Göta

Court of Appeals at Jönköping, he appealed for personal clemency to the King, Oscar I, but though he received royal compliments for his temperance work, he got no redress. Once the law had been invoked, as in the case of the book-burning Eric Janson in Hälsingland twenty years earlier, it had to run its course.

The following year Nilsson left the country under the court decree and thereby started a sharp debate in the Swedish press as well as in the British and American. Protests were sent officially from Paris as well as London and Washington. In an English newspaper, the Reverend George Scott, who had continued his interest in Sweden after he had left under pressure in 1842, wrote that he hoped Nilsson's exile would lead to complete religious liberty in Sweden, which it did seven years later. The law against conventicles was then modified so as to apply only during hours when services were held in the state churches. In the meantime the animus against Nilsson's followers continued, and at New Year's, 1853, a group of twenty-one of them decided to emigrate to America with Nilsson as their guide. He joined them in Denmark where he had served as a Baptist preacher. In New York he was warmly received as a martyr to religious liberty and with his fellow immigrants he was sent to the Middle West where he continued to preach. He founded a number of Swedish Baptist churches, particularly in Iowa and southern Minnesota.

On the eve of the Civil War Nilsson returned to Sweden as a missionary for the Twenty-fifth Street Baptist Church of New York. He was then an American citizen, his term of banishment had long since expired, and the law had been modified so that he was free to preach as he pleased, but to make "assurance doubly sure" he asked the new King, Charles XV, for a formal pardon. This was granted on December 11, 1860, and in proof thereof he received a handsomely engraved certificate with the royal seal and the King's signature, which he proudly displayed at subsequent public appearances. Seldom had martyrdom terminated more triumphantly. When the Civil War was over he returned to the United States and until his death in 1881 he lived in partial retirement at Houston, Minnesota, where in 1853 he had organized a Baptist church and for some years served as its pastor.

The next most important, if less sensational, Swedish Baptist missionary in the United States was Gustaf Palmquist, a better educated man and intellectually superior to Nilsson. Born in 1812 at Solberga parish in Småland, he had become, in 1830, a schoolteacher at Filipstad, in Värmland, John Ericsson's home city. Later he continued this work

at Gustafsberg, near Stockholm. There he became "born anew" as a
Lutheran *läsare* or reader, and after his conversion he did missionary
work among the prison inmates and the very poor of Stockholm. In
1850 he was invited by a group of friendly dissidents from northern
Sweden who, on August 17, were to sail on the schooner *Oden* from
Gävle, to serve as their religious guide. Both Anders and Eric Norelius
were to be on board. At that time he could not leave his work in Sweden
and therefore declined. The next year, however, he crossed the Atlantic by himself and then visited his old friends who had sailed on
the *Oden* and who had by then settled in western Illinois. At Andover,
he also called on the Reverend Lars Paul Esbjörn, who had not only
organized his first congregation at Andover, but had formed little
groups of Lutherans at Galesburg, Moline, and other places. For the
winter 1851–52 Palmquist was asked by Esbjörn to take over the budding Lutheran congregation at Galesburg, which he did.

In Sweden, Palmquist had begun to study Baptist literature as early
as in 1845, and when in the spring of 1852 the American Baptist church
of Galesburg held its annual revival, he followed it with special interest. He then decided that he was more in accord with the Baptist
interpretation of the Bible than with the Lutheran and in the summer
of 1852 he was baptized by immersion at Galesburg. Being well educated and an experienced public speaker, he was at once ordained as
a preacher and set to work among the incoming Swedes. He then
moved to Rock Island, Illinois, where some of the former passengers
of the *Oden,* including Anders Norelius, had settled. Among them
he found ready listeners and, with him as the pastor, three of them
including Norelius formed on August 13, 1852, the first Swedish Baptist
congregation in the United States, only two years after Esbjörn had organized the first Lutheran parish at Andover. A year later the first
church was built, a little white, wooden building, seating about fifty. In
February 1853, the Baptist Home Mission Society came to its aid with
$200.

Within two years Palmquist turned over the charge to Norelius, who
by then had also been ordained a Baptist minister, and accepted an offer
of the Baptist City Mission in New York City to act as its missionary
among the incoming Swedish immigrants, presumably in competition
with the Methodist Gospel propaganda, in the original sense of the word,
promulgated from the Bethel Ship with such success by Olof Gustaf
Hedström. The very next year, 1855, Palmquist, a gentler and better educated man than Hedström, returned to his former congregation at Rock

Island, Illinois. Two years later he sailed for Sweden where, until his death in 1867, he was employed as a distributor of Baptist literature and as an educator of young men to be Baptist preachers. His health was not robust. While walking one stormy evening after a church service from Moline to his home in Rock Island, he had caught a cold, from the effects of which he never recovered. By everybody who knew him he was esteemed as a sincere and deeply devout man.

While acting as a Baptist missionary on the New York waterfront, in October 1854, Palmquist made one decidedly consequential convert, Knut Oscar Brundin, a former Swedish naval, non-commissioned officer, born at Uppsala in 1832, who, under the name of K. O. Broady, became a colonel in the American Civil War and after that an influential religious and educational leader in Sweden for over fifty years. While crossing the Atlantic he had lost by death his young wife, born Charlotta Kloppman, so that when he arrived in New York he was deeply depressed. In his arms he carried a prematurely born child, which survived. From Palmquist he received religious solace and the next year he was baptized in the Tabernacle Baptist Church in New York City.

Being then only twenty-three years old and fairly well educated, he was encouraged by his new American Baptist friends to prepare for the ministry at Madison University (now Colgate) of Hamilton, New York. There in 1861 he received his Bachelor's degree, probably the first one issued to a native-born Swede by an American college, and the same year he married an American girl, Miss Emily Westnedge. Having had military training in Sweden, he had drilled his fellow undergraduates in preparation for the impending war, and upon graduation he enlisted with them in the Union Army, in which on September 19, 1861 he got a commission as captain in the Ninety-first New York Volunteer Infantry Regiment. "He participated in thirty-five engagements," writes Nels Hokanson, "including Chancellorsville, Virginia, May 1-2, 1863, Gettysburg, Pennsylvania, July 1-3, 1863, Bristow, Virginia, October 14, 1863, Mine Run, November 6—December 2, 1863, Wilderness, Virginia, May 8-12, 1864. During the last battle he was transferred to the Sixty-first New York and promoted to the rank of colonel."

He was twice wounded and in the Battle of Reams Station he was in command, under General Winfield Scott Hancock, of three brigades or six regiments and there he was wounded in a leg. When he recovered, the war was so close to its end that he submitted his resignation in order to prepare himself for the Baptist ministry. General Hancock had already recommended him for the rank of brigadier general and hoped he would remain. When Broady declined the honor he was named by President Lincoln a colonel of the regular United States Army and allowed to keep the title for life.

After being ordained he was given his first charge at Ilion, New York, in an American Baptist church, but in 1866 he was persuaded to return to Sweden to become, first, a teacher and then the principal of the new Baptist Bethel Seminary in Stockholm, where, for the next fifty years, or until 1916, he trained Baptist clergymen who subsequently preached to their fellow countrymen, both in Sweden and the United States. At the Bethel Seminary, he introduced the American educational methods he had learned at Madison (Colgate) and being a high-ranking veteran of the American Civil War, he exerted in Sweden, until his death in 1922 at the age of ninety, a strong pro-American, as well as Baptist, influence. Twice he was honored by his New York alma mater with honorary degrees, in 1877 as D.D. and in 1916 as LL.D.

The best educated and most intellectual of the Swedish Baptist pioneers in the United States was, beyond a doubt, the Reverend Anders Wiberg, who, like Esbjörn, had obtained a degree from Uppsala University and in 1843 had been ordained as a minister in the Swedish state church. In 1816 he had been born, like Esbjörn, in Hälsingland and returning there after his ordination as a clergyman, he had become well acquainted with the Eric Janson followers and other types of dissenters. For two years, beginning in 1840, he had edited *Missions Tidningen (The Missionary Journal)*, published in Stockholm by Evangeliska Fosterlandsstiftelsen, a pietistic organization within the state church, and had thus become well acquainted with its leader, C. O. Rosenius, as he had with George Scott and other non-conformist preachers. When he returned as a state church minister to his native province, he began to preach pietistic, revivalist sermons himself, and also to give lectures on temperance, a sure way to arouse the opposition of the conservative wing of the established church. For such unauthorized activities and particularly for serving Holy Communion in a private house, he was suspended for six months in 1850 and then resigned permanently. During a visit to Hamburg in 1851 he had become acquainted with the German Baptists, as Fredrik O. Nilsson had been. He then began to read Baptist books, and also the one by Robert Baird on religious conditions in the United States.

His health being poor, he accepted in the summer of 1852 a chance to get a free trip to America by acting as chaplain to a group of Swedish immigrants sailing from the east coast and while passing through the Baltic he composed a pamphlet on baptism published in Uppsala in 1852. It was destined to be widely read by his fellow countrymen, both in Sweden and the United States. While the ship paused at Copenhagen, he was baptized by immersion by the recently exiled Reverend Fredrik O. Nilsson, then serving in Denmark.

Bearing a letter of introduction from Nilsson, who by his martyrdom had become an international celebrity, Wiberg was well received by the American Baptist leaders in New York and in spite of his halting English was invited to lecture before The Baptist Female Bethel Union on the religious conditions in his own country. By the American Baptist Publications Society he was next employed as a distributor of its books among Scandinavian sailors and immigrants. In March 1853, he was ordained in the Baptist Mariners' Church as a minister, and then set off for the Middle West as a missionary among the Swedish pioneers. In Andover he met Lars Paul Esbjörn, an old friend and fellow temperance advocate in northern Sweden, and in Moline another former comrade, the Reverend Gustaf Palmquist, whom he had recommended in 1850 as a spiritual guide to the passengers on the *Oden.* Together he and Palmquist visited the near-by Bishop Hill and in the colony church, which is still standing, they heard a sermon by Jonas Olson, the self-taught successor to Eric Janson. What the reactions of these two highly educated Swedish Baptist clergymen were is not known.

In June 1853, Wiberg returned to New York to continue his writing as well as preaching. For the next two years he lived in Philadelphia as an editor and translator of religious texts for the American Baptist Publication Society. By his employers, his writings were then distributed both in Sweden and among the Swedish immigrants in the United States.

In 1855 the Society decided to send him to Sweden as its special representative, paying him a salary of $600 a year. Feeling financially secure, he married Miss Caroline Lintemuth, a Philadelphia-born girl of German descent. That summer they sailed together for Sweden on their honeymoon. In Stockholm they helped organize on October 10, 1855, the first Swedish Baptist church in the city and for the next eight years, with American support, Wiberg promoted the Baptist denomination in Sweden. In 1857 a country-wide Baptist Conference was organized on the American pattern. From 1856 to 1874 he edited a new periodical, *Evangelisten,* which he had founded and which he developed into a power in the land.

To solicit funds for a Baptist church in Stockholm and for a school to train Baptist ministers, Wiberg returned in 1863 to the United States, but as the Civil War was then raging, he had to wait three years to accomplish his purpose. In the meantime he once more made a tour of the young and struggling Swedish Baptist congregations in the Middle West, preaching and encouraging. After his return to Sweden in 1866, he never came back and in his native country he died in 1887.

On his final trip to Sweden Wiberg brought with him not only Colonel Broady, but also another well-educated young Swede who had been an American naval officer in the Civil War, Johan Alexis Edgren. Like Broady he had declined an offer of a permanent military career in America, preferring to pursue religious and educational activities. Having been for some years an officer in the Swedish Merchant Marine he had quickly been given a commission in the United States Navy. In the Army, his younger brother, August Hjalmar Edgren, was already an officer. As his main interest was in education, his story will be told in more detail in connection with the Bethel Institute at St. Paul, Minnesota.

Nearly a century has passed since the small beginnings of the Swedish Baptist work at Rock Island, Illinois, in 1852, but the denomination, which since 1945 has been known as The Baptist General Conference of America, now consists of 325 churches with 42,000 members. The Conference is divided into fifteen state and district conferences. The Home Mission work is headed by Reverend Wm. Turnwall and the Foreign Missions by Reverend Walfred Danielson.

The Publication department (Baptist Conference Press) is managed by Reverend C. Geo. Ericson. It publishes the denominational weekly, *The Standard,* of which Reverend Martin Erikson is editor, and several Sunday school periodicals and books. Among the Baptist editors of note have been Dr. Eric Wingren, who from 1885 to 1918 was the editor of *Nya Vecko-Posten,* and Dr. J. O. Backlund, associate editor (1918–1931) and editor (1931–1945) of *The Standard.* The latter is also an author or translator of numerous books. The national headquarters for all the departments, except the schools, is in Chicago. Seven homes for the aged and two children's homes are connected with the Baptist Conference.

XIII

THE MORMONS

In Sweden the Mormons or Latter Day Saints have conducted missionary work, as well as emigration promotion, since 1850. In that year their first representative, Johan Erik Forsgren, who, like the first Baptist preacher, Fredrik O. Nilsson, was a former sailor, was sent there as a member of a missionary group, headed by Erastus Snow, one of the original twelve Mormon apostles. The other members of the group were G. P. Dykes and P. O. Hansen, the latter a Dane. Having been born in Gävle, the northern port on the Baltic from which so many of the early emigrants from Norrland had left the country, Forsgren was sent there to begin work among his own relatives and boyhood friends, but like Nilsson, who that year was exiled by court order, he promptly came into conflict with the Swedish authorities, being accused of spreading religious propaganda in conflict with the pure Evangelical Lutheran faith of the Swedish state church. He was not formally arrested or tried, however; but according to Stephenson was placed on board an American ship and told to leave the country. Since he carried an American passport the Captain let him go ashore, however, and he then told his story to a reporter for a radical Stockholm newspaper which promptly launched a new attack on the Government. When the ship reached Denmark, Forsgren was set free through the intervention of American diplomatic representatives. He continued his missionary activities in Denmark so successfully that when three years later he returned to Utah, where he arrived in October 1853, he had with him a group of about three hundred converts, of whom nearly one-third were Swedes.

Forsgren had been born in 1816 and at the age of nine had gone to sea. He sailed the seven seas before the mast and in 1832 made his first landing in the United States. In Boston he heard sermons by the Latter Day Saints who were then proclaiming the doctrines discovered by Joseph Smith, and in that city he was rebaptized on July 16,

1843. The next year, when Jonas J. Hedström was already active in western Illinois as a Methodist missionary, he joined the headquarters of the Mormon Church at Nauvoo in the same state and there became acquainted with Joseph Smith himself. He even helped construct the original Mormon Temple. After Smith had been lynched by an Illinois mob, he joined the Mormon Battalion to protect the church members on their trek to Utah, and via California he arrived in Salt Lake City, October 1847, only three months after Brigham Young, had announced, "This is the place." When he returned there in 1853 with his group of Scandinavian converts, Brigham Young assigned them as northerners to the development of the Sanpete Valley, which is higher in altitude and therefore colder than the Salt Lake region. This they did so successfully that ever since it has been called the "Granary of Utah." At that time the population of Utah was less than fifteen thousand.

In 1930, according to the United States Census, the number of Swedish-born residents of Utah was 4,017. How many were members of the Mormon Church is difficult to say and, of course, not all Mormons of Swedish descent live in Utah. According to Swedish statistics, the number of Swedish converts to Mormonism between 1850 and 1909 was 17,259, of whom 7,822 emigrated to America, and 5,116 later withdrew from the Church while still in Sweden. In his chapter on the Swedes in Utah, written for *The Swedish Element in America* (1931, Vol. II, p. 243), Andrew Jenson, official church historian of the Latter Day Saints, estimated that about twenty thousand Swedes had been converted to Mormonism and of these some ten thousand had emigrated to America. In Salt Lake City, as in almost every other community in Utah, they are found in good positions. While they have at times obtained the right to conduct religious services in their own language, they have never had any separate church organization. In Sweden itself they are no longer disturbed in their missionary work. On the other hand, attempts by other Swedish American denominations to do missionary work in Utah have yielded only meagre results.

XIV

The Mission Friends

Discontent with religious conditions in Sweden, especially when contrasted with the absolute freedom reputed to prevail in America, was unquestionably one of the contributory causes of the early emigration. After the law against conventicles, or prayer meetings in private houses, had been repealed in 1858, this cause was largely removed. On the other hand, the state church fear of separatist tendencies, including the American-inspired temperance movement, turned out to be only too well founded. As soon as complete religious liberty was established the number of lay preachers, known as colporteurs, and independent mission houses increased by leaps and bounds. Good Templar lodges and other temperance societies likewise grew rapidly in strength and influence.

The split between the state church and its pietistic wing became even more marked after Professor Paul Peter Waldenström became leader of the latter in 1868. A doctor of philosophy from Uppsala University and then a teacher of Hebrew, Greek, and Christian doctrines at junior colleges, he had become converted in 1858 and in 1864 was ordained a minister in the state church from which he resigned in 1882. From 1884 to 1905 he was a member of the Swedish Riksdag, where his dialectic brilliance and his gift of popular oratory made him an ever-influential figure. From 1868 until his death in 1917 he edited *Pietisten,* a widely read weekly, in which his writing powers found full scope. In 1872 he published in this periodical a vigorous sermon in which he expressed firm disagreement with the orthodox Lutheran doctrine in regard to the vicarious atonement, which he declared to be pagan both in nature and in origin. This radical step had wide reverberations both in Sweden and among the Swedish immigrants in the United States. Not only churches and communities but families were divided on this issue. In 1878 the divergence culminated in the formation of the Swedish Mission Covenant Society.

Though an independent religious body, with its own churches and corps of preachers, it is not recognized as an official organization, so that its members continue to remain nominally members of the state church too. In 1946 it had 1,643 congregations with 106,266 members and 655 full-time pastors, or more than twice as many as any other non-conformist group in the country. While decidedly conservative in their private code of morals, its members have always been politically liberal and progressive.

This division in the Lutheran body in Sweden had a corresponding effect among the former Swedish immigrants in the United States. While a majority of the early ones, especially those who came in groups escorted by young dissident pastors of the state church, had been Bible "readers" or religious dissenters in Sweden, they had remained nevertheless devout Lutherans, "quite unaffected by any separatistic intentions, though a few were hopeful of the establishment of a Lutheran Free Church in the new country," as Dr. David Nyvall, the most prominent Mission Friend educator, wrote in *The Swedish Element in America* (Chicago, 1931). By and large this hope bore fruit in the Augustana Synod established in 1860.

Like their predecessors, the New Readers who came over in ever greater numbers after the Civil War, especially from the province of Småland, believed in a personal and complete conversion, and were less insistent on academically educated clergymen, provided their religious zeal was genuine, and less interested in "the parish idea of church constituency" to quote Professor Nyvall once more. At first they attended the already established Swedish Lutheran churches if for no other reason than to hear services conducted in their own language.

In 1868 one of their lay preachers, J. M. Sanngren, arrived in Chicago from Alsheda in Småland, where he had been born in 1837. At once he looked up his fellow Smålänning, the Reverend Erland Carlsson, who was then pastor of the Immanuel Church, founded in 1853, and by him was engaged at a salary of forty dollars a month as a lay missionary among the ever-increasing immigrants in the city. The year before, a fairly large group of New Readers had arrived in Chicago from Småland and had begun to attend the same church. When they heard the young, full-bearded, handsome new colporteur preach at the evening services, they at once recognized him as one of their own and in 1869 they asked him to become their pastor in a new Mission House they then built in the typical Småland style on Franklin Street in Chicago. Though they then withdrew from the Immanuel Church, they still called their new congregation The Lutheran Mission Church of Chicago.

A similar division had already taken place in 1868 in Galesburg, Illinois, and when Sanngren declined a call there, the Reverend Charles Anderson, a Danish-born Lutheran pastor, who also spoke Swedish as well as English, was chosen. He remained, however, a member of the Lutheran Synod of Northern Illinois, from which the Swedes, under Esbjörn's leadership, had withdrawn in 1860. His new church was called The Second Evangelical Lutheran Congregation of Galesburg. Later Anderson became head of the Ansgar Synod of the Swedish Mission Churches and founder of a mission institute, or a ministerial training school which was active from 1873 to 1884, first at Keokuk, Iowa, and then at Knoxville, Illinois.

At Swede Bend, in central Iowa, a similar mission society was formed in 1868, its leader being Carl August Björk, another Smålänning, who was destined to play a leading role in the Mission Covenant Church, serving as its President from 1885 to 1910. In Småland, where he had been born in the parish of Lommaryd in 1837, Björk had been a shoemaker and a soldier. He arrived at Swede Bend in 1864 and while continuing his work as a cobbler, he promptly joined the local Swedish Lutheran church. While he had little educational training, beyond that provided by the elementary public schools of his home parish and by the Army, he had natural intelligence and was a gifted public speaker—a tall handsome man with a military carriage. (Photographs taken of him in his later years suggest a bishop or banker.) On Sundays, when the regular pastor was absent in order to preach in other churches, he was often asked to conduct the services as a lay reader, which he did very well. Instead of preaching, however, he read articles from *Pietisten,* the Swedish devotionalist periodical edited by Rosenius. One Sunday, relates Stephenson (p. 269), the sexton hid the paper, his purpose being to compel Björk to preach extemporaneously. This he did so well that his audience was thrilled. When the regular minister returned and heard about it he was displeased and termed Björk a "heretic." Only ordained ministers of the Lutheran faith were to be allowed to preach, he declared. On July 4, 1868, the day of American Independence, the admirers of Björk formally withdrew from the church and formed their own Mission Society.

By 1873 enough of such separatist bodies had been organized throughout the Middle West to set up in Chicago a Mission Synod with Sanngren as its first President. In 1878, after Sanngren had died while pastor of a Mission church at Lund in Wisconsin, Björk succeeded him as President of the Synod. In 1885 Björk was elected the first President of the new Evangelical Mission Covenant formed that year including the Mission Synod as well as the former members of the dissolved Ansgar Synod and some independent churches. By that time the designation "Lutheran" was permanently dropped while the word "Evangelical" was retained. After 1894 Björk gave his whole time to the central administration, its finances, missionary work, educational problems, etc. In 1910 he retired and in 1916 he died.

A Mission Covenant personality in decided contrast with Björk's was that of Erik August Skogsbergh, a native of Värmland, but educated at the Ahlberg School for Lay Preachers in Småland. He came to America in 1876 to become pastor of a Mission Covenant church in Chicago. There he was warmly greeted by the veteran American evangelist, Dwight L. Moody. Skogsbergh was an able executive who founded schools, built churches or rather "tabernacles," started newspapers and organized revivalist campaigns, but he was first of all a fiery preacher who held his audience spellbound. Popularly known as the "Swedish Moody," he at times conducted joint campaigns with the famous American evangelist, as at the Chicago World's Fair in 1893, speaking to special Swedish audiences in Swedish while Moody himself addressed the general public in English. Professor Stephenson, who knew him personally, calls him (see, p. 277) "the greatest popular preacher the Swedish Americans have produced." From 1884 to 1908 Skogsbergh was active in Minneapolis, where he built a large tabernacle, and from 1908 to 1913 in Seattle, Washington, where he also built a similar structure. At regular intervals he conducted revivalist campaigns in the Middle as well as the Far West. Few Swedes have been more dramatic. He lived until 1939.

When formed in 1885 the Mission Covenant included forty-seven churches, of which thirty-nine came from the Mission Synod and the rest from other sources, while the ministers numbered thirty-eight. In 1947 there were 471 churches, 442 ordained pastors and 40,961 members. Its property was valued at $10,460,311. Since 1933 the Reverend Theodore W. Anderson of Chicago has been President. The official organ of the denomination is the *Covenant Weekly,* of which the Reverend G. F. Hedstrand is editor. For fifty-seven years prior to his retirement in 1946 the Reverend Otto Högfeldt edited *Missions-Vännen,* affiliated with the same denomination. At the age of eighty-seven he died in 1948.

A smaller group of Mission Friends is made up of independent churches which keep the least possible of denominational organizations. Their most influential leader was the late Johan Gustaf Princell, an able and high-spirited man, who used to say that synods were apt to be expressions of organized hypocrisy and that all denominations tended to divide rather than unite Christian believers. His ideal of church government was therefore congregationalist. In the early 1890s, Professor Stephenson records, an attempt was, in fact, made to incorporate all the Swedish Mission churches in the American Congregational Church as a separate conference, but without success. The rather loose organization of the Free Mission churches was first known as The Swedish American Mission Society, a name adopted in 1884, then as The Swedish Free Mission, next as The Swedish Evangelical Free Church, under which name it was incorporated in 1908, and now as The Evangelical Free Church of America. In 1947 it had 175 churches, 173 ministers, and 15,000 members. The President is the Reverend E. A. Halleen of Minneapolis, who is also its missionary director. Its official organ is *Chicago-Bladet,* of which J. C. Olson is the editor. In English it publishes *The Evangelical Beacon;* R. A. Thompson, editor.

Professor Princell, originally a Lutheran minister, was born in Småland in 1845, but emigrated with his family when he was only eleven. In Sweden the father's name had been Gudmundson, but in America he changed it to Gunnerson. The name Princell his son took from the town of Princeton, Illinois, where the family first settled. After attending Augustana College and working on *Hemlandet,* he studied, first at the old Chicago University and then at the Lutheran Theological Seminary in Philadelphia, which was not under Swedish Lutheran control. In 1872 he was, nevertheless, ordained by the Augustana Synod and his first charge was the Gustavus Adolphus Church in New York. In 1878 he was suspended from the Synod after he had announced his acceptance of the Waldenström theory of the atonement. He next served an independent church in Campello, Massachusetts; then became head, at Knoxville, Illinois, of the Ansgar College founded by Charles Anderson, and finally editor of various religious newspapers in Chicago. Being an outspoken and independent-minded man, he fell out in 1885 with the Mission Covenanters as he had with the Lutherans in 1878. He next started in Chicago a training school for ministers which by degrees became the present Bible Institute and Seminary of the Evangelical Free Church. Until 1914 Princell was its principal as well as its main teacher.

If Princell was the intellectual leader of the Free Mission Church, Fredrik Franson, a Swedish-born, world-roaming revivalist who carried neither scrip nor purse and preached to all nations an imminent Second Coming of Christ, was its leading orator, a counterpart to Skogsbergh in the Mission Covenant. Since both Franson and Skogsbergh had been born in the mining region in central Sweden, to which Walloon metal workers had been brought in the seventeenth and eighteenth centuries, it is probable that they both had some Gallic blood in their veins. At least they were both more temperamental than their average countryman and both looked more French than Swedish. While Skogsbergh was born in Värmland, Franson hailed from Nora in Västmanland, the heart of the iron ore district known as Bergslagen. Born in 1852, Franson was taken by his parents to Kansas when he was seventeen, and then to Nebraska. When he was twenty he was converted to the Baptist faith and in 1875 he became a follower of Dwight L. Moody, preceding Skogsbergh by a year. In 1879 he went to Utah to convert the Swedish Mormons to his own faith, but made little progress. After staging an ambitious world conference in Chicago in 1881 to prepare for the Second Coming, he once more returned to Sweden.

Until his death in 1908, Franson roamed all over the world, inspiring missionary activities and preparing his followers for an early end of the world. The two World Wars, which came after his death, would not have surprised him. "He had only a smattering of English, German, and French," writes Stephenson (p. 126), "but that mattered none, for he could pray so fervently in the language of his boyhood parish, that his hearers would burst into tears." His personal faith and consecration still inspire The Scandinavian Alliance Mission which he founded at Chicago in 1890, as well as the Evangelical Free Church of America.

Professor Stephenson (p. 125) calls him "the John the Baptist who prepared the way for Aimee Semple McPherson," who, he believes, had more followers in Sweden than in California. There the Holiness or Pentecostal Movement, of which Franson was a forerunner, is strong and still gaining ground, its Philadelphia church in Stockholm being the largest and best attended religious auditorium in the city. In recent years the Pentecostal Movement has made inroads on the Mission Covenant membership in Sweden as it has on the Baptists, but while it has given rise to a number of independent churches here too, it has created no denominational organization in America. The only church in which its services are conducted in Swedish is the Philadelphia Swedish Pentecostal Church of Chicago.

In the latter half of the nineteenth century several Swedish-speaking congregations of the Seventh Day Adventists were organized in America, principally in the Middle West, but as they were, from the start, members of the American Conference of that denomination, they, too, never had any national organization of their own.

There is also a special Scandinavian unit within the American Salvation Army, which conducts some of its exercises in Swedish. The Eastern department with headquarters in New York includes the New York, Brooklyn and Erie division with thirty-two subsidiary corps. The Central department with headquarters in Chicago has three subdivisions, covering the Middle West, as the Western Territory with headquarters at San Francisco, covers the Pacific Coast. In its ranks there are about two hundred officers and nearly seven thousand workers or "soldiers."

As individuals, many Americans of Swedish descent, whether born in the United States or in Sweden, belong to a great variety of other American religious organizations such as the Unitarian, Christian Science churches, and many others. It is only to the very oldest of the former immigrants that English is now an unfamiliar tongue. And yet as recently as when prohibition was still on the statute books in the United States an old Swedish farmer in the Middle West to whom the overtones of the religious terms his mother had taught him still meant much, is reported to have remarked that a service conducted in English was like drinking near-beer: "It has no kick in it!"

PART THREE

DENOMINATIONAL EDUCATION

===

XV

THE SWEDISH TRADITION

From their homeland the early Swedish settlers brought to America greater interest in religious than in secular education. Compulsory public schools were not established in Sweden until 1842. Some of the pioneer emigrants could therefore barely read and not all could sign their names. But as the Swedish school system progressed, this handicap was gradually overcome, so that among the mass of Swedish immigrants who came after the Civil War, the illiteracy rate was one of the lowest in any nationality. But beyond reading and writing and the rudiments of arithmetic, the main subject taught in the Swedish public schools well into the twentieth century continued to be the principles of Christianity (*Kristendomskunskap*). Since the state church had never conducted Sunday schools, at least not in the country districts from which a majority of the immigrants came, the public schools were expected to serve the same purpose. In their curriculum more hours were assigned to biblical history than to Swedish; the geography of Palestine was taught better than that of Scandinavia; the maps of the Holy Land on the schoolroom walls or printed in the textbooks were more detailed than those of Sweden; every child was expected to learn by heart the catechism of Martin Luther, both the "Little" or Shorter and the "Big" or Longer; more hymns from the official state church psalm book had to be memorized than gems from Swedish lay literature; the supervising visitor was the parish minister and the climax of the school course was the preparation for the first communion, which the minister conducted himself. Thus it may be said that the aim of the public school education in Sweden was rather to train future members of the Lutheran state church than citizens of the country—a circumstance that explains, at least partly, the difficulties the former Swedish immigrants have had in the United States in making themselves felt as a body politically, as well as the lukewarm interest they have often shown in problems of government, whether national or local. In Sweden itself the people have become more highly organized during the past fifty years, both politically and economically, than perhaps those in any other country. The labor unions and the cooperative societies are good examples. The school system has also been changed so that much less emphasis is now laid on religious instruction.

Having thus been trained under strictly religious auspices the newly arrived Swedish immigrants inevitably regarded the church as their primary center of organized activities, just as the Pilgrims had in New England. To both groups theocracy seemed normal. But just as the founders of Harvard, Yale, Brown and other colleges "dreaded to leave an illiterate ministry to their churches," so the Swedish settlers in the Middle West soon founded their own divinity schools, including preparatory courses. In Sweden neither the Methodists nor the Baptists had any clergymen to draw on, as their own denominations had not as yet gained a foothold, and the immigrants who remained Lutheran pleaded in most instances in vain for ministers from their land or origin. Even the subsequently organized Mission Covenant members, who always had set greater store on having their ministers spiritually qualified than professionally educated, have gradually raised their scholastic requirements.

In Sweden the Lutherans had been accustomed to having an academically trained clergy and therefore expected the same in the United States. The state church ministers sent to the colonial churches on the Delaware had been men with university degrees and in their parishes they set up special schools in which at least the Swedish language and the tenets of the Lutheran faith were taught, but as far as is known they founded no secular schools. In the Sunday schools of the early immigrant churches, too, Swedish was one of the first compulsory subjects, though that requirement has long since been dropped. To make use of English, new schoolbooks had to be written and published, rituals as well as hymnal texts translated, all of which took a long time, and improvements are still under way.

"Further back than forty years ago," wrote one of the colonial ministers, the Reverend Israel Acrelius, in the *History of the Swedish Congregations in America* which he published in Stockholm in 1759, "our people hardly knew what a school was. The first settlers, whether

Swedish or Dutch, were poor, humble, and ignorant folk, who brought up their children in the same lack of instruction. That is the reason persons brought up in this country [America] can neither count nor write; very few of them are fit for public service." The good opinion of the Swedes, recorded by William Penn in 1687, was based on their qualities as workers rather than as scholars.

After Penn had arrived in 1682 the first schoolhouses in Pennsylvania were built and it is likely that the descendants of the original Swedish colonists sent their children to them. The Reverend Carl Magnus Wrangel, who served the Gloria Dei Church in Philadelphia from 1759 to 1769, worked out a school program for his parish, but nothing indicates that it was intended exclusively for the children of Swedes. By that time the neighborhood had been populated with Dutch, English and German families, as well as the original Swedish, and they too attended the "Old Swedes" churches which at first were the only ones built.

At the Bishop Hill colony, the founder, Eric Janson, started a school in English for the brighter young men among his followers, and his purpose, too, was religious rather than civic. In Sweden he had educated himself. As a young man he, like the colonists on the Delaware, hardly knew what a school was. But being naturally shrewd he understood that if he was to gain adherents among the non-Swedes in the United States he must reach them through the use of English. Such missionary work was to be done by the graduates of his school. In 1850 his death ended the program.

The Swedish immigrants have always set a high value on the education of their children and for that purpose few nationality groups have made greater sacrifices. In the American public schools, as in various colleges and universities, many Swedes have served as teachers or administrators or both. Where they were among the first settlers they promptly took part in the organization of public schools. In McPherson County, Kansas, for instance, the Reverend Olof Olsson, who arrived there at the head of a large group of immigrants from Sweden in 1869, became the first County Superintendent of Schools, a post in which he was followed by his successor in the church, the Reverend Carl A. Swensson. Fearing political domination by any religious group or sect, the Swedes in America have always been strongly in favor of a strict separation of church and state and they have never tried to introduce the Swedish type of an established or state church.

XVI

Augustana College

The first attempt by Swedish settlers in the United States to educate their own ministers was made in 1855 through the newly organized Lutheran Synod of Northern Illinois, in which both German and Norwegian churches as well as Swedish were members. A Lutheran academy and seminary had been established in 1851 by this Synod at Springfield, Illinois. It was ambitiously named "The Illinois State University," though it was privately owned and was far from being a university in the usual sense of the word. To specialize in the training of ministers for the Norwegian as well as Swedish churches, a special chair was to be provided and called the Scandinavian Professorship, and the Reverend Lars Paul Esbjörn, who had then recently arrived from Sweden, was designated to collect funds for it. By October 1856, he had obtained promises of $2,640 of which $1,373 had actually been paid in. Each church was to contribute $25 annually toward the salary of the professor; interest on the hoped-for endowment fund was to supply the rest. The panic of 1857 delayed further collections and yet in September that year Esbjörn was himself appointed to the chair. (The Reverend Peter Fjellstedt in Sweden had previously been invited, but had declined.) In the fall of the next year, 1858, Esbjörn moved from Andover to Springfield and began to teach. In the catalogue for 1858–59 he was listed as "Professor of Scandinavian Languages, Chemistry, Astronomy, etc." Esbjörn, to be sure, was an expert in mathematics. "He who knows not mathematics is but half a man," he used to quote King Charles XII of Sweden as having said, and as a tutor in that subject he was once engaged by Abraham Lincoln, then a lawyer in Springfield, for the benefit of his son, Robert T. Lincoln. The future head of the Pullman Company was then a junior in the academy and his father was a member of the Board of Directors of the school.

Esbjörn's real mission at Springfield was not to cover all the gaps in the curriculum, but to train young men to become ministers. By the end of his second year, twenty-four of the 120 students were Scandinavians. With William M. Reynolds, who in 1857, had been brought in from Columbus, Ohio, as the new President, Esbjörn came into conflict over both doctrinal and money matters. Originally Reynolds had been a professor at the Gettysburg Theological Seminary in Pennsylvania, from which Seminary Ridge made famous by the battle was named, and had next become President of the Capital University of Columbus, Ohio, another Lutheran academy and seminary at which Eric Norelius was educated. Reynolds objected to Esbjörn's private religious services for his students, which included the celebration of Holy Communion, and Esbjörn wanted to know what had become of the $1,500 which Jenny Lind had contributed in 1854 toward a Scandinavian Chair at the Capital University in Columbus, Ohio, while Reynolds was still its president. The dissension finally grew so sharp that in March 1860, in the middle of the spring term Esbjörn stopped teaching and moved to Chicago, urging his Scandinavian students to follow, which they did. After his departure the "State University" at Springfield gradually disintegrated and since the money Esbjörn had collected toward an endowment of the Scandinavian Chair had been merged with the general funds of the school, that, too, vanished. (The same fate had overtaken the Jenny Lind donation to the school at Columbus, Ohio.)

For the support of the Scandinavian professorship at Springfield, Esbjörn and his friends had decided to ask for a special collection of money in the state churches of both Sweden and Norway, but this request the King of the two countries turned down. A projected personal visit by Esbjörn to collect money for the professorship at Springfield had to be postponed because of "the present state of Europe," according to Synod minutes. The Crimean War was, in fact, then raging and both Sweden and Norway were in danger of being involved. Because of the after-effects of the panic of 1857 and the approaching Civil War it was not easy in 1860 to get funds in America either for the benefit of a foreign-born group.

Another attempt to collect money in Sweden was then decided on and in September 1860, the Reverend Olof Christian Telemak Andrén, who since 1856 had been pastor of the church founded by Esbjörn at Moline, Illinois, was sent there to make personal solicitations. Like Hasselquist and Erland Carlsson, Andrén was a graduate of Lund University and before coming to America had been a minister in the

Swedish state church. He found the Archbishop at Uppsala, Henrik Reuterdahl, decidedly averse to a general church collection for any such purpose. Since there was no Swedish bishop in America to supervise the spending of the proceeds, he said he feared that they would be frittered away. But the new King, Charles XV, and some of his Cabinet members, who were influenced by Peter Wieselgren and other leaders of the new and more liberal element in the state church, were more farsighted and they had the final decision. Two annual collections were authorized, yielding together $10,846, not a large sum, to be sure, from a country of over three million people, but when paid in cash in the midst of the Civil War through the Swedish legation in Washington it was very welcome. King Charles XV himself, to show his interest, donated five thousand volumes from his private library, mostly unbound French books on political subjects he had inherited from his father, Oscar I. (They are still to be found in the Denkmann Memorial Library of Augustana College, Rock Island, Illinois.) After Andrén had finished his missionary work in behalf of the new college, he was offered a pastorate in the state church, which he accepted—a distinct loss to the young Augustana Synod that was hardly offset by the money he had collected for the new college. To promote the second collection, Esbjörn himself returned to Sweden in 1862 and he, too, never came back, an even greater loss to the college, the Synod, and the Swedes in America in general. Having by then lost his oldest son on a battlefield in the Civil War, two wives and a daughter, besides the two little boys who died on the way from Sweden, he was a sorely bereaved man.

An offer of a professorship at the new college failed to bring the Reverend O. C. T. Andrén back. Negative answers were also received from other Swedish teachers of theology such as Sven L. Bring and Paul Peter Waldenström, who later became leader of the Free Mission Church in Sweden. Finally, the Reverend Tuve Nilsson Hasselquist, President of the Synod, took charge of the college too. At that time Esbjörn had become installed as rector of a church in Sweden, and Hasselquist moved the college and theological seminary from Chicago to Paxton, Ford County, Illinois, then an almost uninhabited farming area. In June 1863, the Board of Directors signed an agreement with the Illinois Central Railroad to buy, at $6 an acre, one thousand acres of land, which the railroad had received from the Government as a bounty for new construction. (Twenty years before the top price in Henry County had been $2.50 per acre, paid by the advance agents of the Eric Jansonists at Bishop Hill.) In addition, the college was to get a commission of one dollar per acre for whatever land it could sell at the same price for the first thirty thousand acres and half a dollar an acre on the next thirty thousand. To make the contract operative, at least ten thousand acres had to be sold the first year. While the Civil War was under way, it was difficult to get new settlers who would buy virgin land and after it was over more and more of the Swedes moved to Kansas or Minnesota, where, under the Homestead Act, passed in 1862, Government land was given free to settlers who proved they could live on it for at least five years.

The move to Paxton was not a success. Esbjörn had been right. Chicago was destined to be the great metropolis of the Swedish Americans, he had thought, and there the college should have remained. But back of the move to Paxton hovered the idea of setting up an all-Swedish community with the college as the center. It was the Bishop Hill project all over again, though without any joint ownership of property. Among the few Swedes who had bought land around Paxton, Hasselquist organized a congregation of which, in addition to his college work, he became the pastor. As there were no school buildings, he had to find room in his own house the first year for the five students enrolled, three Norwegians and two Swedes. The next year an old, abandoned public schoolhouse was bought for the recitations and four small frame houses for dormitories. Prior to 1870 the average attendance was thirty-five, but that year it went as high as eighty-nine. At first, all instruction was of the high school grade as none of the students had any previous training except that provided by the public schools in Sweden, which had been only elementary. Instruction in college subjects began as early as 1866, and in 1877 the first class of half a dozen young men were graduated with Bachelor degrees. Among them were Constantin Magnus Esbjörn, a son of the founder of the college, who later became himself its Professor of Theology, and Carl A. Swensson, a son of the Reverend Jonas Swensson, and the subsequent founder of Bethany College at Lindsborg, Kansas. For the first twenty years all instruction was given in Swedish, but Hasselquist early foresaw that there would never be enough Swedes in America to maintain the language permanently and he therefore preferred professors who could teach in English. Since 1890 all instruction, except classes in Swedish and special training courses in the theological seminary, have been given in that language. As long as immigration continued, the ministers of all Swedish churches in America had to be able to preach in both languages, a difficult requirement.

Once Paxton was admitted to be unsuitable, if not hopeless, several places in Illinois were considered for a new site; among them Andover, Galva, and Geneseo, but finally a ridge between Moline and Rock Island, facing the Mississippi River, which there flows west, was chosen. It was a good choice. In 1873 some nineteen acres of ground were bought for $10,000 and the construction of a new college building begun. Again the country had been struck by a financial depression and the first building, a four-story brick structure, was not ready until 1875. To support the college, every communicant in the Synod was asked to make an annual contribution of twenty-five cents, making Augustana in a special sense a people's college.

A decade later a new main building of stone, looking somewhat like a state capitol, was erected. It cost nearly $100,000 and at once outranked the Tower Building at Bishop Hill as the most impressive building erected by Swedish Americans for their own use. Since then a number of new buildings have been added, including a special group for the theological seminary, which are very modern and distinctly "American Collegiate." The ten buildings and the grounds which now constitute the college and seminary plant are valued at over a million and a half dollars while the endowment fund approaches two millions. New departments have gradually been added, including those of science and art as well as music and nursing. High school graduates of both sexes are admitted. The faculty comprises about fifty members and the student body around 1,500. In 1947 the college and the seminary were completely separated. A Phi Beta Kappa rating was won by the former in 1949.

After the death in 1891 of Hasselquist, Olof Olsson, who since 1875 had been Professor of Theology, became President and served for ten years. His successor was Gustav Albert Andreen, who like Hasselquist served for thirty years. He was the son of Andreas Andreen, a pioneer pastor in Indiana and Illinois, and not related to the Reverend O. C. T. Andrén, who had solicited funds for Augustana in Sweden. A native-born American, Andreen was himself an alumnus of Augustana, having been graduated at the head of his class in 1881. After serving as an instructor at Augustana and Bethany successively, and taking a law course (1884–1886), he became a graduate student at Yale in 1893 and in 1898 received his Ph.D. degree in Germanic languages. To prepare himself for a Scandinavian professorship at Yale, which had been offered him, he took a two-year course at the universities of Uppsala, Oslo, and Copenhagen, but no sooner had he begun his teaching at Yale, than he accepted, instead, the presidency of Augustana. Besides being a good linguist who wrote and spoke Swedish and English with equal ease, he was a practical executive, who could raise money for new buildings. Until 1905 he was not ordained. While still in Sweden, he had collected about $27,000 for a professorship at Augustana in science, named in honor of the new King, Oscar II, and not only were the debts of the college paid in full during his administration, but an endowment fund was begun.

In 1935 Andreen was succeeded by the Reverend Conrad Bergendoff, the son of an Augustana pastor at Middletown, Connecticut, a graduate of Augustana College and Theological Seminary, and holder of a Ph.D. degree from the University of Chicago. At one time, like Andreen, he pursued advanced studies at Uppsala University and before being elected President he had served for several years as Dean of the Augustana Seminary. He has formulated his educational program as follows: "My belief is that a Christian college does most for American citizenship when it remains true to the purpose for which it exists, namely, the interpretation of all knowledge in the light of the Word of God."

For a denominational college, Augustana has paid considerable attention to science, a subject with strong appeal to almost all Swedes. As early as 1877, Professor Anders Richard Cervin, brother-in-law of Hasselquist and once his assistant as editor of *Hemlandet*, gave a voluntary course in botany. A native of Kristianstad in Skåne, where he was born in 1823, and holding a Ph.D. degree from the University of Lund, obtained in 1847 when he was but twenty-four years old, he had studied law as well as science and theology. When *Hemlandet* moved to Chicago in 1864, he became its chief editor, but after Hasselquist had been appointed President of Augustana College and moved it to Paxton he joined him in 1868 as one of the teachers. His subjects were Greek, mathematics, and the natural sciences. From 1878 to his death in 1900 he was also the managing editor of the weekly church paper, *Augustana*, and other synodical publications. (His son, Olof Z. Cervin, is now the official architect of the Augustana Synod.)

Cervin's successor as Professor of the natural sciences was another graduate of Lund University, Joshua Lindahl, born at Kungsbacka, Sweden, in 1844, and before emigration a participant as a botanist in several British as well as Swedish deep-sea expeditions. In 1876 he came to Philadelphia as assistant to the director of the Swedish pavilion at the Centennial Exposition. He was the real founder of the science department at Augustana, teaching there from 1878 to 1888, when he became State Geologist of Illinois and Curator of the Natural History Museum at Springfield. In 1895 he was appointed Director of the Cincinnati Society of Natural History. He was a prolific writer on a great variety of scientific subjects, and Volume 8 of the *Geographical Survey of Illinois* is chiefly his work.

In 1888 he was succeeded at Augustana by one of his own pupils, John A. Udden, likewise born in Sweden, but in 1881 graduated at Augustana, where he had been one of the students of botany under Cervin. While a teacher at Bethany College at Lindsborg, Kansas, he found in an Indian grave at Paint Creek, five miles from Lindsborg, a piece of steel-chain mail, which may have been taken by the Indians from one of the soldiers of Coronado. From 1915 to his death in 1943, Udden, who was one of the first to write about sand storms and soil erosion, was Professor of geology at the University of Texas, and as such first suggested the presence under the university's own land of the petroleum deposits from which oil worth several millions has since been extracted.

Among other prominent American scientists first trained at Augustana College have been Anton J. Carlson, the famous "Ajax," Professor Emeritus of physiology at the University of Chicago and former President of the American Association of University Professors; George M. Stephenson, Professor of History at the University of Minnesota; Thorsten Sellin, eminent sociologist and criminologist of the University of Pennsylvania, and editor of *The Annals*, published by the American Academy of Political and Social Sciences; Roy V. Peel, now director of a special graduate school to train city administrators at Indiana University; O. E. Oestlund, State Entomologist of Minnesota; Philip Dowell, head of the department of biology in the New York City school system; and John Edward Wallin, a native of Iowa, who is director of education in mental hygiene in the state of Delaware. In 1932 Augustana College could boast of being the alma mater of one hundred professors stationed in various parts of the United States. Its students likewise come from almost every state in the Union. In 1935 the Wallberg Hall of Science was built from a bequest by Emil and Marie Wallberg of Toronto, Canada, which ultimately may amount to $500,000, the largest gift ever made for educational purposes by a Swedish American family. Superbly situated and well equipped, Augustana College seems assured of a bright future.

XVII

GUSTAVUS ADOLPHUS COLLEGE

During the Civil War the Swedish Lutherans of Minnesota began in a modest way a little school that was to become, step by step, the present Gustavus Adolphus College of St. Peter, Minnesota. In the education of future clergymen for the Augustana Synod it has served as a "feeder" for the Augustana Theological Seminary at Rock Island. The founder of the Minnesota school was the Reverend Eric Norelius who, with his older brother, Anders, had arrived from Sweden in 1850. In 1856, when he was but twenty-three years old, he had been ordained a minister in the new Swedish Lutheran church, together with a few other recently arrived ex-immigrants. The same year he was sent to Red Wing, Minnesota, where a congregation had just been organized. In the fall of 1862, when the War Between the States was in its most critical stage, he began to give private instruction in his own home, at first to a single pupil, J. Magny (father of Clarence R. Magney, former Mayor of Duluth, and now a Justice of the Supreme Court of Minnesota). By the spring of 1863, the number had grown to eleven. The next year the school was moved to an abandoned log church at East Union in Carver County and under the name of Minnesota Elementary School it was put in charge of the Reverend Andrew Jackson, a former Lutheran missionary in Kandiyohi County, who had been forced to abandon his work by the Sioux Indian uprising in 1862. To help support themselves the students once operated a grist mill. The name of Elementary School was an echo of the Swedish term *Elementarskola,* which would correspond to an American junior high school rather than to a public grammar school. In 1867 the name was changed to St. Ansgar's Academy, in honor of the first Christian missionary in Sweden. Like the Paxton site for Augustana College, that at East Union clearly showed itself to be too remote, and in 1872 a committee of the Minnesota Conference of the Swedish Lutheran Church recommended a merger with the University of Minnesota, which was not then the mammoth institution it is today. Only Swedish and the principles of Christianity were to be taught by the academy; all other subjects by the university. The panic of 1873 prevented the merger and in 1876 the school was moved to St. Peter, a German and predominantly Roman Catholic community on the west bank of the Minnesota River, to the northwest of Minneapolis. There a Swedish farmer by the name of Anders Thorson had obtained from the citizens of the town an offer of twenty acres of land and $10,000 in cash. The offer was made and accepted in 1874 and in 1875 the first building was erected. Possibly as an expression of its independence of the Roman Catholic implication contained in the name St. Peter, the school was again renamed and, in honor of the Swedish hero-king in the Thirty Years' War, called Gustavus Adolphus College.

For the first five years the Reverend John P. Nyquist was President and in 1881 he was succeeded by Matthias Wahlstrom, one of the earliest graduates of Augustana College at Rock Island, Illinois. During the next twenty-three years he kept the helm. Since his retirement in 1904 there has been a long succession of presidents, the present occupant of the post being the Reverend Dr. Edgar Magnus Carlson.

The number of students has seldom been over six hundred, but during the Second World War four hundred United States Navy trainees were enrolled. Situated on a high ridge, facing the river and overlooking the city of St. Peter, are thirteen college buildings, and about $100,000 was appropriated ahead for a new library, which was dedicated in the fall of 1948. The total real estate holdings and equipment have been valued at $1,250,000 and the endowment fund has reached $500,000. Among the contributors have been J. J. Hill, the American railroad builder, who gave $40,000, a sum more than matched by C. A. Smith, the Swedish-born lumber magnate, who assigned to the college property worth over $50,000. The late John A. Johnson, Governor of Minnesota for three terms, who had been editor of the St. Peter *Herald,* collected $41,000 toward a woman's dormitory, which in his honor was named Johnson Hall. Of this sum he had obtained $32,500 from Andrew Carnegie. After the First World War the General Education Fund of the Rockefeller Foundation promised $100,000 toward an endowment fund, provided twice that sum was contributed by the alumni and other supporters. By 1925 this was done.

Among the alumni have been two famous Governors of Minnesota; John Lind, the first Swede to be elected to that office, who had been a student while the school was still at East Union, near Carver, and

A. Olson Eberhart, also born in Sweden, who was graduated in 1895, when full college rank had been attained. Other prominent alumni are Henry N. Benson, former Attorney General of Minnesota and now President of the college's Board of Directors; Carl E. Seashore, the music psychologist, who was Dean Emeritus of the graduate school at the University of Iowa, and Admandus Johnson, historian of the Delaware Colony, and founder of the American Swedish Historical Museum in Philadelphia. Among former students who attended the seventy-fifth anniversary in June 1937 were Andrew Holt, Senior Justice of the Minnesota Supreme Court, then aged eighty-five, and Colonel J. A. Lundeen of Washington, D.C., aged eighty-nine, whose service in the United States Army had been begun sixty-nine years earlier. Like Governor Lind, they had attended while the school was at East Union. During the seventy-five-year period of its existence, 10,228 students had been enrolled, of whom 3,488 had been graduated. Of the 1,791 college graduates, 250 had become ministers or missionaries, and 479 teachers in American public schools.

XVIII

BETHANY COLLEGE

Among the various colleges and academies established by the Swedish Lutherans, three others in addition to Augustana and Gustavus Adolphus, have survived and are likely to continue since they serve neighborhood as well as denominational needs. They are: Bethany College in Lindsborg, Kansas, Luther Academy at Wahoo, Nebraska, and Upsala at East Orange, New Jersey. Of these Bethany is the oldest, being founded in 1881 by the Reverend Carl A. Swensson, one of the first graduates of Augustana. He had been born in Sugar Grove, Pennsylvania, near Jamestown, New York, the son of the Reverend Jonas Swensson, one of the early pastors persuaded to come from Sweden. Having entered Augustana in 1873 while it was still at Paxton, Illinois, and followed it to Rock Island in 1875, Carl Swensson was graduated in 1877 with the first group to receive a Bachelor of Arts degree. After taking the seminary course, he was ordained in 1879, and was then called to the new settlement at Lindsborg, Kansas, as successor to Olof Olsson, who had been appointed Professor of Theology at Augustana. Not only at home but in college he was thus trained by people who themselves had been educated in Sweden. He therefore both spoke and wrote Swedish and English equally well. Tall, erect, blond, and full of vitality, he was a whirlwind of energy. He was a writer as well as orator, a teacher and legislator—fond of travel and at the same time determined to build up both Lindsborg and Kansas. While personally a decided Puritan, he had a strong flair for publicity. As a member of the State Legislature he helped keep Kansas "dry"; but he also loved both art and music. The Lindsborg Oratorio Chorus which for the past two generations has sung Händel's *Messiah* at Easter was organized by him and his wife.

Coming fresh from Rock Island in Illinois, he was determined that his new field of endeavor should also have a college. His Swedish fellow pastors in Kansas nodded approval, but took no action. In 1879 his

congregation had set aside certain lots to be sold, half the proceeds
to be used for a Lutheran School and the other half for a church
building, but as land was then plentiful, sales were hard to make. But
Swensson went ahead. As an assistant teacher he engaged his class-
mate from Augustana, Johan August Udden, who had specialized
in science. When the new school opened on October 15, 1881, in the
basement of Swensson's church, the two teachers were there but not
a single pupil. (In Minnesota, twenty years earlier, Eric Norelius had
had on the opening day at least one student.) But Swensson was not
daunted. When farm work was over later in the fall, he rounded up
the young men and the final, first-year attendance went as high as
twenty-seven. While Swensson himself taught Swedish and Christianity, Udden took over all other subjects.

The first year's budget was less than $300. The next year there were
ninety-two pupils and in 1883 the first building was erected. From
the beginning, the training of teachers, both for the parish schools in
Swedish communities and the expanding public school system of the
frontier was stressed. By 1886, when a new main building of brick
had been completed, a full college course of four years was offered and
has been ever since. In addition to the school of music and the college
orchestra, both directed for the past forty years by Professor Hagvard
Brase, who had been trained in Sweden, a school of art was organized
in 1890. It was first directed by Olof Grafström, a prolific painter of
both landscapes and church murals, who later joined the faculty of
Augustana College at Rock Island. He was succeeded by Birger
Sandzén, who in a manner and color all his own has not only painted
the Kansas plains and the Rocky Mountains, but has done pioneer
work in making Kansas and the whole Southwest more art conscious.
Andrew Carnegie contributed $20,000 toward a college library and
C. A. Smith, the Swedish-born lumber baron of Minnesota, offered to
give a certain amount of his lumber, then worth about $25,000, pro-
vided the college could raise $100,000 in cash. In 1929 Presser Hall
was completed as a special auditorium for the annual *Messiah* festivals,
aided by a gift of $75,000 from the Presser Foundation, which had
been established by a music publisher of that name in Philadelphia.
Like the money for the Denkmann Library in Rock Island, this gift
came from a non-Swedish source, indicating that the college and the
Oratorio Chorus had won good-will and confidence in wide circles.
An earlier auditorium had been built with aid from C. A. Smith,
a friend of Swensson, who had already aided Gustavus Adolphus

College in his own state. After Mr. Swensson's premature death at forty-seven in 1904, his assistant, the Reverend Ernst F. Pihlblad, succeeded him as President, a post he held until just before the Second World War. The present occupant of the post is Dr. Emory Lindquist, a former Oxford scholar. The directors, five of whom must be clergymen and six laymen, are nominated by the alumni and elected by the Kansas Conference of the Swedish Lutheran Church, which owns the property. Like Augustana, Bethany fills, however, a wider need than the purely denominational. In 1947 the students numbered 415.

In 1949 Bethany College received, for the construction of a Science and History Hall, a bequest of $100,000 from the estate of Ludwig Nelson of Wichita, Kansas, a former immigrant from Småland, who had died in August of that year, leaving an impressive fortune. He had once been mayor of Lindsborg, the seat of his beneficiary institution.

XIX

Luther College

No sooner had Carl A. Swensson launched the little school at Lindsborg, Kansas, than three of the pioneer pastors of the neighboring state of Nebraska, E. A. Fogelström, J. Torell, and J. E. Nordling, followed his example and on November 10, 1883, the four hundredth anniversary of the birth of Martin Luther, opened a Luther Academy at Wahoo in that state. The number of students the first day was only five, but, as in Kansas, the number grew rapidly after the corn had been husked that fall. At the end of the first term it was thirty-five. By 1930 it had reached 215, but the average attendance in recent years has been slightly less than that. During the Second World War, the six buildings, valued at over $200,000, were used for the United States Air Force Reserve program. The academy section has two parts, a college preparatory course and a general vocational. The junior college, organized in 1925, gives courses in liberal arts, teacher training, commerce and music. At the fiftieth anniversary in 1933 it was estimated that a total of 4,560 pupils had been enrolled and of these 1,305 had been graduated. For the upkeep of the school the Nebraska Conference, which owns it, had by then contributed $235,000 and for the buildings and permanent improvements, $211,000. The Reverend Floyd E. Lauersen is now President as well as Dean of the junior college. The late P. A. Rydberg, who died in 1931 while Curator of the New York Botanical Gardens, was once a teacher there. His study of the flora of the Rocky Mountains is still standard. The most famous alumnus of the music school is Howard Hanson, composer, conductor, and Director of the Eastman School of Music at Rochester, New York, who was born on a near-by farm. In 1945, one-half of the Nebraska contribution to the Centennial Thank Offering of the Augustana Synod, or about $65,000, was added to the endowment fund.

XX

UPSALA COLLEGE

In 1893 extensive celebrations were held both in Sweden and among the Swedish Lutherans in the United States to commemorate the three hundredth anniversary of a conference at Uppsala, Sweden, at which the Protestant Reformation was definitely accepted as the state religion. On that occasion the former emigrants and their descendants in America were visited for the first time by a prelate of the Swedish state church, the Right Reverend K. H. Gez. von Schéele, Bishop of Visby. By that time the stream of Swedish immigrants in the United States had penetrated through the Middle West, the Mountain states and to the Pacific Coast, as well as through New England, New York, New Jersey and central Pennsylvania. In the industrial Eastern communities, in which the more recent arrivals had found work as skilled mechanics rather than as farmers, several Lutheran churches had by then been built. Their earliest ministers were graduates of the Middle Western Swedish colleges, and the East was regarded by the settlers in the Midwest as a missionary field.

The need of an Eastern college was keenly felt, however, and in Rock Island, while attending the celebration of the tercentenary of the Uppsala Convocation, a committee representing the New York Conference of the Augustana Lutheran Synod decided to found a college. This was done the same fall and the Reverend Lars H. Beck, who had a Ph.D. degree from Yale, was selected as the first principal. The first schoolroom was in the basement of the Bethlehem Church on Pacific Street in Brooklyn. At the outset thirty-six students were enrolled and in 1905 four graduates were given B.A. degrees. The next four years the college was housed in a rented building belonging to another church in Brooklyn and after that it was moved to Kenilworth, New Jersey, where a real estate company offered a bonus of $8,000 and a commission on whatever lots the college backers could sell. These terms were not kept and soon the college found itself isolated in a barren district which failed to develop as expected, either as an industrial center or as a residential community. Many buyers of lots became tired of paying taxes and finally abandoned their holdings. Dr. Beck resigned in 1910 and was succeeded by the Reverend Peter Froeberg, one of the first graduates. In two years he managed to collect $23,000 toward paying a debt of $30,000. In 1920 the Reverend Carl G. Erickson, another holder of a Ph.D. degree from Yale, was elected President. In 1924 he moved the college to East Orange, New Jersey, where well-developed, residential property, comprising twenty-eight acres, had been bought for $228,000, by far the most ambitious purchase ever made by any educational institution founded by Swedish Americans. A campaign for funds had yielded $445,000 in pledges. Thanks to the prosperity that followed the First World War the Eastern Swedes were then able to give money. By 1928 the enrollment had reached three hundred, in which many nationalities besides the Swedish were represented. At first several suburban residential buildings were remodeled into dormitories or recitation halls. In 1934 more land was acquired, including space for an athletic field. A special endowment of $100,000 for a professorship in Swedish was collected in 1942–44, and since then a rather ambitious building program has been begun. Four units including Beck Hall were completed in 1948, and plans made for a chapel and a gymnasium. When the war was over the enrollment reached the 1,800 mark. Being situated so near New York and in the heart of one of its best developed and most densely populated suburbs, the college has impressive possibilities. The academy, or high school department, was dropped in 1928. No attempt has so far been made to offer professional training for ministers. Each year, however, several of the graduates continue their studies at the Augustana Theological Seminary at Rock Island or in other divinity schools. The present head of Upsala College is the Reverend Evald B. Lawson, a youthful and enthusiastic administrator, who has an earned Doctor's degree in theology.

For admission, no denominational or racial tests have been applied at any of the colleges founded by Swedes in America, and for a number of years all of them have been co-educational.

At Parkland, Washington, the Pacific Lutheran College was founded in 1920. It is owned by the Pacific Lutheran College Association representing the Pacific district of the Evangelical Lutheran Church and is supported by a number of Lutheran organizations on the West Coast. In 1947 it had eight hundred students and the President was S. C. Eastwold. It is the only four-year Lutheran college in the entire Pacific Coast area.

XXI

North Park College

The early educational problems of the Swedish Mission Friends were more complicated than those of other Swedish denominations. To begin with, there was no unanimity as to whether preachers should be professionally trained at all, spiritual zeal and the gift of oratory being held by some to be sufficient. In the second place, the new denomination had no "mother church" in either Sweden or the United States from which educational traditions could be derived. Many of the early ministers who came from Sweden had had, to be sure, a fair degree of training at special schools for colporteurs, or lay preachers, such as the Ahlgren School at Hvetlanda in Småland, and gradually the educational requirements for all Mission Church pastors were raised.

By offering to help train their preachers, the American Congregational Church made an attempt in 1885 to gradually affiliate with itself the Swedish Mission Friends, just as forty years earlier the American Episcopal Church had tried to absorb the Swedish Lutherans. In the early 1850s the Home Mission Society of the same denomination had likewise given financial aid to the Reverend Lars Paul Esbjörn, the pioneer Lutheran pastor, for his work among the first settlers in Illinois. In 1884 the Reverend M. W. Montgomery of Minneapolis, Director of the Scandinavian Division of the American Home Mission Society, made a visit to Sweden and returned deeply impressed with the moral earnestness and spiritual strength of the Free Church movement in the northern countries. Through letters of introduction from a Mission Friend pastor in Minnesota, the Reverend Erik August Skogsbergh, he had met such religious leaders as Professor Paul Peter Waldenström and after his return he wrote a book entitled, *A Wind From the Holy Spirit in Sweden and Norway.*

When the Mission Covenant was organized in 1885 by the churches of the two older synods, the Mission and the Ansgar, two professors at the Chicago Theological Seminary, a Congregationalist institution, Messrs. Scott and Curtis, approached the delegates and offered to provide a special professorship at the seminary for the training of their future ministers. As the first occupant of the chair they would accept, they said, any candidate nominated by Dr. Waldenström in Sweden. Furthermore, they offered to pay the traveling expenses for the new President of the Covenant, the Reverend Carl August Björk, to carry a letter to Waldenström and then bring back with him whomever the latter would select. These offers were accepted and the new teacher Björk brought back with him was the Reverend Fridolf Risberg, who then became head of the Swedish department of the Chicago Seminary, a post he held from 1885 until it was discontinued in 1917. During this period altogether about three hundred ministers were trained for work among the Swedes. The first year twelve students were enrolled.

While the education given by Risberg and his associates was of the best in a professional sense, the arrangement was not satisfactory to the Swedish Mission Friends because it deprived them of control over the theological doctrines taught their future ministers. As early as 1888 the Mission Covenant therefore offered to provide an assistant to Risberg and to pay his salary. The man chosen was David Nyvall, who ultimately became a leading figure in Mission Church education. Born and educated in Sweden, he had come to Minneapolis in 1886 as an assistant to the Reverend E. A. Skogsbergh, who was his brother-in-law. In Sweden his father had been one of the pioneers among the "New Readers" but he was also a friend of the Reverend Olof Olsson, an "Old Reader," who in 1869 helped establish the Lutheran settlement at Lindsborg, Kansas. Skogsbergh was an eloquent pulpiteer and revivalist and also a firm believer in education. In his own house in Minneapolis he had organized a little divinity school, which in 1885 was moved to an empty store and in 1888, when his new and imposing Tabernacle had been finished, was given quarters there. The same year Nyvall left for Chicago to assist Risberg at the Congregationalist Seminary, where he remained for two years. From 1892 to 1917 another Swedish scholar, M. E. Peterson, assisted Risberg.

Relations between the Mission Covenant and the "Risberg School" in Chicago remained friendly, and in 1890 new "efforts were made," writes Professor George M. Stephenson, "to organize the Mission Covenant into a conference of the Congregational Church." This move the Swedes resisted and at the Covenant Conference in 1891 it was decided to accept Mr. Skogsbergh's offer to make his Minneapolis school, called the Northwestern Collegiate, the denominational training institution for future preachers. It had previously been a general academy with a business school. Now a seminary was added and after Risberg had declined the presidency, it was accepted by Nyvall. Soon the enrollment reached 125. In 1894 the school was moved to Chicago where about eight acres of land had been provided as a site on the North Branch of the Chicago River. The new name was North Park College.

In 1923 Nyvall resigned the presidency to concentrate on the seminary. As President he was succeeded by the Reverend Algoth Ohlson, who had a Master's degree from Harvard. When he retired in 1949 he was succeeded by Clarence A. Nelson. Free of debt the college now owns twelve buildings valued at $1,200,000 and sites for more. In 1947 the number of teachers was over seventy. While full college rank had not been attained, that is only a matter of time. Besides the Junior College, one of the first in the United States, there is an academy or high school division, a divinity school, a school of music and a special summer session including a school of Swedish.

In 1947 the enrollment reached 1,792, then the largest of any college founded by Swedes in the United States, proving the advantage of being situated in or near a large city like Chicago, which the Reverend L. P. Esbjörn had foreseen for the Lutherans as early as in 1861. In 1949, Upsala College, situated near New York, had 1,892 students, a new record for any Lutheran College in the country.

In Minneapolis the Northwestern Mission Association, a district conference of the Evangelical Mission Covenant Church of America owns the Minnehaha Academy, a four-year co-educational high school with an evangelical Christian emphasis. It was founded in 1913 and offers three main courses—college preparatory, general, and business. As part of each course Bible study and chapel attendance are required. The enrollment is limited to 450. The main building, costing about $100,000 was erected in 1922. Until 1949 when he succeeded Algoth Ohlson as head of North Park College Clarence A. Nelson was the President.

XXII

Bethel College and Seminary

Like the other Swedish denominations in the United States, the Baptists had to train a majority of their own clergymen. At first there was perhaps less enthusiasm for such education among the younger groups than among the Lutherans because their traditions in this respect were less strong. "These pioneers who had left the homeland under religious persecution, which was instigated by an educated clergy," says the introduction to a history of the Baptist Bethel College and Seminary in St. Paul, "were not to be easily persuaded that education was the key to the problem."

But among the early Swedish Baptists in America, as among the Methodists and the Lutherans, were a few men who had been educated in Sweden, and they did their best to provide academic training for future ministers. In such work the leading Baptist pioneer was Johan Alexis Edgren, a former sailor, sea captain, and a Union naval officer in the Civil War. He was an older brother of Hjalmar Edgren, also a Civil War veteran who served as a Dean of the University of Nebraska. Both were born at Elvsbacka in the Swedish province of Värmland and since their parents were fairly well-to-do and well educated, they received their early instruction at home. At the age of ten Johan Alexis was sent, however, to the *Elementarläroverk* or preparatory school at Karlstad, but from reading sea stories he became so eager to taste life at sea that at the age of thirteen he persuaded his parents to let him try. He soon had enough of being an ordinary ship's boy, sea cook, and sailor, and between voyages he studied navigation in Stockholm until at the age of twenty-three he had passed not only his captain's examination for both sail and steam, but had qualified to become a teacher of navigation. In the meantime he had explored large areas of the world from Egypt to the west coast of South America as far north as Lima, Peru, and had sailed under English, Swedish, Norwegian, German, and American flags. On his first visit to New

York he had come into contact with Olof Gustaf Hedström, the Methodist missionary to Swedish sailors and the early immigrants; at the Bethel Ship in the North River, where Edgren found a letter awaiting him from his parents, Hedström had prayed with him for the salvation of his soul. On his next visit to New York, after a harrowing experience at sea, he was taken by a friend to the Baptist Mariners' Church near Chatham Square and there on April 29, 1858, he was baptized by total immersion.

At the outbreak of the Civil War he was a mate on a Swedish brig bound from Boston to Savannah and, as it passed the South Carolina coast, in the early morning of April 12, 1861, he saw flashes of gunfire when the Confederates began to fire on Fort Sumter. On a previous trip he had observed at close range the slave labor on the waterfront at Charleston and like Lincoln in New Orleans he had then resolved "to hit that institution hard, if he ever got a chance."

When he got back to Sweden from Savannah, his younger brother, Hjalmar, who in 1860 had received a commission in the Swedish Army, had left for the United States to enlist in the Union cause. At once he got a commission as a second lieutenant in the Ninety-ninth New York Volunteers and being stationed near Fort Monroe he was one of the many spectators on March 9, 1862, at the battle between the *Monitor* and the *Merrimac*. Being like Captain John Ericsson, the inventor of the little *Monitor,* a native of Värmland, he naturally became extra-enthusiastic about its success, and his letter home about the battle so excited his older brother that the latter at once took a German sailing ship from Hamburg for New York to learn more details. After finding his brother at the Rip Raps fortifications near Fort Monroe, he returned to New York and enlisted in the Navy at the Brooklyn yard. Being then twenty-three years old, in good health, having a captain's certificate and several years' experience as a mate, and being an expert in navigation to boot, he was naturally welcome and was at once given a commission. He was ordered to report in Philadelphia for duty on a converted steamship, *Young Rover,* of which he became the navigating officer. Later he was placed in command of another blockading vessel, the *Catalpa,* serving under Admiral John A. Dahlgren in the South Atlantic blockading fleet, and, finally, had charge of a shore battery in the battles for Savannah and Charleston which ended General Sherman's campaign. By a curious coincidence he was also an eyewitness to the re-raising by General Robert Anderson of the American flag over Fort Sumter on April 15, 1865.

Between two enlistment periods in the navy, Edgren attended, during the winter of 1863-64, the Presbyterian Theological Seminary at Princeton, New Jersey, and when the war was over he refused a permanent commission in the Navy in order to enter, instead, the Baptist Theological Seminary at Hamilton, New York, where he spent the scholastic year, 1865-66. There in the spring of 1866 he married Miss Annie Abbot Chapman, whose mother, born Wadsworth, was a first cousin of Henry Wadsworth Longfellow. Their oldest son, Robert Wadsworth Edgren became famous first as an athlete and then as a New York sports editor and cartoonist.

Soon after their marriage Mr. and Mrs. Edgren were sent to Sweden with the Reverend Anders Wiberg and Colonel K. O. Broady, both married to American wives, as Baptist teachers and missionaries. Edgren had known Wiberg in Stockholm when he was a student at the navigation school and had again met him in Philadelphia during the war. Together they founded the new Baptist Bethel Seminary in Stockholm for the training of Baptist ministers in Sweden and there for three years Edgren taught mathematics, physics, geography, and astronomy. After that he continued his own theological studies at the University of Uppsala while preaching in a local Baptist church and enjoying American financial support. Next he preached for a while at Gothenburg, but Mrs. Edgren's health was frail and in 1870 both returned to the United States.

On his arrival in New York, Edgren was at once called to be the pastor of the First Swedish Baptist Church of Chicago and while there he enrolled in the Union Theological Seminary, where he was graduated in 1872. In the fall of 1871 he opened at the same institution a theological department of his own for the training of Swedish Baptist ministers. At first he had only one student, Christopher Silene, but at Christmas he got a second, Nels Hayland. The school was to have been located in the basement of his own church, but on the opening day the church was destroyed in the great Chicago fire.

Overburdened by work, poverty, and poor health, Dr. Edgren was compelled to resign his presidency in 1887 and then retire to California, where he recovered enough to continue at least his literary activities until his death in 1908. (During the Civil War he had suffered a serious sunstroke.) Next to Wiberg, he was the pioneer intellectual leader among the Swedish Baptists, both in the United States and Sweden. In spirit he was a citizen of both countries.

In the fall of 1877 the seminary was moved to Morgan Park on the south side of Chicago and, except for two brief intermissions, it remained there as part of the divinity school of the University of Chicago, until 1914, when it was merged with the Bethel Academy in St. Paul, Minnesota. In 1930 the joint name of the two institutions became The Bethel Institute. Since 1947 a full four-year college course has been offered and the name changed to Bethel College and Seminary. The campus in St. Anthony Park, St. Paul, opposite the Minnesota State Fair Grounds, covers eight acres and has three main buildings. In 1948-49 the enrollment went over seven hundred, with one hundred in the Seminary. Several new buildings are planned. In twenty years the property had reached a value of over a million dollars. A special course for women is offered, leading to the degree of Bachelor of Religious Education.

From 1914 to 1941 G. Arvid Hagstrom was President of the Bethel Institute at St. Paul and in the latter year he was succeeded by Henry C. Wingblade. For thirty years prior to 1921 Carl Gustaf Lagergren, who had been a teacher in Sweden, and educated at Uppsala University, served as Dean. "With the advent of Dr. Lagergren," writes J. O. Backlund, "a new era began in the educational history of the Swedish Baptist denomination." In Sweden Lagergren had been a friend of Anders Wiberg, whom he succeeded as editor of *Evangelisten,* the oldest Baptist publication in the country. For many years before coming to America in 1889 he was a Baptist minister at Sundsvall. With his aid and that of many others, the battle for an educated ministry among the Swedish Baptists was definitely won. The future of Bethel College and Seminary has bright possibilities.

PART FOUR

AMERICAN ACTIVITIES

═══

XXIII

LAWYERS AND PUBLIC OFFICIALS

The respect for law and order which characterizes most Swedes, wherever they live, has deep roots. Ever since they first appeared in history they have formulated rules of behavior and insisted on their observance. An often quoted preamble to one of their earliest provincial codes, on which present Swedish law is based, defines their ideal as follows:

"The law is made for the guidance of all, rich and poor, and to define right from wrong. The law shall be observed and respected, protect the poor, maintain peace for the peaceable; awe and chastise the unruly. . . . The land shall be ruled by law and not by violence."

This concept both the seventeenth century Swedish colonists and the nineteenth century immigrants carried with them to America. When Governor Johan Printz arrived in 1643 to manage the colony on the lower Delaware for the Swedish Government, he had with him a set of written Instructions which were, in effect, the first Constitution of that region. Though with the loss of the colony in 1655 the validity of these Instructions lapsed, the Swedish settlers who remained, continued "to live according to the old Swedish customs." To avoid provoking their native country, which still was powerful in Europe, the Dutch and English permitted a high degree of local self-rule.

As the colony grew under William Penn and his successors and absorbed members of other nationalities, some of the descendants of the Swedish colonists became not only lawyers but judges and holders of other kinds of public office. For many years John Morton, a great-grandson of Morten Mortensson, a Swedish-born colonist, practiced law in Philadelphia and from 1770 to 1774 was a Justice of the Supreme Court of Pennsylvania. As a delegate from that colony he added the decisive signature to the Declaration of Independence, the Pennsylvania delegation itself as well as those of the other colonies being evenly divided.

After the war Alexander Contee Hanson, a grandson of John Hanson
of Maryland who in 1781 was elected "President of the United States in
Congress Assembled," practiced law in Annapolis and was elected, successively, to both the House of Representatives and the Senate. Since
that time such American families of partly Swedish descent as the Bayards, the Keenes, the Rambos, the Paxsons, the Springers, and the
Yocums, have produced both lawyers and public officials for various
parts of the country. Some have served the nation as a whole. The Bayard family, for instance, has contributed no less than five United States
Senators from the state of Delaware, the last one being the late Thomas
F. Bayard, who held the office from 1869 to 1885. He was also Secretary
of State in the first Cleveland administration. As late as the 1930s P. Warren Green, a descendant of Peter Rambo of New Sweden, was Attorney
General of the state of Delaware. The late Colonel George A. Elliott of
Wilmington, Delaware, who traced his Swedish descent through his
mother's family, was a lawyer and also President of the Swedish Colonial
Society. Among his successors in the latter office has been Colonel
Frank D. Melvin, who is a Philadelphia lawyer. A life member of the
Society is Harold L. Ickes, former Secretary of the Interior, who like
the late President Franklin D. Roosevelt, is of partly Swedish colonial
descent. The late Colonel Henry D. Paxson of Philadelphia was also a
lawyer.

Among the nineteenth century immigrants there were, on the other
hand, few, if any, who were either inclined or qualified to be lawyers.
Except Gustaf Unonius none of the first pioneers had had a legal
education, and Unonius chose to become an Episcopal clergyman. In
the practice of law, moreover, ignorance of English was a greater
handicap than in engineering, business, teaching, the practice of medicine, or preaching, especially among fellow immigrants. At first the
Swedish-language press too offered a variety of opportunities to educated men, deficient in English. But to draw up a will or a contract,
prepare a brief, or argue a case in court required a good command of
English and special legal training, to say nothing of formal admission
to the bar. It was also easier to become an architect, an engineer, a
dentist, a research scientist, or even a college professor, than a lawyer.

In Sweden, the legal profession had been but little developed at the
time when a majority of the immigrants left. The number of lawyers
there is still relatively small and in a court any layman may represent a

friend or neighbor. Being fully codified, Swedish law is also easier to understand than either American statute or common law, the meaning of which depends so much on court decisions which only a trained jurist is able to follow. The Swedish permanent jurors (*nämndemän*) who assist the judges in the lower courts are not expected to be lawyers. The judges know the law, it is said, while the *nämndemän* know the litigants.

On the American frontier the early Swedish settlers found a different situation. For all kinds of transactions, from buying land to making a will, the assistance of a lawyer was required, and in city councils and state legislatures, to say nothing of Congress, a layman had little chance to make himself heard. In Illinois, Jonas W. Olson of Galva, the son of one of the founders of the Bishop Hill colony, is supposed to have been the first Swede admitted to the bar. In Chicago, Swan A. Miller, a native of Sweden and a Civil War veteran, who had arrived in 1855, began the practice of law in 1876.

Several of the young Swedes who had been officers in the Civil War became lawyers and public officials. Even before the war began, Hans Mattson, a former immigrant, had become a lawyer in Minnesota. In the panic of 1857 he had lost all his property and to clear up his affairs he had to consult an attorney, Warren Bristol of Red Wing, Minnesota. According to Mattson's *Memoirs* (p. 65), the latter said to him: "You have nothing to do now; you have had enough of speculation. You know the English language, you have some knowledge of our laws, you have had a good education, you are young and ambitious, then why not study law? This is the state and this the county for you to begin in. Come to me and within a year you will be permitted to practice law. After that you will have no difficulty in making a career."

With his young wife, Mattson then moved from Vasa, a community he had helped found, but where his farm was then mortgaged for four times its current value, and in Red Wing he hired a single room, about sixteen feet square, in which they both lived, ate and slept. There he plugged at his Blackstone, Kent and other commentaries. At night he often studied until midnight by an improvised lamp his wife had made from fat saved in her cooking. Kerosene lamps were not then available and tallow candles too expensive. After a year he was not only admitted to the Minnesota bar but was also accepted as a partner of his teacher. In the spring of 1858 he got a job in the office of the local justice of the peace and early in the summer he was appointed bookkeeper for the city at a salary of $12.50 a month. Next he became

County Auditor and as such was elected chairman of a committee to revise the tax laws of the state. In 1860 he campaigned for Lincoln and, in response to the latter's call for men, helped raise a company of volunteers, by whom he was elected captain. During the war itself he was promoted to colonel and placed in command of the Third Minnesota Volunteer Regiment. During his absence his job as County Auditor was held open for him and after the war was over he was three times elected Secretary of State, a record more than equalled in recent times by Mike Holm, another native of Sweden, who has been elected to the office without a break since 1920, regardless of which party has carried the state, and without ever having made a single political speech.

Holm's political strength is jocularly ascribed to the fact that the voters of Irish descent conclude from his first name that he is an Irishman, whereas the Swedish descendants know from his last that he is one of their own. As a matter of fact he has conducted his office in such a way as to win the esteem of a majority of all Minnesota citizens, regardless of national origin.

In view of the relatively large proportion of Minnesota voters who are of Swedish birth or descent (in 1940, however, only 8.2 per cent of the Minnesota population were either born in Sweden or had at least one Swedish-born parent), it is not surprising that the first Swede to be elected to Congress should come from that state. He was John Lind, who had been born in Kånna, Småland in 1854 and brought to America by his parents when quite young. His formal education was therefore wholly American. He was one of the early students at the newly founded Gustavus Adolphus College and later attended the University of Minnesota (1875–76). After that he was admitted to the bar. Ultimately he became President of the State Board of Regents. His first election to Congress took place in 1886 and he was re-elected both in 1888 and 1890, each time on the Republican ticket. In 1896 he became a Fusion nominee for Governor and in 1898 he was elected on such a ticket in opposition to a straight Republican candidate. "He was the first Swede to hold this important office," wrote O. Fritiof Ander in *Swedes in America* (p. 324) "but the Swedes of strong Republican sentiments never really appreciated Lind because he had deserted their own party." After serving one term as Governor, Lind was re-elected in 1902 to Congress, but on a straight Democratic ticket. In 1913 he was sent to Mexico by President Wilson as his personal representative in an effort to clear up the relations with that turbulent country. It was, however, a task beyond his powers. In 1930 he died, a more or less forgotten, disappointed and broken man.

In 1904 John A. Johnson, who was Minnesota-born of Swedish parents, became the second Swede to be elected Governor and under wholly Democratic auspices. He was re-elected both in 1906 and 1908 and only his death in office in 1909 prevented him from becoming a prominent candidate for President in 1912 on the Democratic ticket. The Republican split that year would have assured his election as it did Wilson's. Johnson was not a lawyer, but a newspaperman; he never had any college education, but before being elected Governor he had been editor of the *Herald* at St. Peter, the seat of Gustavus Adolphus College. Because his father had been a man of irregular habits—he had, in fact, died in a poorhouse—Johnson had truly come up the "hard way." Few men of any nationality in the state have been either more highly respected or more dearly beloved than Governor John A. Johnson. Before him only John H. Pillsbury of the flour mill dynasty had been twice re-elected Governor. Both in St. Paul and St. Peter monuments have since been raised to Johnson's memory, and at the Gustavus Adolphus College a dormitory has been named in his honor. By all citizens he is recognized as one of the state's most important men.

In the Republican split between President Taft and ex-President Theodore Roosevelt in 1912 many Swedish-born voters, particularly the farmers in the Middle West, were inclined to follow the latter. When the Farmer-Labor Party succeeded the Democratic as the main opposition party in Minnesota, as it did in neighboring states, many Swedes joined that or at least supported its nominees. In order to secure the election of their candidates the Republicans in Minnesota then began to nominate lawyers of Swedish descent, even some who were of the "Progressive" type. Thus in 1910 Johnson was succeeded as Governor by Adolph Olson Eberhart, a lawyer who was born in the Swedish province of Värmland, and graduated from Gustavus Adolphus College. Despite the Bull Moose defection in 1912, he was re-elected that year, for which the Republican leaders felt deeply grateful. Since then several Governors of Minnesota have had at least some Scandinavian blood in their veins, whether they have been Farmer-Labor men or Republicans. In 1915, when he took up the practice of law in Chicago, Eberhart was succeeded by Joseph Alfred Arner Burnquist, native son of Swedish ancestry, who had been Eberhart's Lieutenant Governor. In both 1916 and 1918 Burnquist was re-elected and has since then served as Attorney General.

In Minnesota the Progressive idea died but slowly and after the great depression had set in, Floyd Björnstjerne Olson, who was of mixed Norwegian-Swedish ancestry and of decidedly radical antecedents, was elected Governor on the Farmer-Labor ticket. Previously he had been a crusading District Attorney in Minneapolis. As Governor he, too, was twice re-elected. In 1936, after being nominated for the Senate, he died in office. Like his predecessor John A. Johnson, he might otherwise have become a national figure.

On the same wave of discontent which swept the Middle West, Ernest Lundeen, another Minneapolis lawyer, born of Swedish parents in South Dakota, staged a political comeback. A veteran of the Spanish-American War, he had first served in the Minnesota Legislature as a Republican and in 1912 and 1916 he had been a delegate to the Republican national conventions. In the latter year he was elected to Congress and was one of the few Representatives who in 1917 voted against American entry into the First World War, an act he was always proud of. (Before voting he had taken a plebiscite in his district.) In the Republican primaries in 1918, however, he was defeated for re-election and thus virtually read out of the party. In 1930 he was nominated by the Farmer-Labor Party for the Senate and in 1936, when he took the late Governor Olson's place on the ticket, he was elected. In his anti-militarist attitude he never wavered. In 1940 he was killed in an airplane accident.

The present Governor of Minnesota is Luther W. Youngdahl, another "domestic" Swede and a former Associate Justice of the state's Supreme Court. First elected in 1946, he was re-elected in 1948, though the Democrats that year won the United States senatorship, electing Hubert H. Humphrey, Mayor of Minneapolis. President Truman also carried the state. Many of the former Farmer-Labor voters of Swedish ancestry have, however, returned to the Republican fold and in the future fewer ambitious Swedes need to become Democrats or Farmer-Labor "insurgents" in order to get nominated for public office.

Prior to Lundeen, Minnesota had been represented in the United States Senate by only one Swede, Magnus Johnson, an able if unconventional political figure, a former glass blower from Värmland, whose lung power was prodigious. In 1922 he ran for Governor on the Farmer-Labor ticket and in July 1923, was appointed Senator to complete the term of the late Norwegian-born Republican veteran,

Knute Nelson. In Washington his Swedish accent as well as his bucolic ways caused amusement, especially his milking contests. The next year a campaign of ridicule, if not outright fraud, prevented his re-election. In 1932, however, he was elected to the House, and re-elected in 1934, but in the midst of the 1936 campaign he, too, died. For all his uncouthness, he was fundamentally a man of high character and considerable political acumen.

The most eminent Minnesota Congressman of Swedish origin was unquestionably the late Charles A. Lindbergh, Sr., father of the aviator, and like him inclined to be independent. Born in Stockholm in 1860 he grew up on a Minnesota farm and obtained his law degree at the University of Michigan. After practicing at Little Falls, he was elected to the House in 1906 and was re-elected four times. In Congress he started the famous investigation of the "Money Trust" and in 1918, like Lundeen, he failed of re-election. In 1919 he wrote a book called *Why Is Your Country at War?* In 1924 he was nominated for Governor on the Farmer-Labor ticket, but died during the campaign. A great deal of the opposition spirit later shown by his son was undoubtedly due to the political and personal hounding to which he had seen his father subjected. The full story of the Lindberghs has not yet been told.

In the House, Minnesota has been represented by several Congressmen of Swedish or mixed Norwegian-Swedish ancestry. (Despite the Swedish spelling of his name, Harold Knutson, the veteran Congressman who in 1948 finally was rejected by his constituents, was born in Norway.) No attempt can be made here to enumerate all of the Swedes, whether born in Sweden or "domestic," who have been members of the state's legislature or have held similar public offices.

Like the Governor's chair, that of Attorney General, which likewise used to be reserved for simon-pure Yankees, has in recent years been occupied by a number of lawyers of Swedish ancestry. Between 1929 and 1936 it was filled three times in succession by such men. Among them was G. Aaron Youngquist, born in the Västergötland province of Sweden and, like Governor Lind, brought to America in his infancy. After graduation from St. Paul's College in Iowa in 1909, he was admitted to the Minnesota bar the same year, and for four years served as District Attorney of Polk County and then as Assistant Attorney General and Attorney General. During the Hoover administration he was appointed an Assistant Attorney General of the United States and put in charge of taxation and prohibition enforcement. As such he argued for the Government upward of seventy cases before the United States Supreme Court and it was under his direction that Al Capone was finally brought to book for income tax evasion. He now practices law in Minneapolis. Others who have held the office of Attorney General in Minnesota have been Henry N. Benson, a graduate of Gustavus Adolphus College at St. Peter and a former state Senator, who held the post from 1928 to 1932, and Harry H. Peterson, who was elected state Senator three times in succession on the Farmer-Labor ticket. He is now a member of the state's Supreme Court.

An Associate Justice of the same court for thirty-one years was Andrew Holt, born in 1855, the son of Johannes Hult, a Swedish pioneer in Minnesota. After attending Gustavus Adolphus College, then at Carver, Holt studied law and after practicing for thirteen years first became a municipal judge in Minneapolis and then a district judge. In 1911 he was elected to the Supreme Court, on which he served until 1942, being regarded for many years as the most venerable jurist in the state. Upon his retirement he was succeeded by Clarence R. Magney, a former Mayor of Duluth, whose father had been the first student at Gustavus Adolphus College. Judge Magney, himself, was graduated from the University of Minnesota and Harvard Law School. Another member of the court is Associate Justice Leroy E. Matson. Since a majority of the Supreme Court Justices at St. Paul are of Swedish ancestry it is sometimes facetiously asserted that when the court really comes to grips with knotty problems of law, it does so in Swedish. As a matter of fact the use of Swedish is rapidly disappearing throughout the state. At one time there were several Swedish weeklies; now there is none.

In Des Moines, Iowa, Eskil C. Carlson, a native of Småland, who has three academic degrees in law, has been City Solicitor as well as a municipal judge. Since 1920 he has taught law at Drake University. In the same state Charles F. Wennerstrum has been a Justice of the Supreme Court since 1941, being also a Trustee of the same university. In the trials of the German war criminals at Nürnberg he was one of the American judges.

In Connecticut, a number of lawyers of Swedish ancestry have served as local magistrates. Among them is Herbert L. Emmanuelson, a native of New Haven and graduate of Yale, who was once secretary to the Mayor of the city. In the Domestic Relations and Children's Court for King's County in New York, Peter B. Hanson, a native of Hälsingborg, Sweden, was a justice from 1927 to 1937. He now practices law. In Brooklyn he has also been a Democratic district leader.

Though the profession of law cannot be said to have any special appeal to Americans of Swedish ancestry, there are now nearly three hundred lawyers of that origin in Minnesota alone. In Illinois the number is even larger and the same proportion to the Swedish population probably obtains throughout the country. While many of them have been District Attorneys or State's Attorneys or even Attorney Generals or other kinds of public prosecutors, few have elected to practice criminal law. The frenzied oratory and courtroom dramatics so often used by defense attorneys to influence juries in criminal cases seem foreign to their nature. In Sweden itself such tactics would not be tolerated for a moment. In other words, the Swedes tend to be lawyers for the state rather than for individual defendants. An example is Governor Earl Warren, of California, the Republican nominee in 1948 for Vice President, who was a District Attorney, then Attorney General, before he was elected Governor in 1942 and then re-elected in 1946 by acclamation, being endorsed by both the Republican and Democratic Parties. His father was born in Norway, but both his mother and his wife were born in Sweden.

In Illinois, where no citizen of Swedish ancestry has so far been elected either Governor or United States Senator, the Swedish proportion of the population being less than three per cent, Oscar E. Carlstrom was elected Attorney General in 1924 and held the post for two terms. From 1921 to 1925 he had been a member of the state's Tax Commission. In 1928 he was a candidate for Governor on the Republican ticket, but withdrew in order to avoid splitting the opposition to Len Small, the Republican Governor then in office.

Other American lawyers of Swedish descent who have served as Attorneys General for their respective states have been, Oscar L. Heltzen in Rhode Island; Joseph H. Peterson in Idaho; Einar K. Mattson in Montana, and Clarence V. Beck in Kansas, to mention only a few.

In Chicago, John A. Swanson, as State's Attorney for Cook County, made a determined effort from 1929 to 1932 to rid the city of its criminals, while at the same time the Federal District Attorney, George E. Q. Johnson, prosecuted both tax evaders and bootleggers. Under directions from Washington, Johnson had charge of the prosecution of Al Capone and his gang for evasion of income taxes. He later served as a United States District Judge. Incidentally, the "Q" in his initials represents only an effort to distinguish himself from the numerous other George E. Johnsons in the City Directory. The "E," however, stands for Emerson, an author greatly admired by his father, John Johnson, a Swedish-born immigrant farmer in Iowa, who arrived in 1868 from Småland. On September 19, 1949, Judge Johnson died in Chicago at the age of seventy-five.

Another native of Småland who has had a distinguished law career in Chicago for over fifty years is Gustaf Bernard Anderson, a graduate of Augustana College and Harvard University. He later studied at Uppsala University in Sweden and became an honorary Swedish Vice Consul in Chicago. A genial host, he has been President of the Chicago Food and Wine Society. His younger brother, George, who was for many years his law partner, is an outstanding expert on Chicago real estate, a subject on which he often lectures before law schools and bar associations.

Another graduate of Augustana College who has had both a political and law career in Chicago is Carl Chindblom. Before being elected to Congress as a Republican in 1918, where he served for seven consecutive terms, he had been a Cook County attorney and Master in Chancery at its Circuit Court. After his defeat for re-election to an eighth Congress term in the Democratic land slide of 1932, he was appointed a Referee in Bankruptcy. He is now engaged in private practice. In Congress he was a member of the influential Ways and Means Committee.

Chicago's most famous judge of Swedish descent was the late Harry Olson. From 1896 to 1906 he was an Assistant State's Attorney of Cook County. In 1906, when the new Municipal Court was organized, he was elected its first Chief Justice, a position he held until 1930 when he too was swamped in the Democratic wave. As a judge he instituted many judicial reforms and was active both in the rehabilitation of criminals and child welfare work.

In an effort to break the career of Chicago's famous chief magistrate, the late Mayor William Hale (Big Bill) Thompson, Judge Olson was twice entered in the Republican primaries, in 1915 and 1919, but each time was defeated by the superior political tactics of a fellow Swede, the late Frederick Lundin, a native of Trollstad in Östergötland, who, as Thompson's campaign manager, proved himself the ablest political manipulator so far produced by the Swedish element in the United States.

Having been brought to Chicago by his parents in 1878 when he was but ten years old, Lundin had learned the art of politics from the ground up. When he died in 1947 at the age of seventy-nine in

Beverly Hills, California, the New York *Times* obituary said of him that he had "wielded more political power than any other individual in Illinois for nearly a decade." His formal education had been of the slightest, but his practical experience all the more thorough. "As a youth," continued the *Times,* "he started blacking boots and selling newspapers in a Loop saloon; then became an errand boy in a clothing store. At the age of twenty he was manager of the store." Thanks to his liberal advertising, especially in the Swedish-language weeklies, of a soft drink extract he called "Juniperade," or in Swedish *Enbärsdricka,* he became widely known and in 1894 at the age of twenty-six he was elected to the Illinois State Senate from a strongly Swedish district in northwestern Chicago. He was not re-elected, but having had a taste of politics, he decided to play the game all the harder and in 1908 he was the first Illinois Swede to be sent to Congress. (In Minnesota John Lind had been elected to his first Congress term in 1886.)

In 1912 Lundin became a victim of the Republican Party division between Taft and Roosevelt and after his defeat for re-election he concentrated on local politics. Together with "Big Bill" Thompson he organized the Lorimer-Lincoln League and after Thompson's election as Mayor of the city in 1915, he acted "the silent boss" behind the scenes while Thompson played a front figure. According to the New York *Times,* Thompson gave Lundin full credit for his victory and "turned over all city patronage to the 'Poor Swede' [Lundin's own term] who set up a City Hall, No. 2, in the Hotel Sherman." An anonymous contributor to *The Swedish Element in the United States* (Vol. I., p. 95) says, "his [Lundin's] political machine was something the like of which Illinois had never seen"; while Oliver Linder, editor of a local Swedish-language weekly, *Svenska Amerikanaren-Tribunen,* who must have known Lundin personally, adds, in the same volume (p. 51), that Lundin "was without a question—and still is—a consummate politician. The part he has played in state and local politics has been on par with most anyone's, if we are willing to give the 'Poor Swede,' as he likes to call himself, his just dues. . . . There is no one to deny that for a time he was the biggest factor in political affairs in Chicago and Cook County."

To offset the influence of Lundin, the opposition Republicans in Chicago selected the "good Swede," Judge Harry Olson, as a candidate for Mayor in the party primaries and in 1915 and again in 1919, but each time were defeated. After the election of Governor Len Small in

1920, Lundin extended his hold on political affairs from Cook County, which includes most of Chicago, to the state itself. He then closed his headquarters in the Hotel Sherman and operated in greater seclusion from his estate at Fox Lake. Later he retired to California. While his countrymen concede that as a practical politician he was an exception, they find it hard to conceal their glee over the fact that at least one "poor Swede" could play the game of American politics and hold his own against all comers.

While relatively few Swedes enter politics to gain a living, a considerable number have gained high public office. If properly urged, they do not disdain the prestige that comes with such responsibility, particularly if they feel they are enrolled in a "good cause." Thus in 1912, they followed ex-President Roosevelt pretty generally into the Bull Moose camp. How many were "New Dealers" under the late Franklin D. Roosevelt is hard to say, but judging by the election results, he must have received quite a number of their votes too. Usually they like a spirit of personal independence rather than party loyalty. When the late Senator George William Norris of Nebraska supported Governor Smith for President in 1928, his prestige was not hurt among the Swedish farmers of that state. How the Swedes will vote is hard to forecast. Minnesota is notoriously one of the most difficult states in the Union to analyze before an election. The surprise in 1948 was no exception.

The first American of recent Swedish ancestry to be elected to the United States Senate was Irvine Luther Lenroot (originally, Lönnrot) of Wisconsin. Born in 1869 of Swedish parents who had arrived in 1854, he began his career as a lumber worker, became a court stenographer, was admitted to the bar in 1897, and was elected to the State Legislature in 1900. For two terms he was Speaker of the House. In 1908 he was elected to Congress and re-elected regularly until 1918, when he was appointed to fill a vacancy in the Senate caused by the death of his predecessor. In 1920 he was elected in his own right, but for only one term, being defeated in 1926. In 1929 he was appointed by President Hoover a judge in the Federal Customs Court and Patent Appeals in Washington, D.C., from which he resigned in 1944. In 1920 he had been selected by his fellow Senators as their candidate for the vice-presidency, but after Senator Harding had been "put over" in the famous smoke-filled room at the Hotel Blackstone in Chicago, the Convention took its revenge by nominating from the floor Governor Calvin Coolidge of Massachusetts. Thus Lenroot, like Governor

John A. Johnson of Minnesota, missed the chance of being the first American President with a Swedish ancestral background. He died at the age of eighty on January 26, 1949. Katherine Lenroot, who has been Director of the Children's Bureau in the Department of Labor since 1934, is his daughter.

Governor Peter Norbeck of South Dakota, who also was elected a United States Senator in 1920 and held the office until his death in 1937, was of mixed Norwegian and Swedish parentage. His political faith was that of the Progressive Republican persuasion, and by profession he was not a lawyer, but a well digger. Early in life he had been a schoolteacher. He was twice re-elected.

In the Democratic Party a similar career as a United States Senator has been made by Edwin C. Johnson of Colorado, whose father was a pioneer farmer, first in Illinois and then in Kansas, where the son was born. Originally a telegrapher and train dispatcher, the future Senator moved early to Colorado to improve his health. There he became, first, a rancher and the manager of a cooperative store. Next his cooperative friends sent him to the State Legislature and after that he was elected Lieutenant Governor and then Governor. In 1936 he received, as candidate for the United States Senate, the largest majority ever given to anyone in his state. He was re-elected in 1942 and again in 1948.

As Governor of Colorado Johnson was preceded by another Swede, George Alfred Carlson, a former football captain, Phi Beta Kappa member, and star debater, who, before his election in 1914 as a Republican, had been another "fighting District Attorney." He had been born in Iowa, both his parents being natives of the Halland province in Sweden. His promising career was suddenly cut short by death in 1926.

Early death also ended the career of John E. Erickson, who had grown up in Kansas and later moved to Montana where he became a lawyer, then a prosecuting attorney, next a district judge and, finally, from 1925 to 1933, Governor. In the latter year he was appointed to fill a vacancy in the United States Senate.

On the Pacific Coast the first Swede to reach high public office was Albin Walter Norblad who, after serving one term in the Oregon State Legislature, was elected Governor in 1929. Born in Sweden, he had gained dubious fame by introducing in the legislature during the First World War a bill making it illegal to print practically anything in any language except English—an expression of the wartime xenophobia. Needless to say, it was not passed.

Either the voters on the West Coast who are of Swedish descent are less devoted to the Republican Party than those of the Middle West and the East, or the Democratic Party managers of that region too find it pays to nominate candidates of Swedish ancestry, particularly in such states as Washington, where one-third of the population is supposed to be of Scandinavian origin. At any rate, since the Democratic resurgence began with the first election of Franklin D. Roosevelt as President in 1932, an unprecedented number of candidates of at least partly Swedish descent have been elected to Congress from the Northwest. From the state of Washington both Monrad C. Wallgren and Martin F. Smith were elected to the House in 1932, 1934, and 1936. Each time both were re-elected with increased majorities. In 1932 Smith, who is only partly of Swedish stock, was the first Democrat ever to carry the Third Congressional District. In 1940 Wallgren was appointed a Senator to complete the term of L. B. Schwellenbach, who had entered the Cabinet. In 1945 he resigned to become Governor, being succeeded in the Senate, as he had been in the House, by Warren G. Magnuson, who had been a zealous District Attorney in Seattle. In the Senate, Wallgren became a close friend of Harry S. Truman and was reputed to have been his personal choice for presidential running mate in 1948. At the Democratic Convention in Philadelphia he seconded Truman's nomination but in the election he was defeated for the Senate while Truman himself carried the state. Wallgren's nomination by President Truman on February 3, 1949, as Chairman of the National Security Resources Board was tabled by a Senate Committee, seven to six, as unwarranted by his business experience. In October, 1949, he was confirmed as a Federal Power Commissioner. From Oregon, William Alexander Ekwall was a Democratic Congressman who became a Federal Judge in New York.

Despite the New Deal wave, Frank Carlson of Kansas, the son of a Swedish-born farmer, was elected to Congress as a Republican in 1934 and re-elected five times. In 1946 he was elected Governor of Kansas and re-elected in 1948. The corresponding office in neighboring Nebraska is held by Val Peterson, another Republican, who was also re-elected in 1948. In New England, where most of the former Swedish immigrants and their descendants, though not formally, organized as such, are apt to be Republicans, only Pehr G. Holmes, former Mayor of Worcester, Massachusetts, has been elected to Congress, where he served from 1930 to 1939. Born in Sweden in 1881, he is by profession an electrotype manufacturer. In New Jersey Frank L. Sundstrom, a former all-American football player from Cornell, was elected to Congress in 1942 as a Republican and was re-elected in both 1944 and 1946, but defeated in 1948. His father was of Swedish descent.

The first American of Swedish immigrant ancestry to be appointed to a post in the Cabinet was a Democrat, Clinton P. Anderson, from New Mexico. He was born in South Dakota, usually a "Progressive" state. Originally his father came from Falun in the Swedish province of Dalarna. For reasons of health the son moved early to New Mexico and has lived there since. His record includes the work of a newspaperman, insurance official, international Rotary President, State Treasurer and member of Congress from New Mexico. At the end of the Second World War he succeeded Chester Bowles as United States Food Administrator and was then appointed Secretary of Agriculture—a post from which he resigned in 1948 to run against General Patrick Hurley, former Republican Secretary of War, for Senator from New Mexico. He was easily elected.

Until recently few Swedes have served in diplomatic posts. Few have had the professional training required of career men and even fewer have had the political background required as a rule for the key posts. In 1924, President Coolidge did appoint Alfred John Pearson, Professor and Dean at Drake University in Des Moines, Iowa, and a native of Landskrona in southern Sweden, to be United States Minister to Poland and a year later to the corresponding post in Finland. A graduate of Bethany College of Lindsborg, Kansas, Pearson held a Ph.D. degree from Yale. Later he returned to his academic work. He died in 1939.

During the First World War Colonel Oscar N. Solbert (later a general) was a United States Military Attaché in London, serving for five years under three different Ambassadors. He then became Military Aide to President Coolidge and in 1924 was appointed the official travel escort to the Prince of Wales. Both in 1926 and 1938 he performed the same duty for the Crown Prince and Crown Princess of Sweden. Born in Sweden, brought up in Worcester, Massachusetts, and a high honor graduate of West Point, he is in private life an official of the Eastman Kodak Company of Rochester, New York.

During the Second World War Major General John M. Hilldring, born of Swedish parents in New Rochelle, New York, was appointed an Assistant Secretary of State to handle relations with Germany. Resigning in 1947, he was once more chosen for the same office. On

August 5, 1949 Major General John E. Dahlquist, a native of Minnesota and of Swedish ancestry, was announced as the new commander of the First Infantry Division of the United States Army, called the "backbone of the occupation forces in Germany," traditionally a high post of honor. At the end of the war General Dahlquist was in command of the division to which Hermann Goering surrendered. Among the younger career men in the American diplomatic service there are now several who are of Swedish descent, just as there are among the younger officers in both the Army and the Navy.

As permanent officials, technicians and researchers, even more are employed in the Government departments, especially in that of Agriculture and the Forestry Service of the Department of the Interior. One of the most important permanent non-political officials of the former is Eric Englund, Assistant Chief of Research in the Bureau of Agricultural Economics. Born in northern Sweden, he went to sea as a boy, worked for Swedish farmers in Texas and then in Oregon, where he managed to get his college education. Subsequently he became a Master of Science at the University of Wisconsin and a Ph.D. at Harvard. During the Second World War he was a veritable Joseph in the handling of the world's wheat supply. He is now on a special mission to Sweden as an Agricultural Attaché at the American embassy in Stockholm.

During the Second World War Professor Theodore Andersson of Yale University held a post in the Cultural Relations division of the State Department. Nils Gösta Sahlin, Director of the American Swedish Institute in Minneapolis, and Nils W. Olsson of the University of Chicago, both born in Sweden, were officials at the American legation in Stockholm, while Erik T. H. Kjellstrom, a Swedish-born economist, now with the National Association of Manufacturers, served in the Economic Warfare division in Washington.

In July, 1949 Dr. Eric Cyril Bellquist became First Secretary of the American Embassy in Stockholm. He had previously been Professor of Political Science at the University of California and Acting Chairman of the Department. During the war he was a regional specialist on northern Europe for the OWI and later in the Department of State. He was born in 1903 of Swedish parents in New Jersey, brought up in Tennessee, and educated in California. In Stockholm he was to serve as Chief Information Officer. He once studied at the University of Uppsala in Sweden.

A truly remarkable, if typically American, Government career has been made by Mary Anderson, who for twenty-five years was head of the Women's Bureau in the Department of Labor. Born on a farm near Lidköping in the Swedish province of Västergötland, she emigrated at sixteen, worked first as a domestic and then as a stitcher in a shoe factory. Wholly self-educated, she became an important official in the Shoe Workers Union and during the First World War was appointed to Federal office by President Wilson. When she retired in 1944 at the age of seventy-one, President Roosevelt called her work "a monument of constructive achievement in the best interest of millions of wage earners." He added that they "owe much to her fine spirit of leadership, rich common sense, fidelity to their best interests and her successful championship of practical rights and programs"—an achievement proving that America is still a land of opportunity.

While most American policemen and police officials are supposed to be of Irish extraction, a surprising number of Swedes have made police careers. To them maintenance of order and the suppression of crime is a natural occupation. The Sheriff Olson stories by G. M. Chute in the *Saturday Evening Post* typify the spirit. In such Swedish centers as Jamestown, New York, and Rockford, Illinois, both police and fire officials of Swedish origin have served for protracted terms. In 1940, August Edward Bargren (Berggren), who was born in Sweden in 1863, retired after fifty years' service in the Rockford Police department, during forty-six of which he was head of the force. In Boston the late Eugene C. Hultman, whose father was Swedish, served as a Metropolitan Police Commissioner in the 1920s. Until he became an army major in the Second World War, Harold Anderson, son of Swedish immigrant parents, was Chief of Police in Kansas City, Missouri, a post to which he returned when the war was over.

An even more notable example of a successful American police career from patrolman to Commissioner was made by Arthur W. Wallander of New York City. Originally appointed by the late Fusion Mayor, Fiorello H. La Guardia, in 1945, he was continued in the office by the new Democratic Mayor, William O'Dwyer, a triumph of personal merit. Having under his command over seventeen thousand uniformed men, charged with keeping order in the country's largest city, he had duties in comparison with which those of an average major general are simple. Born of Swedish parents on Manhattan Island, he rose from the ranks. His wife, another native New Yorker, is of Irish descent. In 1947 he was decorated by the King of Sweden, with the insignia of Commander of the Order of Vasa. He resigned his post in February 1949, being then entitled to a pension, but was able to accept more lucrative private employment.

The "dean" of Swedish mayors in American cities is Samuel A. Carlson who from 1908 to 1938 served almost continuously as chief executive in Jamestown, New York. The late Professor Charles A. Beard, the American historian, called his autobiography "a living document in the history of popular government." Early in his career he had to make a hard fight for a city-owned electric power plant which was then called a "Socialistic innovation." As an adventure in public ownership, it may have been inspired by the Swedish example. Now the whole city is proud of it.

On June 13, 1949, Eric G. Hoyer, a native of the Swedish province of Västergötland, was elected Mayor of Minneapolis, the first one of Swedish origin to be so honored. For thirteen years he had been a member of the City Council and during the final six he had been President. As such he automatically succeeded Hubert H. Humphrey, elected United States Senator in November 1948. Mr. Hoyer represents the Democratic-Farm Labor Party.

Next to law enforcement and municipal administration, the Swedes have shown the greatest interest in the public schools, a system to which they had become accustomed in their land of origin. On the Midwestern frontier their first public offices were usually those of Superintendent of Schools. In Kansas the Reverend Olof Olson was the first to hold such a post in McPherson County. In 1893 Robert Lindblom, who had been President of the Board of Trade in Chicago, was appointed a member of the Board of Education, and in 1898 of the Civil Service Commission. In 1913 the late Charles S. Peterson was appointed a member of the Chicago Board of Education and after that held various city offices. In 1927 he was elected Treasurer. The number of public school officials of Swedish descent in the Middle West is very large.

In the old city of Brooklyn, the late J. Edward Swanstrom, an attorney who was the son of a Swedish-born clergyman, became President of the Board of Education and after the consolidation of the other boroughs he was reappointed as head of the school system for Greater New York. In 1901 he was elected President of the Borough of Brooklyn, which alone had over a million inhabitants. He died in 1911.

In 1936, Mayor La Guardia appointed Mrs. Johanna Lindlof, a veteran grade teacher, to be a member of the New York Board of Education; and in 1948, Mayor William O'Dwyer, appointed Andrew G. Clauson President of the Board. By profession he is a public accountant, and both his parents were born in Sweden. Such services are typical of other Swedish descendants in smaller communities in which Swedish immigrants settled.

Even in the South an occasional Swedish name appears. Thus on September 28, 1946, the New Orleans *Item* printed an editorial which read as follows: "Another of the framers of Louisiana's present constitution goes to his rest—Emil Sundbery [Sundberg]. He was a splendid citizen whose memory will be honored by those who knew him. An immigrant from Sweden, he settled in Louisiana in the 'nineties and became a leading figure in the lumber industry. But he also took an intelligent part in public affairs and fought steadily against corruption in politics. He helped pave the way for a check on the Behrman machine by his efforts to elect John Parker and to reform the constitutional mare's-nest under which the state was then operating. If it be true that one takes to the hereafter what one has given to others, Emil Sundbery did not go to his reward empty-handed." Until his death his existence had been unknown to practically all his Northern countrymen.

In legislation, law enforcement, and in the private practice of law, descendants of immigrants from Sweden seem likely to play an increasingly important part as they become better educated and less handicapped by language difficulties. Back of them are long traditions in lawmaking and administration which are bound to make themselves felt. The Swedes in general are jealous of their legal rights and, while not litigious, they will fight long and hard for what they consider their due. Instinctively they love order and justice just as they do cleanliness and beauty.

XXIV

Architects and Builders

A future dictator, if intelligent, would assign all Swedish men in America to build houses and all Swedish women to improve the fare in public eating places. Which the country needs most is hard to say. But just as the latter have the knack of making food taste good, so the former have a natural aptitude for carpentry and house construction. The severe Swedish winter climate and the abundance of building materials such as lumber, stone and iron have developed through the ages that kind of skill. In the United States the Swedes have had an even greater opportunity to use their talents. No sooner had they arrived on the lower Delaware in the seventeenth century than they began to build in the traditional Swedish manner the snug log cabins that in the nineteenth century became a common symbol of the American frontier. Only the Cape Cod cottage has been more popular.

That the log cabin type of construction had first been used in New Sweden and not in New England or by the Indians, was not generally realized, however, until very recently. In 1928, Fiske Kimball, Director of the Philadelphia Museum of Art, wrote in his book, *American Architecture,* as follows:

"The log houses of horizontal logs notched together at the corners and chinked with clay, which has been ignorantly assumed to have been borrowed from the aborigines by the first settlers, was unknown either to the Indians or the English colonists. It seems to have been brought in from the [European] Continent by the Swedes of the Delaware, the first settlers from Northern Europe, where it was also known by the Swiss and Germans who followed."

The case has since been clinched by a Boston architect, the late Harold R. Shurtleff, whose book *The Log Cabin Myth,* was published posthumously by the Harvard University Press in 1939, as edited and completed by Samuel Eliot Morison, Professor of American History at Harvard.

Conversely, it cannot be said that since the colonial days either Swedish architecture or Swedish building methods have had much influence in America. There has never been a "Swedish" style of building like the "Dutch Colonial" or the "English Georgian" or "French Provincial." What the nineteenth century Swedish immigrants brought with them was manual skill rather than experience in mass production or the knowledge of architecture. The colonial "Old Swedes" churches in Wilmington and Philadelphia, for instance, are unmistakably Swedish, but very few of either the churches or the homes of the more recent Swedish immigrant-pioneers show any such influence. While their workmanship may be Swedish, the designs have usually been copied from examples in the neighborhood. Either the immigrants had not taken much interest in architecture at home or they preferred not to stress their national origin. In recent years the churches built by congregations they founded are more likely to show Swedish influences and in some instances, as in New York, Providence, and Worcester, architects trained in Sweden have been employed. The houses in which the Swedes live, on the other hand, seldom have any Swedish characteristics except neatness and order, inside and out.

American architects of Swedish ancestry are relatively numerous, but as a group they have so far utilized little of the Swedish tradition or style. Modern Swedish architecture is, of course, too new to be generally accepted in America and the more pretentious of the older public buildings in Sweden were usually copied from foreign models anyway. The houses at Bishop Hill in Illinois, for instance, which the first Swedish pioneers constructed, do not suggest any buildings these country people from northern Sweden could have seen at home. Even their brickmaking was learned in America; and the designs they used are said to have been made by a German architect, who had done similar work for a German religious colony in Iowa. They resemble, in fact, German city buildings rather than Swedish farm houses.

In Illinois there are today, it has been shown, twice as many architects of Swedish descent per capita as of any other nationality. The first one of note was Lars Gustaf Hallberg, born in 1844, in Sweden and educated both there and in England. He arrived in Chicago immediately after the great fire in the fall of 1871 and then found an abundance of work. He was a pioneer in the use of reinforced concrete and built churches and apartment houses as well as private homes. His son, Lawrence G. Hallberg, a graduate of Cornell, has followed in his footsteps, but has specialized in factory buildings, of which the Stewart-

Warner plant in Chicago is an example.

Colonel John A. Nyden of Evanston, Illinois, was a native of Moheda parish in Småland, where he was born in 1878, but his education was principally American. A graduate of the art school of the University of Illinois, he was an engineer as well as an architect, and he designed and built such Chicago hotels as the Admiral, the Commonwealth, the Melrose and the Fairfax, not to mention several bank buildings and the stadium at Springfield, Illinois. During the First World War he was a major in the Quartermaster Corps in charge of forty-two general and debarkation hospitals. In 1920 he became a colonel in the reserve. In 1938 he died. In the design of the American Swedish Historical Museum in Philadelphia, largely financed by Illinois businessmen, he tried, in his own words, "to express the Seventeenth Century architecture of Sweden in American colonial terms." Few other American architects of Swedish descent have so far attempted anything similar, but for the future there is much to draw on.

Another Swedish-born architect who has set his stamp on a large number of Chicago buildings is Eric Edwin Hall, born in 1883 in the province of Östergötland. Having had some technical education in Sweden, he arrived in Chicago in 1904 and, while working as a mechanic, studied architecture at the Armour Institute of Technology. After graduation he designed several hotels, apartment houses, bank buildings and municipal edifices, including the Criminal Courts Building and Jail as well as the hospital buildings of Cook County and, finally, the Chicago Stadium. In 1915 he was appointed official architect of Cook County.

A somewhat similar role has been filled in New York, both in Albany and New York City, by Carl William Larson, a native-born American of Swedish parentage and a graduate of Harvard. After working for various firms in Boston and New York, he became in 1926 chief designer in the office of the New York State Architect in Albany. As such he had charge of the plans for the New York State Office Building in New York City, the State Teachers College at Buffalo, the College of Home Economics at Cornell University, and a number of state hospitals, normal schools, prisons and barracks as well as field houses for various state parks.

Another Harvard graduate born in Boston in 1891 of mixed Swedish and Danish ancestry who has specialized in college buildings is Jens Frederick Larsen, who first worked as a designer, successively, in Montreal, Glasgow and London. During the First World War he was a captain in the Royal British Air Force. Since then he has drawn plans for college buildings at Dartmouth, Wabash, Marietta, Colby, Bucknell, Washington and Jefferson, and the University of Louisville. He was also the architect of International House at University City in Paris, financed by the Rockefeller family, and of the Field Institute for Advanced Studies at Princeton. Included in his more recent work have been plans for future expansion at Upsala College at East Orange, New Jersey, where a new dormitory, Beck Hall, was completed in 1949. He is the author of *Architectural Planning for American Colleges.* For Colby College he designed the memorial church given by the late George Horace Lorimer, editor of the *Saturday Evening Post,* in memory of his father.

Harry John Carlson of Boston has designed both the Normal and the Latin School groups of buildings in that city and dormitories for both Harvard and Wellesley. Furthermore, he is the architect of the Bates College Chapel in Maine and the library at Hamilton College, Clinton, New York. A native of St. Paul, Minnesota, he received his training at the Massachusetts Institute of Technology and in Paris. He is a past President of the Massachusetts Institute of Technology Alumni Association, and a life member of both the Massachusetts Institute of Technology Corporation and the Alumni Council. In the 'nineties he was the architect of Dreamwold, the famous estate of the late Boston financier and promotor, Thomas W. Lawson, situated at Egypt on the South Shore.

In New York City and vicinity Harrie Thomas Lindeberg, who was born in New Jersey of Swedish parents from Stockholm, has specialized in sumptuous suburban homes and country clubs as well as in monumental public and college buildings in various parts of the country, including American Government buildings abroad. He was the architect of the North College building at Wesleyan University in Middletown, Connecticut, and of the Astor Memorial Building at Rhinebeck, New York. He has, in fact, executed commissions in twenty-six states and was the architect of the United States legation buildings in Helsingfors, Finland, and Managua, Nicaragua, as well as of the proposed American embassy building in Moscow, which has not yet been erected.

In and around Milwaukee, Wisconsin, Herbert W. Tullgarn, born in Chicago in 1889 of mixed Swedish and Norwegian parentage, has designed during the past thirty years both public and private buildings ranging from cathedrals and theatres to schoolhouses and garages. Among them are the Cathedral of the Wisconsin Consistory at Milwaukee, the Astor Hotel in the same city, and the Lorain Hotel at Madison.

Los Angeles is the home of George Edwin Bergstrom who was born in Wisconsin of Swedish parentage in 1876 and educated at Yale and the Massachusetts Institute of Technology. Since 1913 he has had an independent West Coast practice. In 1921-23 he was President of the Allied Architects Association of Los Angeles and in 1941 was appointed chief consulting architect of the United States War Department. As such he was chief designer of the Pentagon, the gigantic War Department Building, in Washington, D.C.

A Harvard graduate in architecture who was born in Kansas City, Missouri, is C. Theodore Larson, who in 1929 was awarded a Harvard Traveling Fellowship for study in both northern Europe and the Mediterranean area. Since then he has been an editor of the *Architectural Record* in New York and has written for a number of other magazines. He is now employed as consultant for an Ohio housing concern.

During the past twenty years there have been several American students of architecture who have been given American fellowships for study in Sweden and some have written extensively on the modern Swedish style. Among them is G. E. Kidder-Smith, a descendant of F. Hopkinson Smith and a graduate of Princeton, who in 1948 was appointed to the faculty of architecture at Yale. An expert photographer, he has given much attention to the new public schools in Sweden.

Designing school buildings for Chicago has been the specialty of Arthur Hussander, a Cornell graduate, born in Chicago of Swedish descent. He has been employed by the Chicago Board of Education in the designing of such important buildings as the Nicholas Senn High School, the Carter Harrison Technical High School, and the Lindblom High School, named in honor of the late Robert Lindblom who came from Sweden in 1864 and for a generation was a leader in both business and civic affairs.

If American architects of Swedish descent have not developed any distinctive style, they have done much useful, sound and artistic work.

It was in fine carpentry work and building construction that the Swedish immigrants came into their own, especially in Chicago and vicinity. Nationally, too, some of them have made an impressive record. An example was the late Nils Persson Severin who came to Chicago in 1888 from Skåne in southern Sweden where he had had some experience in house construction. In Chicago he erected literally hundreds of buildings. His list of large projects throughout the nation includes the $350,000 Presbyterian Church of Evanston, Illinois; the Masonic Temple and the Y.M.C.A. buildings in New Haven, Connecticut; the United States Customs House and Post Office at Honolulu, Hawaii; the territorial Capitol at Juneau, Alaska; the $3,000,000 Post Office at Baltimore, Maryland; the $5,000,000 Post Office in Boston, Massachusetts, and the $15,000,000 central arch of the Arlington Memorial Bridge in Washington, D.C. As late as in 1927 he supervised the remodeling of the White House itself and for his work was personally thanked by President Coolidge, who took a keen interest in such things. At the age of eighty-three Severin died in 1945. He was truly a national American builder.

Much was contributed to the creation of modern Chicago, the "shovelling, wrecking, planning, building, breaking, rebuilding," that Sandburg sings about, by two Ericsson brothers, Henry and John E., born, like Colonel Nyden, in Moheda parish in Småland. Both were appointed Building Commissioners of the city, Henry in 1911 by Mayor Carter Harrison, and John E. in 1931 by Anton J. Cermak. The name of Henry Ericsson is inscribed on the conspicuous water tower near the Tribune Building where North Michigan Boulevard crosses the Chicago River. When he arrived in the city in 1881 at the age of twenty, he had had some technical as well as practical education in Sweden. At first he worked as carpenter in the Chicago suburbs and there became acquainted with Andrew Lanquist, a bricklayer, who had arrived the same year from the province of Västergötland.

In Sweden Lanquist had had some practical engineering experience on the Swedish state railroads under an army officer by the name of Major Franklin. When he came to Chicago, however, he had only three dollars in his pocket and was glad to get work as a bricklayer at eleven cents an hour. When he was assigned to the construction of new way stations for the Chicago, Western and Indiana Railroad his experience in Sweden began to count and soon he was appointed a foreman. In 1882 he formed a partnership with Henry Ericsson and together they remodeled an old church on Polk Street in Chicago into a terminal for the railroad. Next, they began to construct private houses, schools, apartment houses, office buildings and factories. In 1891 they jointly put up the Monon Building, one of the first skyscrapers in Chicago.

Each found new partners in 1897 and the company formed by Ericsson then erected such noted Chicago buildings as the Manhattan, the Harvester, the Gossard, the Twentieth Century, the Liquid-

Carbonic, the Morton, City Hall Square, the Garland, the Conway, the Bloom, the Pittsfield, the Chicago Trust Company, the Cort and the Roosevelt theatres, not to mention factories, warehouses and at least thirty-six public schools. During the First World War, the Ericsson company built Camp Grant at Rockford, Illinois, involving a cost of some $8,000,000. "He, literally, not only saw Chicago grow up, but helped form its appearance," wrote C. Theodore Larson in his chapter on "Architects and Builders" in *Swedes in America*.

In 1902 Ericsson was joined by his younger brother, John E. who, as a youth of sixteen had arrived with his parents in Minnesota and after doing farm work for a year, learned how to lay bricks, and became a foreman on building construction in Chicago. From 1906 to 1919 he too was a partner of Lanquist and then began his own operations, which led to his appointment as Building Commissioner for the city in 1931.

By 1905 Lanquist had become head of Lanquist & Illsley and among the buildings this firm erected were the Commonwealth-Edison, the People's Gas, the Railway Exchange, the Mallers, the Kesner, the Majestic, the North American and the Kimball, the Y.M.C.A. hotel, the State Bank Building, the Wrigley, the Crane Company, the Marshall Field Men's Building, and the United States Steel Company plant at Gary, Indiana. Outside the Chicago area the firm built the Marine National Bank of Buffalo, the First National Bank and the Bell Telephone Building in Milwaukee, the Whitney, the Stroh, the Real Estate Exchange, the Bok and the Dime Savings Bank buildings in Detroit; the Bell Telephone Building and the First National Bank in Omaha; the Memphis Trust Company in Memphis, Tennessee; the Bell Telephone Building in Minneapolis, the Allsworth Building and the St. Louis County Courthouse in Duluth, the Wrigley Field Baseball Park in Los Angeles, two glass factories in Toledo, Ohio, and many others. In 1937 a special Builders and Manufacturers Room was dedicated to Lanquist's memory at the American Swedish Historical Museum in Philadelphia. In his address on that occasion former Congressman Carl Chindblom of Chicago said, "The contracts for these buildings frequently involved amounts of from five to ten million dollars each. In many instances no bond or security was required beyond Mr. Lanquist's personal responsibility."

Henry Ericsson's immediate successor as Building Commissioner in Chicago was Charles Boström, another large-scale contractor, who had been born in the Swedish province of Värmland. He came to America in 1891 at the age of nineteen and first worked as a carpenter in Michigan. After only two years he started as a builder in Chicago, where he specialized in private housing, including apartment buildings, but he also put up several industrial plants. In his spare moments he studied architecture and thus learned to be his own designer. His special interest was city planning and for Chicago he laid out a zoning system and then served for many years as Chairman of the Zoning Board. His career was typically American—that of a Swedish-born carpenter who reached the top of his profession and finally was entrusted with official responsibility.

Another Swedish-born large-scale builder of private houses in Chicago and its suburbs was Louis M. Nelson, who came from Värmland in 1882 at the age of twenty-three. In his birthplace, Sunne in Värmland, made famous in fiction by Selma Lagerlöf, he helped maintain during his later life a children's hospital.

In 1897 Eric E. Skoglund arrived in Chicago from the central Swedish province of Närke, which, otherwise, has furnished only a few American immigrants, and after some training in architecture and structural engineering became, first, a specialist in stone work and then a general contractor. Among the buildings erected by him or his firm are the Apollo Theatre, the Illinois Telephone Building, the Lake View Trust & Savings Bank Building, the Sheridan Road Building, containing 130 apartments, the Orrington Hotel at Evanston and many others.

A Swedish-born specialist in hospital construction was Eric P. Strandberg, born in the northern province of Jämtland, who came to Chicago in 1882 at the age of twenty-two. In Sweden he had been trained as a carpenter and cabinetmaker. In partnership with his son of the same name he built the New Augustana, the St. Luke's, the Englewood, the German and the Norwegian Deaconness hospitals, as well as the Bankers Life Insurance Building, the Cloister apartment house containing eighty-four units, as well as the American Swedish Historical Museum in South Philadelphia.

Another native of Västergötland in Sweden, is Adolph Lindström of Wilmette, a Chicago suburb, who came there in 1901 at the age of seventeen. With the aid of as many as ten thousand Swedish-born carpenters and masons at a time, he has built apartment houses, hotels and business buildings worth many million dollars. Among the prominent Chicago structures he has erected are the McCormick Hotel, the De Witt and Whitehall apartments, and the new building of the Chicago *Daily News.*

E. C. Carson, a native of the Åland Islands, which are mainly populated by Swedes, came to America in 1882. Though a sailor by training, he first worked on a farm in Iowa and then moved to Chicago. Besides hundreds of private houses, he has built ten grammar schools, three high schools, some of the Northwestern University buildings, the Chicago Business College, the Breakers Business Building, the Second Regiment Armory, and the Winnebago County Courthouse in Rockford, Illinois.

In New York the Swedes have been less prominent either as architects or general contractors, but have specialized more on foundation work and such details as flooring. Many of the structural steelworkers who run up the frames of the skyscrapers are former Swedish as well as Norwegian sailors.

The steelwork on such early New York skyscrapers as the old Manhattan Life Building, erected in 1893, and the thirty-four-story City Investing Building at 165 Broadway, completed in 1908, was done by holm Technical College, who came to the United States in 1890. After Gustave A. Sandblom, a native of Sweden and a graduate of the Stock- working for the Fuller Company, famous as builders of New York skyscrapers, he became associated with Francis H. Kimball, a New York architect, and together they built several New York theatres as well as office buildings. On December 21, 1948, Mr. Sandblom died in New York at the age of eighty-one.

The distinctive McGraw-Hill Building on West 42nd Street was built by Andrew H. Peterson, who was born of Swedish parents in East Boston, Massachusetts. He also constructed the $12,000,000 Palmer House in Chicago, the $14,000,000 General Motors Building in Detroit, the $11,000,000 Union Trust Company building in Cleveland, the impressive Field Museum on Michigan Avenue in Chicago, and scores of other commercial, educational, and industrial structures in Illinois, Ohio, Pennsylvania, Minnesota, New Jersey, Rhode Island, Massachusetts, and British Columbia. During the First World War he was one of the three executives in charge of the construction of Camp Upton at Yaphank, Long Island, as well as of the $78,000,000 Government powder plant at Nitro, West Virginia. During the postwar depression he was head of the P.W.A. in Massachusetts, and to that work, too, he brought as much success as was humanly possible.

Building contractors, carpenters, and masons of Swedish birth or descent are to be found in almost every American city. In Kansas City, Missouri, Godfrey C. Swenson, born at Vimmerby in Småland in 1876 arrived in 1896. Ten years later, after he had worked as a mason, foreman, and sub-contractor, he organized the Swenson Construction Company which has since put up several hundred buildings, "including some of the largest structures in Kansas City and the adjacent territory of Oklahoma as well as Kansas." In Salt Lake City, Utah, the Fryberg Brothers, born in Gothenburg, are building and grading contractors on a large scale.

In New York City and vicinity one of the biggest building firms is John A. Johnson & Sons, the founder of which was born in 1865, in Södra Lundby, Västergötland, Sweden, and arrived in the United States on his twenty-third birthday, May 17, 1888. In 1896 he started his own business, specializing at first on two-family houses and, later, apartment houses in the Bay Ridge section of Brooklyn. When his two eldest sons were old enough, they joined him and the firm was then incorporated under its present name. Mr. Johnson died in 1938 but his sons have expanded the business until today it is one of the largest contracting firms in the country. For the New York World's Fair in 1939-40 it put up or did the woodwork for a majority of the buildings, including the central Trylon and Perisphere—the symbols of the Fair. The Swedish pavilion was entirely built by this firm and so were over a score of the other buildings. During the Second World War the Johnson company built Camp Dix and Camp Kilmer in New Jersey, the Sampson Naval Training Station at Geneva, New York, and the Postal Concentration Center in Long Island City, which served the whole European theatre of war. Both preceding and during the war the same firm was entrusted with a large proportion of the contracts for the construction of the Oak Ridge atomic experimental station in Tennessee. It likewise constructed all of the buildings for the Japanese village in Utah which was destroyed to test the bombs which were to be used to defeat Japan. The houses were replicas of those in Japan, complete in every detail even to the furnishings. The speed with which these houses were constructed received a special commendation from the Government. Since the war the Johnson brothers have concentrated on general construction work for the Government, such as veterans hospitals and public housing projects. It also builds private houses known as "Johnson Quality Homes" of forty different types. They have been shown complete in the John

Wanamaker store in New York. The total value of the buildings erected by them prior to 1949 exceeded $350,000,000.

On the railroad construction in the Middle West and Northwest the immigrant Swedes did a tremendous amount of work. When the late J. J. Hill started to build the Great Northern he is supposed to have said: "Give me Swedes, snuff and whiskey, and I'll build a railroad through hell." Originally the Swedish workers were chiefly pick-and-shovel men and when they had saved enough of their earnings they usually bought land along the new routes and developed farms. Those who returned to Sweden often used their savings to buy farms there. Among those who remained were some who became construction foremen, engineers and sub-contractors. As early as in the 1840s Polycarpus von Schneidau did some of the preliminary surveying work on the first railroad from Chicago to Galena now a part of the Illinois Central. For the Burlington road in western Illinois the Swedish colonists at Bishop Hill did some of the grading work around the city of Galva (Gävle).

"During the railroad building boom in the early years of this century," writes Svante J. Löfgren in the 1947 *Year Book* of the American Swedish Historical Foundation in Philadelphia, "when the eastern railroads were racing to reach tide water on the Pacific Coast, thousands of Swedes were employed by Swedish contractors, such as Axel Holman, who with the help of 5,000 men built the Chicago, Milwaukee, St. Paul and Pacific Railroad across the Cascade Mountains. Another contractor was Charles J. Johnson, who had started as a 'pick and shovel' man and then worked himself up to be one of America's leading railroad builders. Alone or in partnership with others, Johnson constructed over three hundred miles of railroads. During the building of the Chicago, Milwaukee, St. Paul and Pacific Railroad he had the biggest contract to be let up that time to any contractor in the state of Washington. It included eighty miles of road through the Cascade Mountains, two-thirds of which had to be built through rock, involving the blasting of four tunnels, measuring together three thousand feet, as well as the construction of all bridges on 110 miles of the route."

"Another of the early railroad contractors," continues Mr. Löfgren, "was P. P. Johnson who came to the State of Washington in 1889 and there started to work for the Oregon Railroad and Navigation Company. Later he went into partnership with another Swede, Martin Nelson, and together they too built many miles of railroad for the

Great Northern and other railroad companies. One of these included the construction of a tunnel, a half mile long, at the Devil's Canyon. [Perhaps this was what J. J. Hill had in mind.] It was completed without a single accident."

A former member of the engineering department of the Great Northern who later helped construct sections of the Canadian National, the Canadian Pacific, the Grand Trunk and the Algoma Central Railroad was Oscar W. Swenson, who died at the age of eighty-four on December 17, 1948, at Mount Kisco, New York. He was a native of Center City, on Chisago Lake in Minnesota, where his parents had been among the first Swedish settlers. After graduating from Carleton College at Northfield, Minnesota, Mr. Swenson became a railroad builder and then entered the employ of Foley Brothers, Inc. of St. Paul, originally a lumber and milling firm, which had branched out as general contractors for heavy work including railroad construction. After having been promoted to field manager and Vice President, Mr. Swenson became in 1930 President of Foley Brothers in Pleasantville, New York, originally a branch of the St. Paul firm, but by then an independent concern. As such he had charge of the building of several piers on the New York waterfront, grade-crossing eliminations on Long Island and the construction of the foundations of the piers on the New Jersey side of the George Washington Bridge. In 1946 he received a scroll from The Moles, an organization of tunnel and heavy construction men, for "outstanding achievements."

Another kind of construction in which the Swedes have participated is shipbuilding, ranging from warships and large freighters to racing yachts. "The leading contractor for many years on the Pacific Northwest," writes Mr. Löfgren, "was Charles J. Erickson. He erected buildings of all kinds, including lighthouses and churches, and a $2,000,000 dry dock for the United States Navy at the Bremerton yard near Seattle; he graded or re-graded miles of streets in Seattle, laid sewers and water mains, built railroads and sawmills, and during the First World War constructed the ten largest steel ships built in the Northwest during the war period."

The first Swedish-born shipbuilder in the state of Washington of whom there is a record available was Ole Engblom, born in 1823 at Attmar, near Sundsvall. In 1839 he set out as a sailor for England. In 1856, when he had sailed a schooner of his own on the Pacific, he became a gold miner in California. From there he went to Puget Sound and in 1864 started shipbuilding in Port Orchard and later in Port Blakely, where he constructed several sailing vessels both large and small. In 1870 he took up Government land near Seattle and lived on it until 1883, when he moved to a smaller farm in Kent, Washington, where he died in 1890.

Another early Swedish shipbuilder in the Northwest, was the late John Lindström. Born at Ockelbo in the northern province of Gästrikland in 1867, he landed in New York when he was twenty, and then found his way to Eureka, California, the westernmost city in the United States, and there got work as a laborer and general helper in a shipyard. A few years later he went up the coast to Aberdeen, Washington, where two Nelson brothers, also Swedes, had already founded a shipyard. In a few years Lindström had a yard of his own and began doing repair work, as well as "constructing sailing ships with three, four and five masts, steam schooners, steamers, tug boats and other deepwater craft. For many years the steam-schooners he had originated were the most popular lumber carriers on the west coast." He also took part in the government of his city and once served a term as Mayor. In 1908 he was killed in an accident. Lindstrom Street in Aberdeen was named in his honor.

"By the first of this century," writes Mr. Löfgren, "shipyards owned by Swedes were to be found in nearly all seaports in the State of Washington." One of them was owned by Ivar Chilman who had come to the United States via Australia. He had learned the art of shipbuilding on the west coast of Sweden. Having found employment in a yard at Hoquiam, Washington, then a new sawmill town, he was soon able to buy the yard and has operated it ever since. More than a hundred ships, including tug boats, fishing boats, steam schooners, and barges have been built, and during the First World War Chilman constructed two steamships for the United States Government."

As late as in 1945 the oldest shipyard on Puget Sound under the same management was the Ballard Marine Railway of Seattle, which had been owned since 1909 by the three Fryberg brothers, the oldest of whom, Charles, had been brought to the West Coast by his parents from Sweden when he was but three months old. The other two, William G. and Henry F., were natives of Washington. Their father, Captain Hans Fryberg, arrived in a sailing vessel with his wife and child in 1874. "From their yard came a continuous stream of vessels," writes Mr. Löfgren, "steamships, tug boats, refrigerator ships, fishing schooners, pile drivers, and motor ships." Among its customers were the United States Bureau of Fisheries and Biological Survey. The last ship finished before the two surviving younger brothers retired in 1945 was a navy refrigerator ship of the tuna-clipper type.

During the First World War Captain John L. Anderson, who for some years has owned steamboats and automobile ferries on the twenty-eight-mile-long Lake Washington, near Seattle, became a shipbuilder and converted an old picnic ground on the lake into a modern ship-yard in which he then built ocean-going vessels for French and Nor-wegian customers. In 1918 he sold the yard and during the Second World War it was used to construct large steel ships for the United States Government. Anderson was born in Sweden in 1868 and came to Seattle in 1888.

How many Swedes have worked in shipyards on other coasts than those of the Northwest will never be known. The Todd Shipyards Corporation, which has repair and construction yards in many ports besides New York, employs a large number of them. In New England the Swedes have been specialists in the building of racing craft and pleasure boats. In 1911 Bror Tamm arrived in America from Skåne, which has many shipping yards. By 1916 he had been employed by the George Lawley & Sons shipyards at Neponset, near Boston, the "biggest little ship builders in the world." Gradually Tamm came to be regarded as one of the best designers of sailing rigs and was given charge of the spars and rigging for such well-known sport-sailing vessels as the *Yankee,* the *Whirlwind,* the *Jubilee,* and the *Vanitie.* He finally became assistant general manager of the firm.

There have been a number of other Swedish specialists in various kinds of building equipment. As chief engineer of the Otis Elevator Company, the late David Lindquist, born and educated in Sweden, developed the gearless-traction electric elevator, which in the words of C. Theodore Larson, "has since become the standard for all build-ings requiring elevators of high rise and great speed. It revolutionized the whole system of vertical transportation. During the early part of World War I he developed the automatic system of self-leveling elevators which replaced the old type that had to be adjusted to the floor by hand. In 1922 he introduced the automatic-signal control which requires the operator only to press a set of buttons. The importance of such elevators in the development of the American skyscraper can-not be over-emphasized." Mr. Lindquist came to the United States in 1902 and became the Otis chief engineer in 1911. He employed so many assistants trained in Sweden that it used to be said that every engineer had to know Swedish in order to work for the Otis Company. One of his collaborators was the late August Sundh who for forty-six years was employed by the Otis Company.

A high ranking specialist in the heating and ventilation of large buildings was the late Werner Nygren, also born and educated in Sweden. In 1898 he began his work in Boston. "During his career," writes Mr. Larson in *Swedes in America* (p. 433), "he designed the heating and ventilating systems for the Woolworth Building in New York, the American Telephone and Telegraph Building, St. Patrick's Cathedral, Hunter College, the R. H. Macy Department Store, the Columbia-Presbyterian Medical Center, the Los Angeles Public Library, and the Travelers Insurance Building in Hartford, Connecticut. He was president of the New York Heating Board of Trade and of the New York Association of Consulting Engineers."

Such building details as metallic, fireproof doors were developed by the Charles Dahlstrom Company of Jamestown, New York, and several other firms in that city organized by Swedes, including one making ornamental bronze doors for banks, cemetery vaults, etc. Metallic ready-made store-fronts, as well as windows, portholes, and escalators were designed and manufactured by the late Francis J. Plym, a native of Småland, who was an architect before he became a manufacturer. In Niles, Michigan, he built not only factories, but hotels and apartment houses. He even owned the local newspaper. The wallboard known as Celotex and other insulating materials for buildings was developed by Bror G. Dahlberg, another native of Sweden, who is the founder and President of the Celotex Company.

Two Swedish-born and trained engineers have been pioneers in new building materials: the late John G. Bergquist, who developed the method of making cement from the slag of blast furnaces, and Karl P. Billner, a native of Skåne, who has invented the "vacuum" type of cement for use in housing. Bergquist, who came to the United States at the age of twenty-four, was employed by the Portland Cement Company until 1912. After that he was President of the American Gas Accumulator Company of Elizabeth, New Jersey, which made the roadside "blinkers" as well as the automatic beacons invented by the Swedish winner of a Nobel Prize, Nils Gustaf Dalén. Billner, a graduate of Chalmers Institute in Gothenburg, came to the United States in 1906 and was first employed as a bridge builder and highway and irrigation engineer on the West Coast. The first cement bridges in Oregon were designed by him. Next he helped develop the porous type of cement known as aerocrete and then he originated the vacuum type concrete which has been used in the construction of such Government buildings in Washington as the Social Security Building, the Pentagon, the Railroad Retirement Board Building, the Census Building, the Central Library building, two National Guard armories, and many others. Since the Second World War he has specialized in the construction of low-cost housing. While lumber is sure to be more and more scarce and more and more expensive, he contends, as long as consumption exceeds regrowth, cement can be produced without limit, the ingredients being so abundant.

A similar attempt to solve the low-cost housing problem of America by the use of enameled steel, corresponding to the all-steel bodies of automobiles and railroad coaches, has been made by another native of Sweden, Carl Gunnard Strandlund of Columbus, Ohio, President of the Lustron Corporation which in the summer of 1948 built such a house as a sample in a vacant lot at Sixth Avenue and 51st Street, near Rockefeller Center in New York. Backed by a $15,500,000 Government loan, large-scale production had by then been started in a former war plant at Columbus, Ohio, where an early output of 150 homes a day or one every nine minutes was anticipated. Previously Mr. Strandlund had been general manager of the Vitreous Enamel Product Company of Chicago, makers of gasolene pumps, and during the war he had developed, with Government backing, a method of reducing the processing time on armor plate for tanks from fourteen hours to eight seconds, one of the most important ordnance contributions made in the Chicago district. He was then backed in building a new type of house. Strandlund had come to the United States with his parents from Sweden when he was only four. His father became a development engineer for the John Deere Company in Moline, makers of agricultural machinery, and in its behalf developed over three hundred patented improvements in agricultural implements. Once an engineer himself, the son put the farm tractor on rubber tires and reduced its weight to make it practical. Cost reduction through mass production has been his passion ever since. The Lustron four-room house which needs no paint is the climax of his career.

Whether architects, engineers or plain house carpenters the immigrant Swedes and their American-born sons have contributed rather more than their share to building construction in America and in the future seem likely to hit on some procedure by which all the people may be decently housed at reasonable costs. Originally adept in the use of wood, they have learned to employ other materials. Besides erecting houses and office buildings they have been leaders in the manufacture of furniture, notably at such centers as Jamestown, New York, Grand Rapids, Michigan, and Rockford, Illinois. In the creation of designs they have so far been inclined to follow current public tastes, rather than to originate new forms. In that respect their contemporary colleagues in Sweden have made more progress. The American furniture style known as "Swedish Modern" is a re-adaptation of designs made in Sweden.

XXV

Scientists and Educators

Inasmuch as most Swedes are highly skilled in trades or practical occupations and do not need a higher education to make a good living, it was once assumed that, except for a few professionals in law, theology, medicine, and engineering, the number of American Swedes who had attended college or a university was small. But this is not the case. An impressive number are to be found, not only in the industrial laboratories, in state and Federal experimental stations, and in the forestry and wild-life conservation services, but also in our higher institutions of learning, as teachers, research scientists, or administrators. University professors of Swedish lineage are found in all parts of the United States, even where the proportion of other citizens of Swedish extraction is exceedingly small or practically non-existent. They teach not only science and engineering, for which the Swedes have special predilections, but also languages, literature, history, religion, and philosophy. Many have won distinction in our botanical gardens, museums of natural history, and observatories. Usually a Swede likes flowers, animals, and stars. The educated Swede, particularly, is likely to be fond of the solitude and quiet required for study and research—it suits his temperament—and if left alone he is apt to bury himself among books and scientific apparatus even deeper than the average scholar.

The total number of American teachers of Swedish birth or lineage will probably never be known, but it is certainly large, including, as it does, not only hundreds of unsung grammar school teachers of both sexes, but scores of high and grammar school principals, elementary school supervisors and superintendents, dozens of college and university presidents and deans, and hundreds of professors in the higher institutions of learning, of whom there are nearly two hundred of full professorial rank in institutions like Harvard, Yale, Columbia, Princeton, and the universities of Chicago, Wisconsin, Minnesota,

Illinois, Iowa, California, and Washington. At the University of Minnesota alone there are approximately a hundred instructors and professors of Swedish extraction, though the proportion of "Swedish" population in the state is less than ten per cent. Fritiof O. Ander, Professor of American history at Augustana College, wrote in 1938, in *Swedes in America* (p. 282), that there were then "nearly three hundred superintendents and principals of schools of Swedish ancestry in Minnesota and Illinois alone," and that in Minnesota "approximately seventeen of the county superintendents" were of Swedish origin, with a smaller number in such states as Wisconsin, Iowa, Illinois, Kansas, Nebraska, Colorado, Arizona, California, and Washington.

Over a century ago, in 1844, on the recommendation of Longfellow, the Swedish-born Maximilian Scheele De Veere (1820–98) became Professor of modern languages at the University of Virginia, a position he held for fifty-one years. He taught German and Italian, wrote a French as well as a Spanish grammar, inaugurated the study of Anglo-Saxon, and became one of the founders of the American Philological Society. He was learned in most European dialects, including the Slavic, and his *Outlines of Comparative Philology* appeared in 1853. When the Swedish novelist, Fredrika Bremer, came to America in the 'fifties, she visited his home in Charlottesville, Virginia. He was born in Växjö, Småland, and before his appointment as professor edited a German periodical in Philadelphia, *Die Alte und Neue Welt*. During the Civil War he was sent to Germany in behalf of the Confederate States.

The works on American natural history written in the eighteenth century by Peter Kalm have already been mentioned. In the nineteenth century, a Swedish nobleman and pioneering scientist, Gustaf Wilhelm Belfrage (born in Stockholm) became a naturalist of the American frontier. In Texas he collected so many insects that at his death he was able to leave over thirty-six thousand "pinned specimens in good order," besides those preserved in paper, sawdust, and alcohol. And in the interim, from 1868 to 1873, he had sent valuable collections of insects to educational repositories in London, Stockholm, Cambridge, Brussels, Boston, and St. Petersburg. In 1882 he died in Texas.

Being countrymen of the great Linneaus, Swedes have shown a natural taste for botany, particularly the utilitarian phase of it. A typical example was the late Alexander P. Anderson (1862–1943), an economic botanist and chemist whose work contributed to the breakfast tables of America puffed cereals, rice or wheat, which even children will sometimes eat when they get tired of the cooked or shredded varieties. He was born in a sod hut in Minnesota, became a professor at the state university and after making approximately fifteen thousand experiments with cereal grains and starch, he discovered a method of blowing them up by firing them from guns. From his discoveries he became wealthy and was able to donate large sums to various charities.

Another botanist of Swedish descent is Hugo L. Blomquist, Chairman of Duke University's botanical department. He has discovered in seaweed a substance suitable for preparing agar, the indispensable fungic and bacterial culture medium used in every hospital and biological laboratory. This had previously been a Japanese monopoly.

The venerable and venerated Gustavus A. Eisen, born and educated in Sweden, who died in New York in 1940 at the age of ninety-one, was a botanist, zoologist, archaeologist, scientific horticulturist, as well as a prolific writer on the Holy Grail, the history of glass, and dozens of other subjects. In order to preserve the giant trees of California, he succeeded in getting the United States to make a national park of the Sequoia territory. In California he also started the cultivation of figs.

Fascinating, too, but tragic is the story of Per Hjalmar Olsson-Seffer, of Swedish-Finnish parentage, a specialist in the flora of sand dunes and in agricultural botany, who, in April 1911, was murdered by armed bandits near Cuernavaca, Mexico, when he was only thirty-seven years old.

Outstanding in the history of botany in America are Per Axel Rydberg (1860–1931), once Curator of the New York Botanical Garden in the Bronx, and Henry Knute Svenson, a native of Sweden, who, in 1936, became Curator of the herbarium in the Brooklyn Botanical Garden, and is now on the staff of the American Museum of Natural History in Manhattan. Another prominent American botanist of Swedish descent is Professor Felix G. Gustafson whose best known work has been done on the structure of the sex organs of plants.

To the knowledge of the more practical aspects of plant life such as agriculture, forestry, and horticulture, a number of other American Swedes have made notable contributions. Many are employed by the United States Government, others by the different states or cities. In the Department of Agriculture, for instance, there is a large number of scientists of Swedish as well as other Scandinavian origins.

The editor of publications issued by the department's Bureau of Diary Industry is A. B. Nystrom, while Rudolph O. Gustafson, who has a Master of Forestry degree from Yale, is a specialist in wildlife refuges, especially those for migratory waterfowl. In the same department, Ralph Melvin Linden is a plant pathologist engaged in the control of fungus action on trees, just as Leonard W. Melander is trying to eradicate the effects of barberry rust on grains.

An Assistant Editor of the second edition of Webster's *Unabridged International Dictionary,* as a specialist in biology, was Dr. Erik F. B. Fries, son of J. E. Fries, the steel engineer. He received his Ph.D. degree at Harvard and is now Assistant Professor at the City College of New York.

A branch of the exact sciences which has attracted many Swedes in the United States as well as in Sweden, the home of Jöns Jakob Berzelius and Karl Wilhelm Scheele, is chemistry. Probably the most eminent in America was the late Otto Knut Olof Folin (1867–1935), a native of Småland, who from 1907 to 1934 was Professor of physiological chemistry at Harvard. An international figure, he was honored by many countries. Equally prominent at Yale University is Professor Rudolph J. Anderson, an authority on the chemistry of bacteria, especially those of tuberculosis. In 1947 he received an honorary Doctor's degree from Lund University in Sweden. The President of the Yale Chemical Society, which meets in Berzelius Hall, from 1930 until his death in 1942, was Carl O. Johns, who was a specialist in the chemistry of petroleum. There is hardly a university or chemical research institute in the country which does not have at least one professor or advanced research worker of Swedish birth or extraction.

An honorable place among American chemists was earned through his own efforts by the late Emil Osterberg. In Sweden, where he was born, he had received a high school education and was then employed as a clerk in a brewery. When he arrived as an immigrant in Connecticut he had to work at first as a blacksmith and during the depression of the early 'nineties, he lost even that job. Being married and the father of several children, he then accepted a post as janitor in the Judd Hall Experimental Laboratory at Wesleyan University in Middletown at $25 a month. He soon proved that he was no ordinary janitor; the bottles he washed were so chemically clean that he was asked to assist with the experiments in physiological chemistry then conducted in the basement of Judd Hall with an Atwater-Rosa calorimeter, an instrument for determining caloric food values. In fact, he became the principal "subject" for those pioneering experiments. At night he studied chemistry by himself and eventually became such an expert in the analysis of urine and the determination of nitrogen that he was asked to join the staff of the Cornell Medical School in New York City. He never received any academic degree, but his experimental skill was phenomenal. After retirement he died at the age of seventy-five in Florida.

Another Swedish favorite field in science has been that of geology and geography, including exploration. Ernst Valdemar Antevs is a Swedish-born glacial geologist working in Arizona, who by counting the annual glacial deposits is able to estimate the age of the soil, and by measuring the thickness of the layers can determine the average temperature each year, even the prehistoric. A pupil of the pioneer Swedish geo-chronologist, Baron Gerard De Geer, he had previously done similar research work in Sweden as well as on Bear Island and Spitzbergen. He has also been associated with the Carnegie Institute in Pittsburgh and Harvard University.

The late Waldemar Lindgren (1860–1943) was a native of Småland, who for many years was head of the department of geology at the Massachusetts Institute of Technology, while Johan August Udden was a former immigrant educated at Augustana College, who became a famous geologist of the Southwest. As a professor of the University of Texas he was credited more than anyone else with making possible "the utilization of the petroleum wealth, partly realized, but mostly still unexploited, of Texas." W. Elmer Ekblaw, Professor of Geography at Clark University, Worcester, Massachusetts, and editor of *Economic Geography,* was a former explorer of Grant and Ellesmere Land in the Arctic. For several years he lived with the Eskimos in those regions and a mountain peak in the Antarctic has been named in his honor. He was born in 1882 of Swedish parents on a farm in Illinois. He died in 1949.

A self-educated, Swedish-born geologist of unusual attainments was the late Olof O. Nylander of the state of Maine, the son of a cobbler and himself a house painter by trade. But he liked rocks and fossils and though without even the rudiments of a formal education he studied by himself and ultimately discovered the first fossil specimens unearthed in Aroostook County. (As a boy he had received some encouragement from a scientist in Sweden.) Before he died his writings appeared in scientific journals, the University of Maine gave him an honorary degree of Master of Science and in 1938 a museum was built at Caribou to house his collections. In 1943 at the age of seventy-nine he died in the same city.

Of the many college and university professors of physics and nuclear chemistry, who are of Swedish descent, only the following can be mentioned. Henry Anton Carlson was formerly Chairman of the Department of Physics at the California Institute of Technology. Glenn T. Seaborg (b. 1912) of the University of California at Berkeley, nuclear expert and chemist, co-discoverer of plutonium, curium, americum, and neptunium, was awarded in 1947 the $1,000 American Chemical Prize; in 1948 the William H. Nichols Medal of the New York section of the same Society, and the same year the John Ericsson Medal, issued every two years by the New York Society of Swedish Engineers. In 1946 Dr. Seaborg was appointed by President Truman to "serve on the nine-man General Advisory Committee of the Atomic Energy Commission, and was named 'Chemist of the Year' in an informal poll conducted by *Chemical and Engineering News*." His mother came from Sweden at the age of seventeen, while his father was born of Swedish parents in Ishpeming, Michigan, where the son too, drew his first breath. Another specialist in atomic physics is John Bertrand Johnson, a native of Sweden, who in 1917 received his Ph.D. in physics at Yale and who has since been employed by the Bell Telephone Laboratories in New York in research work on electrons.

The most famous of all American nuclear physicists of Swedish ancestry is, of course, Carl David Anderson of the California Institute of Technology, who in 1936 won the Nobel Prize in Physics for his discovery of the positron. He is a native of New York City.

Elmer William Engstrom, a Vice President of the Radio Corporation of America in charge of research and President of the Industrial Research Institute at Princeton, New Jersey, received on June 15, 1949 an honorary degree of Doctor of Science from New York University. "His personal contributions to radio and electronic development," read the citation, "notably the incredible progress of television command the respect of his scientific peers." He was born in 1901 at Minneapolis, Minnesota, both parents being natives of Sweden.

Astronomy and meteorology are likewise sciences that have attracted the attention of the Swedes, both in the United States and in their land of origin. The late Salomon August Andrée, the would-be polar explorer by air, whose body with those of his two young companions, was recovered in the ice on an island off Spitzbergen in 1930, was a physicist and meteorologist whose reason for learning to fly was the belief that aviation could aid both those sciences. His first balloon trips were made at the Centennial Exposition in Philadelphia in 1876.

From 1917 to 1946 Gustaf Strömberg, an astronomer holding degrees from the universities of Stockholm and Lund, was a member of the research staff at the Mount Wilson Observatory in southern California. At the New York World's Fair in 1939–40 his name was listed on the "Wall of Fame" as one of the American citizens of foreign birth who had made "outstanding contributions" to American civilization. He is the author of *The Soul of the Universe* and *The Searchers*.

In 1940 Gustave S. Lindgren, a native of Stockholm, retired as head of the Albany, New York, office of the United States Weather Bureau. He died in 1942. Carl Gustaf Rossby, who in 1947 was appointed to a new chair in meteorology at the University of Stockholm, had previously been professor in the same subject at the University of Chicago. He has long been rated as one of the world's leading authorities in weather study, which has recently gained new importance because of aviation.

Of the many American scientists who received their early training in the pioneer Swedish American institution, Augustana College, probably the most colorful and interesting is Anton Julius Carlson, formerly Professor of physiology at the University of Chicago, popularly known as "Ajax," a man of unusual character, physical strength, and personality; a good showman, whose pupils never cut classes. At the age of seven he started earning his living in Sweden as a shepherd. He knows all about the scientific aspects of hunger, digestion, and alcoholism; never accepts a report of any kind without scientific evidence; and believes that everybody, old and young, should work for a living. He has the revolutionary idea that babies should be fed when they are hungry instead of at regular four-hour intervals and ridicules the notion that monkey glands can rejuvenate a human being. Incidentally, he has no use for food faddists; nature knows best what you should eat, he says, but suggests that, if possible, every one's diet should be varied.

In addition to men of scientific achievements we find many Americans of Swedish stock who have become college and university administrators.

Among the descendants of the Delaware Swedes, was Charles Janeway Stillé (1819–99), Provost of the University of Pennsylvania from 1868 to 1880.

Probably the most distinguished of all American university administrators of Swedish ancestry was the late George Norlin, President of the University of Colorado (1919–30). He was born in 1871 of

Swedish immigrant parents, in a primitive farm house near Concordia, Kansas. A brilliant speaker, thinker, and writer, and the recipient of many academic honors, he was Theodore Roosevelt Professor of American Life and Institutions at the University of Berlin (1922–23), an Elector of the Hall of Fame, and a member of the Board of Trustees of the Carnegie Foundation for Advancement of Teaching. His special subject was Greek, in which he received his Doctor's degree at the University of Chicago. For the Loeb Classical Library he translated the works of Isocrates.

The late William Anthony Granville (d. 1943), a noted mathematician of Swedish descent, and once an instructor at Yale, was for thirteen years (1910–23) President of Gettysburg College, Pennsylvania. His textbook on calculus was once widely used.

In 1946 Reuben Gilbert Gustafson, nationally known chemist and public speaker, who until then was Vice President of the University of Chicago, was elected Chancellor of the University of Nebraska.

Another descendant of the nineteenth century Swedish immigrants was Elam Jonathan Anderson, former head of Linfield College in Oregon, who at his death in 1944 was President of the University of Redlands, California. In 1946 W. S. Carlson, a specialist in the Arctic regions and a former colonel in the United States Air Force, who calls himself a "hybrid Scandinavian," was appointed President of the University of Delaware. Victor Raymond Edman, formerly a professor of history and a missionary in Ecuador, became in 1941 President of Wheaton College in Illinois. Even more Swedes have possessed the qualities required for college or university deanships. From 1908 to 1936 Carl Emil Seashore, a Swedish-born, nationally known psychologist, whose specialty was the psychology of music, was Dean of the graduate college at the University of Iowa and in 1942, when he was seventy-six, recalled as Dean *pro tempore,* an unusual honor, considering his age. He died October 16, 1949.

Carl Christian Engberg (d. 1939), a native of Sweden, was for many years Professor of mathematics and executive Dean of the University of Nebraska, where the late August Hjalmar Edgren was once Dean of the graduate school. The Swedish-born Frans August Ericsson of Upsala College, East Orange, New Jersey, one-time Acting President of that institution, is now Dean, while Arthur Wald, also born in Sweden, was for many years Dean of Augustana College at Rock Island, Illinois.

To make a selection among the numerous American college and

university professors who were either born in Sweden or of Swedish parents in the United States is not an enviable task for there is an embarrassment of riches. Such men are to be found not only in the Middle West or the Far West, the regions usually associated with the Scandinavians, but in practically all parts of the country.

At Yale, for example, there were in 1947, besides the teachers of lower rank, at least ten permanent members of its teaching staff (full or associate professors) of Swedish origin: Dr. Bert G. Anderson (dental surgery); Professors Rudolph J. Anderson, a research chemist who has had no teaching duties for the past twenty years; Theodore Andersson (French); Adolph B. Benson (German and Scandinavian); Einar Hille (head of graduate instruction in mathematics); Helge Kökeritz (English, expert in Shakespeare and the history of the English language); Dr. Grover F. Powers (pediatrician), whose father's name was originally Johnson; Philip G. Laurson (civil engineering); Dr. Gustaf E. Lindskog (surgery, and Lieut. Commander USNR); and Harry Rudin (modern European history). Four of these were born or educated in Sweden. And it may be worth while to point out that by 1947 more than sixty Swedish Americans had won their doctorates in philosophy at Yale.

Among the college or university teachers of Swedish blood who have passed on were Arthur E. Christy (Christopherson) (d. 1946), editor, and Professor of American literature at the University of Illinois, born in China of Swedish missionary parents; Ulric Dahlgren (d. 1946), Professor of biology at Princeton, and sometime Director of the Marine Laboratories at Woods Hole, Massachusetts, and Mt. Desert Island, Maine, a grandson of Admiral Dahlgren of Civil War fame; Arvid Reuterdahl (d. 1943), born in Karlstad, Sweden, physicist and mathematician, who in 1922 was appointed President of Ramsey Institute of Technology at St. Paul, Minnesota; George Herbert Ryden (d. 1941), born in Kansas City, Missouri, who was an authority on the colonial Swedes, State Archivist of the state of Delaware and Professor of history at its university; A. A. Stomberg (d. 1943), Professor of Scandinavian at the University of Minnesota; and David F. Swenson (d. 1940), a Swedish-born Professor of philosophy at the same institution, through whose remarkable translations of Kierkegaard that Danish philosopher was first introduced to the American public.

In such special fields as physical education, covered in another chapter, and vocational training, especially home economics, and a fine art, like music, teachers of Swedish origin have made perhaps their greatest contributions. In musical education the outstanding names are Howard Hanson, Director of the Eastman School of Music at Rochester, New York, as well as a composer; and Edgar Andrew Nelson, President of the Chicago Conservatory of Music. Former members of the Metropolitan Opera Company such as Marie Sundelius and Karin Branzell, devoted themselves after their retirement to the training of younger singers, the former at the New England Conservatory of Music in Boston and the latter in New York.

In vocational fields the following are representative: Dr. Leonard Lundgren, Director of adult and vocational education in the public schools of San Francisco, California; the late L. W. Wahlstrom of Chicago, who at the Francis W. Parker School helped rehabilitate veterans of the First World War; G. A. Glyer, Supervisor of training for the distribution trades in the public schools of Delaware; and Carl E. Karlstrom, who is Supervisor of vocational education in the public schools of Detroit, Michigan. At Wayne University in the same city, J. H. Trybom is Director of vocational education.

J. E. Wallace Wallin of Delaware, leader in modern psychological education, has been particularly interested in handicapped children; Arthur E. Lindborg organized in 1924 the Virgin Island Educational Association; John L. Stenquist has been Director of the Bureau of Educational Research of the public schools of Baltimore; and Cora Lee Danielson, writer on educational topics, has supervised in Los Angeles the education of exceptional children. Emanuel Ericson, a native of Sweden, is Director of industrial education and extension service at the State College, Santa Barbara, California.

In the field of agricultural education, Carl E. Rosenquist of the University of Nebraska; Dean E. P. Sandsten of Colorado Agricultural College; R. B. Jeppson, the state Supervisor of agricultural education, Nevada; and both John O. Christianson and T. A. Erickson of the College of Agriculture, University of Minnesota, have played important parts. For about twenty-five years the latter was chief organizer of the 4-H Clubs in the state of Minnesota and thus became known to thousands of farm children as "Daddy" Erickson.

The former Swedish immigrants have always been staunch supporters of the American public schools, a system to which they had become accustomed in Sweden, and, in conflicts between the parochial and the public grade schools, have regularly defended the latter. Whenever the Augustana Synod, for instance, has taught Swedish or the Lutheran faith in schools of its own, it has always done so in summertime, so as not to interfere with the work of the public schools. American voters of Swedish origin have invariably supported financial legislation in favor of the public schools and many of the teachers and officers of such schools have been of Swedish descent.

Obviously it is impossible to list all such teachers in the elementary and secondary schools, whether public or private, or those in the state normal schools or the teachers' and junior colleges. Public school superintendents of Swedish descent are, or have been, most common in Colorado, Illinois, Iowa, Nebraska, Michigan, Idaho, Wyoming, Utah, Minnesota, Wisconsin, Kansas, and several other Midwestern states.

Several of the state teachers' colleges, both in Illinois and Michigan, have had at times as many as five faculty members who were of Swedish origin. Typical of them was the late Blenda Olson who at the age of eleven came from Småland to be a nurse girl for her aunt's children living on a farm in western Illinois and who in 1905 was graduated as an honor student from the University of the state at Urbana. At first she taught in local high schools and then obtained a Master's degree at Columbia's Teachers College in New York. After that she taught German at the Western Illinois State Normal School until that subject was dropped during the First World War, but nothing daunted she then took up French and by attending summer courses at the University of Chicago, at Grenoble in France, and the Sorbonne in Paris, she qualified as a teacher of French at the same normal school renamed the State Teachers' College. This work she continued until 1938, helping train teachers for the public schools of the state. She died in 1942.

Another striking career in the American public schools has been made by Agnes Samuelson in the neighboring state of Iowa. From the rank of a rural public schoolteacher she advanced by degrees until in 1927 she was appointed State Superintendent of public instruction for the state and in 1935 she was elected President of the National Educational Association, the central organization of all American public school officials and teachers. In 1945 she became its Assistant Director of public relations with an office in Washington, D.C.

Among the many Swedes who have served on the boards of education in the large cities—the most conspicuous have been the late Charles S. Peterson of Chicago, and Mrs. Johanna Lindlof, who served for a decade on the Board of Education in New York City. When appointed by Mayor La Guardia in 1936, the latter had taught elementary subjects for thirty-five years, and her appointment caused "wide reverberations." She proved to be a militant educational leader and successfully advocated the construction of playgrounds for children and other improvements. In her appeals to the public, she made use of the radio, visited schools, and addressed meetings of parents and teachers as well as those of taxpayers.

Like most teachers, the librarians are modest individuals who get little credit for their labors. Among the best known of those of Swedish ancestry are Edwin H. Anderson, who up to 1934 had been a director for twenty-one years of the New York Public Library; Pearl Gertrude Carlson who in 1935 became Librarian of the Jamestown College Library, North Dakota; and William Hugh Carlson who in 1937 was chosen Librarian of the University of Arizona, then became associate Librarian of the University of Washington, and is now Director of libraries of the Oregon state system of higher education. Then there is Einar Söderwall, formerly Librarian of Northwestern University, Evanston, Illinois; and Adam Julius Strohm, formerly head of the Detroit Public Library, who in 1930–31 was elected President of the American Library Association. At Detroit he was succeeded by Ralph Adrian Ulveling, who is also of Swedish extraction.

Another prominent librarian of unusual ability and character was Harry Lyman Koopman, whose father was Swedish. Mr. Koopman was a poet, editor, and a professor of bibliography who had been associated with the libraries of Columbia, Cornell, Rutgers, and the University of Vermont before he became chief Librarian of Brown University in 1893, a position held until 1930. He died in 1937.

Probably the foremost American librarian and bibliographer of exclusively Swedish origin was the late Aksel G. S. Josephson, who for many years was connected with the New York Public Library. In 1944 he died at the age of eighty-four. Born in Uppsala, Sweden, he came to the United States in 1893, attended the Library School at Albany, New York; became in 1894, cataloguer for the Lenox Library, New York, chief cataloguer of the John Crerar Library, Chicago in 1896, and consultant cataloguer in 1928. He was an organizer and officer of the Bibliographical Society of America, a member of many learned organizations, and a prolific writer and compiler.

Who's Who in Library Service contains many other names of Swedish origin. In addition to those mentioned we can cite only two more: Miss Edith M. L. Carlborg, a native of Linköping, Sweden, who holds two university degrees and is now a cataloguer in the Brown University Library; and Torsten Peterson, born in Trelleborg, Sweden, who is a bibliographer in the Princeton University Library.

In practically all forms of education, as well as scientific research, the former Swedish immigrants and their American children have made important contributions. Teaching is a form of work that requires, above all, patience, diligence and accuracy—qualities characteristic of the Swedes. The same may be said of research. As a rule they are also good disciplinarians and have themselves been trained to observe regulations. In teaching as in all their other work, they dislike slipshod ways. In the future more and more of them are likely to qualify as educators.

For an additional list of American scientists and educators with a Swedish background, see *Swedes in America,* published by the Yale University Press in 1938.

XXVI

Health Specialists

In America, Swedes and their descendants have practiced some kind of medicine or given some form of health service for over three hundred years. When they first arrived on the lower Delaware in 1638 medical knowledge was possessed by only a few men. And yet on the *Fama*, the ship that had brought over Governor Printz in 1643, there arrived the following year a "barber-surgeon" by the name of Hans Janeke, who was probably of German origin. Before his arrival another medical practitioner of the same kind, known as Jan Peterson of Alfendolft, had attended the Swedish colonists. He was undoubtedly of Dutch origin.

The best known of the early Swedish barber-surgeons was Timon Stidden (also spelled Stedham or Tyman Stidham), who had been born north of Sundsvall in northern Sweden. He sailed from Gothenburg in 1649 and the records show that in 1656 he was ordered to prepare a report on "the cure of some soldiers on the South River" (the Delaware). Ultimately he became owner of a large portion of the land on which the city of Wilmington, Delaware, is now built, and his descendants are scattered throughout the United States. Once when an old man had been killed by the Indians, the records show that Dr. Timon Stidden was called to examine the body. He lived at Upland (now Chester) in Pennsylvania, and a fully authenticated metal case in which he carried his instruments has been preserved by his descendants.

All the early colonial doctors, whatever their nationality, had been trained in Europe, but, in the eighteenth century, one Adam Kuhn was Professor of *materia medica* and botany at the College of Philadelphia, which later became the University of Pennsylvania. Though probably a German, he had been a student under the famous Linnaeus at Uppsala, in Sweden. A diploma signed by him and granted to one John Archer in 1768 is still displayed at the College of Physicians and Surgeons at Baltimore, Maryland, where it is regarded as the oldest in the country. In honor of Kuhn, Linnaeus named an American plant, the *Kuhnia eupatorioides,* just as he named the *gardenia* in honor of Dr. Alex. Garden, a native of Charleston, South Carolina, who died in 1791. "Thus through Kuhn," wrote Dr. David L. Tilderquist of Duluth, Minnesota, in *Swedes in America* (p. 340), "there was exerted an indirect influence on early American medicine by the great Linnaeus of Sweden."

Among the outstanding nineteenth century leaders in American medicine were the two Stillé brothers, Alfred and Moreton. They were partly of Swedish colonial ancestry, being direct descendants of Olof Peterson Stillé who was born in the Roslagen district north of Stockholm. He had left for America in 1641. A graduate of the University of Pennsylvania School of Medicine in 1836, Dr. Alfred Stillé became a professor there in 1864. His textbook, *The Elements of General Pathology,* was first published in 1848. He was the first Secretary of the American Medical Association and in 1867 became the President. Sir William Osler gives him credit for being the first to define the difference between typhus and typhoid. Born in 1813, he died in 1900. His brother, Moreton Stillé, who was also a noted teacher of medicine, is famous as the first American writer on medical jurisprudence. Together with a lawyer, Francis Wharton, he wrote the earliest known work on the subject in America.

An even more prominent medical practitioner, as well as teacher and writer, was Dr. William W. Keen, also of Philadelphia. Born in the same city in 1837 he lived to be ninety-five. His earliest known American ancestor was Jöran Kyn, a Swedish soldier who came with Governor Printz in 1643. Dr. Keen's *System of Surgery* in eight volumes is still a standard work and he has been called the "Father of Surgery" in America. When he retired in 1907 he was a professor at Jefferson Medical College in Philadelphia. On a boat anchored in Buzzards Bay, off Cape Cod, Massachusetts, he once secretly performed an operation for facial cancer on President Grover Cleveland, which was entirely successful; neither physical nor political complications ensued. Having been at various times President of the American Surgical Association and the Congress of American Physicians and Surgeons, he was able, as late as 1920, to preside over the International Congress of Surgery in Paris, a city in which he had studied as a youth. A member of the Baptist Church, he wrote at the age of eighty-four a book entitled: *I Believe in God and Evolution.*

Among the early nineteenth century Swedish pioneers were only a few men who had studied medicine in Sweden. Gustaf Unonius had taken a course in the subject at Uppsala University, but had never practiced. One of his companions, William Polman, had likewise been a medical student at Uppsala, where he had learned enough to become a medical practitioner on the Midwestern frontier. Others took up the study of medicine soon after they arrived. Among them was Dr. Johan Arvid Ouchterlony, who had been born in Sweden in 1838 and who had had a good preparatory education before he arrived in the United States in 1857 at the age of nineteen. He obtained his medical degree in the United States in 1860. The following year he became an army surgeon and was at once assigned to wartime hospital work at Louisville, Kentucky. In 1864 he became a lecturer on clinical medicine at the University of Louisville, and in 1865 began private medical practice. In 1876 he was one of the founders of the Louisville Medical College and until his death in 1908 he continued his medical teaching, first at the Kentucky School of Medicine and then as a professor at the University of Louisville.

Dr. Maurice F. Lindquist, another native of Sweden and a medical officer in both the Mexican and the Civil Wars, and before that a sailor and world-wide roamer, established himself after the two wars were over in private practice at New Haven, Connecticut, where his son, Dr. M. F. Linquist, continued his work until his own death in 1947 at the age of eighty. Father and son had by then served the same community for a total of 108 years. In 1867 Dr. Carl Petter Tigerhjelm arrived in Vasa, the little Swedish community founded in 1855 by Hans Mattson in Minnesota, and began to practice there. He had previously followed his profession in the Jämtland and Härjedalen district of north-central Sweden. Gradually other Swedish-trained physicians began to settle in other Swedish communities, in New England, New York and California. After that many sons of the immigrants studied medicine in America and took up professional work in almost every field.

The same was true of the dentists of Swedish descent who practically without exception have been trained in the United States. Several of them have in fact, carried American dentistry methods to Sweden, as others have to other European countries. In 1936 the late George Eastman, founder of the Kodak firm, established in Stockholm a dental clinic named in his honor. It has contributed much to improving the dental care of the Swedish people, especially the school children.

While Swedish immigrants have not founded any medical schools of their own, they organized early a number of hospitals as well as orphanages and old people's homes, most of them under either religious or fraternal auspices. Members of the Lutheran Augustana Synod alone have founded in various parts of the country eleven such hospitals and they serve all patients without discrimination. As early as the middle 'sixties the Reverend Eric Norelius started a home for waifs in a private house at Vasa, Minnesota, which later became a large orphanage. Under Swedish Lutheran auspices there are now eleven such homes for children. For immigrants and sailors the early churches of the Swedish pioneers set up missions in New York, Boston, San Francisco, and Seattle, some of which are still active. For young working women in the large cities ten hospices have been provided and at Axtell, Nebraska, there is a Lutheran home for incurables, founded in 1913 by the Reverend K. G. William Dahl, which has been called a "Miracle of the Prairies." Altogether eighty-six welfare institutions are now to be found in the different states—founded, supported and managed by Swedish settlers or their descendants. At Englewood, Colorado, there is a Swedish non-denominational sanatorium for the tubercular. The list includes sixteen children's homes, thirty-eight homes for the aged, eighteen hospitals, twelve hospices, the rest being sailors' missions or similar institutions. The capital value of the buildings has been estimated at over $23,000,000. How much has been spent on maintenance is not known.

All the hospitals, as well as the training schools for nurses, have been run according to American standards and practices rather than the Swedish about which little knowledge was brought over by the country people who constituted a majority of the early immigrants. But as they were often exhausted by their travels they easily fell victims to epidemics, especially cholera, and medical care was essential. Since public hospitals were then rare, if not non-existent, such care had to be provided by their own countrymen. During the cholera epidemics, for instance, the early Lutheran parsonages at both Andover and Chicago, became emergency hospitals and out of the latter grew the Augustana Hospital, now one of the most important in Chicago. For such purposes the Swedish people in the United States have always been generous. In recent years American hospital designs and techniques have been closely studied in Sweden.

Having been brought up, as a rule, on a high standard of cleanliness, the Swedes take deep interest in sanitation work. An outstanding example is the truly impressive work done in the Hawaiian Islands during the past twenty years by Dr. Nils P. Larsen, a native of Stockholm, who was brought to America by his parents while a child. (His father, born at Brunskog in Värmland, was originally named Larsson.) After graduating from the Cornell Medical School in New York in 1916, Dr. Larsen became a medical officer in the One-hundred-sixth Regiment during the First World War and for exceptional bravery under fire in France was decorated and then cited in the General Orders of the United States War Department. In 1922 he became Superintendent of Queens Hospital in Honolulu and under his direction it was raised from the fourth to the first rank. He next started a clean-up campaign throughout the islands which resulted in a greatly lowered infant mortality rate and an improved control of epidemics. As Superintendent of Queens Hospital he was succeeded in 1936 by Dr. Gustaf W. Olson, who had had his medical training in Minnesota and California.

Another Swedish medical specialty for which there seems to be a permanent need in the United States is physiotherapy, including "Swedish" massage. Practitioners of this art, whether born in Sweden or not, are to be found in practically every city and sometimes in rural districts. For reducing purposes and general re-invigoration as well as in the treatment of various ailments it has shown itself to be beneficial. A number of men and women who were originally physical culture specialists in Sweden have become physiotherapists in the United States. Several have even taken medical degrees and some have been appointed professors at American medical schools.

The Swedish system of health culture goes back to the exercises developed by Per Henrik Ling, an early nineteenth century Swedish poet and university graduate, who wanted to raise the physical standard of his countrymen as a means to revive their national spirit after the loss of Finland to Russia in 1809. After studying languages, gymnastics and sports in various countries, including Denmark, Ling returned to Sweden in 1813. He then founded in Stockholm the Royal Central Institute of Gymnastics. The young men and women he trained taught the system not only in Sweden but in many other countries including the United States.

It is worth noting that Mark Twain spent the summer of 1899 in Sanna, Sweden, where his daughter, Jean, sought aid for an epileptic ailment by taking the "Swedish movements" taught by Henrik Kellgren, a local *sjukgymnast,* or physical culture specialist. Mr. Clemens became so enthusiastic over his daughter's improvement that he took treatments himself. After his return to America he recommended the system to his friends. In New York he placed his daughter under the care of a Minnesota-born physician of Swedish descent, Dr. Frederick Peterson.

The new system of exercises was first introduced in Chicago by Polycarpus von Schneidau, a former Swedish army officer, who had originally arrived at Pine Lake, Wisconsin, in 1842 but had moved to Chicago in 1845. There, besides fencing and dancing, he taught Swedish gymnastics to classes of women as well as men. In New York the Ling exercises were introduced in 1855, ten years later, at a hydropathic institute conducted by Dr. George Taylor. In 1856 his younger brother, Dr. Charles Taylor, made a study trip to London and Stockholm to learn more about the new exercises and a son of the latter, Per Henrik Taylor, was named in honor of the Swedish founder of the system. He likewise used the Swedish method in his practice as an orthopedic surgeon. For many years there existed in New York a Zander Institute, founded by a Russian *emigré* by the name of Wischnewetzky but named in honor of Jonas Gustaf Vilhelm Zander, founder of a similar medico-mechanical institute in Stockholm. In many American hospitals the Zander type of machines for mechanical physiotherapy were installed, but gradually their use has diminished, "probably because of the lack of trained operators," to quote the late Captain Theodore A. Melander in *Swedes in America* (p. 358). In both New York and Stockholm the Zander Institutes have long since been closed.

In Boston the Ling system was launched with even greater *éclat* by a handsome young Swedish army officer, Baron Nils Posse, who arrived there in 1885. At first he taught the teachers of the Boston public schools and gradually "setting-up" exercises became part of the daily program in almost all American public schools. Before long Baron Posse was able to interest a Mrs. Hemenway, a philanthropic Bostonian, who, in 1890, founded The Boston Normal School of Gymnastics with the former Swedish army officer as one of the instructors. The next year, however, he opened his own gymnasium from which about thirty new instructors in the Ling system were graduated each year. After Posse's death in 1895, it was conducted for some years by Harry Nissen and was then renamed the Posse-Nissen School of Physical Education. It offered a four-year course in gymnastics and physiotherapy and on both subjects Posse wrote books.

In 1887, or only two years later than Posse, Claes Enebuske, who had likewise been educated in the Ling gymnastics in Stockholm, arrived in New York and began to teach at the Brooklyn Normal School of Gymnastics, where many young Swedes became his pupils. In the summer he taught at the Chautauqua Institute near Jamestown in western New York. After Posse's resignation Enebuske was appointed his successor as an instructor at the Boston Normal School of Gymnastics. In Boston the Swedish system was strongly supported by a Dr. Hartwell who for two years had studied it himself at the Royal Central Institute in Stockholm, and it was partly through his influence that the exercises were introduced in the public schools of the city. From there they spread throughout the country. While teaching in Boston Enebuske earned a degree at the Harvard Medical School and then retired from gymnastics to become a general practitioner of medicine.

The same course was followed by his assistant and successor at the Boston Normal School of Gymnastics, Carl Collin, who was born in the Swedish province of Blekinge in 1864 and likewise was trained at the Royal Central Institute in Stockholm, but even after he had become a doctor of medicine at Harvard, he continued to teach gymnastics at Wellesley College and, after that, at the School for Physical Education at Battle Creek, Michigan, and finally in Chicago. He taught at the Boston Normal School for over twenty years and at the end of his career he retired to a farm in New Hampshire.

At Wellesley, Collin was succeeded by William Skarström, born in 1869 in Stockholm. Having arrived at an early age in New York, he first taught Swedish gymnastics at the New York Y.M.C.A. and then at Pratt Institute in Brooklyn. He next took a course at the Boston Normal School, and in 1901 he, too, obtained a medical degree at Harvard. After that he taught physical culture successively at the noted private preparatory school at Groton, the Massachusetts Institute of Technology, and the Boston Normal School of Gymnastics. He then became Professor of physical education at Columbia University in New York, where he remained until 1912. Next he succeeded Collin at Wellesley College and there for nearly twenty years, or until 1931, he remained a highly appreciated teacher. He was the author of *Gymnastic Kinesiology* and *Gymnastic Teaching*.

Dr. Enebuske's work at the Brooklyn Normal School as well as at Chautauqua was carried on by Jakob Bolin, who was a graduate of the Lidbeck Institute in Stockholm. At Chautauqua a special large building on the Swedish pattern and with Swedish equipment, called the Bolin Gymnasium, was built, and in his summer courses he trained pupils from almost all parts of the country. Bolin next became an instructor at the Savage School for Physical Education in New York and in 1910 Professor of physical education at the University of Utah. In 1914 he died. Since then there have been a number of other Swedish-born teachers and practitioners of both gymnastics and physiotherapy, on the West Coast as well as in the East and Middle West.

"The few institutions that still use the Ling System to any extent," Captain Melander, who had founded in 1916 a Swedish Institute of Physiotherapy in New York, wrote rather bitterly at the end of his chapter in *Swedes in America* (p. 365), "are some military academies and Catholic schools, in which seriousness and discipline prevail. American youth in general and especially in the Eastern states, where so many nationalities are mixed, do not care much for attention and discipline—two things absolutely necessary for the Swedish system. The same laxity seems to prevail, sad to say, also among the younger generations of Swedish descent. This proves that our health gymnastics, despite hard and time-sacrificing work by many, have not succeeded in establishing itself in the United States. At the same time, however, it is gratifying to see that massage and physiotherapy according to the original Swedish principles are always in demand and have gained appreciation from the medical profession as well as from the population in general."

Except for the physiotherapists, a certain number of nurses and a few of the early medical practitioners, most of the American doctors of Swedish descent have been trained in the United States. Sweden has seldom had doctors to spare and some Swedes who have studied medicine in America have at times found it worth their while to return to Sweden, where their American training has been highly appreciated. To an even greater degree this has been true of the dentists. Conversely, a certain number of American-trained specialists have made studies in Sweden where a considerable amount of practical experience has been available, especially in the field of social welfare work. Toward the eradication of certain maladies such as tuberculosis and the venereal diseases greater progress has likewise been made in Sweden than in the United States and, thanks in part to less expensive hospital care, the Swedish infant mortality rate is also lower than the American.

Additional names of American doctors and physiotherapists of Swedish descent may be found in *Swedes in America* (New Haven, 1938).

XXVII

WRITERS

Because of their historical and sociological importance the writings of former immigrants have begun to receive attention in America. "Melting-pot literature," they have been called, that is, literature written in America and primarily in the immigrant's own vernacular. Generally of mediocre literary merit, it has been frowned upon by some critics who refuse to call it literature at all. This, we believe to be wrong for we must judge such writings from an immigrant's point of view. His expression of contentment, hardships, hope and despair—has been of greater moment than literary *form*. In this chapter, therefore, we shall first consider briefly what we may term Swedish literature in America, remembering that this pioneer writing is, at least potentially, American literature.

The late Ernst Skarstedt listed in *Pennfäktare* (*Scribblers*), 1930, 575 Swedish American writers, the vast majority of whom wrote in Swedish. Professor Joseph E. A. Alexis in *La Littérature Suèdoise d'Amérique,* a smaller but more selective compilation made the same year, furnished a bibliography listing works by seventy-seven Swedish-writing authors, of whom twenty-two were chosen for special consideration. A large proportion of them were journalists, or writers who started out as such; but we find among them not a few clergymen, some educators, and several who had pursued other professions. Some of them wrote almost exclusively on scientific, historical, religious, or outright denominational subjects, but most of them, including a number of women, had ventured at some time in their lives into belles lettres. Here we are concerned chiefly with the latter.

The aggregate quantity of verse and prose produced by these "Scribblers" in their native language is amazingly large, and some of it —especially in consideration of backgrounds, handicaps, and material circumstances—of surprisingly good quality. Though much, of course, is of an inferior grade, enough deep, melancholy, and beautiful thoughts have been expressed by Swedish American immigrants in poetic phraseology and with sufficiently admirable workmanship to deserve more attention than can be given in this volume. In fact, a few of the poets wrote well enough to break down the prejudice in Sweden against the literary work of former emigrants and to receive from their homeland both royal and academic honors.

The poetic themes treated most frequently were nature, religion, and a resigned and often hopeless yearning for the country left behind. Most immigrants of any nationality have probably shared this feeling of being divided in sympathy between the fatherland and the land of adoption. Among the Swedish Americans this feeling was a serious one, since from the first they had made up their minds to become permanent settlers and citizens of the New World. There was no retreat or return. And so this heartrending dualism becomes a stirring theme in Swedish American verse. In prose, we note particularly descriptions of the "dog's life" of the immigrant in America, realistic but entirely loyal narratives of the experiences of the Swedish "greenhorn," whether in factories or farms of the East or on the prairies of the Middle West or in the mines and forests of the Northwest. Sometimes plays, short stories, sketches, and novelettes about Swedish American life, were written in an amusing mixture of Swedish and English. In brief, Swedish immigrant literature endeavors to describe the birth pangs and growing pains of assimilation known as Americanization.

As we examine Skarstedt's list of writers, most of them natives of Sweden who have long since gone to their reward, we meet a motley variety of personalities. There are, for instance—listed alphabetically —Carl Bruhn (b. 1869 in Stockholm), a gifted international adventurer, who wrote both verse and prose in Swedish, English, German, or Spanish. He also made a translation into Swedish of Owen Wister's *The Virginian;* Gus Higgins (d. 1909), a humorist, artist, caricaturist, and musician à la Bellman, who, as he claimed, had been forced by some Irish boardinghouse comrades to change his name of Lindström to Higgins; Emanuel Schmidt (b. 1868 in Hudiksvall, d. 1921 in Minnesota), preacher, Professor of Hebrew, and religious writer, who was honored by the Swedish Academy for his Swedish translation of Longfellow's *Hiawatha;* and Edward Sundell (d. 1929), who in 1911 became secretary to Senator Chauncey M. Depew, of New York and who later edited the Senator's memoirs, lectures, and speeches.

Several other Swedish immigrants wrote, like Bruhn, in both Swedish and English: Olof Jacob Bonggren (b. 1852 in Dalsland), a learned, venerable poet on the staff of *Svenska Amerikanaren* in Chicago, who divided his poetic and philosophical writings among Sweden, the United States, and the home, and who was called a "typical Swedish American poet"; Oliver A. Linder (b. 1862 in Skåne), editor of the same paper and a specialist in the sonnet, who also wrote short stories and criticisms, as well as articles on American and Swedish American subjects for the Swedish encyclopedia, *Nordisk Familjebok;* the Reverend Emil Lund, editor, clergyman, and religious writer, who in addition to other accomplishments spoke Latin and Hebrew and lived to be a nonagenarian; Carl Adolf Lönnquist, theologian, hymnodist, and composer, who in Skarstedt's list is credited with eleven volumes of verse, some of it humorous and satirical; Ernst Wilhelm Olson (b. 1870), editor and translator, who, in addition to a biography of Olof Olsson and numerous other works, has written a history of the Swedes in Illinois; and as late as June 1947, was working enthusiastically in the editorial rooms of the Augustana Book Concern. (A collection of his poems, including translations, was published in 1947 as *Valda Dikter*) and Carl Fredrik Peterson (d. 1901), a native of Södermanland, a translator of Swedish verse into English, as well as a journalist, historian, astrologer, Swedenborgian, and political writer who wrote, in Swedish, a history of the United States that was translated into both Finnish and Norwegian and used as a textbook in many schools of those countries.

Probably the most prolific of all Swedish American writers was the late Oscar Leonard Strömberg, a Methodist minister of Nebraska, who was born in Arboga, Sweden (1871). He wrote poems and short stories but chiefly novels, of which thirty-eight are listed by Alexis. His books were light, entertaining, religious narratives, with noble tendencies, which never mention alcoholic drinks, as Strömberg was an ardent champion of temperance. Most of his novels were published in Sweden, and at least one was translated into English.

Chronologically, one of the first Swedish American poets was a native of Värmland, August Hjalmar Edgren (1840–1903), a Civil War veteran, teacher and scholar, "whose pathetic, alternate longing for Sweden and America constantly set him traveling between the two countries until, finally, Sweden won out." He was also a philologist and lexicographer of international repute and probably the first Swede to earn a doctorate at Yale University (1874) as well as to teach there. He was perhaps best known for his faithful poetic translations from the Sanskrit and of works by Poe, Longfellow, Whittier, Bryant, and Lowell. He rendered *Evangeline* into Swedish, parts of *Hiawatha,* and a selection of poems from Tennyson. In his own writings he shows himself to be both a thinker and a master of form. His style was classic, academic, yet simple and effective. He longs for America, but once there he yearns still more for his fatherland. On both continents he was, successively, a professor in several institutions and he possessed a natural gift for language and literature, an exquisite esthetic sense, and was a sincere painstaking interpreter of life who scorned all hypocrisy and superficiality. Dignity of subject and harmony of words and phrasing were two of his outstanding literary qualities. "Edgren was a restless, almost tragic figure," says another writer, "and represents the heartrending inner split and dualism in the Swedish American immigrant."

Magnus Henrik Elmblad (1848–88) a native of Småland was one of the most gifted of the Swedish American poets who wrote in Swedish. Constantly torn mentally, like Edgren, between two physical worlds, and addicted to the excessive use of alcohol, he finally succumbed to the vice and died in Sweden in great poverty. He wrote easily and lucidly in both verse and prose and was considered an exceptional translator of verse. At an early age he had translated Ibsen's *Brand* and after he arrived in America he made one of the best translations into Swedish of "The Star-Spangled Banner." He wrote entertaining sketches for the newspapers, made translations from the German and English, and selected his poetic themes from two hemispheres. *Allan Roini,* an epic poem dealing with the struggle for independence of Herzegovina against the Turks, was awarded a prize by the Swedish Academy. It glorified love of family, country, and nature. Throughout life Elmblad had a profound sympathy for the lower classes of society.

Another Swedish American poet was Ludvig Holmes (d. 1910), a native of Skåne and a clergyman. Two volumes of poems, pure in both form and content, came from his pen, in 1896 and 1904. Without striking originality or depth, he versified easily and made his verse readable. He chose a great variety of subjects, serious as well as humorous, but probably succeeded best in those of a religious character.

Johan Alfred Enander (1842–1910), famed editor of *Hemlandet,* the first Swedish newspaper in Chicago, came to America in 1869. Primarily a journalist, he was also a college teacher, political orator, and for many years the Grand Old Man of Swedish American cultural life, who exerted a vast and wholesome influence on his fellow countrymen.

He extolled American law and liberty, urging everybody to obey the former so that the latter might survive. He wrote a few poems on Sweden, the Swedish language, as well as on the Chicago fire, but his forte was prose. He was the recipient of the medal *Literis et Artibus* from Sweden, and many other honors. His admonition to Swedish immigrants to regard their native country as a mother, and love their new one as a bride has become proverbial, at least among the Swedes. As an editorial writer and orator, Enander was effective in confirming his countrymen in the Republican faith.

The hybrid Swedish American dialect has been successfully used by several authors to make faithful pictures of the influence of English upon Swedish, and vice versa. The most popular writers of this genre have been Anna (Aina) Olson (b. 1866) and Gustaf Nathaniel Malm, a son of Småland, who was born in 1869 and died in 1928. The latter, a singer and artist as well as a writer, was gifted with power of observation, a good-natured tolerance, and the ability to discover really humorous situations. He has immortalized himself in *Charli Johnson, Svensk-Amerikan* (1909), a character who moves among the Swedish immigrants of Kansas and Nebraska and speaks their hybrid dialect.

The most active collector of Swedish American literature and leading specialist on the subject was the late Gustaf N. Swan of Sioux City, Iowa. Born in Östergötland, 1856, he was a businessman, banker, Swedish Vice Consul, and also contributor to many magazines, annuals, and newspapers. His collection of six thousand books and pamphlets, which, in addition to more classical items, contains many Swedish American literary products, was donated to the Denkmann Library of Augustana College, at Rock Island, Illinois. Mr. Swan, who died in 1938, had been decorated with the Royal Swedish Order of the North Star and held a L.H.D. degree from Augustana.

One evening about twenty years ago, a committee of four men and a woman met in New York, to act as judges in a literary contest. When the woman member made a passing reference to window curtains one of the men, a short, scraggly bearded, and modestly dressed person, whom the rest had believed to be half asleep in a corner, suddenly raised his head, opened his eyes and abruptly asked in Swedish: "Who mentioned curtains? *I* want no curtains; *I* want the *sun!*" The man was Ernst Skarstedt (1857–1929), probably the ablest and in many respects the most original Swedish American writer. He wanted no darkness, metaphorical or otherwise; no obstruction of any kind to light. Both physically and mentally he was a pioneer. The son of a professor at the University of Lund, he had received a good education, but his spirit of *Wanderlust* drove him westward. A poet and a master of descriptive, realistic prose, he recorded his "dog's days" in America (*Mina hundår i Amerika*) with unforgettable vividness and poignancy. A productive author on a variety of subjects, he wrote with a critical acumen which commanded the respect of foe and friend alike, pricking the bubbles of social and political sham. He tried to work with other people, as, for instance, in newspaper offices, and he was both a husband and a father, but was happiest of all when alone with nature, raising chickens or playing his violin. He was a philosopher and hermit. As an apostle of reason and justice, he rejected all forms of narrow dogmatism and hated convention, pretension, and falsity with a holy hatred. At the same time he sympathized sincerely with all honest endeavors.

Several American Swedes have essayed to describe in Swedish the bitter struggles of the Swedish pioneer in America in fiction form. The best and most pretentious work of this genre is *Nu blommar prairien* (*Now the Prairie Blooms*), by Albin Widén, who was until 1947 head of the Swedish Information Bureau in Minneapolis. As a prize-winning novel, it was published in Sweden; it deals with the toil, aspirations, and tribulations of a group of Swedish settlers in Minnesota. There are some romantic and some humorous episodes; still more work, worry, and religious tribulations, and also enough crop-destroying grasshoppers to discourage any pioneer farmer. The hero is a young clergyman, and the story ends semi-happily, with a caravan of Swedes leaving Minnesota for points still further west. The work recalls the well-known novels of O. E. Rölvaag, which deal with Norwegian settlers in the Northwest.

Of invaluable social, cultural, and political service, both to the Swedish immigrant and to the American melting-pot process in general, have been the weekly Swedish-language newspapers and kindred publications. They have helped immeasurably to make the Swedish pioneer feel at home during his period of transition and readjustment, and unless the immigrant felt reasonably at home he would not make a good citizen. The newspapers in his native tongue acted as a comforting stabilizer until his feet were more firmly planted in the new, foreign soil.

The Swedish press in the United States has had an influential and honorable history for almost a century. *Det Gamla och Nya Hemlandet*

(*The Old and the New Homeland*) was established by the Reverend Tuve Nilsson Hasselquist in Galesburg, Illinois, in 1855 and then moved to Chicago. In New York *Skandinaven* had appeared irregularly during the years 1851–1853. They were followed by a surprisingly large number of weeklies and monthlies. O. A. Linder estimates in *Swedes in America* (p. 186) that by 1910 the total number of such publications, big and small, had exceeded one thousand, a majority of them being denominational in character. "The number of weeklies with a secular program, most of them published for short periods, was about 250," adds Mr. Linder. Eighty-six cities in twenty-seven states contributed to this list, which, incidentally, tells us something about the number, distribution, and reading habits of Swedes in America. In 1938 thirty-five Swedish publications were still appearing in the United States and Canada, and the *American-Swedish Handbook* for 1945 lists twenty-five, not counting the organs of fraternal organizations.

The heyday of the Swedish American press came during the first twenty-five years of this century. The Swedes were then prosperous, and about 250,000 subscribed to Swedish-language publications. One of the weeklies had 80,000 subscribers; another 70,000.

Besides the weekly newspapers, a few magazines and annuals have been published in Swedish. Examples of the former were *Valkyrian* of New York (1897–1909) and of the latter, *Prairieblomman,* which appeared at Rock Island, Illinois, for several years early in the twentieth century.

Partly because of the pressure for rapid Americanization that accompanied the First World War and partly because of the immigration restrictions that followed it, the Swedish-language press, like practically all other American newspapers in other languages than English, has had to fight hard ever since for its existence. The American-born children of the immigrants read, as a rule, only publications in English. Several Swedish-language weeklies have either ceased publication or have been absorbed by more vigorous competitors; a few have followed the example of the churches and have either become bi-lingual or have turned to English entirely.

Ultimately, the journalistic medium of Americans from Sweden is bound to be English. *The American Scandinavian Review,* a literary quarterly published since 1911 by The American Scandinavian Foundation, New York City (Henry Goddard Leach, editor), and *The American Swedish Monthly,* published in New York by the Swedish Chamber of Commerce of the USA (Olof Ollén, editor; Lillian Carlson, associate editor), are examples of the trend. Other harbingers of the future are annuals like the *Year Book* published by the American Swedish Historical Foundation in Philadelphia (Marshall W. S. Swan, editor) and quarterlies like the *Bulletin* published by the American-Swedish Institute at Minneapolis, Minnesota (Nils G. Sahlin, editor).

The Dictionary of American Biography claims Swedish colonial or early Swedish American ancestry for several literary Petersons of a century ago. In one Peterson family there were five sons. Three established in Philadelphia the noted publishing firm T. B. Peterson Brothers, and Charles Jacob Peterson (1819–1887), the oldest, was a poet who became famous both as an editor and a publisher. For forty-seven years he edited *Peterson's Magazine,* first called *Lady's World.* In the 'seventies it had a circulation of 150,000. Its editor enjoyed contacts with all the prominent *literati* of the day, especially those living in Philadelphia. He himself wrote several historical novels and other books including *The Naval Heroes of the United States* (1850). His cousin, Henry Peterson (1818–1891), poet and historical novelist, edited the *Saturday Evening Post* for twenty-five years. Their earliest American ancestor's name is given as Erick Pieterson, the godson of a Swedish archbishop.

In 1937 Roy W. Swanson, editorial writer and reference librarian on the St. Paul *Pioneer Press and Dispatch,* was asked to write a chapter for *Swedes in America* on American journalists of Swedish antecedents. He did so, but pointed out the difficulties of the task, because of lost or Anglicized family names and the large number of such English-writing journalists. Furthermore, they were distributed, he said, from New York to Alaska. Take New York City. There was first of all "Ted" Wallen (Theodore Clifford Wallen) of the New York *Herald Tribune,* whose reporting won for him an LL.D. degree, though he died (1936) at the age of only forty-two. Born in New Britain, Connecticut, of Swedish parents, he had received his political training on the Hartford *Courant,* and for the *Herald Tribune* he became first Albany correspondent and then covered several national party conventions, presidential tours, as well as the Naval Disarmament Conference in Washington in 1922. In 1930 he was appointed head of the *Herald Tribune* Washington bureau.

A native of Sweden was William Axel Warn ("Baron" Warn) of the New York *Times,* late dean of the legislative correspondents at Albany, an erstwhile sailor and globetrotter, who first became a contributor to the Brooklyn *Daily Eagle* and in 1902 began to cover the

Criminal Courts Building for the *Times*. In 1912 he was sent to Albany, where he had the opportunity to report on the careers of such men as Charles Evans Hughes, Alfred E. Smith, Franklin D. Roosevelt, and Herbert H. Lehman. Other American Swedes of past or present associations with the New York *Times* have been: Alma Louise Olson, formerly its literary correspondent in Scandinavia, who holds the Vasa Medal from Sweden; George M. Palmer of the *Times* sports department; the late Oscar Cesare, cartoonist; and the Swedish-born Godfrey N. Nelson, a lawyer and authority on taxation, who is Secretary of the *Times* corporation and regularly contributes to it articles on taxation and finance.

Neil Harmon Swanson, the historical novelist, has been, since 1941, executive editor of the Baltimore *Sun* papers. He has been connected with these papers since 1931, and before that worked on the Minneapolis *Journal* and then became managing editor of the Pittsburgh *Press*. Ferdinand Lundberg, author of *Imperial Hearst* and *America's Sixty Families,* was for ten years associated with Chicago and New York papers. Oliver Carlson, another Swedish critic of Mr. Hearst, and joint-author of *Hearst: Lord of San Simeon,* was born in Sweden and grew up in Michigan, where he got his newspaper training. He is a free-lance writer, now living in California, who has written feature articles for the New York *Post* and Philadelphia *Record,* and has contributed articles to various magazines on political and economic subjects. He has also written several books including a biography of Arthur Brisbane.

Mauritz A. Hallgren, author and journalist, born (1899) in Chicago of Södermanland parentage, has been a commentator on politics and economics. After working for newspapers in Chicago and other cities, he was for several years a Washington and European correspondent for the United Press, and later associate editor, first of *The Nation* and then of the Baltimore *Sun* (1934–38). He is the author of several books, including *Seeds of Revolt* (1933) and *The Tragic Fallacy* (1937), as well as *All About Stamps* (1940).

Elmer T. Peterson, a native of Iowa who was from 1927 to 1937 editor of *Better Homes and Gardens* at Des Moines, had captured during the First World War the *Editor and Publisher* gold medal for the best editorial in relation to the Fourth Liberty Loan. He had then had twenty years of experience in Kansas journalism, culminating in the editorship of the Wichita *Beacon*. He is now associate editor of the *Daily Oklahoman* of Oklahoma City. Besides a novel, *Trumpets West,* and several contributions to national magazines, Mr. Peterson has published *Forward to the Land* (1941), and *Cities are Abnormal* (1944).

Another native of the Middle West with a Swedish background is Albin E. Johnson, who served in the American Navy during the First World War, then became a reporter for the United Press and later foreign editor, successively, of the Philadelphia *Public Ledger* and the New York *Evening World*. For the latter paper and a few others like the Kansas City *Star* and the Los Angeles *Times* he covered during the next ten years the activities of the League of Nations in Geneva and other attempts to establish peace. He actually described the rise of Mussolini, Hitler, Franco and other dictators. After returning to America in the late 1930s he became a foreign commissioner for the New York World's Fair and as such visited many countries to arrange their participation.

A third Midwesterner of Swedish ancestry is Elmer W. Peterson (not to be confused with Elmer T.), who was born in Minnesota. After serving on the Minneapolis *Tribune,* he became an Associated Press correspondent in Stockholm and after that covered several countries, in the Far East as well as in Europe. Next he became a news commentator for the National Broadcasting Company, first in New York and then in California. He is also popular as a lecturer on world events.

The editor of *The American Swedish Monthly* from 1936, when he succeeded Johan Liljencrants, until 1946, was Victor Oscar Freeburg (Fredberg), born in Iowa and educated in Kansas, as well as at Yale. He once taught English at the United States Naval Academy, at Haverford College, and then at Columbia University in New York. In the First World War, he served as an ensign and from 1922–25 he was assistant Director of the American Swedish News Exchange, Inc. He is also a painter, and now lives on Cape Ann, Massachusetts.

For the *Monthly* Holger Lundbergh writes on the arts. A collection of his incidental poems was published in 1948 under the title of *Word Business*. He is now Assistant Director of The American Swedish News Exchange, founded in 1922 by Dr. Börje H. Brillioth of Stockholm, who later became editor-in-chief of *Stockholms Tidningen* in Sweden. Since the Second World War the general manager has been Allan Kastrup, a journalist born and educated in Sweden.

Other notable American magazine and newspapermen of Swedish descent are: Erik Oberg, editor of *Machinery,* a native of Värnamo, Småland, who arrived in the United States in 1901 after having re-

ceived both an academic and an engineering education (He worked
for a while as a designer of machine tools and manufacturing equipment for the Pratt & Whitney Company in Connecticut); John Gustaf
Goldstrom, pioneer aviation reporter, who in 1910 made a flight with
Glenn M. Curtiss, has written a history of aviation, and has had a
street in his native Pittsburgh named for him; Everett Kallgren, a
native of New Haven and formerly city editor of the New Haven
Journal Courier, who in 1935 became night editor of the New York
Herald Tribune; J. Harold Swanson, a Cornell graduate, who until
its merger with the *Journal* in 1940, was editor, secretary, and general
manager of the Jamestown (N.Y.) *Post;* and Harvey Ellsworth Newbranch (originally Nyquist or Nygren), editor and Vice President of
the Omaha *World-Herald,* who in 1919 was awarded the Pulitzer
Prize for the best editorial of that year; and George E. Akerson, born
in Minneapolis and educated at Harvard, who from 1928 to 1930 was
secretary to President Herbert Hoover. After working on the Minneapolis *Tribune,* he was sent, in 1921, to Washington to cover the Naval
Arms Conference.

Several Swedish American newspapermen have served both the
Swedish- and English-language press, usually in that order. Among
such journalists—influential emissaries of Swedish culture in the United
States—have been: Victor Nilsson, Edwin August Björkman, and Johan
Ludwig Wallin. Dr. Nilsson (d. 1942), nationally known interpreter
of Scandinavian music was for over thirty years music critic on the
Minneapolis *Journal;* Mr. Björkman, a native of Stockholm, inter-
nationally known translator, novelist, and essayist, served on several
newspapers in Minneapolis, New York, and Asheville, North Carolina,
before devoting himself exclusively to translating and other literary
tasks; Mr. Wallin, who died in 1936, served for thirty years as music
critic of the Oregon *Journal.* After the Civil War, Colonel Hans
Mattson, tried his hand in both fields; for a time he edited the *North,*
a business publication in English for Scandinavian Americans.

The Swedish representatives of the so-called rural press are many.
In Minnesota, for example, the late Governor John A. Johnson, had
been editor of the St. Peter *Herald;* N. P. Olson of the Red Wing
Daily Eagle, was a native of Kristianstad, Sweden, who in 1943, after
over sixty years of publication service, passed away at the age of eighty-
nine; and Victor Emanuel Lawson, editor and publisher of the Willmar

Daily Tribune, who in 1937 was elected President of the Associated Press of Minnesota.

Chicago journalism has had many Swedes, besides Carl Sandburg. The most sensational reporter in America of Swedish blood, was the late Hilding Johnson, born in Sweden, whose personality furnished the basis for the popular newspaper melodrama and motion picture *The Front Page* (1928). For twenty years "Hildy," as he was called, was Criminal Courts Building reporter for the Chicago *Herald and Examiner.* He was said to have known everybody worth knowing in the political as well as in the criminal world of Chicago and thus became a legendary example of the American "hard-boiled" newspaperman. He "often played poker," it was rumored, "with condemned murderers the night before they were to hang."

Among other American journalists of Swedish ancestry who deserve mention are: George Axelsson, New York *Times* correspondent in Stockholm, his native city; Herman G. Nelson, leading staff writer of the Rockford (Ill.) *Morning Star;* Bernard Peterson, a native of Glimåkra, Sweden, who served for many years on the editorial staff of the late Boston *Evening Transcript,* now assistant editor of *Industria,* organ of the Associated Industries of Massachusetts; Bertil Stolpe, public relations representative of the Des Moines *Register and Tribune;* Everett Norlander, managing editor, Chicago *Daily News;* George L. Peterson, columnist and editorial writer, Minneapolis *Star;* Jalmar Johnson, Sunday editor, *The Oregonian,* Portland, Oregon; Laurence C. Eklund, Washington correspondent, Milwaukee *Journal;* and Gene Lindberg, feature writer, Denver *Post.*

Several of the journalists mentioned above are also, as noted, authors of novels, short stories, poems, etc. Neil H. Swanson, for example, has published numerous works of fiction including *The Judas Tree* (1933), *The Phantom Emperor* (1934), *The First Rebel* (1937), *The Silent Drum* (1940), and *The Perilous Fight* (1944), all based on episodes in American history. Like Douglass Freeman, once editor of the Richmond *Times Leader* and a prominent historian, Mr. Swanson writes his books before breakfast, beginning at four A.M.

Another author with a journalistic background is Herman Landon, born in Stockholm, who in 1933 had fourteen novels to his credit, besides serials, short stories, and novelettes. After being associated with the Chicago *Record Herald* (1910–14) and the Washington (D.C.) *Herald* (1915–17) he turned to mystery fiction. Some of his novels are *The Gray Phantom, The Unknown Seven,* and *Hands Unseen.*

Arthur Peterson (1851–1932), sometime editor of the *Saturday Evening Post,* of which his father, Henry P., was publisher, was the author of *Songs of New Sweden* (1887), *Collected Poems* (1900,) *Sigurd* (1910), and *Andvari's Ring* (1916). Mr. Peterson was once in the United States Navy, and served on the U.S.S. *Baltimore,* under Admiral Dewey. Charlton Lawrence Edholm, whose father was born in Sweden, a poet, artist, and writer of light fiction, has turned to the wild and unruly West for such titles as *Doomed Cowboy, Reckless Road,* and *Wildcat.*

About ten years ago *Our Daily Bread* caused a stir among the reading public. The author, Gösta Larsson, was a young Swedish immigrant educated in Sweden as an engineer, whose manuscripts, it was said, had been rejected in Sweden and who had therefore, with characteristic Scandinavian persistency, decided to try his hand in English. He came to America; mastered the language; and his first novel surpassed expectations. It is cheerless but interesting, describing with much enthusiasm the drab surroundings of a workingman's life in Sweden. It was followed by *Fatherland, Farewell!, The Ordeal of the Falcon,* and *Ships in the River* (1946), which was sold to be filmed. Mr. Larsson has also been a contributor to various magazines. He now lives in New Hampshire. As an author of cookbooks, Anna Olsson Coombs of Carlisle, Massachusetts, has been successful. She was once a teacher in Sweden where she was born and educated.

Among other American writers of Swedish descent who have made their mark in English are: Skulda Banér, born in Ironwood, Michigan, the daughter of Gustaf Runesköld Banér, who was a writer of verse in English as well as Swedish. Her *Latchstring Out* is an account of her childhood in Upper Michigan. She now lives in California and though totally blind is at work on four additional books; Nelson Algren, a native of Chicago, whose two grandfathers arrived there during the Civil War. His novels include: *Somebody in Boots, Never Come Morning,* and *The Man With The Golden Arm,* and a collection of short stories, *The Neon Wilderness;* Daniel Lundberg, a writer of Swedish descent who once lived in Mexico. He has published one novel, *River Rat,* and is now a script writer in Hollywood; and Edita Morris (née Toll), who was born in Sweden and married to a son and namesake of the late Ira Nelson Morris, for eight years American Minister in Stockholm. Originally a short story writer for the fashionable magazines, she has recently published two novels, *My*

Darling from the Lions, and *Charade,* as well as a collection of short stories, *Three Who Loved.* Another fiction writer who is of mixed ancestry, including Swedish, is Margaret Lee Runbeck, whose work has appeared in most of the large circulation magazines. She has also written several novels of which *Our Miss Boo* was the most popular.

Stuart David Engstrand made his debut in the early 'thirties with *The Invaders;* then published in 1939, *They Sought Paradise,* based on the Swedish Bishop Hill colony in western Illinois. His next book was *The Sling and the Arrow,* a psychoanalytical study of the modern type, which in 1948 was translated into Swedish.

It is difficult to do full justice to the late Dr. Frederick Peterson (d. 1938), professor, alienist, collector, traveler and author. Dr. Peterson was a poet who could find inspiration in a cactus plant, and, in fact, once wrote an ode to one. He was a connoisseur of art; an author of educational and medical works; and an authority on Oriental plants, use of colors and mysticism. When his *Chinese Lyrics* appeared in 1916, and received the acclaim generally given to an unknown but newly discovered foreign-born poet, no one suspected that the pseudonym "Pai Ta-shun" concealed the name of an American Swede from Minnesota—Peterson—who practiced psychiatry in New York. Both of his parents were Swedish. *Who Was Who in America* lists eight volumes by Dr. Peterson, including textbooks and translations from the Swedish. Some of his literary talent was inherited by his daughter, Virgilia Peterson-Sapieha (Princess Sapieha of Poland) who in 1940 published *Polish Profile* and in 1942 a novel, *Beyond This Shore.*

The most eminent American author of Swedish descent is, of course, Carl Sandburg, free-verse writer, Lincoln historian, and troubadour extraordinary. His father—a poor, devout, hard-working blacksmith, who, while he could "read his Bible after a fashion" could hardly sign his own name—came from Sweden to Illinois in the 'seventies; got a job on a railroad; changed his name of August Johnson to August Sandburg, for there were already too many August Johnsons in the neighborhood; married Clara Anderson; and proceeded to raise a family. Carl who was born in Galesburg, was one of four children, and in the course of time he became, in turn, a bootblack, hobo, milk-driver, farmer, barber, dishwasher, salesman, and a dozen other things. He roamed all over the Midwest. He took part in the Spanish–American War; attended Lombard College, but did not stay long enough to get his diploma; was secretary to the Socialist Mayor of Milwaukee;

and then began his real career. He first engaged in newspaper and magazine work, including an assignment for the Chicago *Daily News* as its correspondent in Stockholm (1918). In the meantime he had received a prize for poetry; his *Chicago Poems* had appeared in 1915, and were followed, among others, by *Cornhuskers* (1918), *Smoke and Steel* (1920), *Slabs of the Sunburnt West* and *Rootabaga Stories* (1922), *The American Song Bag* (1927), etc; more prizes were then awarded him and invitations to speak in public began to pour in. He lectured at several educational institutions, including the universities of Chicago and Hawaii. In 1928 he was Phi Beta Kappa poet at Harvard, and in that same year received the first of several honorary degrees.

Carl Sandburg offers something intensely original, not to say unique, in rugged, interesting, and picturesque personality and bold, vivid writing. Always a champion of the lower classes, he has found poetry in cities, among toiling laborers and washerwomen, amidst smoking chimneys and other drab surroundings; here was a crusader who knew poverty; here was satire, wisdom, and love of America; and here was a guitar- and mandolin-player who turned out to be a new, enthusiastic type of collector, interpreter, and recitalist of American folk songs. Sandburg's verse, by the way, was really a motley collection of images, thoughts, and wholesome propaganda, now tender, now thundering, in rhythmical, but very uncommon, super-vigorous phraseology.

But his greatest fame will probably rest on the painstaking historical research he has done on the Great Emancipator. His monumental biography of Abraham Lincoln began to appear in 1926 with *The Prairie Years,* followed in 1939 by *The War Years,* in four volumes, which in 1940 captured the Pulitzer Prize—and placed Sandburg definitely in the front rank of American historians and biographers. Critics agreed that his work on Lincoln was not only a "crowning achievement," but one of the best biographies of all time. And the biographer has much in common with his subject: he is earnestly human, sensible, and sympathetic; his language is daring, simple, and unforgettably realistic; his object is truth; his words are pregnant with ideas and love of humanity; he has an ever-happy mingling of humor and seriousness; and, above all, a sound philosophy.

Carl Sandburg has also been successful as a popular speaker, columnist, and radio commentator, and his influence on the public mind is probably much greater than is generally realized. A sworn enemy of all oppression and totalitarianism, he proceeded during the Second

World War to expose sincerely, convincingly, but dispassionately, the evils of Naziism, and all other isms akin to it. His speeches taught first of all the principle without which no true democracy can exist, namely, that personal freedom and independence demand discipline and responsibility, both collective and individual. This moral and political philosophy was, in part, inherited from his Swedish ancestors.

While the art of writing is not, like engineering or even linguistics, a Swedish specialty, several of the former immigrants from Sweden and a surprising number of their descendants have contributed to American letters. Originally the former wrote only in Swedish but having enjoyed as a rule a fairly good education in Sweden they had an opportunity as journalists to interpret for their less fortunate countrymen not only their own background but also the customs and institutions of their land of adoption. How long the Swedish-language press or any publication intended for a specific nationality group will survive in America is anybody's guess. So far all predictions of an early demise have not been borne out. During the Second World War, for instance, the American attitude, including the official, toward publications in other languages than English was quite different from that on the First.

For a list of current American weekly newspapers in Swedish and the names of their editors, as well as publishing houses and booksellers, see *American Swedish Handbook* (Augustana Book Concern, Rock Island, Illinois).

XXVIII

MUSICIANS AND ACTORS

When Willa Cather created, in 1915, her musical heroine, Thea Kronborg (*The Song of the Lark*), she gave her a Swedish ancestry. This is not without significance, for Miss Cather knew her immigrants and Midwestern pioneers. While from an international viewpoint, the Swedes have not been as prominent in the art of musical composition as in some other fields—they have produced no Beethoven, Grieg, Sibelius, or Verdi—they have won well-deserved acclaim as vocalists. Swedish singers, including what may seem an almost disproportionately large number of opera stars, are widely known both in Europe and America. The first prima donna of the New York Metropolitan Opera was a Swedish girl from Småland, Christina Nilsson, who on October 22, 1883, dedicated this famous palace of song by singing Marguerite in *Faust*. She was followed at the Metropolitan, over a course of years, by twenty-four other Swedish sopranos, contraltos, tenors, and basses. And earlier than any of them Jenny Lind had come to America in 1850 and made singing tours that became epoch making in American musical tradition. Every American knows the name of at least two opera singers—Caruso and Jenny Lind.

As for Swedish quartets, male choruses, and mixed choirs, they abound in every American community where there are enough Swedes to form a vocal group. The American Union of Swedish Singers alone is composed of seventy male choruses with a membership of about 1,500.

Practically every American home with a Swedish background can boast of at least one musical instrument. To the Swede a piano is something more than just another piece of parlor furniture. Usually he is musical; his fondness for the art includes, however, the popular variety, especially if it is of Swedish origin, and his love of dancing and light entertainment may some day threaten the more serious forms. Nevertheless, the history of the Swedes in America contains names of many good, and some excellent musicians, violinists, cellists, pianists, organists, teachers and conductors, not to mention experts on the harmonica, flute, ocarina, saxophone, and accordion. But with few exceptions, they have not approached the heights reached by the Swedish vocalists.

We know little about music among the colonial Swedes, but when they emigrated to America they must have brought with them at least the standard Swedish hymns and folk songs, and we do know that they had no objections to instrumental music even in the churches, in regard to which they differed from certain other early settlers. In the Swedish churches, in fact, good singing was insisted upon and was not considered an innovation of the devil. John Tasker Howard, in *Our American Music: Three Hundred Years of It,* tells how the Reverend Andreas Sandel of the Gloria Dei Church at Wicaco imposed a fine of six shillings on certain members of his congregation for "untimely singing," which proves, presumably, that "timely singing" was in order. At the dedication of the Gloria Dei in 1700, the Swedes invited a group of German priests to furnish music and this church may very well have been the first house of worship in America to install an organ. At all events, about 1703 the church had an organist. And the fact that Gustaf Hesselius was probably the first builder of organs and spinets in the land (*c,* 1742) would seem to indicate a general liking and demand for organ music. The character of it was, of course, religious.

We may assume that this situation continued among the colonial Swedes as well as among the early nineteenth century Swedish immigrants until about the time of the Civil War. There probably were a few church organists and music teachers of Swedish ancestry before that time, but we have as yet no records of them. The late Victor Nilsson, music editor and critic of the Minneapolis *Journal,* mentions a Victor Williams, born (1816), in Sweden, who taught music in Cincinnati for more than twenty years, usually as part of his public school work. We know, too, that C. J. L. Almquist, a bizarre, romantic, Swedish author, who in the 'fifties sought refuge in America for personal reasons, was a lover of music, and before he left the United States in 1865 he had collected Indian melodies in the vicinity of Niagara Falls. The only prominent Swedish name, however, that was definitely associated with musical life in America prior to 1875 was Jenny Lind, "The Swedish Nightingale," as her contemporary and sincere but often sentimental admirers called her.

In 1875 Gustavus Johnson came to Minneapolis and became a musical pioneer in the state of Minnesota. He had been born in 1856, in England of a Swedish father and an English mother. An organist, pianist, and college musical director, he founded in 1898 at Minneapolis the Johnson School of Music, Oratory, and Dramatic Art. His compositions consisted of ensemble pieces, a rather pretentious piano concerto, and a "piano school" course of music based on the touch system. He lived to be seventy-six. Another organist and composer of sacred music was John Victor Bergquist, a native of St. Paul, Minnesota (d. 1935), who had received his training abroad under Guilmant; August Elfåker, also an organist, arrived in Chicago in 1855, and while living there composed a symphony and several songs for solos and mixed choirs; Hugo Bedinger, a brilliant composer and organist, also born in Skåne, Sweden, returned there, as did Elfåker, after having taught instrumental music at Bethany College, Kansas, where Hagbard Brase (1877), a native of Rada, near Stockholm, and educated at the Royal Swedish Conservatory of Music, was a teacher and conductor from 1900 to 1947. As director of the Lindsborg Oratorio Society, Brase gave throughout this period superb service to music in America. In addition to Brase there have been several other noted musicians connected with Bethany College, who have helped train the members of the famous Oratorio Society, which annually renders Händel's *Messiah* in a way that has made musical history in the Midwest.

An American musician of Swedish descent is Arne Oldberg, born (1874) in Ohio, a recognized composer and "pedagogue of solidity and distinction." He has studied under Leschetizky in Vienna, and others, specializing in composition and the piano. From 1897 to 1941, he was professor of these subjects at Northwestern University, at Evanston, Illinois. "He cultivates both classical form and spirit," writes a music critic, "and his compositions show sincerity, warmth, and excellent technical workmanship." His works have been played by symphony orchestras of Chicago, Philadelphia, and Minneapolis, especially his "Paolo and Francesca" overture. His two symphonies in F minor and C minor have both won national prizes. His forty or more compositions include a piano concerto, a horn concerto, "Academic Overture," "Symphonic Variations," a rhapsody, a quintet for piano and strings, and a piano sonata.

The foremost American composer of Swedish descent is, however, Howard Hanson, since 1924 Director of the Eastman School of Music in Rochester, New York. Both his parents and grandparents came from Skåne, the southernmost province of Sweden, while he himself is a native of Wahoo, Nebraska, where he was born in 1896. His honors and accomplishments have been numerous. In 1921 he won the first Prix de Rome for study at the American Academy in the Eternal City; he has often been guest conductor of orchestras both in Europe and in the United States; he is a Fellow of the Royal Swedish Academy of Music, as well as of the American Academy at Rome; in 1944 he was awarded the Pulitzer Prize, for "distinguished musical composition." On December 2, 1943, his Symphony No. 4 (Opus 34), was performed by the Boston Symphony Orchestra and in 1945 he received the Ditson Award for "distinguished service to American music." When the Festival of Music opened at Columbia University, in May 1945, Howard Hanson was the conductor. He is the composer of several symphonies, concertos, symphonic poems, and other musical compositions. He composed his first *Nordic Symphony* in California, where he had been Dean of the conservatory of fine arts of the College of the Pacific. His third symphony, first performed in 1937, was later broadcast on "Everybody's Music Hour." A unique achievement in Hanson's career was *Merry Mount,* an opera written on request for the Metropolitan Opera Company of New York. It had a brilliant première in 1934, requiring some fifty curtain calls. It was chiefly a choral work dealing with the conflict between New England Puritans and Cavaliers. Hanson has been called a "blending of the North and South, or East and West, a cosmopolitan and an individual." Like most Swedes, he indulges in no great extremes; he is a romanticist, with a serious spirit, yet carefree, humoristic, and balanced.

Among other Swedish American composers or directors are: Axel W. E. Austin, composer of marches; Henry Hallstrom and Per Olsson, associates of the American Guild of Organists; John Theodore Erickson, Mus.D.; Conrad Forsberg, and Arvid Samuelson, eminent church organists; Oscar Ekeberg, former Director-in-chief of the American Union of Swedish Singers; Nanny Strand, born and educated in Stockholm, who is a Hollywood band leader; Hjalmar Nilsson, who was a leading promoter of Swedish vocal music in America (d. 1937); and Ebba Nylander Sundstrom, violinist and former Directress of the Women's Symphony of Chicago.

Of the many Swedish American music teachers we can mention only: Greta Torpadie a voice teacher who was the wife of Theodore Björksten, tenor and teacher, who accompanied Christina Nilsson on her last tour of the United States; Augusta Öhrström-Renard, once a member of the Royal Opera in Stockholm who opened a music school in New York in 1897, and who did more perhaps than any other person to make American audiences acquainted with Swedish songs (d. 1921); and Samuel Youngquist, a former student at the Stockholm Conservatory of Music, who has had some operatic experience and whose tenor voice has been heard in Finland, Sweden, and America. He is now (1948) Professor of vocal music at Upsala College in New Jersey. In addition, he gives private lessons in his New York studio. Formerly a church soloist, he frequently appears in concerts, accompanied by his wife, Helen Lindström Youngquist.

But it is primarily as singers that Swedish musicians have become known in foreign lands. Such recognition came definitely a century ago with the appearance of Jenny Lind (1820–87), an operatic soprano born in Stockholm. After she had made an unusually favorable impression in England and on the Continent, the American showman-promoter, Phineas T. Barnum, set about inducing her to make a tour of the United States. He offered her $1,000 per concert— later allegedly raised to $2,000—an unheard-of guarantee a hundred years ago. Miss Lind, with her entourage of European musical assistants, landed in New York, September 1, 1850, and, largely because of Barnum's aggressive advertising, received the most boisterous welcome ever given any singer anywhere, either before or since. Nor had New York ever witnessed anything like it in honor of anybody. Triumphal arches, ovations, and serenades were the order of the day, and before long, foods, wearing apparel, and all manner of goods, including cigars, were named for the Swedish visitor. Barnum had conceived the idea of auctioning off the choice reservations in advance. The first sale for the first concert in New York brought $225; the offer made the purchaser famous, and, indirectly, prosperous. Later, in Boston, Providence, Philadelphia, and New Orleans, the best seats sold for as much as $725, $625, and $575. America had gone music mad. Before she had fairly started Jenny Lind had become a cult, a legend. The net proceeds of her first concert in New York, September 11, at the old Castle Garden, later the Aquarium—an appearance outside of the main schedule—amounted to $10,000, and was immediately donated by Miss Lind to various American charities, which, naturally, did not harm her popularity. In reality, she was very generous. In New York she appeared in six concerts before packed houses, which, it is said, "produced considerably more than $100,000." Eventually, under the Barnum contract, she gave ninety-three concerts in the United States and Cuba, but after these were over both singer and impressario were tired physically as well as dissatisfied with the arrangement. The general enthusiasm for her art then enabled her to make forty more appearances without Barnum's assistance. In Boston, she was married on February 2, 1852, to her accompanist, Otto Goldschmidt; her honeymoon she spent in Northampton, Massachusetts, and on May 28, bade America farewell. It had been a unique visit with astonishing results. Though details are unknown, she had apparently put Barnum on his financial feet, and had not done so badly for herself, despite the fact that she everywhere gave away thousands of dollars to religious as well as charitable enterprises, or gave extra concerts wholly for benevolent purposes. In 1920, the centennial of her birth, appropriate commemorative exercises in her honor, with Jenny Lind costumes, songs, and other reminders, were held both in Sweden and the United States. Among her favorite concert numbers sung in America were the "Casta Diva" aria from *Norma,* Händel's *Messiah,* and the Norwegian "Echo Song." At her first American concert she sang, besides the first and last of these, a duet with Belletti from Rossini's *Il Turco in Italia,* and "Greetings to America" by Bayard Taylor, set to music by her conductor, Julius Benedict.

Since Jenny Lind's voice was not adequately recorded, we have no way of comparing her art with that of modern singers; but in general both critics and the American public were enthusiastic, though here and there, a discordant note of dissent was heard. In England, for instance, Thackeray had not been able to listen to more than one act of one of her performances, but that may have been the exception that proves the rule. In most places the worship of Jenny Lind resembled a mania. Even statesmen like Daniel Webster were carried away. It should be remembered, too, that in America she made her success, not because of enterprising ballyhoo, but in spite of it. In many concert halls where she appeared the audiences were at first visibly cold, even hostile, because of Barnum's high charges for the tickets and his lack of sound experience in concert affairs. The singer had to overcome this handicap which she invariably succeeded in doing with possibly one exception. She was not considered physically beautiful, but her personality, artistry, religious character, and generosity endeared her to most listeners. Dozens, if not hundreds, of poems were written in her honor; volumes appeared about her in prose, and it was Jenny Lind more than anyone else before her time who brought consciousness and appreciation of music to America.

About the time when Jenny Lind was contemplating her first tour to America, a poor peasant girl of seven, Christina Nilsson, sang and played the violin at village fairs in Småland, Sweden. She attracted the attention of music lovers, was educated at their expense, first in Sweden and then abroad, and finally made a triumphal debut in Paris (1864), as Violetta in Verdi's *Traviata.* For her Ambroise Thomas wrote his opera *Hamlet,* in which she created the part of Ophelia. Her success was almost as sensational as that of her countrywoman. From France she went to England, and from there, in 1870, to America, where the Swedes of New York gave her a rousing welcome. Her first concert was given in Steinway Hall, which was packed. Her aria from *Hamlet* was described as "electrifying," and in two years she gave 261 concerts in fifty-four cities. On November 13, 1870, she gave a benefit concert in North Bridgewater (now Brockton), Massachusetts, which netted $2,000 for the new Swedish Lutheran church, and some parishioners wanted to name the church after her, but compromised on *Nilsson* Street. After two years she returned to England, where she was married to a French banker, Auguste Rozeaud, in the famous Westminster Abbey. During her second visit to America in 1874–1875, she gave 157 concerts; and in 1882 she came back again for a third tour; and finally in October 1883, as already stated, Miss Nilsson was chosen to sing the heroine's role, that of Marguerite in Gounod's *Faust,* at the dedication of the Metropolitan Opera House. She left for Europe in 1884, never to return. A critic wrote of her: "Her voice [a dramatic soprano] was marvellously sweet, brilliant and even, and she possessed great skill in vocalization. In her acting she showed great individuality, fine intuition, rare charm and excellent power of expression." In 1887 she married a Spanish count, De Casa Miranda. For many years she lived at Cannes but she died in 1921 at Växjö, near her birthplace in Småland.

At least twenty-five Swedish stars—not counting temporary guest artists—have appeared on the New York Metropolitan stage. As a rule they had gained reputations in Europe before coming to the United States; they have had an extensive repertoire, singing in any language required, whether Romance or Germanic; and, naturally, they have been especially successful in Wagnerian roles. And once, at least, even Swedish was sung at a Metropolitan performance. On January 16, 1936, Gertrude Wettergren was called upon at short notice to substitute for Rosa Ponselle in the role of Carmen. Mme. Wettergren was unprepared to sing it in French, so the manager told her to sing

it in Swedish, which she did, with "sensational success." Other Swedish Metropolitan stars, listed alphabetically, have been: Sigrid Arnold-
son, a coloratura soprano, who made her American debut in 1894;
Joel Berglund, who in February, 1946, made an honored name for
himself in the role of Wotan in *Die Walküre;* Jussi Björling, who has
sung leading tenor roles more than fifty times; Karin Branzell, who
entered the Metropolitan circle as Fricka, in 1924, and for twenty
years made a distinguished career in several roles; Julia Claussen,
who sang Delilah to Caruso's Samson (1917), followed by the roles
of many Italian and Wagnerian heroines; Johannes Elmblad, a basso
profundo of 1888; John Forsell, who in 1904 had been soloist with
the Lund University Singers in their tour of America and who made
his debut as Telramund in *Lohengrin* (1909); Olive Fremstad, born
in Stockholm of a Norwegian father and Swedish mother, who after
her American debut in 1903, became one of Metropolitan's greatest
attractions; William Gustafson, an American-born bass singer, who
after 1920 sang kingly parts in *Tristan, Aïda, Lohengrin,* and other
works; Eyvind Laholm, born in Wisconsin of Swedish parents, who
after a successful career in the Berlin opera, made his American debut,
1939, first as soloist for the New York Philharmonic, and then at the
Metropolitan, December 7, 1939, in *Die Walküre;* Nanny Larsén-
Todsen, who first appeared as Brünnhilde, 1925; Göta Ljungberg, who
made a sensational debut as Sieglinde Jan. 25, 1931, and in 1934 created
the part of Marigold in Howard Hanson's *Merry Mount;* Alice Nielsen,
of Swedish and Irish extraction, who appeared with various opera
companies and came to the Metropolitan as Mimi in *La Bohème* (1909);
Jennie Norelli (Norelius), who in 1904 sang in *Rigoletto* with Caruso;
Martin Öhman, who for a short time in 1924 was a member of the
Metropolitan company; Sigrid Onegin, born in Stockholm of French-
German parents, who made her debut as Amneris in *Aïda* (1922);
Thorsten Ralf, of a Swedish family of tenors, who with great acclaim
introduced in 1946 a new *Lohengrin* to the Metropolitan audience,
after having sung the part in Europe over a hundred times; Hjördis
Schymberg, Sweden's youngest court singer and one of five musical
sisters, a coloratura who was engaged direct from Stockholm and made
her debut at the Metropolitan in February 1947; Marie Sundelius,
a popular soprano with a charming personality, who joined the Metropolitan in 1916; Set Svanholm, whom Olin Downes of the New York
Times has characterized as "one of the most accomplished Wagnerian
tenors that the Metropolitan has presented to the public in the decades

of its existence"; Blanche Thebom, an American-born mezzo-soprano, of Swedish ancestry, whose interpretation of Fricka was enthusiastically received at her appearance in 1944; Kerstin Thorborg, Swedish-born contralto, who for some years has been a mainstay of the Metropolitan in both Wagnerian and other roles; and the Stockholm-born Astrid Varnay, who at the age of twenty-three, successfully stepped into a Wagnerian role on short notice in 1941, without having "so much as carried a spear on any operatic stage."

It is an impressive list of singers and the Metropolitan audiences as well as the New York critics have long since given them their approval. Most of these artists were born in Sweden, and a majority have stayed here long enough to become real Americans. Incidentally, a Texas-born Swede, Christine Lindberg, a mezzo-soprano, made her debut in 1947 at the Royal Opera in Stockholm.

Probably because of the common belief that music could come only from southern climates, some Swedish singers have Italianized their names: Norelius became Norelli; and Harald Lindau, Aroldo Lindi. The latter was born in Småland and after many successes in Europe, where he was hailed at times as a second Caruso, collapsed on the stage in San Francisco (1944), while singing the role of Pagliacci, and died a few moments later. In recent times, however, no Swedes have been obliged to change their names to get engagements, either in America or elsewhere.

Swedes love *a capella* chorus singing, and it is in this field probably more than in any other that they have made a substantial contribution to the appreciation of good music in America. Swedish male singing societies, like the university student choruses from Lund and Stockholm, have toured America; American Swedish musical organizations have toured Sweden; and their choruses are constantly appearing in concerts in America. Swedish glee clubs abound in the North, East, and West. The American Union of Swedish Singers, already mentioned, the successor of an older organization of an all-Scandinavian character, was organized in Chicago on the initiative of the Lyran Singing Society of New York in 1892, with Professor John R. Örtengren as Director-in-chief.

Generally the members take their work seriously and practice once a week. Each group has its own director. In 1926 (May 31 and June 1) the Union sang on the stage of the Metropolitan Opera House in honor of the Crown Prince and Crown Princess of Sweden, having serenaded President Coolidge at the White House on May 29 just before the unveiling of the John Ericsson Monument in Potomac Park.

But neither the male choruses nor the mixed church choirs have carried off all the honors. In fact, as in the case of Jenny Lind, the Swedish women singers came to America first. Some people vaguely remember a certain Swedish Düring Ladies Quintet, and The Swedish Ladies' Octet of 1887; but they seem to have completely forgotten the earliest of them all, The Swedish Ladies Vocal Quartet, which, before coming to America, had toured Europe, including Russia (in St. Petersburg the members had been the guests of Alfred Nobel, future donor of the prizes), and in several capitals had sung before royalty. This quartet toured America in 1876–77, the year of the Centennial, giving concerts in Philadelphia, New York, Brooklyn, Boston, and other cities. On January 15, 1877, for instance, the quartet sang in the Boston Music Hall, in honor of the Norwegian violinist Ole Bull, at the invitation of such a literary and intellectual elite as Longfellow, Lowell, O. W. Holmes, and E. E. Hale, all of whom had signed the invitation. The members of the quartet were Bertha Erixson, Inga Ekström, Amanda Carlson, and Ingeborg Löfgren. Everywhere the tour was a success, and the participants continued their appearances in the United States for several years, or up to 1883. Eventually all were married and then remained permanently in America. Only recently the final survivor of the group, Mrs. Inga Ekström-Olund, passed on, leaving some of her musical talent to her two daughters.

Most Swedes like the theatre, even if in certain Swedish American circles there is still an echo of religious scruples against it. Half a century ago, when most of the immigrants spoke better Swedish than they do now, almost every large American city had a troupe of Swedish American players, who presented very ambitious programs in their native tongue, and sometime with artistic success. The number of performances was surprisingly large. On the other hand, it took some time before Swedes appeared on the American stage in English-speaking roles, and, except on the screen, the *number* of "Broadway luminaries" of Swedish descent has never been great. The quality of their work, however, has been high.

In the "Gay Nineties" a conspicuous pioneer appeared in this field. He was Arthur Donaldson, born (1868) in Norsholm, Sweden, who had come to America at the age of fourteen and had first acted in Swedish-language companies. It was he who made famous the lead character in *Yon Yonson,* a comedy based on a Swedish greenhorn's oft-ridiculed difficulty of distinguishing between a "j" and a "y." "Yumping Yimminy, vat a yump!" exclaimed Yon Yonson after some successful stunt, and the audience roared. Holger Lundbergh in *Swedes in America* credits Donaldson with 350 parts including classics, melo-dramas, and light operas under a single management. The part that made him really famous was that of the hero in the *Prince of Pilsen,* a role which he created, and in which he appeared 1,345 times. This operetta had its première at the Broadway Theatre, New York, in March 1903, under the management of Henry W. Savage, and ran uninterruptedly for more than one thousand times. Donaldson made a gay, dashing, handsome, athletic young prince. He has also appeared in the movies and, in fact, was the first actor to appear in a sound film. "At 8 o'clock one Sunday morning in the early part of 1926," the first sound picture ever made was filmed in the Teka Studio at Third Avenue and 48th Street in New York in Swedish. It was a short play by Hans Alin, called *The Verdict,* which had been written for the experiment, the scene being a Swedish country courtroom. The theme was the murder of a farm girl. Donaldson directed the picture and played five different parts, including that of the accused, a gypsy, who was found to be innocent. The part of the judge was played by Eric Sylvan. The picture was shown a week later at the Brooklyn Academy of Music, and being regarded as a "remarkable achievement" was later re-sounded and played in English under the title of *The Retribution.*

Then came Martha Hedman, a native of Östersund, in the Swedish province of Jämtland, who had made her debut in Helsingfors, Fin-land, under the tutelage of Siri von Essen, the first wife of August Strindberg. After appearing in Sweden, she was persuaded by the late Charles Frohman, whom she met in England, to come to New York, and there she made her American debut in 1912, in *The Attack*. It met with so much success that other appearances followed, includ-ing engagements in England. She toured with John Drew as Simone in *The Prodigal Husband;* in 1915 she played Jane Carson in *The Trap;* in the same year David Belasco cast her in the role of Xelva in *Boomerang.* It was an immediate success and the engagement lasted over four years, bringing the Swedish-born actress a national reputa-tion. She was regarded as the most beautiful woman on the American stage, and her clothes and manners were copied by American girls. The "Hedman Swirl" became as much of a fashion as did the Garbo long bob later on. Eventually Miss Hedman appeared in other plays, collaborated with her husband in the writing of a comedy, and in 1942 made a successful come-back in *The First Crocus,* but has spent most of her later years in retirement in her Connecticut home. In 1949, she published a novel, *Uncle, Aunt and Jezebel,* about a family in Finland.

The best known and most versatile male actor on the Broadway stage who is at least partly of Swedish descent is Glenn Anders, a native of Los Angeles, whose father was Swedish and his mother a daughter of Vermont. Of his father he remembers most vividly his insistence on the Swedish setting-up exercises, originated by Per Henrik Ling. He is a graduate of Columbia and his stage career began with the Los Angeles Stock Company in *Macbeth.* Since then he has appeared in well over a hundred productions ranging from farce to melodrama and as a member of road companies has played in practically every American city. The list includes Eugene O'Neill's *Strange Interlude, Dynamo* and *They Knew What They Wanted* as well as plays based on works by Ernest Hemingway such as *A Farewell to Arms* and *Soldier's Wife.* During the 1948–49 season Anders played the role of an erratic theatrical director in Moss Hart's comedy *Light Up The Sky.* He has also been a film actor, appearing with Orson Welles and Rita Hayworth in *The Lady from Shanghai.*

In Hemingway's *Get Away Old Man* Anders shared honors with Richard Widmark who had made his New York debut in 1943 in George Abbott's *Kiss and Tell.* Before going on the stage he had taught acting at Lake Forest College in Illinois and after coming to New York in 1938, he had appeared in some thirty radio plays. In 1947 he had a part in a film *The Kiss of Death.* Since then he has appeared with Lionel Barrymore in a whaling film and many others. His native heath is Sunrise, Minnesota.

Another Minnesota-born Broadway and Hollywood actor who has made good is Clinton Sundberg, who hails from Appleton, where his father, Charles Sundberg, was auditor for a lumber company. He is a graduate of Hamline University at St. Paul and once taught English in Uruguay as well as in Minnesota. His stage career began in a stock company in Portland, Maine, and after appearing in various road companies, including London productions of *She Loves Me Not* and *Boy Meets Girl,* he came to New York in *Room Service* and then had a part in a musical, *Stars in Your Eyes.* He next acted the newspaper reporter in *Arsenic and Old Lace* and after appearing in *Over 21* and *The Rugged Path* was signed up for the films without even a screen test.

Various Oriental roles, like those acted in the films by Warner Oland have been played on the stage by another Swedish-born actor, Arvid Paulson, as in *The Willow Tree, Curiosity* and *The Yellow Jacket*. A widely experienced Broadway actress who has appeared in dozens of plays is Nydia Westman, who is a third generation descendant of Swedish Midwestern immigrants on her father's side, while on her mother's she is a descendant of Sir Christopher Wren, the famous English seventeenth century architect. During the 1948–49 season she appeared in *The Madwoman of Chaillot*.

But the greatest histrionic successes achieved by Americans with Swedish backgrounds have been in the films. For forty years "even Swedes," as one writer humorously puts it, have been engaged in the cinema. As early as in 1907 Linda Arvidson tried her hand collaborating as a writer with that moving picture pioneer David W. Griffith. In fact, Linda was Mrs. Griffith.

Then in 1911 an artist's model from New York, born in Ystad, Sweden, began her screen career. She was Anna Q. Nilsson, an attractive blonde, who became popular in the silent westerns and melodramas. She retained her popularity until her acting was ended for all time, it was thought, by an accident in 1930. But in 1947 she reappeared in *The Farmer's Daughter,* and was signed for a supporting role in *It Had to Be You,* at the Columbia Studios. Another early Swedish-born favorite was Sigrid Holmquist.

A motley group of Swedish-born actors and directors invaded Hollywood in the 1920s. The first big name was that of Victor Seastrom (Sjöström), an actor as well as a director of high standards, who possessed a genius for interpretation. In Hollywood he directed such successes as *Name the Man* and *He Who Gets Slapped*. Later, when back in Sweden, he played the hero in a film based on the life of John Ericsson as well as many others.

Then came Lars Hanson, Einar Hanson, and Nils Asther. The first one was regarded as Sweden's foremost screen actor when he arrived in America to work for the Metro-Goldwyn-Mayer studios. His stay in Hollywood was brief, but it was long enough to establish his reputation. His outstanding pictures were *The Flesh and the Devil,* in which he played opposite Greta Garbo, *The Scarlet Letter,* with Lillian Gish; and, under Seastrom's direction, *Captain Salvation*. These were silent movies, and a Swedish accent, or even the use of Swedish as in *The Scarlet Letter,* made little difference.

Einar Hanson came to the United States about the same time as his namesake Lars Hanson. He already had a European reputation, and in a short time, "he appeared," according to Leonard Clairmont, "in more pictures than all the other Swedes put together." In 1927, however, his promising career was suddenly ended by an automobile accident. Mr. Clairmont continues: "Soon afterwards Nils Asther came, saw, and conquered. He was the type to please feminine admirers, and the producers quickly realized that Asther was especially suited for leading roles of a more sophisticated nature. Twice he played opposite Greta Garbo, and at other times with other prominent stars. His climb to fame was swift and without many difficulties, but later, through being cast in spiritless and insignificant parts, he became weary and resumed his work in Europe." He has since returned to Hollywood.

A more permanent career was that of the late Warner Oland (Johan Verner Ölund), in the role of a Chinese detective, Charlie Chan (based on stories by Earl Derr Biggers). He first appeared on the screen in 1931. Here was the amazing example of a man born in the northern part of Sweden taking the part of an Oriental and doing it supremely well. "By a muscular contraction of his eyelids, and by brushing the ends of his eyebrows up and the ends of his moustache down, he was able, almost without make-up, to look like a genuine Oriental," wrote Mr. Clairmont. When traveling in China or Japan, he was mobbed by admiring fans, and a Chinese actor in Shanghai made a specialty of imitating Oland's looks and acting.

He was followed by literally dozens of actors and actresses of Swedish blood: June Carlson, Shirley Grey (Agnes Zetterstrand); Ruth Peterson, Greta Granstedt, young May Carlson and Frances Peterson, Evelyn Knapp, Agnes Anderson, Veda Ann Borg, Arthur Pierson, Eric Linden, Allyn Drake, Gustav Wally (Wallenberg), Henry Hunter (Jacobson), Jane Novak, Knut Rahm, Van Johnson, Winifred Westover, Emory Johnson, once a director, and many others. Some of them have concealed their own origin behind an Anglo-Saxon stage name. There is, for instance, that well-known screen actress Jean Rogers, "the most beautiful natural blonde in California," whose parents came from Malmö, Sweden. Her real name is Elinor Lövgren. Astrid Allwyn is also of Swedish parentage, born in Boston.

Among other Hollywood Swedes (1948) are: the California-born Leif Erickson, son of a sea captain, who once played the dashing "brother" of Greta Garbo in *Conquest;* Dorothy Peterson, who in *The Country Doctor* played the motherly nurse of the Dionne quintuplets; Björn Holmström, who has appeared with Signe Hasso; Frank

Sundström, who in 1947 started work on *Tragic Symphony* based on the life of the Russian composer Tchaikovsky; Alf Kjellin, a young character actor who had made his mark in Sweden as the unhappy schoolboy in *Torment;* and Märta Torén, a pupil of the Royal Dramatic Theatre School in Stockholm who after a trial performance with Cary Grant received a long-term contract from Universal Films.

Two other film actresses trained in Sweden and having considerable experience back of them, both on the stage and the screen, have recently come to Hollywood. They are Signe Hasso and Viveca Lindfors. Both are former pupils of the school for actors run by the state-supported Royal Dramatic Theatre in Stockholm. Miss Hasso, who arrived early in the Second World War, has appeared in *The Seventh Cross, Assignment in Brittany,* and *The House on 92nd Street.* Miss Lindfors came after the war was over, but has acted in *Adventures of Don Juan* with Errol Flynn and *To the Victor* with Dennis Morgan.

The list of Hollywood actors and actresses who can claim only fifty per cent or less of Swedish blood includes: Gloria Swanson, Myrna Loy, Larry Blade (Lorenz Lundberg), Leonard Clairmont (Asplund), and Anna Sten, whose mother was Swedish. Mr. Clairmont, claims that the cinema industry could hardly get along without the "multitude" of Swedish motion-picture technicians—cameramen, designers, architects, and craftsmen. Olga Celeste, born near Lund in Sweden, teaches, for instance, wild animals how to behave before the camera, and "Swede" Lindell trained such illustrious film actors among horses, as Flicka, Smoky, and Thunderhead.

Despite her absence from Hollywood for several years Greta Garbo has continued to be ranked as the number one screen artist of the world, the queen of the cinema. She has been called glamorous, magical, illusive, aloof, even unapproachable; but her acting has become legendary, like the singing of Jenny Lind, who like her was born of poor parents in Stockholm. At first she worked as a sales girl in a department store, and then managed to be accepted as a pupil in the famous school of acting at the Royal Dramatic Theatre. Her first major part was that of Countess Dohna in a film version of Selma Lagerlöf's story, *Gösta Berling's Saga,* produced under the direction of the late Mauritz Stiller. This film was seen by a Hollywood scout and in 1926 both Stiller and Miss Garbo were invited to California. Soon her popularity rose to unprecedented heights. Few will forget her characterizations of Camille, Queen Christina, Mata Hari, or Anna Karenina. Her real name is Greta Lovisa Gustafson, and she will long be remembered as one of the most remarkable of all Americans from Sweden.

But even the fame of Greta Garbo was to be outshone by that of another Stockholm girl and former pupil at the Royal Dramatic School, Ingrid Bergman. At one time three of her films were shown simultaneously on Broadway, *Spellbound, The Bells of St. Mary's,* and *Saratoga Trunk.* She is both a stage and a screen star, as well as an outstanding radio performer. Despite her Swedish birth and education she was able to appear in the English talking films almost as soon as she reached Hollywood. Her simplicity and enduring charm soon gained the hearts of millions.

Her invitation to Hollywood was due to her acting in a Swedish film, *Intermezzo,* together with the late Swedish actor, Gösta Ekman. For her first presentation to American audiences this film was remade in California with the late Leslie Howard as her partner. It was released in the spring of 1939, and at once established her rank. She next appeared on the New York stage in Molnar's *Liliom* and then resumed her film work in Hollywood.

Among her best known films have been *Dr. Jekyll and Mr. Hyde, Adam Had Four Sons, Rage in Heaven, Casablanca, For Whom the Bell Tolls,* and *Gaslight.* In her most recent film roles as in *The Arch of Triumph* and *Joan of Lorraine* she has scored greater popular and financial than artistic successes. Her playing in the stage version of the latter was, on the other hand, an all-round triumph. Neither honors nor criticisms have turned her head. In the future her career should continue to be interesting.

To the development of radio and television the Swedes in America have made greater contributions as engineers and technicians than as actors or broadcasters. But since such work is usually done behind the scenes, little personal credit has been won. Even Vin Lindhe, who directs the Glee Club of the Radio City Music Hall in New York, is little known. He is of Swedish descent, born in Chicago. Once he was musical director of a radio station in Texas.

The leading name of Swedish origin in American radio, however, is that of Edgar Bergen, born in Chicago as John Edgar Berggren, best known as the creator of Charlie McCarthy, Mortimer Snerd and other wooden dummies who have come to seem more like living personalities than most human beings. Through his work in radio Bergen may be said to have elevated ventriloquism from vaudeville to fine art. Charley McCarthy's original name was "Kalle," the Swedish diminutive of Karl or Charles, and Bergen claims that he still is Swedish in everything except his name. Fundamentally he is, of course, in the tradition of Tom Sawyer and Huckleberry Finn—a concentrate of the small-town American boy as seen in fond retrospect. Both Bergen's parents came from Hässleholm in Skåne and he was born in Chicago on February 16, 1903. Originally he intended to be a doctor, but while a pupil at the Lakeview High School in Chicago, he began to act during vacations in vaudeville shows as a ventriloquist to earn expense money. Then he went abroad and performed his act in a number of countries including Sweden. When he got back he was invited to be a guest on the Rudy Vallee radio program and before long he had his own show. He has also acted in several films, both with and without Charlie. Like most Swedes he is inherently shy and self-conscious, but by speaking through his dummy he has been able to create almost the opposite, an impudent and abrasive individual, the eternal urchin. His occasional sketches in Swedish American dialect are highly appreciated both by his sponsors and the public.

Another radio actor of Swedish descent who has so far stuck to that medium is Karl Swenson, who for the past ten years has acted in such National Broadcasting Company serials as *Lorenzo Jones, Linda, Cavalcade of America, Inner Sanctum, March of Time,* and several others. For Lincoln's birthday celebration, in 1948, he played for the radio audience the title role in *Abe Lincoln in Illinois* which was followed by *Abe Lincoln in Washington.* Like Bergen, he had originally hoped to be a doctor, and he once took a pre-medical course at Marietta College in Ohio, but as a child, despite his shyness, he managed to appear in school theatricals and gradually got into radio work. He was born in Brooklyn, where his father was a building contractor, hailing from Västergötland. His mother had been brought as a child from the province of Blekinge to New Britain, Connecticut. In New York he is himself a commuter, living with his wife and four children at Irvington-on-the-Hudson.

A staff artist on the Columbia network is Alice Frost who for many years has played Mrs. North in the weekly feature *Mr. and Mrs. North.* She is a native of Minnesota, where her father, John Frost, was a Lutheran clergyman, born in Småland. Her mother came from the adjoining province of Östergötland.

No American of Swedish descent has so far gained national reputation as a radio commentator or "moulder of public opinion," with the possible exception of Carl Sandburg, whose work on Abraham Lincoln has earned him a sound reputation as an interpreter of America. As a radio comedian Edgar Bergen is in a class by himself. Through his dummy, Charlie McCarthy, he can say some of the sharp things the late Will Rogers used to say and do it without causing resentment. In the field of song, on the other hand, Swedish opera stars have won a wide renown. Some of them, like Jussi Björling and Blanche Thebom, appear on the best sponsored radio programs and also give concerts. As stage actors few Swedes can claim to be really eminent, while in the cinema they have been near the top from the very first. Perhaps the fact that the films were originally silent encouraged them more, being free of the language barrier. In recent years, however, they have shown that they can clear that too, as witness Greta Garbo and Ingrid Bergman. First-class male moving picture actors have been scarcer. In this connection it is worth noting that all of the brightest Swedish film stars were not only born in Sweden, but that they had there enjoyed the advantage of a thorough training in the art of acting.

XXIX

ARTISTS

In 1922 a group of American students and teachers, including an American-educated young Japanese woman, toured Scandinavia. At the end of the trip the Japanese girl was asked what had impressed her the most in the various northern countries, whereupon she promptly replied: "the people of Denmark, the scenery of Norway, and the art in Sweden." This reference to Swedish art is not without significance. Sweden has long been interested in art, especially since the Thirty Years' War when the victorious Swedish commanders, returning from Germany with honors and booty, began to collect art and to have their portraits painted. Swedes in general are fond of both portraits and landscapes; names like Zorn, Liljefors and Carl Larsson, are household words. Among Swedish sculptors, Carl Milles, now an American, is the most famous. This love of beauty and artistic expression was brought across the sea by many of the Swedish immigrants. As painters, sculptors, illustrators, wood carvers, interior decorators, and masters of various handicrafts they have contributed their share to art in the United States.

Swedish artists appeared early in America. One of the most famous portrait painters in the American colonies was Gustaf Hesselius (1682–1755), a native of Dalarna, Sweden, a cousin of Emanuel Swedenborg, and a brother of two pastors in the original "Old Swedes" churches on the Delaware. He arrived in Philadelphia in 1712. Later, in Maryland, he appears to have executed the first commission for a public building in this country, an altarpiece for St. Barnabas Church, Prince County, which he called "The Last Supper." He specialized in portraits and religious subjects, painted two Indian chiefs for Governor John Penn in 1735, and became one of the first artists of consequence in America. He was also skilled in mechanical construction and built one of the first organs in this country. As one of the first artists of our earliest period, his life and work have been summarized in the

Dictionary of American Biography. His son, John Hesselius (1728–78), followed in his father's footsteps; many of his canvases are scattered throughout the East, some of them having been wrongly attributed to his father. John Hesselius is reputed to have given the first lessons in painting to Charles Willson Peale, the early American portraitist.

Another early Swedish artist was Adolph Ulric Wertmüller, an imitative, conventional painter, who came to America in 1794. A man of charming manners and a certain ability, he became a portrait painter of some distinction and as such found many patrons among the influential families of Philadelphia. About 1795 he painted a well-known picture of George Washington. His canvases are found in the National Museum of Stockholm, in the Academy of Fine Arts in Philadelphia, and in the American Swedish Historical Museum of the same city, as well as in several private collections. For a while he returned to live in Sweden, but soon came back to the United States, married Miss Elizabeth Henderson, bought an estate on the border between Delaware and Pennsylvania and lived there until his death in 1811.

The pioneer artist in what we may call modern Swedish American history was Lars Gustaf Sellstedt (1819–1911), whose life was indeed stranger than the proverbial fiction. Born in Sundsvall, Sweden, he left home with his mother's knowledge at the age of twelve and for several years literally sailed the seven seas. In 1834 he set out for America as a cabin boy, served in the United States Navy for three years, and finally settled down in Buffalo in 1842. He had already studied drawing and while a sailor had drawn figures and sketched scenes on whale teeth from seamen's life—a form of art known as scrimshaw work. After 1845 he was able to devote most of his time to art and literature. Though self-taught, he painted portraits of many notables, including Presidents Fillmore and Cleveland. He was the principal founder, for twenty-six years the superintending Director, and from 1876 to 1877 President of the Buffalo Academy of Fine Arts. In 1875 he became a member of the National Academy. At the age of eighty-five he published a remarkable autobiography, *From Forecastle to Academy,* and in 1910 when he was ninety-one, *Art in Buffalo.* A poet as well as an artist of ability, he represented the Swedish love of both art and adventure, including the ability to conceive and attain high aims.

Peter M. Almini, a native of Stockholm, was the first Swedish artist to settle in Chicago (1852) where he soon earned a name as a practitioner of fine art as well as an interior decorator. His specialties were fresco and mural paintings, of which he executed many for churches as well as assembly halls in Chicago and other cities.

Henry E. C. Peterson was a prominent Swedish American artist of the modern pioneer days, who in his youth had studied art in Stockholm. After serving for over three years in the American Navy during the Civil War, he settled in Chicago and took up painting as a profession. Later he continued his art education at the Julien Academy in Paris. After his return to Chicago he painted portraits of such men as Brigham Young and several bishops of other churches and later continued the same kind of work in New York.

Another Swedish veteran of the Civil War, Colonel Fabian Brydolf of Iowa, learned to paint with his left hand after he had lost the right one in the Battle of Shiloh. Born in 1819, he had been educated in Sweden, emigrated in 1841 and first settled in Cleveland, Ohio. He moved to Iowa in 1846.

Olof Krantz was a self-taught, Swedish-born veteran of the Civil War who produced American primitive art in the form of farming scenes and savage portraits of the members of the Bishop Hill colony in western Illinois. These paintings, whose existence had been forgotten, have recently been exhibited in both New York and Chicago. They were found in the loft of the original community church which is now preserved by the state authorities of Illinois as a public monument.

In the course of time, several centers of Swedish American art were developed. The first of these was Lindsborg, Kansas, where in the 1880s the Swedes had founded Bethany College. In 1890, Olof Grafström, a landscape painter, born in 1855 in Medelpad, in northern Sweden, became head of the newly established art department, and as such he continued until 1897, when he accepted a similar position at Augustana College at Rock Island, Illinois. He was best known for his altarpieces. In 1928 he returned to Sweden, and there he died in 1933. In New York his daughter, Ruth, became a successful fashion illustrator.

His successor at Lindsborg was Carl G. Lotave, who had been educated in Sweden and France. After a few years he moved to Colorado Springs where he produced many notable portraits as well as landscapes, and then, after moving to New York, won high credit for portraits of international celebrities such as Marshal Joffre, King Albert of Belgium, General Pershing, Venizelos, and Marshal Foch. When he died in 1924 his dust was entombed, pursuant to his own request, on the top of Pikes Peak in Colorado.

Even better known among the Lindsborg art masters is Sven Birger Sandzén, who was born in Sweden (1871), and educated in Stockholm and Paris, an independent artist of international reputation. He is both a painter in oil and a lithographer; his favorite subjects have been the mountain landscapes of the Southwest. "No one," writes Oliver Linder in *Swedes in America* (p. 495), "has surpassed him in reproducing the grandeur and strength of peaks, crests, and rugged mountain sides. Sometime his paintings are visions of form and color. He is at times a realist, and at other times a dreamer. In his prints one finds the same inspiration and brilliant execution." His style is definitely personal and his canvases have won many merited awards. They are found not only in the public museums of Chicago, Washington, and New York, but abroad in those of Gothenburg, Stockholm, London, and Paris. As a teacher at Bethany College and as a lecturer as well as working artist, Sandzén has done much to make not only Kansas but the Middle West and the Southwest more art conscious.

Another landscapist of the first order was John F. Carlson of the Woodstock colony in New York state, who also had a studio in New York City. Born in Småland, Sweden, he was brought to this country at the age of eleven and here he ultimately became known as one of the world's best painters of trees. A lover of the woods, he found trees, which he called his friends, to be the most fascinating "sitters." To him they had character, ambitions, whims, strivings, and idiosyncrasies. A member of the National Academy, he was also an officer of several art organizations and the recipient of many prizes. He was also a writer of books, lecturer, and teacher. His canvases hang in the galleries of many museums and institutes throughout the United States, and it is no exaggeration to say that he established an improved school of landscape painting. His "Woods in Winter" was long ago acquired by the Corcoran Gallery in Washington, D.C. He died in New York in 1945.

Another Woodstock colony member of high rank is Henry Mattson, who came to America from Gothenburg in 1906. Largely self-educated, he won his success the long and hard way. "In his landscapes he does not," says a critic, "copy Nature to the point of tiresomeness. He paints mostly from an inner perception of the subject matter." He has won some very substantial prizes; the Guggenheim award ($1,800); the Corcoran Prize ($1,000); and third prize at the International Art Exhibition in Pittsburgh in 1935. His "Wings of the Morning" has been purchased by the Metropolitan Museum of Art.

A self-taught artist who had unusual ability and experience was the late Carl Oscar Borg, an erstwhile seaman, born in 1879 in Grinstad, Sweden, who became an associate member of the National Academy. In company with the scientist and art connoisseur, Gustaf Adolf Eisen, he took part in archaeological research in Egypt, and at various times he painted in many parts of the world, including Spain, Morocco, Italy and the Nile Valley, as well as in Central America and the North American Southwest. Settling in California after his return from Egypt, he was commissioned by the University of California to paint the Pueblo Indians of Arizona. Thereafter he specialized in sketches of Indians in their home surroundings as well as in desert motifs, in both of which he achieved marked success. When Hollywood needed an expert on Hopi Indian villages, for instance, it turned to Borg for expert advice. He was also a master etcher. His canvases are very widely distributed in France, Sweden, and in the United States, especially in California and Arizona. The number of honors that came to him—prizes, medals, honorable mentions, and memberships in various societies and clubs—is very large. He died in Santa Barbara, California, in 1947.

That several Swedish-born artists should choose to paint marines is only natural, being, like most Scandinavians, lovers of water and the sea. One of them, Leon Lundmark, who was born (1875) in Småland and educated in Stockholm, emigrated to America about 1905. He had a great appeal for both critics and the public, painting the sky and water with a clever technique and instinctive coloring. To sell his pictures he drove around the country, accompanied by his wife, in an automobile with a trailer and thus found many buyers. His production was very large. In 1942 he died in California.

The outstanding marine painter among the Swedish Americans was Lieutenant Commander Henry Reuterdahl, the naval artist, who was born in Malmö, Sweden, in 1871 and died in the United States in 1925. A self-educated man with much natural ability, he was engaged by an American magazine during the Spanish-American War to accompany the United States fleet and make sketches of the operations. Later he was commissioned in the United States Navy. In the National Gallery in Washington hangs his large canvas, "The Combat between the *Monitor* and the *Merrimac*," and not less than ten of his marines are in the Naval Academy at Annapolis. His career is summarized in the *Dictionary of American Biography*.

Oscar Brousse Jacobson is a versatile artist who came from Sweden in 1890. He was educated, first, at the Yale School of Fine Arts and then in Paris. A noted teacher, lecturer, and art judge, he was appointed, in 1915, Director of Art and Music at the University of Oklahoma. His work has been shown in Stockholm, and in several cities in the United States. He has traveled and painted in the Sahara Desert and in 1931 he was awarded the gold medal of the Mid-West Art Exhibition in Kansas City. One of his better known works is "Grand Canyon"; and his portrait of Governor Williams hangs in the state Capitol at Oklahoma City.

One of the early portrait painters was C. F. von Saltza, born in Sweden in 1858, who arrived in the United States in 1891. For a long time he had charge of the department of painting at the Museum of Fine Arts in St. Louis and later headed the corresponding department at the Art Institute in Chicago. He died in 1905.

Arvid F. Nyholm arrived in Chicago from Stockholm the same year as Von Saltza. A disciple of Anders Zorn, and like him fond of clear and distinct colors, he too became a portrait painter; but he also did good work in landscapes. He painted first in New York and then in Chicago, where he died in 1927. He was a member of the National Academy of Design.

Another member of the National Academy was the late August Franzén (d. 1938), a native of Norrköping, Sweden, who became a noted illustrator as well as a portrait painter. He was an unusually aristocratic-looking man who had won many medals. Among other works he executed an excellent portrait of President Taft, owned by Yale University. He was a member of the Lotus and the Century clubs of New York, and of the Union Interallié of Paris, formed during the First World War.

Among the Swedish painters who have worked in the United States the most famous was easily the late Anders Zorn, who was also one of the greatest etchers of all time. Five times he came to America to paint portraits and to discuss art problems with his colleagues. That a man of his strong temperament and great genius should fail to exert an influence is unthinkable. Among the portraits he painted were those of President and Mrs. Cleveland, Vice President Sherman, Senator Aldrich of Rhode Island, Andrew Carnegie, Adolphus Bush of St. Louis, the Deerings of Chicago, and many others.

One of the best private Swedish art collections in the United States is that owned by George N. Jeppson of Worcester, Massachusetts, including, as it does, works by Zorn and Liljefors as well as by Carl Larsson and Gustaf Fjaestad. He has also been a generous supporter of the Worcester Art Museum.

Another noted American art collector of Swedish descent was the late Dr. Frederick Peterson of New York City, a poet as well as a pioneer psychiatrist. He specialized in Chinese art. The large collection of paintings from Ch'ing period distributed, under a gift from William Bingham, among Princeton University and colleges like Amherst, Bowdoin, Dartmouth, and Williams, had originally been collected by him.

Like so many of their fellow citizens in Chicago, the Swedes living in that metropolis are proud of their interest in art. To encourage painters and sculptors of Swedish origin the Swedish Club of Chicago has for many years held an annual exhibit of their work.

The greatest living American sculptor of Swedish birth is, of course, Carl Milles. Of recognized international stature, and yet modest and courteous, he is one of the foremost sculptors of any age or land. It is impossible to indicate here, even superficially, the scope and quality of his numerous masterpieces which grace so many public places in Sweden, England, and the United States.

Milles was born in 1875; studied under Rodin in Paris; won a prize in 1902 for a Sten Sture monument; became in 1920 Professor of sculpture at the Royal Academy of Art in Stockholm; and since 1929 has been an artist-in-residence at the Cranbrook Academy of Art in the Bloomfield Hills of Michigan. No one who has ever seen Milles' statue of Gustavus Vasa in sitting posture or his many fountains, such as the Orpheus figure before the Concert Hall in Stockholm or the Fountain at St. Louis, Missouri, will ever forget the independence and originality of their creator. It was natural that Milles should be selected to design the New Sweden Tercentenary Monument, executed in black Swedish granite, and erected in 1938 on the Rocks at the original landing place at Wilmington, Delaware. In 1936 he was awarded an honorary Doctor's degree by Yale, and in 1947 he was elected one of twelve new members of the National Institute of Arts and Letters.

On February 9, 1945, the New York *Times* announced the death of Francis Peter Hedlund, a sculptor and interior decorator of Wilkes-Barre, Pennsylvania. Born in Worcester, Massachusetts, of Swedish parentage, he was educated at the Beaux Arts Academy in New York; then studied abroad and finally in New York under Gutzon Borglum, the noted Danish American sculptor. By the *Times* he was credited "with aiding in the designing and in the laying out of the sizes for the Rushmore Memorial in North Dakota." He had also worked for Borglum on the Stone Mountain Memorial in Georgia. An expert on gold leaf, he spent two years on the golden tower of the Fisher Building in Detroit. Hedlund had traveled extensively in the United States and Europe and did considerable work in England, Ireland, and Sweden.

An artist of an unusual personality as well as originality, both as a sculptor and a philosopher, was the late David Edström of Los Angeles (d. 1938). A native of Småland, he came to America at the age of seven. His creations were allegorical, psychological, and symbolistic; in fact, impregnated with thought suggesting Strindberg. His many prizes and other tokens of recognition indicated a widespread appreciation of his art. In 1937 he published his autobiography, *The Testament of Caliban*—a significant title; the book is also a record of Swedish artists during the preceding fifty years. Students of character as well as art will find his bold and honest *Testament* both provocative and instructive.

Charles Haag, born (1867), in Norrköping, arrived in America in 1893, after studying sculpture in five European countries. With a firsthand knowledge of poverty, he was able to portray this misfortune in art. His best group is perhaps "The Emigrants," an impressive tragedy of newcomers. One of his sculptures was the first by a Swedish American artist to be accepted by the Metropolitan Museum of Art. He also carved fifty wood statuettes, entitled "Spirits of the Forest," sixteen of which were exhibited in 1946 at the American Swedish Historical Museum in Philadelphia.

Olaf Björkman was a native of Stockholm (1886), who studied in Paris under the Norwegian artist, Christian Krogh, and others. His work had a spiritual quality and a "lasting and intense beauty of form." Among his most noted works were: "The Titan," a study of Beethoven; "The Doomed Sphinx," a portrayal of Lincoln; Edgar Allan Poe and the raven; and a memorial for Auguste Rodin in Paris. He died in New York on February 24, 1946.

Carl Halstahammar, born 1897, came from Västerås, in Sweden. In his chosen specialty of wood sculpture, he has few equals. A pupil of Zorn—who, it may be recalled, was also a sculptor—Halstahammar carves with taste, humor, and natural realistic form. Six of his life-sized figures in wood adorned the General Motors Building at the

Century of Progress Exposition in Chicago and after an extended study of the red man, he carved a group of Indians which gained high rating. In 1937 he received, with a gold medal, the Frank Logan Prize ($500). He is an author and lecturer on wood carving, as well as a director of an Academy of Wood Sculpture bearing his name. His home is in Chicago. The group of Swedish sculptors in America includes several women such as Mrs. Vicken von Post Totten of Washington, D.C., who is represented in the Metropolitan Museum of Art, and Agnes Fromén of Chicago, who once executed a bust of Washington Irving for a school in Bloomington, Illinois.

Probably the first prominent American illustrator of Swedish birth was Bror Thure de Thulstrup, born 1848. His father was at one time Minister of War in Sweden, and he himself was educated in both Stockholm and Paris. An account of his life is found in the *Dictionary of American Biography*. Though he studied drawing in France, he was self-taught as a painter. In New York he made illustrations for such periodicals as *The Graphic, Leslie's Monthly*, and *Harper's Weekly*. Among his honors was a royal decoration from Sweden. He died in 1930.

Other Swedish artists who have been successful illustrators in the United States are: Ben Albert Benson of Chicago, born in Bollnäs, Sweden, in 1901, who specializes in magazine work; Douglas Borgstedt of Bryn Mawr, Pennsylvania, formerly an illustrator for the *Saturday Evening Post, Collier's*, and other magazines, later photography editor of the *Post* and, occasionally, a cartoonist for both the *Post* and *Collier's;* the late Oscar Cesare, who died in 1948, as a cartoonist for the New York *Times*. Before joining the *Times* he had worked for the New York *World*. He was born in Sweden. Robert W. Edgren, a former athlete who became a popular sports editor and artist, who died in 1939; Ruth Sigrid Grafström, whose fashion drawings have appeared in *Vogue*, the *Delineator*, and the *Woman's Home Companion;* R. John Holmgren, of New York City, a Minnesota Swede, who has made illustrations for the *Cosmopolitan, The American*, and *Collier's;* and the late Abian Anders Wallgren (d. 1948), the famous "Wally" of the *Stars and Stripes* during First World War, and later a cartoonist for the *American Legion Monthly*. According to an obituary, "Wallgren was credited by General John J. Pershing with keeping up the morale of thousands of doughboys by his travesties of officers and his humorous treatment of the difficulties and problems of the soldiers," as Bill Mauldin did in the Second World War.

The notion that Swedes lack a sense of humor is further belied by the success of Carl Ed, born in Moline, Illinois, of Swedish immigrant parents from Småland. Since 1919 he has drawn the comic strip *Harold Teen* for the Chicago *Tribune* syndicate, which has been reproduced in both films and radio. A former student in the art department of Augustana College, Ed lives at Evanston, Illinois.

The most gifted and successful of the straight illustrators is Gustaf Tenggren, a book and film artist, who was born in Sweden in 1896, and who received his education there. Among his best known book illustrations are those of the *Ring of the Nibelungs* (1932) and the hundred drawings used in Helen Dike's *Stories from Great Metropolitan Operas* (1943). Mr. Tenggren later became art director for the Disney studios in Hollywood.

Another Swedish-born artist who has been a successful illustrator of both books and magazines in the United States and England, as well as in Sweden, is Einar Nerman. *A Child's First Book,* illustrated by him, had a sale of 100,000 copies the first month.

In addition to the wielders of brush, pen, and chisel, miscellaneous Swedish artists have worked in the United States with knives and other tools on wood, leather, linoleum, and metal. They are not only carvers of various kinds, but are also modelers, decorators, and teachers of Swedish *sloyd,* i.e., arts and crafts. Some of them have become known as sculptors. One of them is Thorsten Sigstedt, a Swedish-born wood carver (1884) who after restoring some masterpieces for the Swedish Academy of Antiquities, settled in America to execute Gothic ornaments for the Swedenborgian Cathedral at Bryn Athyn as well as several panels for other churches and institutions including the American Swedish Historical Museum in Philadelphia. His specialty is ornamental figurework in wood.

Another wood carver of note is John Torell, a native of Arvika in Värmland, who emigrated in 1921. Besides reliefs, busts, and statuettes, he has helped carve the decorations for the Tribune Tower and the Furniture Mart in Chicago, as well as for the elevator doors of the Palmolive Building. He has, furthermore, designed and carved imposing panels for the Edgewater Presbyterian Church and once executed a portrait bust of the late Mayor Anton Cermak.

In 1910 a boy of thirteen, who had run away from his home in Närke, Sweden, watched a Buffalo Bill show in Copenhagen, Denmark. When the performance was over, the lad sought out his American hero and asked him for a job on his ranch. Buffalo Bill, amused, replied in the affirmative and probably promptly forgot about the matter; but after four years at sea, the young man, Edward H. Bohlin, appeared at the ranch to claim his job. There he became a galloping, larruping cowboy; next an actor and craftsman. His riding trappings were always artistic, and he soon started to carve in both leather and silver. One day, while playing a cowboy part for a Wild West film, a dispute arose about costumes appropriate for the Daniel Boone era. "While waiting his turn before the camera, he hastily sketched designs for buckskin breeches and fringed jackets. During the lunch hour he showed them to the producer," with an estimate of the cost. He was immediately offered $22,000 for the three hundred outfits needed, accepted the offer, hastily hired leather-worker assistants, and filled the contract. He then gave up both ranching and acting in order to devote himself exclusively to his new art. Taking his motifs from the flower and animal life on Catalina Island, he carved, for example, a saddle for P. K. Wrigley, for which he was paid $5,250. Colonel Tim McCoy paid him $4,350 for another. Among his other achievements is a carved telephone set made for Mae West.

In 1935 Lord and Taylor's Fifth Avenue store in New York exhibited a two-in-one Swedish apartment, designed by William Pahlman, an American interior decorator of Swedish ancestry. Pahlman had traveled in many parts of Europe, and found, he said, in Swedish designs, furniture, and colorings his ideal for home furnishings. They seemed to him to be not only modern but attractive and sensible. He works with fabrics, rugs, chairs, tables, and paint, and his work evinces an unfailingly sound taste. In Swedish furniture, he says he feels the essence of a "hospitable, gracious liveability." In the introduction to America of the modern Swedish industrial art Tage Palm of Chicago and New York has done pioneer work.

An expert in metal work is Hugo O. E. Carlborg of Providence, Rhode Island. An instructor in modeling at the Rhode Island School of Design as well as a designer and sculptor in the art department of the Gorham Manufacturing Company, he has modeled a large number of metal memorials, including tablets for the United States war monument in France, a tablet for the Canadian National Railways, the Thigpen tablet in New Orleans, and several tablets for various churches, educational, municipal, and business organizations. His father, Otto Carlborg, a former engineer, is a native of Sweden who is a sincere lover of art. Since his retirement he has taken up the hobby of carving birds in wood, painting them in their natural colors, and in general reproducing them with such fidelity to both form and plumage that they have won the admiration of expert ornithologists. At the age of eighty-nine he continues his carving and thereby gains happiness.

In manual training Sweden has done pioneer work, and when Boston established a special *Sloyd* Training School in 1888, the moving spirit of the enterprise was a Swede, Gustaf Larson, who became its first principal. Over four hundred teachers of arts and crafts were sent out from that school, and ten subsidiary centers were established as far away as in Mexico and in South India. Mr. Larson was born in Västergötland in 1861 and died in 1919. He had been educated in the Swedish Normal School of *Sloyd* at Nääs in Sweden, and for some years was the editor of *The Sloyd Record* in America.

In the development of American arts and crafts, including occupational therapeutics, many opportunities are offered to teachers with a Swedish background or training. An example is the career of Ruth L. Hallén, who at an early age came from Sweden to the United States and first studied at a trade school for girls and then at the art museum of Worcester, Massachusetts. Then she returned to Sweden to study weaving, needlework and similar crafts. When she came back to America she brought with her a Swedish loom, "big as a barn door." It aroused the suspicion of the customs authorities and so did the weaving designs in her notebook which looked like hieroglyphics. But once admitted she was quickly hired as an occupational therapist at the Grafton State Hospital near Worcester, where the value of manual training as an aid to mental recovery had been recognized. Next she was employed as a consultant by the New Hampshire League of Arts and Crafts and then in 1937 by the United States Government as director of arts and crafts in an experimental school at Arthurdale, Virginia. A number of other weaving teachers trained in Sweden are employed in different parts of the United States.

Most Swedish artists in the United States have been teachers of art, whether of the "fine" varieties or the more practical or industrial kind in which the Swedes in Sweden have made such notable progress, especially during and since the First World War. In art work, as in other occupations, Swedes are apt to be sound and thorough rather than sensational or strikingly original. Instinctively they observe the classic injunction: "Nothing to excess."

XXX

INDUSTRIALISTS

The earliest industry to which the Swedes applied themselves in America, whether as colonists on the lower Delaware or pioneers in the Middle West, was farming. For this they had been trained in Sweden, where agriculture had traditionally been the main source of livelihood. "By general consent," writes Dr. Eric Englund, an official of the United States Department of Agriculture, in *Swedes in America* (p. 75), "the American farmers of Swedish extraction are recognized as among the better farmers of their respective communities. The testimony of county agents in regions where Swedish stock constitutes a substantial part of the rural population amply confirms this point. Of forty-six Master-Farmer awards made by *The Farmer* of St. Paul, Minnesota, to farmers of that state during the years from 1926 to 1932, nine, or practically one-fifth, were made to farmers of Swedish descent, whereas the Swedes, as listed by the Census of 1930, constituted only one-tenth of the whole rural-farm population." Swedish inventions such as the De Laval cream separator, made by Carl Gustaf Patrik De Laval in 1877, and new varieties of grain such as Victory Oats and Hannchen Barley, developed at the Swedish experimental station at Svalöf in Skåne are likewise listed by Dr. Englund as important contributions to American agriculture.

In his chapter on "Pioneers of the Northwest," in *Swedes in America,* the late Professor Andrew A. Stomberg of the University of Minnesota, quotes his colleague, Professor Helge Nelson of the University of Lund in Sweden, to the effect that the area cleared and cultivated by former Swedish immigrants in the United States exceeds that of the soil tilled by their kinsmen in Sweden. According to Professor Nelson there were in 1920 in the United States "60,461 farmers who were born in Sweden and of these about 85 per cent owned their farms." In addition, according to American Government statistics, there were about 10,000 more

Swedish-born American citizens who operated farms of which they were not the owners. "Swedish-America is the most important conquest ever made by Swedes," wrote Ernst Skarstedt, the ablest Swedish-born author in America.

Among the other industrial occupations in which the early immigrants were qualified to participate were logging, mining and railroad construction. "It was faith in the Swedes and their kinsmen, the Norwegians," writes further Professor Stomberg, "which greatly encouraged the railroad executives to extend their lines further and further into the new sections; they felt certain that these people would settle along the new lines (which they had helped construct) and build new communities. This faith was fully justified, and it was frequently attested to by James J. Hill, the famous railroad builder and executive. In a notable address, in 1902, he pointed to the splendid revenue his company was annually reaping from typically Swedish and Norwegian settlements."

The story of the newly arrived Swedes working as lumberjacks ever further into the Northwest reads the same way. Some writers contend that several of the feats attributed to the legendary Paul Bunyan were originally based on the "tall" stories told by or about the early Swedish timber cutters. Their own boasting was, of course, but a reflex of their social inferiority feeling as foreigners, though many of them were possessed of great strength. In time, they became also operators of lumber mills. "The biggest sawmill business in the Middle West during part of the era in which the lumber industry flourished," writes Professor Stomberg, "was built and managed by C. A. Smith, a native of Sweden. His employees were nearly all Swedes."

From logging and railroad construction to house building and other industries requiring manual skill the step was not long and as the country's "infant" industries grew at a forced tempo under the stimulus of the high protective tariff, it soon became profitable to make furniture and other industrial goods. In such enterprises the Swedes were prepared to join, first as manual workers and later as entrepreneurs.

In the general industrial development of the later decades of the nineteenth century and the early ones of the twentieth many engineers as well as mechanics trained in Sweden had an important share. In such work the language handicap was not serious. "I came here to work and not to talk," one of the graduate engineers is quoted as having said when refused a raise because of his unfamiliarity with English. To the growth of American industry such men became as valuable as the

Swedish-trained officers had been to the Union armies during the Civil War. Whether mechanics or engineers, thousands of them gradually found employment in all types of tool and machinery shops such as the Deering Harvester Works at Moline, Illinois, and later in the automobile and airplane plants at Detroit and other points in the Middle West as well as in New England. It is, for instance, just as difficult to imagine a Ford or Chrysler automobile factory at Detroit as a Pratt & Whitney airplane plant in Connecticut without Swedish specialists in precision.

At the Pratt & Whitney plant in East Hartford, a large number of Swedish engineers have been employed since 1885, led by the late Bengt N. W. Hanson, who became its President. Originally he was a gunmaker or rather a designer of machinery for the making of guns, which before the First World War were sold by Pratt & Whitney to Government arsenals in practically all parts of the world. In 1915 he was appointed a civilian member of the United States Machine Gun Board and then became general manager of the Colt Fire Arms Company, for which he had charge of gun production during the remainder of the conflict.

In the Second World War such men once more became a military asset. An example was the late Carl Gustav Swebelius of Hamden, Connecticut, formerly an engineer for the Marlin Firearms Company of New Haven. To make machine guns for the British he reorganized in 1939 the High Standard Manufacturing Company of Hamden, Connecticut, where he employed as many of his former associates at the Marlin plant as he could find. When the United States itself entered the war, his speed and efficiency in production were widely cited by the American War Department as an example to other manufacturers. Among his many inventions made during the First World War was the synchronization of machine-gun fire with the airplane propeller which was so delicate that bullets could be fired between the blades. Personally a "kindly, big blue-eyed Swede with a feeling for guns," Mr. Swebelius was known to his employees as Gus, and yet he was credited with knowing more about automatic weapons than any other man in America. At the age of sixty-eight he died October 18, 1948 and in his will he left an estate of three and a quarter million dollars for research on cancer and epilepsy.

Another arms manufacturer of Swedish birth who put new vigor into an old New England plant is Carl R. Hellstrom, who in 1946 was elected President of Smith & Wesson, the old revolver firm of Springfield, Massachusetts. Born in Stockholm in 1895, he was educated at the University of Christiania in Norway, and the École Polytechnique in Paris. While a student at the latter during the First World War he was sent by the French Government to the United States to supervise the production of shells. In 1917 he was transferred to United States Ordnance, was given a commission as captain and American citizenship at the same time. During the 1920s he was in the coal business but in 1931 he became, first, chief engineer and then general manager for the Smith & Wesson firm. During the Second World War he stepped up its production from about a hundred guns daily to 1,100; altogether the firm made some two million revolvers for the Allied forces. After the war Hellstrom designed a new kind of factory built outside of the city and prepared to withstand atomic warfare. As such it was much publicized as a model for other manufacturers.

A few Swedish-trained engineers arrived early in America. In the seventeenth century, Peter Lindeström, a specialist in fortifications wrote a geography and drew the first map of the Lower Delaware region, and in the eighteenth, Colonel J. C. Senf built a canal in South Carolina. Even the Reverend Nicholas Collin, the last of the Swedish-ordained pastors in the "Old Swedes" churches, who arrived in 1770 and lived until 1831, was an inventor and amateur mechanic. About 1840, Lorentz August Berg, a Swedish-trained pharmacist, born in 1803, came to Connecticut and for J. W. Williams of North Manchester compounded the formula for the first Williams Shaving Soap; for its production the first factory was built in 1847 at Glastonbury, Connecticut.

The most famous Swedish-born engineer and inventor of the nineteenth century in America was, of course, John Ericsson, who during the Civil War gave the Government the plans for the *Monitor* which broke Confederate power at sea. From London, where he had vainly demonstrated his improvements of the propeller, he came to New York in 1839 and lived there until his death in 1889. In 1926 the United States Government erected a monument in his honor in Potomac Park, Washington, D.C. In the early 'fifties he was visited by another young Swedish-born inventor, Alfred Bernhard Nobel, the prize donor, who by his high explosives was to revolutionize not only warfare but industrial techniques, especially railroad and highway construction. What they discussed is not known.

Another prominent engineer of Swedish birth and education who came to the United States before the Civil War was John William Nyström. His *Treatise on Screw Propellers and Their Steam Engines* was published in Philadelphia in 1852 and other technical works by him continued to appear for half a century. One of them ran through eighteen editions. According to Dr. Amandus Johnson, Nyström was "for a time acting chief engineer of the United States Navy." The most noted designer of American ordnance used in the Civil War was Admiral John Adolph Dahlgren, whose father had come from Sweden to Philadelphia soon after the War for Independence. After the turn of the century the number of Swedish-trained engineers and other technicians increased at an even higher rate than Swedish immigration in general.

As in agriculture, the Swedish immigrants were prepared to take part in mining, Sweden's next oldest industry. In the mining of coal, as in Pennsylvania, iron ore in Upper Michigan and the Mesabi Range in northern Minnesota, or copper in Butte and other places in Montana, they have taken an important part, not to mention the exploration for gold in California and later in Alaska.

Among the earliest American mining engineers trained in Sweden was John Uno Sebenius, born in 1862. He came to the United States in 1888 and in 1901 was made superintendent of explorations for mineral-bearing land on the Mesabi Range for the Oliver Iron Mining Company. During thirty years he was a general mining engineer for that company. He was also an honorary major on the staff of Governor John A. Johnson of Minnesota and a colonel on the staffs of Governors Eberhart, Hammond, and Burnquist.

Among the many other specialists in mining only a few can be mentioned. Axel E. Anderson is a mining engineer for the Du Pont interests at Seattle, Washington; Robert Carl Beckstrom, a petroleum expert and professor in the subject at the Colorado School of Mines, where his specialty is the recovery of oil from oil-bearing sands; Milton S. Lindholm is a geologist and mining engineer for the Calumet and Arizona Mining Company. (In 1914–18 he conducted mining operations in West Africa.)

In the technique of locating new deposits of both metal ores and petroleum two Swedish-trained engineers, the late Karl Sundberg and his associate, Hans Lundberg, a resident of Canada, did important pioneering work. By their use of a magnetic device, which may be called a truly scientific "divining rod," they had found, before coming to America, the copper, gold and silver ore at Boliden in northern Sweden. Using the same method they then located a new vein of lead ore at Buchans

Mine in Newfoundland. In the finding of gold-bearing ores in northern Ontario, and in many other explorations of the earth's sub-surface in various countries, including petroleum deposits, their methods are still used with success.

In the smelting of ores, which logically came next, the Swedes have also been prominent. In such work they had long traditions back of them, especially in the production of iron and steel. In Pittsburgh, for instance, Thorsten Berg was selected by Andrew Carnegie as chief engineer at the Homestead Works; for the Tennessee Coal and Iron Company, also a subsidiary of the United States Steel Corporation, the late J. E. Fries, a well-educated Swedish engineer, was placed in charge of its Birmingham, Alabama, plant and there built the first electrically operated mill.

For the Bethlehem Steel Company, of which he was once chief engineer, Casimir von Philip, made many improvements in rolling mill machinery, just as in coke-oven operations Ragnar Berg, chief engineer for the Koppers Company of Pittsburgh, developed a number of labor-saving devices. A. G. Witting, for many years chief engineer of the Illinois Steel Company, did the same at Gary, Indiana. For the Carnegie–Illinois Steel Corporation at Munhall, Pennsylvania, A. W. Söderberg, its chief mechanical engineer, has made several inventions that have benefited the steel industry, principally the "rocking type" of heavy plate shear which eliminates the "shear bow" or arching of the plate along the cut edge. In 1936 John Brunner, also employed by the Illinois Steel Company, received the John Ericsson Medal of the American Society of Swedish Engineers for his "perfection of the so-called 'normalizing' steel treating process which substantially prolongs the life of railroad rails."

In the nickel industry, the late Noak Viktor Hybinette, born at Falun, in Swedish Dalecarlia in 1868, was a pioneer and the inventor of the electrolytic process for the refining of nickel and its alloying with steel. In 1892 he became general manager of the Oxford Copper Company at Bayonne, New Jersey, and when that concern was absorbed by the International Nickel Company in 1904, he became chief metallurgist of the latter. As such he inspected nickel mines and planned new developments all over the world. In 1937 he died at Palermo, Italy.

As chief engineer for the Mesta Machine Company of Pittsburgh, Gustav L. Fisk, later a consulting engineer in New York, designed many modern rolling mill features, including the "Fisk" cooling bed for merchant mill stock.

At the Bell Telephone Laboratories in New York, Gustaf Waldemar Elmén has been a specialist in making iron, nickel, and cobalt alloys. For steel mills Carl P. Åström invented a new type of hot-metal car that keeps the metal in molten form for as long as fifteen hours, making it possible to transport in that state as much as two hundred tons at a time over fairly long distances. While chief engineer for the Ludlum Steel Company, N. Axel V. Paulson, later employed by the Avesta Steel Works in Sweden, made inventions that greatly improved the quality of tool steels. Such achievements illustrate the Swedish share in the development of metallurgy in America.

Next came the use of metals and one of the earliest was the construction of railroads and bridges, mentioned in a previous chapter. One of the Swedish-born American experts in bridge building is Oscar F. Dahlstrom, employed by the Chicago and Northwestern Railroad. The long vehicular bridge across the Mississippi at Rock Island, Illinois, was designed by Ruben N. Bergendoff, a brother of Conrad Bergendoff, President of the near-by Augustana College. The even longer Huey P. Long Bridge across the same river just above New Orleans was planned by the late Nick F. Helmers, another engineer of Swedish descent.

On the Pacific Coast the Isaacson Iron Works of Seattle specializes in making equipment for ships such as anchor and propeller shafts; it also makes bulldozers, road scrapers and other heavy machinery. It was founded in 1906 by John Isaacson, who had been born in 1875 at Indal, in the northern Swedish province of Medelpad. At the age of fourteen he began to work in his father's blacksmith shop but remained for only two years. He then emigrated to Montana where he worked as a blacksmith for twelve years and then moved to Seattle where he was employed at the Young Iron Works, already owned by a brother-in-law. Soon he started his own foundry though he could employ but one helper, but before long he had five hundred. He died in 1939; in 1944 one of the Liberty ships was named in his honor. During the Second World War, under the management of his son, Henry, the plant was greatly expanded so that the employees numbered thousands.

To the design of modern American locomotives and railroad cars several Swedish engineers have contributed. Among them was the late Carl J. Mellin, born in 1851 at Hagelborg in the Swedish province of Västergötland. As chief engineer at the Richmond Locomotive Works in Virginia he designed "various kinds of compound locomotives which so greatly increased the pulling capacity of steam locomotives that he may be said to have laid the ground work for a new period in American railroad history." The new type of engine earned him in 1901 the highest award at the Pan-American Exposition in Buffalo and in 1904 a gold medal at the St. Louis Exposition. For the U.S. battleship *Texas* he designed a new type of triple expansion engines which began a new era in ship propulsion and for the U.S. cruiser *Vesuvius* he planned its dynamite-gun machinery, including a revolving turret and gun-operating gear, which made possible machine-controlled firing. In 1902 he became consulting engineer for the newly founded American Locomotive Works at Schenectady, New York, and as such he continued until his death in 1924.

Another Swedish engineer and inventor who helped improve American railroads was Karl F. Elers. He created equipment which had "a cushioning effect on the starting and stopping of trains, as well as on jolts due to bad track conditions." His type of elastic coupling was also installed in electric locomotives to reduce wear and tear. In the control of heavy machinery used in mines and steel mills it was found to be valuable and it is also used in the operation of the locks in the Panama Canal. Mr. Elers was originally employed by the Westinghouse Company at Pittsburgh, but later worked in that city as an independent consulting engineer.

The electric locomotives used to pull ships through the Panama Canal were designed by C. W. Larson, an engineer of the General Electric Company. For years he has been one of that company's specialists in designing locomotives for mines and industrial plants.

The "Lindstrom" hand brake used in so many American railroad cars was designed by Charles Lindstrom, a Swedish engineer first employed by the Pennsylvania Railroad and then by the Pressed Steel Car Company of Pittsburgh.

Nils D. Levin, chief engineer of the Jeffrey Manufacturing Company of Columbus, Ohio, who was born and educated in Sweden, holds about two hundred patents or applications for patents related to electrical locomotives and various kinds of electrical apparatus.

Another prominent railroad engineer who was an inventor as well as a writer of books on locomotive boilers was Carl A. W. Brandt, who died in New York in April 1942. He had been born and educated in Stockholm, came to America in 1902, and the same year was employed by the Lake Shore and Michigan Southern Railroad. In 1910 he was appointed assistant chief engineer for the Cleveland, Cincinnati, Chicago and St. Louis Railroad. Later he became chief engineer for the Superheater Company and in 1940 he was awarded the Melville Gold Medal of the American Society of Mechanical Engineers. Among his books are *The Design of Locomotive Boilers and Superheaters* (1928) and *The Locomotive Boiler* (1939).

In the building of power plants several engineers of Swedish birth have specialized. The most eminent is Carl Richard Söderberg, Professor of mechanical engineering at the Massachusetts Institute of Technology, at Cambridge, Massachusetts. Born at Ulvöhamn in northern Sweden in 1895, he was graduated from Chalmer's Institute of Technology at Gothenburg, Sweden, and in 1922 joined the engineering staff of the Westinghouse Company. There he made "numerous inventions in connection with turbines, particularly devices for balancing very large rotary machinery, spring mountings for machinery subject to vibration and many features in the design of turbo-generator rotors." In 1934 one of the largest capacity turbines ever constructed (183,000 kw.) was installed under his direction by Westinghouse for the Philadelphia Electric Company. He is the author of numerous contributions to technical journals both in the United States and Europe.

The chief designer of electric power plants for the General Electric Company in Schenectady was the late Oscar Junggren, a native of Landskrona, in southern Sweden, born in 1865. Trained at the technical school at Malmö, he came to the United States in 1889. When he died in 1935 he had to his credit about one hundred and thirty patents, most of them relating to steam turbines. Between 1924 and 1932 he designed for the General Electric Company thirty different turbines, which meant on the average a new turbine every four months. "Nearly one-half of all the electric power in the world created by steam turbines," said a company statement in 1938, "comes from those manufactured by the General Electric under Mr. Junggren's guidance." In 1931 he received the Charles A. Coffin award as a "designer and creator of large turbine units and especially for his invention of the triple compound turbine, a distinct advance in the art." He was also given the title of an "Associate Edison Pioneer."

A specialist in the design of large pumping engines, employed by the Allis Chalmers since 1901, is Gustaf L. Kollberg, born at Ljusne in northern Sweden in 1878. He arrived in the United States in 1895 and some of his training was obtained in Chicago. Besides oil-line pumps and high pressure pumps, he has aided in the design and installation of a large number of triple expansion and compound reciprocating pumping engines for municipal water works in various parts of the country.

A Swedish-trained hydroelectric power station specialist, now an electro-chemical engineer for the American Cyanamid Company in New York, is Eric A. Lof, born in 1879 at Trollhättan in Sweden, and a graduate of Chalmers Institute of Technology in Gothenburg. He is the author of a book on hydroelectric power stations, but his specialty is exploration for new projects.

In 1946 the Westinghouse Company's highest distinction, the Order of Merit, was awarded for "his skill in testing," to Carl W. E. Wallin, a native of the Swedish province of Uppland, who since 1903 had been employed as an engineer at its generator works at Pittsburgh. He had charge of the mounting of the company's gigantic generators at the Boulder, or Hoover, Dam, as well as the Grand Coulee Dam in the state of Washington.

In the electrical industry an even larger number of engineers and inventors of Swedish ancestry have been and are employed. In this field William Mattson Bager, born of Swedish parents in Copenhagen, holds some twenty-eight patents with others pending. He was educated in Sweden as an electrical engineer and for many years was a vice president in charge of sales and engineering for the Bucyrus-Erie Company of Milwaukee. Some of his inventions have revolutionized certain types of excavating machinery.

A noted developer of new electric motors for the General Electric was Sven Robert Bergman, formerly in charge of the company's experimental plant at Lynn, Massachusetts. He was born in the province of Skåne, was graduated from the Royal Institute of Technology in Stockholm and joined the General Electric in 1902. In 1934 he received the Charles A. Coffin award for his contributions to rayon-spinning machinery. His "reinforced, high-speed bucket for rayon spinning is capable of making as much as 12,000 revolutions a minute," the citation said. Previously the high speeds required for this work had too often burst the buckets.

To the improvement of electric lamps two American-born engineers of Swedish extraction employed by the Westinghouse Company at

Bloomfield, New Jersey, have made important contributions. In 1928 Albert Ferdinand Lindström, a graduate of Wesleyan University, received the company's annual award for solving the problem of making colored electric light bulbs and in 1931 the same award was given to Waldemar E. Anderson, native of Stamford, Connecticut, and a graduate of the Sheffield Scientific School at Yale, for inventing the "Christmas tree indicating lamp," a bulb that continues to glow after the filament has been burned out. During the Second World War Mr. Anderson designed shock proof electric light bulbs for battleships and submarines.

One of General Electric's light bulb specialists is Sven Kahlson, born in Sweden and graduated in 1924 from Chalmers Institute in Gothenburg. His speciality is the dull-etched lamp. The Pitney plant at Cleveland, of which he is the general superintendent, can make a thousand such glass globes a minute, or about 2,500,000 a day, which is about one half of the entire American consumption. When he first arrived in Cleveland after graduating from Chalmers as a chemical engineer he had to work at first as window cleaner at sixty cents an hour. Next he got a job at the General Electric as a foreign-mail clerk, then as a laboratory assistant and finally as a specialist in glass production. The Pitney plant, which he helped design, is so highly automatic that in spite of its great output it employs only 320 workers.

The most prominent of all Swedish engineers in America is unquestionably Ernst Fredrick Werner Alexanderson, former chief engineer of the General Electric Company and a pioneer in wireless telephoning, broadcasting and television. He holds over three hundred United States patents, including those on "the Alexanderson high frequency alternator, the multiple-tuned antennae, vacuum tube radio telephone transmitter, and the tuned radio frequency receiver," all of which are now in general use. He also did pioneer work in electric ship propulsion, railroad electrification, including the re-generation of power. "His idea of employing the high power tube for relaying and modulation is the basis of *all* broadcast transmitters," says a General Electric statement. The Radio Corporation of America was originally formed to exploit his invention during the First World War of the ship-to-shore telephone, now available on both trains and motor cars. Born and educated in Sweden he came to the United States in 1902. He had read about the work done for the General Electric Company by the late Charles P. Steinmetz, its chief engineer, and ultimately he became his successor.

While in the automotive field no Swede has been able to give his name permanently to a car, such as the Studebaker, Franklin, Dodge, Ford, Nash, or Chrysler, several have created crucial parts. The most basic was probably the precision gages made by the late Carl Edward Johansson, a native of Sweden, who after the First World War became an associate of Henry Ford in Detroit. Thanks to his measuring blocks which are so delicate that in using them the body heat of the operator has to be taken into account, it became possible to make even the most refined parts interchangeable and then assemble them in a central plant—the foundation of all mass production. During the First World War the American Government declared the Johansson gages standard equipment in the manufacture of munitions and in the Second mass production was applied even more widely, especially in the manufacture of airplanes. In 1918 Mr. Johansson himself came to America and in 1923 he joined Mr. Ford. In Detroit he lived for many years, but he died in Sweden during a visit in 1943. The blocks made by Johansson were placed by Mr. Ford at the disposal of all American manufacturers.

At Poughkeepsie, New York, precision gages of the Johansson type have been made since 1925 by the Standard Gage Company of which Erik Aldeborgh, who had been associated with Johansson in Sweden, is the founder and President. In 1942 it won both the Army and Navy Efficiency Production Awards.

In Attleboro, Massachusetts, Frank Mossberg, a former Swedish immigrant, made at an early date an electric automobile that could go sixty miles at twenty miles an hour on a single battery charge. That was several years before Henry Ford launched his internal combustion engine, but at that time no Massachusetts capitalist could be convinced that there was a future for any kind of horseless carriage. Mossberg then returned to his original inventions field, jewelry, tableware, textiles, fog signals, machine tools, roller bearings, reels and spools for the wire industry, and a great varity of other things, in all of which he has obtained a total of over two hundred patents. His braider carrier is used in nearly all braiding machines all over the world.

In Michigan, Charles Herman Blomstrom, whose parents had come from Svenarum in Småland to Lisbon in that state in 1865, constructed a horseless carriage as early as 1892 and in 1900 he built another which he described as "a buggy with an engine." In 1901 the Blomstrom Motor Car Company was organized in Detroit and until 1905 it made a car known as The Queen. The plant was then one of the largest in the city and its output went as high as thirty to forty cars a week. In 1906 a larger car named The Blomstrom was launched. It had four cylinders whereas originally The Queen had had only one. After it had failed to win a sufficient market, Blomstrom helped design such cars as the Gyroscope, the Griswold, the Lion, and the Rex, as well as the Frontmobile, the first front-drive car to be made in production lots in the United States. It was produced at Camden, New Jersey. All these models are now museum pieces and the name Blomstrom all but forgotten. His son, Lowell C. Blomstrom, became chief engineer for the Federal Mogul Corporation in Detroit, makers of bearings.

A Swedish-born automobile executive whose work had permanent results was the late John Björn, a native of Värmland, who from 1916 to 1926 was general manager of the Nash Motor Works of Kenosha, Wisconsin. He helped develop both the Jeffery and its successor the Nash, but he never had any car named for himself. Before emigrating Björn had worked as a railroad engineer in Lapland, but when he arrived in the United States he had to perform, at first, the most menial work. Then he got a job with Gormully & Jeffery in Chicago, makers of the original, high-wheeled bicycles. With this firm he remained through the rest of the bicycle era and well into the automobile age. According to The Swedish Element in America (Vol. III, p. 322), he "was instrumental in inventing the 'clincher' tire which made Mr. Jeffery a millionaire."

Another high executive in automobile construction was Earnest W. Seaholm, who in 1913 joined the Cadillac Company and in 1921 became its chief engineer. This position he held for over twenty years, during which the Cadillac as well as the La Salle were brought up to a high state of both elegance and mechanical perfection. During the Second World War he had charge of making tanks in the Cadillac plant at Detroit. Born near Lidköping in Sweden he was brought to America by his parents at an early age. At first his family settled in Hartford, Connecticut, and then in Springfield, Massachusetts, where he was graduated from the Mechanics Arts High School.

A pioneer in the making of automobile bodies was Carl Birger Parsons of Detroit, who while still in his 'teens landed penniless and alone in New York in 1901. At first he worked on a farm, drove a milk wagon, but when nineteen years old got a job with the Kimball Coach Company of Chicago, which was then constructing a customs-built automobile body for the Czar of Russia. This fired his imagination and after taking a course in a technical school in New York in "carriage and automobile design," he became a specialist in designing automobile bodies and as such was employed by several of the early manufacturers. Then he formed a company of his own for the making not only of bodies but of other automobile parts. Since 1928 he has manufactured, in addition, a kitchen combination of his own design which includes a stove, a refrigerator, a sink and a food storage bin, called the Parsons' Pureair Kitchen. During the Second World War he made munitions.

For the Chrysler Company of Detroit, Tore (Ture) Franzén, born at Lund, in Skåne, and educated in Sweden, has been an experimental engineer for many years. During the Second World War he was a lieutenant colonel of the United States Engineering Corps in France. The design of the "fluid drive" used by the same company was made by Emil Anderson, another engineer of Swedish origin.

Several fundamental contributions to automobile development were made by the late Vincent Bendix, a native of Moline, Illinois, where his father, the Reverend John Bendix, born at Färgeryd in Småland, was a Methodist minister. At sixteen Vincent Bendix ran away from home and, like Henry Ford and Thomas A. Edison, he never got any formal education, but early tinkered with bicycles and similar contrivances. In New York he met Glenn Curtiss, who was to be a pioneer in aviation and by him he was introduced to motorcycles. In 1907 he became a salesman for the Holsman Automobile Company of Chicago and in 1908 he designed and built his own car, the Bendix. While like the Blomstrom, it did not survive, it did have a small but important detail which has remained a permanent fixture in all cars, the Bendix spring. While its existence may be unknown to most car owners, it is however, an integral part of the self-starter which enables so many millions, including women, to be drivers. It connects a battery-driven electric motor with the gasoline-driven main engine and as the latter gathers speed it automatically lets go. Bendix also helped develop the four-wheel brake. A reveler in blue prints, he bought and developed many ideas of other inventors. At one time the Bendix Development Company was reputed to own over fourteen thousand patents. He was also one of the early promoters of aviation and the Bendix speed race for which he gave the first trophy is still a fixed annual event. The town of Bendix in New Jersey was renamed in his honor. Toward the end of his career he concentrated on the Bendix washing machine, which became a posthumous success. Until his death in 1945 he also dreamed of a safe family airplane.

Curiously enough another fundamental device used in practically all motor cars, the disc clutch, which makes the internal combustion engine flexible in its application of power to the car itself, was made by another son of former Swedish immigrants living in Moline, Illinois. His name is George William Borg, Board Chairman of the gigantic Borg-Warner Corporation. Like Vincent Bendix and many other successful inventors, he failed to get a technical education, but in Moline his father, a former sailor and a skilled mechanic, had a small machine shop in which Marshall Beck, a local lawyer and amateur inventor, was his partner. In this shop the disc clutch was first made for the Velie car, now likewise extinct, and then for the Jeffrey trucks and cars made in Kenosha, Wisconsin. Gradually all car makers had to use it. After that Borg expanded into refrigerators, knitting machines, clocks, bathroom scales, airplanes and television tubes, as well as into cattle, barley, and alfalfa.

Another detail of the modern automobile which had its origin in a Swedish mind was the Stromberg carburetor introduced in 1906 and later developed by Bendix. It was not invented by either Stromberg or Carlson, founders of the Stromborg-Carlson firm, still famous as manufacturers of radio receivers, but by one of its employees, John S. Gullborg, a Swedish-born mechanic who had been a gunmaker at the Huskvarna Works in Småland. Born in 1863 in Västergötland, Gullborg came to Chicago in 1886 and at first worked on bicycles and then on telephone devices for the long since defunct Swedish–American Telephone Company, which he helped organize. Next he joined the Stromberg-Carlson combination and while affiliated with it made a number of new inventions and improvements in old ones. In 1912 he perfected, for instance, an automatic alemite die-casting machine which became the basis of a new industry. Another standard implement he created was the grease gun for the lubrication of automobiles now used in practically all American garages.

Two other Swedish-born employees of the Stromberg-Carlson firm who later launched a manufacturing business of their own were the Bodine brothers, Carl D. and Paul J., who had arrived in Loomis, Nebraska, in 1886, and in 1905 began in Chicago the manufacture of fractional horsepower electric motors used in electric clocks, dental drills, moving picture projectors, and electric refrigerators.

The A. B. Modine Manufacturing Company, founded by Arthur B. Modine and situated at Racine, Wisconsin, and La Porte, Indiana, makes such vital automotive parts as self-starters, carburetors, clutches and ignition equipment, though its real specialty is heating and air-conditioning equipment.

Both Alfred Stromberg and Andrew Carlson, founders of the Stromberg-Carlson firm, were born in Sweden and were originally telephone men. Stromberg, born in Stockholm in 1861, was once an employee of the L. M. Ericsson Telephone Company of that city, widely known makers of automatic centrals and other telephone equipment, and in 1885 he obtained employment with the Bell Telephone Company in Chicago. In 1890 he joined the Chicago Electric Protective Company and for it designed the Stromberg system of burglar alarms. In 1894 he formed a partnership with Carlson, who was born in Västergötland in 1854 and previously employed by the Deering Harvestor Works in Moline, Illinois, and then by the Chicago Telephone Company. Each invested $500. The next year the company was incorporated for $50,000, and in 1901, or only six years later, its output was valued at over a million dollars. In 1902 the company moved to Rochester, New York. The financial control as well as management has long since passed out of the original hands.

For various automobiles the Metal Equipment Company of Jamestown, New York, has produced as many as half a million radiators a year and almost as many heaters. The President and general manager of this company is Oscar A. Lenna (Linné), born in Hälsingborg, in the Swedish province of Skåne. When he was but seven years old, his father left for America, intending to dig gold in California, but was never heard from again. Mr. Lenna is also the head of a company making washing machines, the Blackstone, as well as of a foundry. In all three plants he employs chiefly workers of Swedish birth or descent.

An important toolmaker for automobile production was the late Otto Lundell, a native of Floby in Sweden, who as President and chief owner of the Michigan Tool Company made the machinery that took the "grind" out of automobile gears, making them accurate to one ten-thousandths of an inch. He also invented and made many other devices which helped make automobiles run more smoothly and last longer. Originally he had worked in a machine shop in Rockford, Illinois, at twelve cents an hour. (For designing a new drill press he once received $20.) He was, however, a graduate of the Chalmers Institute of Technology at Gothenburg and after working for a while on a Minnesota farm for $25 a month and board, he got a job in another Rockford machine shop and soon was made a foreman. In 1912 he moved to Detroit and began developing his precision gear cutting machinery, working at times as much as eighteen hours a day. Before he died in 1939 he had made a fortune.

Another Detroit plant serving the automotive industry is the Detroit Broach Company, founded and managed by five young Swedish engineers, headed by Gustaf von Reis, a descendant of an old Gothenburg family. Most of them are graduates of Chalmers.

The Indian Motorcycle, whose speed is still unsurpassed, was originally designed by Carl Oscar Hedström, born in 1871 in Småland. Like the original Lindbergh airplane, *The Spirit of St. Louis,* one of the early models made by Hedström in a small shop in Springfield, Massachusetts, is permanently exhibited at the Smithsonian Institution in Washington, D.C.

To American manufacturing and transportation an important contribution has been made by the ball and roller bearings made by the SKF Industries of Philadelphia, a subsidiary of the original *Svenska Kullagerfabriken* of Gothenburg, Sweden. During the Second World War, the American manager, W. L. Batt, who is not of Swedish descent, was Vice-President of the War Production Board in Washington.

A few of the other engineers and inventors who have made significant contributions to American industry have been such men as: Carl Gabrielson of Syracuse, New York, chief designer of the L. C. Smith typewriter; Gideon Sundbäck of Meadville, Pennsylvania, born in Jönköping in Småland, who in 1913 devised a type of zipper known as the Talon Fastener as well as automatic machinery for the making of it. The Sundstrand brothers, Gustaf David and Oscar Joseph, originally makers of machine tools at Rockford, Illinois, where the Sundstrand Stub Lathe is still produced, perfected in 1913 an adding machine on which they had worked for years. In 1927 it was bought by the Underwood, Elliott-Fisher Company of Hartford, Connecticut, with which Oscar Joseph Sundstrand then became associated as a consultant engineer.

Another adding and calculating machine which also multiplies and divides, extracts square roots and cube roots, and other mathematical operations that save human thinking, was invented by the late Carl M. Fridén, who was born in 1891 at Alvesta in Småland and died in California, April 28, 1945. After running away from home at the age of eleven he supported himself in Stockholm as an errand boy and then as laboratory assistant while getting an engineering education. When the First World War broke out he was in Australia, building a factory for the Swedish Match Company, but until he could get a birth certificate from Sweden he was placed in confinement and thus found time to think out a new type of calculating machine which ultimately made him a millionaire. He arrived in California in 1917 and at San Leandro he built a handsome modernistic, flower-surrounded factory in which 1,500 people are employed. During the Second World War they made munitions. The Fridén Calculating Machine Company has its own sales offices in 250 American cities.

Other engineers and inventors of Swedish origin have been men like George E. Swenson of the Celotex Company who holds many patents on roofing and insulating materials; Emil F. Johnson, who as an analytical chemist helped devise an effective system of milk control for New York as well as for other cities; Carl Axel Robert Lundin (1851–1915), lensmaker for such observatories as the Lick, the Lowell, and those at Amherst and the University of Cincinnati, not to mention the one at Pulkova in Russia. Lundin was born and educated in Sweden and in 1906 was given full charge of the optical work at the Alvan Clark & Sons Company at West Somerville, Massachusetts. His son of the same name became manager of the optical division of the Warner & Swasey Company of Cleveland, Ohio, makers, among many other things, of telescope lenses of all sizes including those used in submarine periscopes.

Even more romantic was the career of John Nelson, who came to Rockford, Illinois, as an uneducated carpenter in the early 1850s and there found work in a furniture factory. At the Chicago Exposition in 1867 he saw an automatic knitting machine making men's socks which intrigued him so much that he decided to construct one that would make *seamless* hosiery of all kinds. After working six years he perfected a type that is still used. In Rockford alone, six large mills produce annually millions of seamless stockings for women as well as men. Nelson himself died before any big profits were made but out of his invention members of his family as well as other early investors have reaped fortunes.

In Providence, Rhode Island, the late George Berkander, a native of Västergötland, originated the production of plastic jewelry which has since reached surprising proportions. At his factory as many as fifty new designs are created daily and before he died in 1937 his machines had stamped out, for instance, as many as 145,000 plastic bracelets in a day. Once he used 100,000 bushels of Cape Cod pine cones to make low-priced novelties for sale in five and ten cent stores. He also made poker chips by the million and the demand continues. At one time prison inmates in various parts of the country used to write him for pieces of the celluloid scrap, out of which they then created additional novelties. By selling them as souvenirs they obtained extra expense money.

At Pomona, in southern California, two Fernstrom brothers, Fritz O. and Erik, have run since 1925 a paper mill using Swedish-made machinery and chiefly Swedish pulp which turns out enough colored tissue paper and wrappers to cover over three billion oranges a year. In addition to the trade marks they have printed on them recipes for the use of the fruit. The firm also has customers in Australia, New Zealand, Mexico, and the West Indies as well as in California and other American fruit-growing states.

Niles, Michigan, is an industrial town once dominated by a single inventor and manufacturer of Swedish birth. He was the late Francis J. Plym, who was born in Småland, where his father had been a soldier, and brought to America by his parents when an infant. He grew up in Aledo, Illinois, where he became a highly skilled carpenter and cabinetmaker. By working double time he was able to obtain an education as an architect and in 1897 he was graduated from the University of Illinois. After further study at the National Academy of Design in New York, he became, first, a practicing architect at Lincoln, Nebraska, and then in Kansas City, Missouri. Specializing in store interiors, he invented a ready-made hollow metal store front, patented in 1905. To make it, he built a factory at Niles, Michigan, and there he soon began also to make bank and store fixtures, metal casement windows for ships and lighthouses, parts for automobiles and airplanes, and escalators such as those used in Rockefeller Center, New York. Out of his brain he created a new American industry. In his own name he obtained over a hundred patents and several more in conjunction with others. In Niles he owned the only newspaper and the main hotel, which he called The Four Flags. To the town he gave a hospital and sports fields. At the University of Illinois he maintained two $1,200 fellowships for postgraduate study of architecture abroad, and for his native town, Bäckaby in Småland, he provided an old people's home as a memorial to his parents.

An inventor and industrialist of Swedish birth who began his American career as a railroad hand is Colonel Emil Tyden of Hastings,

Michigan. While working for the Union Pacific Railroad, he invented a self-locking metal clip for the sealing of freight cars. It is made in the largest carseal factory in the world with a daily production capacity of a million seals. Ninety-five per cent of all American railroads and many foreign ones use the Tyden device and by 1938 over 2,250,000,000 of them had been manufactured. It has also been adopted by the customs authorities of both the United States and Canada. At Hastings, Colonel Tyden, who earned his title in the American production service during the First World War, started the manufacture of piston rings and of the Viking automatic sprinklers.

At Kewanee, Illinois, the late Peter A. Waller, born in Swedish Gästrikland, of Walloon descent, who arrived in America in 1885, made millions of the coarse cotton gloves used by farmers and other outdoor workers. When he died he was President of the Boss Manufacturing Company which had plants in fifteen cities, including Kewanee, the largest concern of its kind in the country. His first job had paid him $1.25 a day.

In Brooklyn, New York, Edward Magnuson, an ex-sailor from Kalmar in Småland, has a factory which makes 220 special cleaning compounds for over three hundred different kinds of industries. From coast to coast in the United States as well as in Canada he has distribution centers.

In Chicago, J. P. Seeburg, a native of Gothenburg, once made mechanical player pianos; he now makes coin-operated phonographs, popularly called "juke-boxes." His firm also manufactures parking meters and automatic vending machines for the sale of ice cream and soft drinks and a number of similar commodities.

In the same city Herbert R. Hedman, son of a Swedish-born father, manufactures his own inventions, the F. & E. Lightning Check-Writer, the Lightning Coinchanger and the Sign-O-Meter, which records automatically the number of checks a corporation official signs for his company. He was one of the first to promote television commercially, and is a director of the Western Television Corporation.

In Charleston, West Virginia, Oscar Nelson, born in Sweden and educated in its public schools, has made an even greater success as a manufacturer of the carbon black which became a prime necessity in the Second World War when artificial rubber had to be produced. It is also used in making ink, as well as paint, crayons, and stove polish. Since 1925 he has been President and general manager of the United Carbon Company which before the Second World War made two-thirds of the carbon black used in the United States. As a hobby he runs at Lewisburg, West Virginia, an immense stock farm called Morlunda in honor of his birthplace in eastern Småland. The annual sales of blooded stock are high society events.

Another industrial magnate of Swedish extraction is Walter Nord, President and Treasurer of the United States Automatic Corporation of Amherst, Ohio, and an inventor of steel traps, hydraulic testing valves, greasing equipment, and automatic vegetable washing machines. He was once Mayor of Amherst and the first President of its Rotary Club.

In May 1946, the will of the late Carl G. Nelson was probated in Chicago and the subsequent tax report showed that he left over a million dollars. He had once been a penniless immigrant, but had been one of the founders and principal owners of the Illinois Tool Works. To the Illinois Institute of Technology he had left $50,000 and an equal sum to the local Christian Science church.

Another Illinois manufacturer of Swedish birth is Albert Ivar Appleton, who has specialized in the electrical field. He also has a plant in Wisconsin. He was born in 1872 in the province of Halland and came to the United States as a very young man. Originally he had only two employees.

In the making of the Yale locks, automatic door checks and other builders' hardware, at Stamford, Connecticut, many Swedish workers have been employed. Several improvements are due to their inventions. The same is true of the American Hardware Corporation of New Britain, Connecticut, which, in addition to screws, locks and hinges, once made "a full jewelled automobile," the Corbin, which did not survive. The Stanley Tool Company of the same city likewise has many Swedish-born foremen as well as workers.

As a furniture center Rockford, Illinois, ranks with Jamestown, New York, and Grand Rapids, Michigan. It also produces machine tools, locks and builders' hardware as well as knitting machines. As far back as in 1893 there were over twenty furniture factories in the city owned and operated by Swedes. The Grand Old Man of the Rockford furniture business was the late P. A. Peterson who had come from Sweden in 1852 at the age of six. When he died in 1927 he had investments in nearly fifty plants and was the head of nine. At various depression times he had tided over fellow Swedes by signing their notes. When the panic of 1893 struck he owed $300,000 on such notes and after turning over all his assets to their creditors he went on the road as a salesman, vowing to pay back every cent, which he ultimately did. The banks soon found that without Peterson the plants they had taken over were not worth much but under his supervision they were gradually able to pay off their obligations.

The principal founder of the machine industry in Rockford was Levin Faust, a Swedish-born mechanic, who in 1890 organized, together with three other Swedish metal workers, the Mechanics Machine Company. It was the beginning of the Mechanics Universal Joint Division of the Borg-Warner Corporation which now occupies an impressive modern factory in Rockford. Faust also built the main hotel in Rockford which bears his name. In 1930, there were seventy-two factories in Rockford owned by Swedish residents including the National Lock Company, the city's largest, founded in 1903 by Faust, Frank S. Hogland and Emil C. Traner with the backing of P. A. Peterson. In Rockford Nils F. Testor, a native of Stockholm, makes the glue bearing his name which is sold in five and ten cent stores in tinfoil tubes at the rate of 30,000,000 a year. In Sweden it was originally called Karlson's Klister, a name now used only for the shoe cement.

Another plant in Rockford managed by Swedes makes the Super Maid Cook Ware, used in hospitals, hotels and clubs as well as in homes. It is designed to retain food values by cooking without water. The company, now called The Advance Aluminum Castings Corporation, has another factory at Chicago. It was founded by E. G. Grundström, born in 1882 in Sweden, and Nils Shoan, also born there in 1884. Its annual sales have reached millions of dollars.

In Brockton and Lynn, Massachusetts, the Swedes were among the first skilled shoemakers, some having arrived as early as 1843 or 1844. In Waltham, Massachusetts, and Elgin, Illinois, they have helped make the watches which made those towns famous. At Elgin, William Henry Samelius is Dean of the Watchmakers College. In Rhode Island they make silverware and jewelry. At East Berlin, Connecticut, is the plant of the W. W. Mildrum Jewel Company, which now specializes in guides for fishing rods, a unique business since it may prosper during depressions, when more people have time for fishing. It is owned by a Benson family and operated by five Benson brothers, Oscar, Olof, Victor, Edwin, and Arthur, while the sixth brother, a co-author of this book, is a stockholder. Other relatives are employed as assistant managers and operators. In fact, all five brothers work at the plant. In Worcester, Massachusetts, this family combination is outdone by the Oslund Brothers Machine Company, makers of bottling machinery. It is owned and operated by a father and seven sons, Charles H., Walter, Edwin, Robert, Henry, Fritz, Ernst, and Elmer.

Worcester, Massachusetts, called the heart of Massachusetts, is also an important Swedish industrial center. Several plants, producing machinery or other metal products, including wire goods, are owned and managed by Swedes, whose natural aptitude for precision work comes to good use. This is particularly true of the Norton Company, the world's largest maker of grinding machinery and abrasives, "used for cutting stones, grinding lenses, leveling off humps on railroad rails, for sharpening the lumberman's axe, the hunter's knife and the surgeon's scalpel, in the finishing process of ladies' watches, as well as in huge gun-grinding machinery for the largest American battleships," as Bernard Peterson of the Boston Transcript wrote in *Swedes in America*. At no time were the Norton products in greater demand than during the Second World War when precision machinery was all important. The Norton plant was then run seven days a week in three shifts and the number of employees went over twenty thousand. The company has subsidiary plants at Niagara Falls, in Canada, England, France, Germany, and Italy.

In the founding of this industry two Swedish potters from Höganäs in Skåne had a part, Sven Pulson, who in 1869 began to work for Franklin B. Norton, a Yankee potter, who in 1858 had moved a small pottery shop he had inherited at Bennington, Vermont, to Worcester, Massachusetts, and Pulson's brother-in-law, John Jeppson, who while working as a potter at Taunton, Massachusetts, was invited by Pulson to help him fire the clay for an experimental emery wheel. Later Pulson left Norton to work for other potters who were interested in his experiments with grinding wheels, but Jeppson remained to develop the vitrified grinding wheel and in 1885 became the first superintendent of the Norton Company, a post he held until his death in 1920. The skills these two men had acquired in mixing clays at the old pottery works at Höganäs in Sweden, thus became the basis for an American key industry, a good illustration of the benefit the United States has derived from some of its Swedish immigrants.

George N. Jeppson, a son of John Jeppson, born and educated in Worcester, and once a student at the Royal School of Mines in Stockholm, entered the Norton Company's employ in 1898 to learn the business from the ground up, an example followed shortly before the Second World War by his own son, John Jeppson, a graduate of Amherst and the Harvard Business School. In 1906 George N. Jeppson became works manager and a director of the company. In 1933 he was elected a vice president in charge of production and in 1941 President. Since 1946 he has been Chairman of the Board. In the fall of 1948 his son, John, became manager of a new division with five acres of floor space, costing $4,300,000 in which new methods are used for the manufacture of grinding wheels. At the dedication ceremony, August 30, 1948, George N. Jeppson presented Milton P. Higgins, his successor as President, with the ten millionth grinding wheel already made by the new process.

It is a striking fact that in all American industries either owned or managed by men of Swedish birth or descent there have been so far few, if any, labor conflicts. The relations between management and workers have usually been kept on a personal basis, the Swedish-born industrialists being, as a rule, fellow workers rather than absentee stockholders. A good example is the Norton Company, which pursues an enlightened and highly successful labor relations policy, including high wages, old age and disability pensions and a variety of social benefits. About twenty per cent of its employees are of Swedish origin.

In a single chapter it is obviously impossible to mention all the industrial achievements of former Swedish immigrants and their American-born children, but the examples cited indicate their variety and scope. In mechanical efficiency and inventive ingenuity the Swedes rank high.

XXXI

AVIATORS AND AIRPLANE BUILDERS

Having been sailors and navigators for so many centuries the Swedes could be expected to be intensely interested in the conquest of the air. Being also mechanically minded they took naturally to airplane construction, as they had to that of automobiles. This was particularly true of those born or brought up in the United States, where the opportunities for research and mass production were so much greater than in a country with the limited resources of Sweden. And in Sweden itself the inspiration for both flying and airplane building as well as motor car construction came from America. It was at the Centennial Exposition in Philadelphia in 1876 that Salomon August Andrée, the Swedish meteorologist and physicist who in 1897 was the first man to try to reach the North Pole by air, received his first lessons in flying from John Wise, an early American balloonist.

"They [the Scandinavians] crossed the Atlantic, everybody knows, long before Columbus," wrote the late William Seabrook in *These Foreigners,* "then Lindbergh flew it first [New York to Paris]; and it is a fair guess, if they ever get to tinkering with the Goddard rocket, they will be the first to reach the moon." It was, however, the Germans, rather than the Swedes, who a few years later perfected the rocket plane and jet propulsion.

The first former Swedish immigrant to make aviation history in the United States was Eric Nelson, who was the engineering officer on the first New York-to-Nome flight in 1921 and one of the pilots of four army planes which in 1924 made the first air trip around the world. Only two of the planes made the whole distance and one of them was flown by Nelson. Incidentally, he was the only member of the expedition who was not a native-born American. That was three years before Lindbergh made his non-stop flight to Paris.

Nelson was born in Stockholm, where his father was an engineer and where he himself studied at the Institute of Technology to become one. In 1905, when he was seventeen years old, he went, instead, to sea, first on a training ship and then on commercial sailing routes all over the world. He was therefore personally familiar with the various parts of the globe when he first proposed the army flight in 1921. In 1909 he decided to leave Sweden for the United States. His first job was that of a rigger in a shipyard at Greenwich, Connecticut, and the first summer he spent on a pleasure schooner as a member of the crew. Next he became a testing driver of new automobiles. Having seen on Long Island his first planes in flight he obtained a job as a mechanic for Victor Vernon, an American pioneer aviator, who flew a Curtiss "F" flying boat. Next he was given a chance to work in the experimental motor department of the Curtiss Aeroplane Company at Buffalo, New York, and thus became prepared for his later work as flight engineer. In 1917, when the United States entered the First World War, he tried in vain to enlist in the air forces of both the United States and Canada only to be rejected because he was too old—twenty-nine. He was finally admitted to the ground school at Cornell University as a mechanic. There he managed to get up in the air and before long he was sent to Ellington Field, in Texas, to be trained as a pilot. As such he made such progress that he was kept as an instructor and when the war ended he was in charge of teaching aerial acrobatics.

After the war he took part in the first expedition to photograph the Grand Canyon from the air and then in a country-wide exhibition flight to popularize aviation. This led to the New York–Nome project. Without making a forced landing four planes covered eleven thousand miles, a record at the time. For the round-the-world flight, which came next, he helped Donald W. Douglas, the California airplane builder, prepare special machines, fit for use over water as well as land, and on April 6, 1924, four of them took off from Lake Washington at Seattle, with two pilots in each. One crashed in Alaska, another was forced down in the North Atlantic. "Other men will fly around the world," said Admiral Robinson, when the two remaining planes arrived at the starting point, "but never again for the first time." Not only was Nelson promoted in army rank, but by a special act of Congress he was awarded the Distinguished Service Medal, and then decorated by several foreign governments, including that of Sweden.

In Seattle he had become acquainted with Philip G. Johnson, a young graduate of the engineering school of the University of Washington, who had been born in Seattle of Swedish parents hailing respectively from the provinces of Värmland and Dalsland. In 1917 Johnson became an employee of the Boeing Aircraft Company of Seattle, which in the Second World War was to build the Flying Fortresses, the Super-Fortresses and Stratocruisers, that later crossed continents and oceans. In 1919 he was made superintendent of production and in 1926 President. With him were associated a number of other executives and engineers, as well as mechanics, who were of Scandinavian extraction. In 1928 Nelson was induced to resign from the Army and become sales manager for Boeing. In 1933 he was appointed a vice president in charge of sales and under the Johnson-Nelson regime the company pioneered in the building of large passenger planes and mail carriers, including the Boeing Model 247, a forerunner of the large war planes. In 1936 Nelson resigned, got married, built a home on Lake Washington and did some travel in foreign countries, including Sweden. When the Second World War began he re-entered the American Army as an expert in aviation, serving both in Europe and the Orient. When it was over he was a brigadier general with a chestful of ribbons. Once more he then retired to the Reserve with permission to serve as technical adviser to the Scandinavian Air Lines connecting the North with all continents. The Atlantic crossing, which a hundred years ago required from two to three months, was then made in less than twenty-four hours.

Having become President of the Boeing Company in 1926 when he was only thirty-two years old, Philip Johnson was one of the youngest executives in the American aviation industry. He was also President of three other corporations, including the United Air Lines. In 1934, after the fracas over the airmail contracts, he temporarily left the country at the invitation of the Canadian Government to become vice president in charge of operations for the Trans–Canada Air Lines. (Being an American citizen he could not become President.) When the Second World War began he returned to his post as head of Boeing in Seattle by whom the powerful warplanes already mentioned were then built. Exhausted by overwork he died in 1944 at the age of fifty.

The third great name of Swedish origin in American aviation history is that of Colonel Charles Augustus Lindbergh, Jr. Born in Little Falls, Minnesota, the son of a Canadian-born mother and a Swedish-born father, who became a United States Congressman, he inherited certain traits that may be said to be typical of both those countries, personal modesty, mechanical skill and a spirit of adventure. His pioneer flight to Paris in 1927 began a new era in American aviation and more than any other man he popularized the new means of transportation. He also tasted the two extremes of popular favor and popular aversion, not to mention the personal tragedy of having his first-born child kidnapped and killed.

From both his father and grandfather he has inherited political traditions. The latter was originally an untutored farmer who by his own ability rose to the leadership of his "Estate" in the Swedish Riksdag. When his father was a member of Congress, he usually had the boy with him in Washington. He is himself an able popular speaker and for a man of so little formal education he writes well. In his most recent book, *Of Flight and Life,* he renounces his earlier faith in science and appeals for a return to moral and spiritual values. That he was unwise in allowing himself to become a mouthpiece for the isolationists is clear, but during the Second World War he also rendered important services which some day may be fully known and acknowledged. Tragically tested, adulated and abused as few living men, he has gained a new outlook and a new philosophy.

Another American air specialist, born in the Middle West of Swedish parents, is Vice Admiral Charles E. Rosendahl, whose recent retirement from the Navy may be described as relative. He is still the country's leading expert in lighter-than-air dirigibles, the continued construction of which was decided in 1948 by Congress—a personal triumph for Rosendahl. "His faith paid dividends to his country in the war in helping to clear the German submarines from our coast and eventually from the Western Atlantic," wrote the New York *Times* editorially when he nominally retired in 1946. "He gave thirty-six years of unselfish service to the Navy. . . . Unhampered by the red tape and the bureaucratic inertia that sometimes afflict our armed services between wars, it may well be that Admiral Rosendahl, as a civilian, will be able to promote his specialty better out of service than he was ever able to in uniform."

Admiral Rosendahl was born in Chicago in 1892, both his parents having come from Sweden. His early boyhood was spent in Topeka, Kansas, and the latter part of it in Cleburn, Texas. He was graduated in 1914 from the Naval Academy, and after that he did sea duty during the First World War. In 1921 he returned to Annapolis as an instructor and in 1923 volunteered for special training on the first large rigid dirigible, the *Shenandoah,* which had been built in Germany as part of the war reparations. As one of its officers he was on board when it crashed during a storm in Ohio in 1925, breaking in two. By skillful navigation he landed one part safely, saving some members of the crew as well as himself. After that his fame became world-wide. The next year he was given command of the *Los Angeles,* which had also been built in Germany, and for three years he conducted training expeditions in various parts of the country, including the first non-stop flight to the Panama Canal and a safe landing on the aircraft carrier *Saratoga.* He was then put in charge of the Navy's rigid naval airship training with headquarters in Washington. In 1931 he was given command of the new airship *Akron* and, after a turn of sea duty on the battleship *West Virginia,* he became commanding officer of the Naval Air Station at Lakehurst, New Jersey, where he was in charge when the *Hindenburg* exploded May 6, 1937. On the old *Graf Zeppelin* he had flown around the world in 1929 and on the *Hindenburg* he had crossed the Atlantic four times. He has spent more time aloft on various lighter-than-air craft than any other American. During the Second World War he once more returned to sea duty and was promoted to Rear Admiral. In the Eastern Pacific battles he commanded the cruiser *Minneapolis.* When retired for physical disability he was promoted to Vice Admiral. As the country's leading proponent of dirigibles, which he regards as necessary for the national defense, he has made frequent lecture tours, written magazine articles and books, as well as appeared before Congressional committees to advocate continued construction regardless of the repeated disasters. In 1948 he finally won out. Among his books have been *Up Ship!* and *What About Airships* (1938). His interest in the historical background of the United States Navy as well as in his own background is indicated by his acceptance in 1948 of the presidency of the John Ericsson Society of New York.

Though civilian, an even more romantic career as an American aviator was that of the late Martin Elmer Johnson, companion-explorer of Jack London, and in his own right a famous photographer of wild life, naturalist and lecturer. Like both Lindbergh and Rosendahl he was born in the Middle West of Swedish stock. (His father, born in Stockholm, had been brought to America in his infancy.) He himself was a native of Rockford, Illinois. While still a boy, Johnson was taken by his family first to Lincoln, Nebraska, and then to Independence, Kansas. As a photographer he accompanied, in his 'twenties, Mr. and Mrs. London on their cruise in the *Snark* to the South Sea Islands, later described in a book by London. Then under the sponsorship of the American Museum of Natural History and in the company of his wife, the former Osa Helen Leighty, whom he had married in 1910, he circled the globe by air six times, flying his own planes. His films and lectures on the wild animal life of Africa, Borneo, and other faraway places made both of them known to thousands if not millions of people, all over the United States. On January 12, 1937, when he was fifty-three years old, Johnson was killed in an airplane crash in California. Mrs. Johnson recovered from her injuries and was able to continue their work. Among their books were *Camera Trails in Africa*. Their contention had always been that the jungle was safer than civilization.

The pioneer aviator of the northern route to Europe, which after the Second World War became a commonplace run, was Colonel Bert R. J. Hassell, another son of the Middle West born of Swedish parents. Though he crashed in Greenland on his projected flight from Rockford, Illinois, to Stockholm in 1928, he and his companion pilot, Parker Cramer, returned to America convinced that the northern route could be made safe. During the Second World War he was placed in charge of the Army Transport Command Base at Goose Neck Bay in Labrador and had the satisfaction of seeing his previous contention proved true. Even the wreck of his little plane, which he had named the *Greater Rockford,* was sighted on the Greenland ice cap by American Army fliers.

In many respects Hassell's early career resembled that of Colonel Lindbergh. He was born in 1893 at Marinette, Wisconsin, and his parents, who had come from the Swedish province of Värmland, later settled in Rockford, Illinois. In the late 'nineties they spent a few years in Sweden where the boy had his first schooling. He later attended both Rutgers and Valparaiso universities. When he was twenty years old he learned to fly an old Curtiss "one man pusher"—truly a "crate." For several years he was a test pilot, always a dangerous occupation. In 1913 and 1914 he was a stunt flier, touring the country, particularly its fair grounds, for circus performances. In 1914 he made an emergency landing in a Curtiss flying boat in Lake Michigan and thereby earned the nick-name "Fish." In 1915 he was employed by the United States Army as a civilian instructor in flying and in 1917, when the country had entered the First World War, he was appointed a second lieutenant in the Army Signal Corps. Throughout the war he served as an instructor and test pilot at McCook Field.

In 1919 he was discharged as a first lieutenant and placed in the reserve. He then, like Lindbergh, became an airmail pilot. In 1928, inspired by Byrd, Chamberlain and other trans-Atlantic fliers, as well as Lindbergh, he obtained backing from fellow Swedes in Rockford, Illinois, for a flight from that city to Stockholm. His first take-off in June 1928 ended in an almost immediate crash landing, the plane being overloaded with fuel, but by August he had his plane repaired and on the twenty-eighth set off again. Being off his course over Greenland and out of gasoline he made a safe landing on the ice cap and by walking over the glaciers for two weeks he and Cramer finally reached the arctic study camp of Professor William H. Hobbs of the University of Michigan and thus got home. Then after serving as a salesman for the Rockford Screw Products Corporation, largely owned and managed by Swedes, he once more entered active army duty early in 1942 and was assigned to the northern regions he had explored in 1928.

Another American veteran stunt flier, who was born in the Swedish province of Småland, is Aron Fabian "Duke" Krants, who for several years has been the chief pilot for the reporters of the New York *Daily News*. He came to the United States in 1915 when but fifteen years old and at first worked on a farm in Illinois. When the United States entered the First World War in 1917 he tried to enlist in the Air Corps, but was refused admission because he knew too little English and was not a citizen. By 1919 he had overcome both difficulties and became a sergeant at Kelly Field in Texas. A commission was refused him, however, because he lacked an American high school diploma. After leaving the Army in 1922 he became stunt performer for the Gates Flying Circus but not until 1928 did he obtain a license as a pilot. He then remained in the air for 177 consecutive hours, breaking a record established by the very same officer who had refused him a commission at Kelly Field in 1919. In 1934 he joined the *Daily News* and has since helped cover from the air many events such as the burning of the *Morro Castle*.

A pioneer American journalist of Swedish descent to specialize in aviation was John Gustaf Goldstrom, a native of Pittsburgh, Pennsylvania, who began flying in 1910 and twenty years later published *A Narrative History of Aviation*.

One of the first air stewardesses of Swedish ancestry was Clara Johnson, whose father was a native of Malmö, in southern Sweden. She once gained the distinction of being the first woman to fly a million miles. The roster of other Americans of Swedish descent who have helped place the United States ahead in aviation is a long one.

To the building of American planes the late Vincent Bendix made important contributions. He was president of the Bendix Aviation Corporation and as such produced many accessories such as landing gear, flying instruments and self-starters, etc. The annual race for the Bendix trophy which he donated is still one of the main competitive events in the air. Another manufacturer who was once himself a famous pilot is Captain Hugo Sundstedt, director of production for Air Parts, Inc., of Bridgeport, Connecticut. Born in Sweden in 1886, he made, in 1914, the first non-stop flight from Stockholm to Paris.

A postwar development in which many Americans of Swedish descent participated was that of the Scandinavian Air Lines in which Denmark and Norway as well as Sweden are combined. With the use of American-built planes, practically daily trips have been made in each direction between New York and the Scandinavian capitals. The first New York manager of the service was Tore Nilert. Traffic began in 1946 and in 1947 the line carried 12,555 persons to or from Europe. There is also a regular service from the Scandinavian countries to South America and other continents.

In a scientific and engineering achievement such as aviation, the Swedes in the United States were certain to take an important part, whether as pilots or manufacturers. Being inclined to make careful preparations, they have had a minimum of flying accidents. Colonel Lindbergh has been a typical example. In the civilian air traffic of the future they are likely to become more and more active. Of their prowess as military pilots the record of Major Richard I. Bong, chief American ace in the Pacific theatre of war, was an illustration.

XXXII

Businessmen

By nature a Swede is more inclined to be a producer than a trader; to him the making of goods is more congenial than their distribution. And yet he realizes that commodities have to reach consumers and in recent years more and more of the educated young men brought up in Swedish American homes have gone into business.

The early Swedish settlers on the lower Delaware were expected to develop, first of all, trade with the Indians. That New Sweden became an agricultural colony rather than a trading post, like New Amsterdam, was a reflection of both their capacities and their shortcomings. Since all attempts at trading were directed by the officials of the chartered Swedish-Dutch company, particularly by those of Dutch origin, the opportunities for private business enterprise were at first limited. This remained true also after the Swedes had taken over all the company shares and sent over Lieutenant Colonel Johan Printz as an official governor.

And yet there was a beginning of private business. Before long one Jonas Nilsson, who had come over with Governor Printz in 1643 as a soldier, built for himself a stone house at Kinsessing, now West Philadelphia, and in it he started a store in which he traded with the Indians as well as with his fellow colonists. Skins were the principal goods of the aborigines. This trading post was said to be the busiest spot in the colony until the arrival of William Penn in 1682. Nilsson may thus be regarded as the first Swedish businessman in America. He died in 1693, leaving seven sons and four daughters. Among his descendants are members of several prominent Philadelphia families: Jones, Chew, and Paxson.

During the remainder of the seventeenth and throughout the eighteenth century Sweden sent over to its former colony not only ordained clergymen, but also economic and scientific explorers such as Peter Kalm, who arrived in 1748 to look for dyestuffs and plants that might be useful in Finland and Sweden, and Baron de Hermelin, who came in 1782, principally to explore for minerals but also to investigate commercial opportunities.

The first individual Swedish businessman who came of his own accord for the express purpose of making money for himself was Henrik Gahn, who arrived in Philadelphia on May 13, 1794, in the company of Adolph Ulric Wertmüller, the Swedish artist who later painted a comparatively famous picture of George Washington. They had met in Cadiz, Spain, where a relative of Gahn was the Swedish Consul. What Gahn had in mind was colonization on a large scale, but after an exploratory trip through New York state and New England he gave up the idea and together with an American friend by the name of Mumford he opened a store in New York City, married an American girl, and as early as in 1796 became an American citizen. In 1797 he was appointed the first Swedish Consul in New York and throughout his life he kept in close contact with all visitors from his native country. Some of his descendants still reside in Brooklyn, according to Dr. Amandus Johnson in Volume IV of *The Swedish Element in America* (Chicago, 1934).

Swedish raw materials such as copper and iron were sent to America as early as 1648 and during the War for Independence when the revolutionists needed supplies from other European countries than England, Swedish naval stores such as tar and pitch as well as handwrought iron reached them through various ports on the Atlantic seaboard. Contemporary newspaper advertisements show that Swedish iron was for sale, for instance, at Providence, Rhode Island. The first commercial treaty between Sweden and the new United States signed in 1783 put the stamp of legality on a trade that had been going on for some time.

After that not only direct shipping and a certain exchange of goods continued, but a few individual Swedes, usually former sailors, began to settle and some of them set themselves up in business. Thus John Lindmark, who came to New York some time before 1817, and who for a while served as a sailmaker in the United States Navy, opened a retail store in lower Manhattan as a "victualler" and perfumer and eventually became wealthy. A great-grandson is now a dealer in rare books in Poughkeepsie, New York.

The career of S. M. Swenson as a business man in Texas and New York has been described in a previous chapter. Another early Swedish businessman in Texas was Anders Johan Nelson, who had been brought over by his parents in 1854. In the real estate and cattle business he was so successful that among his countrymen, who sometimes had to borrow money from him, he became known as "Rich Nelson." His sons, too, have carried on his enterprises.

The earliest known Swedish businessman in the Middle West was Raphael Widén, who as early as in 1814 was appointed a justice of the peace in St. Clair County, Illinois. He was also a politician and in 1826 was elected President of the Illinois State Senate. Between 1843 and 1846 Gustaf Flack, a former sailor and farmer, had a store near the Clark Street ferry landing in Chicago, and sometime after 1838 Olof Gottfrid Lange, also a former sailor, who had arrived in Boston in 1824, opened a drugstore in Chicago. Later he, too, began real estate promotion in Milwaukee and then became an insurance agent and finally an operator on the Chicago Board of Trade. Even more famous as a member of the Board of Trade was Robert Lindblom, who for thirty years was a civic and business leader in Chicago and at one time President of the Board. In 1864, when he was twenty-one years old, he had arrived from Sweden and before coming to Chicago in 1877 he had been a grain dealer in Milwaukee, Wisconsin. To the guarantee fund for the Columbian Exposition in 1892-93 he was able to pledge half a million dollars. A Chicago high school is named in his honor.

To the Pacific Coast the Swedes came early as sailors and then as gold seekers, first in California and then in Alaska. Their full story has not yet been written. An early fur trader, homesteader, lumber dealer, and finally banker on the Olympic peninsula in the state of Washington is K. O. Erickson, who since 1912 has lived at Port Angeles. Born in 1867 at Mora in Swedish Dalecarlia, he went to sea at the age of twelve, intending to become a gold prospector in Australia. After failing twice to get there, he finally rounded Cape Horn, reached his destination, but finding no gold continued to New Zealand, where he was equally unsuccessful. After three years "down under" he set out for Alaska and in the spring of 1888 reached Puget Sound, the gateway to the new gold fields. What he did after exploring the country was to charter a schooner and begin trading in furs with the Indians. Seal skins were his main source of income. In four different villages he established fur stores, calling the central one "Mora" in honor of his birthplace. He even learned the Indian language and in 1923 was made a member of the Quillayute tribe and honorary chief under the name of White Bear. For several years he was a County Commissioner in Washington and as such was able to get the first road built across the Olympics to the Pacific. At Port Angeles he founded a savings and loan association, the first bank of its kind in Calallam County. When he resigned the presidency in 1942 it had assets worth over half a million dollars. At the New Sweden Tercentenary in 1938 he officially represented both the state of Washington and the territory of Alaska. His fellow Swedes call him the "Dean of the Northwest."

In Alaska many Swedes as well as other Scandinavians have long been active not only as gold hunters, but as farmers, fishermen, missionaries and businessmen. The families that remained permanently at the Government-sponsored settlement at Matanuska, opened as a depression remedy in the early 1930s, were almost all of Scandinavian origin. Most of them had come from farms in Minnesota and adjoining states.

In many American cities and especially in Swedish American communities there are numerous retail stores run by Swedes, many dealing in Swedish food specialties, which in recent years have won a market outside Swedish circles. Swedish restaurants have likewise sprung up and they have benefited from the popularity of Swedish cooking. Not every *smörgåsbord,* however, is authentically Swedish. Over some of them, a young, disillusioned Stockholm newspaper correspondent in New York has suggested, a warning should be displayed: "All resemblance to Swedish food is purely accidental." Along the tourist highways one finds more and more Swedish coffee houses (*kaffestugor*) as well as overnight camps advertised as "Swedish"—a promise of cleanliness.

The Swedes are fond of good food and the production as well as the distribution of it is a natural specialty. One of the biggest food distributors in the Middle West, if not the country, was Carl A. Swanson of Omaha, President of C. A. Swanson & Sons, and known as the "Turkey King." He was born in 1879 in the Swedish province of Blekinge and arrived practically penniless in Omaha in 1896 when he was sixteen. In Sweden he had worked in a store but since he knew no English and had no other education, he had, at first, to do farm work and other menial chores. By driving a delivery wagon for commission houses he became acquainted with John Jerpe, a fellow countryman already in that business. In 1899 he became his partner and thirty years later, after both Jerpe and another partner by the name of Frank E. Elisson had died, the sole owner. The firm has buying stations in forty-two states and customers all over the country. Its employees number over 3,000 and the assets are valued at more than $4,000,000. During the recent World War practically every man in American uniform was served some of Swanson's canned turkey and other poultry products.

Mr. Swanson died in October, 1949, and was succeeded by his two sons. In Los Angeles a profitable Farmers' Market has been run for the past ten years by Roger Dahlhjelm, a native of Ortonville, Minnesota.

Many of the former Swedish immigrants soon learned how to combine with business their native love of flowers and a more or less scientific knowledge of plants. In various parts of the country they developed profitable nurseries. The pioneer in such work was the late P. S. Peterson of Chicago, popularly known as "Rosehill Peterson." He had been born in 1830 at Nöbbelöf in Skåne—the parish in which the first known Nobel first saw the light. There at an early age he had learned to be gardener and after emigrating in 1851 and coming to Chicago in 1854, he leased in 1856 a few acres of flat land which he imaginatively called The Rose Hill Nursery. When he died in 1903 it occupied five hundred acres and he himself was a millionaire. He was the first professional nurseryman in the Middle West and probably in the country. He was also reputed to have been the first in the country to master the art of moving large trees successfully.

In Chicago the two most important parks, the Lincoln and Union, were laid out and developed soon after the Civil War by two other natives of Skåne, Sven Nelson and Olof Benson, both born in the parish of Fjeckstad, in 1828 and 1837, respectively. In 1852 both came to Chicago and while Nelson at once engaged in the landscape and gardening work he had learned in Sweden, Benson became at first a typesetter. In the Civil War he enlisted early and served for three and a half years. When it was over he joined Nelson, who in 1865 had won a $1,500 prize from the city for the best lay-out of the two new parks. Both men then worked together on the parks as well as on other landscaping projects until in 1874 their partnership was dissolved and Benson became Park Superintendent for the city while Nelson continued in private work. In 1882 Benson retired, but lived until 1909. Another successful Chicago florist born in Sweden was the late William Adolphus Peterson, who ultimately became a banker.

In 1870 still another beauty-loving immigrant from Skåne, the late A. N. Pierson, arrived at Cromwell in central Connecticut, where he married a comely young widow who owned a house with some land and also had a little money. He was industrious, religious and business-like. By borrowing some more money he was able to build a little greenhouse on his wife's land and by degrees it grew until it covered 1,200,000 square feet and it is still growing, the largest establishment under glass in the country under individual ownership and management. During the

Easter month of 1948, for instance, the Pierson Nurseries shipped over a million roses, or as many as 84,000 on a single day, and, in addition, delivered 125,000 gardenias, 32,000 orchids and 38,000 potted flowering plants. From his development of so many new varieties of roses, and winning so many prizes at flower shows in New York, Pierson became known as the "Rose King of America." When he died in 1925 he was succeeded by his son, Wallace Pierson, who had become a state Senator in Connecticut. The business is still run by members of the same family.

Many other greenhouses and florist shops were started by Mr. Pierson and then turned over to men who had worked for him at Cromwell. The Rose Garden in Elizabeth Park in Hartford, Connecticut, which has been the official testing ground for the American Rose Society, was developed by three of Pierson's former pupils.

Many prizes for orchids have been won at the New York Flower Show by the Lager nurseries and greenhouses at Summit, New Jersey. They were started by the Swedish-born John E. Lager, who died in 1937 at the age of seventy-six. Before emigrating to America in the 1890s, he had studied horticulture in London and Paris and had taken part in orchid-hunting expeditions to South America. From a plant found in Colombia, he once developed a pure white blossom. Another time he sold an orchid plant for $10,000 to a European nursery which in turn sold it to Baron Aaron Irman Lambeau, who then kept it in his private hothouse.

Another originator of new flowers—roses and chrysanthemums—is the Swedish-born Ivar Ringdahl of Rome, New York, and in 1905 a Swede, Oscar Winberg, left Chicago to grow oranges in Alabama. There he became an authority on orange culture and is said to have sixty-five varieties in his groves.

A name often seen in flaming letters on American drugstores is "Walgreen." It originates from another farm boy, born of Swedish parents in Knox County, Illinois, and baptized Charles Rudolf Wallgren. While working in a shoe factory at Dixon, Illinois, he had his hand injured, and the physician who attended him suggested that he would be less handicapped working in a drugstore. When his hand had healed he did get such a job and without being especially interested in drugs, he became a successful retailer in other things people need in a hurry, such as sandwiches, soft drinks, coffee, cosmetics, notions, bandages, clocks, and the thousand other things sold in the modern American drugstore. When he started he was $5,000 in debt and his wife made the first sandwiches. He had observed the importance of

prompt and courteous service and before he died in 1939 his company
had over five hundred drugstores in thirty-one different states and
130 cities, as well as warehouses, ice cream plants, and laboratories,
serving 1,200 additional retailers. In 1939 he was succeeded as President
by his son, Charles R. Walgreen, Jr. As a successful businessman he
was shocked by the doctrines of Communism his daughter studied at
the University of Chicago, and as a result of a famous newspaper
controversy he set up at the University "The Charles R. Walgreen
Foundation for the Study of American Institutions."

The art of compounding drugs, in the strict sense of the word, fits
the Swedish temperament and many young men of Swedish ancestry
have become professional pharmacists.

Another line of business in which Swedes have been successful has
been the making and sale of clothing. Along Fifth Avenue in New
York the producers of made-to-order clothes for the most well-to-do
or most fastidious are apt to be Swedes, usually trained in London as
well as in Stockholm. One of them, Carl Victor Backstrom, used to
regard his tailoring of the suit Woodrow Wilson wore when inaugurated President as his crowning achievement. Fine boot making
is another specialty. Swedish cutters and designers are found in nearly
all factories. The "shoe-rebuilding" business of "B. Nelson" in New
York, which was once a one-man Swedish cobbler shop, has been taken
over by non-Swedish capitalists and expanded into a nationally advertised business.

In the making and retailing of ready-made as well as made-to-order
clothing, several Swedes have been successful. In Omaha Otto Swanson,
who in 1947 was elected President of The National Association of
Retail Clothiers and Furnishers, is the head of the Nebraska Clothing
Company. In Chicago Alfred Blomquist, who in 1893 arrived from
Småland, and then started as a journeyman tailor, became eventually
President of the H. M. Stevenson Company. In Boston Charles J. Erickson, who in 1885 came from the same province, and began as a cutter
for Dunne & Company on Washington Street, became in 1929 part
owner and President. Near by is the large clothing retail store of
Scott & Company, Ltd., occupying an entire building. Its owner and
general manager is Emil J. O. Danielson, a native of Stockholm, where
his father once had a clothing store on Drottninggatan. When sixteen
years old he accompanied his family to Kansas, where he attended
the University of Kansas at Lawrence. In 1894 he moved to Providence,
Rhode Island, and then to Boston where he first worked for the old-

time firm of Hibbard & Mason. Next he was invited by Collins & Fairbanks, another old Boston house, to join their new venture, Scott & Company, of which he gradually acquired the ownership. The firm has its own manufacturing plant in which all its clothes are made. "We sell nothing we do not make and make nothing we do not sell," is its slogan. In 1935 Mr. Danielson was appointed honorary Consul of Sweden and as such served several years. The present occupant of the post is Arthur J. Anderson, an insurance official and President of the Board of Trustees of Tufts College, of which he is a graduate.

In the business of retailing, the most prominent figure of Swedish origin is Walter Hoving of New York, former head of Lord & Taylor and an ex-President of the Fifth Avenue Association. Born in Stockholm, the son of Dr. Johannes Hoving, who later practiced in New York, he is a graduate of Brown University, where he once played football. He now heads an amalgamation of warehouses and department stores called The Hoving Corporation, which has been reported to have an annual turn-over of $150,000,000. Another retail executive is Edwin T. Chinlund, a former President of the Postal Telegraph Company, who became a vice president of the R. H. Macy Department Store in New York. In 1949 Göran Holmquist, formerly of Nordiska Kompaniet in Stockholm, was also appointed a vice president of Macy's.

Probably the leading American theoretician of retail selling is Professor Paul Henry Nystrom of Columbia University, a native of Wisconsin, who has been President of the Limited Variety Stores Association since 1934. He is a popular public speaker and a prolific writer. Among other publications, he is the author of *Economics of Retailing* which by 1930 had reached its third edition.

In the advertising business most of the Swedes have been technicians, i.e., artists, lay-out men and printers rather than contact men or general executives. The best known of the latter was Alfred W. Erickson, one of the founders of the large McCann-Erickson Agency in New York. He was born in 1876 at Farmers Mills, New York, where his father was a Swedish engineer. Later he attended schools in Brooklyn. At his death in 1936 the New York *Times* called him "a dominant figure in the American Association of Advertising Agencies." Once upon a time he had been advertising manager for McCutcheon's, the linen store on Fifth Avenue, and later for the Congoleum Company, the Barrett Roofing Company, etc. He was also one of the founders of the Audit Bureau of Circulation. In New York, Sigurd S. Larmon, whose father was a Swedish-born banker in Omaha, is President of the Young and Rubicam Advertising Agency, while George P. Johansen, publisher and owner of *Nordstjernan,* the New York Swedish-language weekly, is Vice President and part owner of the Peck Advertising Company and of its subsidiary, The Advertising Distributors of America. His grandfather, the original publisher of *Nordstjernan,* came from Småland.

A prominent Chicago advertising man is Charles S. Younggren, a native of Kansas, who traces his Swedish ancestry via Germany and Canada. He was once publisher of the *Kansas Farmer* at Topeka and later advertising and sales manager for the Case Plow Company of Racine, Wisconsin. An aviation officer in the First World War, he is a former President of the International Advertising Association. In St. Paul, Minnesota, Martin Trollen, a native of Lund in southern Sweden, is Vice President in charge of production at the Brown & Bigelow Corporation, an advertising and sales organization.

Printing is more of a Swedish specialty than advertising. It has back of it the inherited Swedish manual skill and love of detail and also a long and distinguished tradition in typography. Books printed in Sweden have a certain touch of elegance, each page being a pleasing composition. In Chicago the late Charles S. Peterson, once Treasurer of the city and chief backer of the Century of Progress Exposition in 1932–33, was a printer by trade. When he died he was Vice President and manager of the Inland Press. In the same city Charles J. Stromberg is President of the Stromberg-Allen Company, printers and lithographers. In Denver, Enoch Peterson, a native of Värmland, who is publisher of *Western News,* once a Swedish-language weekly, owns a large plant at which a number of other newspapers are printed. In San Francisco the twin brothers, Louis and Charles Traung, California-born sons of a Swedish sea captain who arrived in 1848, owned for many years the Stecher-Traung Lithograph Corporation. Their father lived to be ninety-four. In 1937, when the brothers were seventy, they visited Sweden together, both for the first time. In Brooklyn, New York, the late Eric Adolf Johnson, a native of Gothenburg, acquired in 1914 ownership of the Paragon Press, the largest Swedish American printing plant in the Greater City, and after his death in 1929 his two sons, Victor E. and Harold N., have run it. Another master printer is Axel Edward Sahlin of Buffalo, who was educated in Sweden. According to *The Inland Printer* for January, 1949, he has won twenty-five international prizes and a British medal for excellence in typography.

Most of the book publishing by and for Swedes in the United States has been done by their various religious organizations and they have naturally specialized in religious works and Swedish textbooks. In Chicago the Engberg–Holmberg Publishing Company, the founders of which had originally been publishers for the Augustana Synod, was incorporated in 1874 as an independent publishing firm and until its dissolution during the First World War not only imported and sold books printed in Sweden but also published several hundred titles of its own. Its members were Jonas Engberg and C. P. Holmberg. It was the first Swedish American publishing house. In 1911 the Swedish firm of Albert Bonnier of Stockholm opened a book store in New York, offering Scandinavian books of all kinds, and have kept it open ever since. Gradually it was expanded into a retail store for the sale of art and handicraft goods as well as American books in English.

Being meticulous and fond of detail, the Swedes have a natural aptitude for map making. The New York map man, *par excellence,* is Andrew G. Hagstrom, a native of Västergötland province in Sweden, of whose maps over a thousand are sold in the city daily. They include subway charts, tourist guides, and automobile maps. For the Standard Oil Company and its various affiliates and subsidiaries almost all road maps are made by the General Drafting Company of New York of which Otto Lindberg, a descendant of Sweden, via Finland and Russia, is President.

While in finance no American of Swedish descent has become nationally prominent, several have made notable careers as bankers. Their proverbial honesty and attentiveness to detail makes them ideal cashiers and, in various parts of the country, a number have risen to executive positions.

In Minnesota the first prominent banker of Swedish descent was the late Edgar L. Mattson of Minneapolis, a son of Colonel Hans Mattson, the Civil War officer, Secretary of State and immigration promoter. While his parents were in Sweden in 1871 on immigrant business, he was born, as his father had been, at Kristianstad in Skåne, but he grew up in Minnesota and at the age of nineteen began his career as a messenger in a local bank. Eventually he became President of the Midland National Bank and Trust Company of Minneapolis and at one time served as President of the Minnesota Bankers Association, not to mention other honors in both the United States and Sweden.

In Chicago the pioneer Swedish bankers were John R. Lindgren, the son of a former Swedish sailor who in 1849 had "washed for gold" in California, and then built up a shipping business in Chicago, and

Henry S. Henschen, a native of Brooklyn, whose father was a leader of the Swedish Methodist Church. In 1891 they formed the State Bank of Chicago, which ultimately went under during the depression that began in 1929. In succession, both men served as honorary Swedish Vice Consuls.

Since 1893 the firm of Nielsen & Lundbeck, originally composed of the late Sophus Nielsen, born a Dane, and G. Hilmer Lundbeck, a native of Uppsala, Sweden, has carried on a private banking business in New York, specializing in the transfer of funds between the United States and Sweden.

In Worcester, Massachusetts, George N. Jeppson, is Chairman of the Board of the Guaranty Bank and Trust Company, an outgrowth of the Scandia Credit Union which he helped organize in 1915. In 1948 its assets amounted to over $23,000,000. From 1941 to 1947 Nils Björk, originally the Treasurer of the Credit Union, was President of the bank. He was succeeded by Roland A. Erickson.

Since November, 1948, Joseph Austin Erickson, a native of Lynn, Massachusetts, has been President of the Federal Reserve Bank in Boston. Ellis G. Hult, who was born in Worcester, was already a Vice-President. Gustaf Magnuson is head of the Foreign Department of the Shawmut National Bank.

Though many Swedish immigrants participated in railroad construction, especially in the Middle West and the Northwest, and a large number of their descendants have since been employed by various railroad companies, none of them has as yet reached the presidency of any of the larger systems. Charles Edwin Carlson was, however, President of the Duluth, Mesabi & Iron Range Railway Company, and as such he received in 1944 the annual safety medal of the American Museum of Safety in recognition of the rate of accident reduction on that line. In Los Angeles, California, Nelson Kinell, a native of Sweden and the son of A. Kinell, a pioneer Swedish Lutheran minister in California, was appointed in 1920 an assistant general passenger agent of the Southern Pacific Railroad.

For many years Colonel Otto Fredrick Ohlson of Anchorage was general manager for the Government railroad in Alaska. He was born in the Swedish west coast province of Halland in 1870. In 1944 he was succeeded by another Swede, Colonel John F. Johnson, who in 1941 had been sent by the United States Army to Iran to organize its transportation system. In 1945 his experience as a railroadman was put to use during the invasion of the Lingayen Gulf in the Philippines.

In bus transportation, on the other hand, a top position has been won by Carl Eric Wickman, President of the Greyhound Lines. He is a native of Mora in Dalecarlia, and in 1904, at the age of seventeen, he came to the United States. His first job was in a sawmill in Arizona. He then found work in the iron mines at Hibbing, Minnesota, and during the First World War, when the miners were paid high wages, he opened a motor car agency and then hit on the idea of providing quick transportation for them by a "jitney" service which he began to operate with a single, secondhand automobile. From this idea grew the Greyhound bus system which now covers the country. From its center in Chicago, Mr. Wickman has kept his hand on all the subsidiary Greyhound companies in different regions and may, therefore, be called the *Bus King* of America. With him have been associated a number of other Swedes. Thus in 1933 Swan Reuben Sundstrom, also a native of Sweden, was elected President of the Pennsylvania Greyhound Lines.

In American water transportation the banner name of Swedish origin is that of the Matson Line, whose passenger liners have run between San Francisco and Honolulu since 1901. In West Coast shipping it is a pioneer organization. Its founder, William Matson, was of true Viking descent, being born in 1849 at Lysekil, an old fishing port on Sweden's west coast, from which many of the Northern sea marauders originally set out. Orphaned at an early age he went to sea for a year when he was only ten and before he was eighteen he reached New York on a sailing vessel, the *Aurora.* Three years later he rounded the Horn under canvas and thus reached San Francisco two years before the first transcontinental railroad was completed. The city then had only twenty-five thousand inhabitants and no cable cars were running. When he was twenty-one he set out for the North Pacific as captain of a schooner, the *William Frederick,* and a few years later he had his own scow schooner, the *Mission Canal,* in which he trafficked between San Francisco and the Puget Sound ports. His next goal was the Hawaiian Islands and in 1882 he commanded as part owner the *Emma Claudina,* a three-masted two-hundred tonner, carrying general merchandise outbound and, on the return trip, raw sugar, pineapples, coffee and hides. In 1877 he had built a brigantine, the first *Lurline,* a name since borne by three successive vessels of different types, the latest being a luxury liner of the highest rank. As the traffic with Honolulu grew, both in freight and passengers, more and more ships were added, and when Captain Matson died in 1917 he was a millionaire.

His *Rhoderick Dhu* was the first sailing ship to be equipped with electric lights and a cold storage plant. In ten days it regularly made Hilo, in Hawaii. His first steamship, the *Enterprise,* bought in 1902, was the first off-shore ship on the Pacific to burn oil instead of coal, as his *Hilonian* was the first on the Pacific to use wireless telegraphy, and the *Maui,* built in 1917, was the first to use a gyro pilot and compass. His use of oil as fuel put him in conflict with the railroads which refused to deliver the oil. He then built the first California pipeline from his own oil wells at Santa Maria to the coast. Next he constructed a much longer line from Coalinga to Monterey and was thus able to deliver, for the first time, fuel oil to North Pacific and Alaskan ports. In 1905 he sold his oil wells for $3,450,000.

New York is served by many freight lines from Sweden and also by the Swedish American Line which specializes in passengers. It was not organized until 1915; so that throughout the peak period of emigration, Sweden had no steamship line of its own to America. During the Second World War its motor liner, *Kungsholm,* which had become popular as a cruise ship to the West Indies, was sold to the American Government as a troop ship and when it was over was bought back for the Italian–South American service. At various times during the war its older sister-ship the *Gripsholm* was used to exchange disabled war prisoners as well as to carry diplomats and repatriate Americans from the Far East. It was justly called a "mercy ship." From 1915 until nearly the end of the Second World War, G. Hilmer Lundbeck was the American managing director and in 1944 he was succeeded by his son, G. Hilmer Lundbeck, Jr.

Tourist travel to Sweden has been fostered since 1920 by the semi-officially sponsored Swedish National Travel Office, of which Birger Nordholm is the manager. Since the beginning of the Second World War the Bureau has also distributed documentary films about Sweden. The best Swedish entertainment films have been circulated in the United States for the past thirty years by Ernest Mattson, President of Scandia Films of New York. Recently Swedish features have also been imported by Rudolph Carlson, likewise of New York.

Since 1907 importers of Swedish goods, chiefly wood pulp and metals, have been organized in the Swedish Chamber of Commerce of the U.S.A. At the end of the Second World War it set up a subsidiary in San Francisco. Since 1926 Oscar G. Marell, formerly editor of its *Swedish American Trade Journal,* has been secretary and general manager. As a successor to the *Trade Journal,* the Chamber publishes the *American Swedish Monthly*. The first President of the Chamber was A. E. Johnson, a former land commissioner for a railroad in Minnesota, and later a general steamship passenger agent, with offices in New York, Chicago and Minneapolis. In 1898 his firm took over the American agency for the now defunct Scandinavian American Line, a Danish concern. When he died in 1919 he was seventy-eight. In 1916 he was succeeded as head of the Chamber by John Aspegren, who in 1912 had been elected President of the New York Produce Exchange, "the first foreign-born and the youngest man to head that organization." When Aspegren suddenly died in 1924 at the age of forty-eight he was followed by G. Hilmer Lundbeck, who held the office for twenty years. His successor was Nils R. Johaneson, a pulp importer, born in Stockholm. The senior Vice President is Alex J. Pagel, President of Pagel, Horton & Company, also importers of wood pulp and other goods. He, too, was born in Stockholm, but came to the United States as a boy and was graduated from the University of Pennsylvania. Another Vice President is Elon V. Ekman, Board Chairman of the Electrolux Corporation, manufacturers of the air cleaner known by that name, and a director of Servel, Inc., which makes the silent, gas-burning Electrolux refrigerator—a Swedish invention. Sigfrid K. Lonegren, a member of the Chamber, born and educated in Sweden and a resident of New Jersey, was an American naval officer and a diplomatic representative in Stockholm during the Second World War. He is an importer and manufacturer of Swedish wallpaper. One of the founders of the Chamber was Colonel Hans Lagerloef, whose honorary title was bestowed on him by the Seventh Regiment of the New York National Guard. He is a second cousin of Selma Lagerlöf, the famous Swedish writer, and in his own right a noted philatelist whose stamp collections have won many prizes.

As retailers, importers, bankers, steamship men, advertising and transport executives, a considerable number of former Swedish immigrants and their sons have made their mark in America. While some of them have become quite wealthy, they have not so far been able to follow in the steps of the Carnegies, the Russell Sages, or the Rockefellers as large-scale benefactors of either humanitarian or educational activities. The late Carl Gustav Swebelius, the arms manufacturer of New Haven, who in 1948 left his estate of three and a quarter million dollars for research work on cancer and epilepsy, was an exception. While several have given considerable sums to various good causes, especially churches and hospitals, they have as a rule been rather indifferent to cultural needs. In education, in particular, they have so far retained the Swedish tradition that the community, rather than the individual, no matter how affluent, should carry the burden. At the same time, there are no more ardent champions of private enterprise than American capitalists of Swedish origin.

XXXIII

CHARITIES AND OTHER ORGANIZATIONS

Since time immemorial the Scandinavians have been taught to stand on their own feet. Only in a case of extreme necessity will they solicit charity for themselves. The typical Scandinavian is no parasite, and to avoid beggary he usually saves something for a rainy day. But at the same time he has an instinctive sense of mercy and responsibility for the needy who suffer through unfortunate circumstances. Nor would a Northerner in a foreign land, except in a dire emergency such as the cholera epidemics in the 'fifties, expect aid from anyone outside his own ethnic group.

Consequently, when the Swedish pioneers in their American dugouts and cabins encountered unforeseen difficulties, they naturally first sought help from their neighbors. If the parents in a struggling Swedish family died, for instance, their neighbors unhesitatingly provided a home for the children. It is not surprising, therefore, that in addition to the building of churches and schools, the Swedish pioneers began early to establish orphanages, hospitals, hospices, and old folks' homes, institutions which, though founded by settlers of Swedish stock, and usually by members of the same denomination, are now in most cases practically undenominational and in all respects wholly American. And, whether religious, social, fraternal, or professional, in origin, all the organizations founded by Swedish settlers in America have justified their existence.

Of the many social service institutions founded by Swedes in the United States we can name only a few: The Immanuel Deaconess Institute of Omaha, Nebraska; the Children's Home of New Britain, Connecticut, organized by the late Reverend J. E. Klingberg, who later established another home in Chicago; the Augustana Home for the Aged, Chicago; The Bethany Home and Hospital, St. Paul, Minnesota; the Lutheran Hospital of Moline, Illinois; the Emanuel Hospital of Portland, Oregon; the Swedish Hospital of Seattle, Washington;

Fairlawn Hospital, in Worcester, Massachusetts; and the Swedish Lutheran Immigrant Home of New York which in the heyday of immigration served to greet the incoming Swedes. Besides founding a number of colleges and theological schools, the churches have engaged in a diversified social welfare and charity program that covers almost every phase of human needs.

"Aside from national federations," writes Julius Lincoln, in *Swedes in America* (p. 144), "a large number of local and special organizations have knit Swedish Americans together for laudable aims. . . . In them power is generated and stored, ready for release whenever a call comes for action in behalf of the public good. Social clubs for the preservation of quaint, colorful customs and old-time memories —singers' unions, orchestras, art clubs, athletic associations, historical societies, literary guilds, political leagues, engineering societies, crafts circles, press associations—cover almost the entire range of physical and mental activities. Without these diversified bodies and societies, there would not now be the story to tell of a people in America that, in per capita support of educational and charitable institutions, stand close to the top."

The Swedes have promoted all types of security and protection, whether from death, sickness, or the elements of nature. Mutual fire, hail, and storm insurance companies have flourished in Swedish American centers. In the Middle West there was, for example, the Swedish American Fire Insurance Company of Kansas, a corporation which, incidentally, had not encountered during the fifty years of its existence prior to 1938, "a single suspected case of arson." The Mutual Life Insurance Company of Illinois—formerly the Scandinavian Mutual Aid Association of Galesburg—counts its obligations in force in nine figures, and the Swedes have been a strong factor in the Lutheran Brotherhood Life Insurance of Minnesota. Building, loan, and savings associations are "favored mediums of reaching a stable status," and cooperative societies, based on Swedish and other Scandinavian models, are particularly common among American farmers with a Swedish background.

It might be mentioned, too, that to keep track in some measure of their history and preserve the record of their achievements in the United States the Americans of Swedish descent have founded several historical societies—in Rockford and Rock Island, Illinois; in St. Peter and Minneapolis, Minnesota; in Seattle, Washington; and in several other places. The outstanding organization of this type, besides the Swedish Colonial Society with headquarters in Philadelphia, is The

American Swedish Historical Foundation of that city, which publishes a *Year Book* and directs the activities of the American Swedish Historical Museum, which was founded in 1926 and managed for many years by Dr. Amandus Johnson. His successor was Dr. Marshall W. S. Swan, who is of mixed Swedish and New England colonial ancestry, a graduate of Harvard and a former Assistant Professor of English at Tufts College. In 1949 he got leave of absence to join the State Department.

Among the directors of Swedish American charitable institutions, we must mention the Reverend Axel C. H. Helander, formerly Superintendent of the Swedish Lutheran Immigrant Home of New York, who retired in 1947 at the age of seventy-six, after thirty-three years of service in behalf of his immigrant countrymen. Thousands of them have been met and comforted at Ellis Island by this clergyman from Småland, who during the First World War was the only Lutheran missionary of any nationality to be admitted to that "island of tears," and—hope.

There is one more name that will live in the history of charity: a welfare worker of international scope who was born in St. Petersburg, where her father was the Swedish Minister to Russia, and who late in life became a resident of the United States, Mrs. Elsa Brändström-Ulich of Cambridge, Massachusetts. She was known the world over as the "Angel of Siberia" because of her relief work among the prisoners of war in that region during the First World War; as well as for her humanitarian labors in Germany after that war was over, such as the establishment of orphanages and workmen's institutions for returning prisoners; and, in America, for her labor in the interest of war refugees in general and of the Finnish Relief and "wings for Norway" in particular. A recipient of many international honors, she was one of the first three international figures—the others being John R. Mott, President of the World's Committee of the Y.M.C.A., and Brigadier General Sir John Kennedy of Great Britain, to receive in 1945 the "Prince Carl" gold medal established by King Gustaf V of Sweden in honor of his brother's forty-year service as head of the Swedish Red Cross to be given for "effective national or international humanitarian activity." She died in 1948 at the age of sixty.

Besides the church, welfare, and historical institutions, several fraternal orders have been established by Swedish immigrants and their descendants. Their welfare work has also been impressive. Among these is the Scandinavian Fraternity of America, in which the Swedes have played a major role. It has 206 lodges in various parts of the

United States. This Fraternity pays out "approximately $150,000 per year" in sick and death benefits.

The Independent Order of Svithiod, founded by Swedes in 1880, has during its existence paid out over five million dollars in pecuniary aid. Its present financial resources are over two million, and for its members the Order maintains an old people's home at Excelsior, Minnesota. In the fall of 1944, this Order sponsored a special War Bond drive for $175,000 to purchase a hospital sea plane for the Navy.

The Independent Order of Vikings is another benefit society, organized by American Swedes in 1899. It issues so-called benefit certificates in amounts of from $100 to $1,000.

The largest Swedish American benefit organization is the Vasa Order, which has a membership of over fifty thousand. It is primarily a benevolent society, founded in Connecticut in 1896, but its program is also fraternal and cultural. The number of its lodges in 1946 was 408 in America and nine in Sweden. Its assets amount to nearly two million dollars, and the Order has, in addition, an old age fund of about a quarter of a million.

Many Swedes have joined the Masons, Odd Fellows, and other American fraternal orders. Even the American branch of the International Order of Good Templars which was introduced by Americans to Sweden in 1879 has in recent years been dominated by members who are of Swedish origin. The Grand Lodge in Sweden has the largest membership in the world.

Among the business organizations the Swedish Chamber of Commerce of the U.S.A., established in 1907, serves as a commercial link between Sweden and the United States. Its headquarters are in Rockefeller Center, New York, and it has a subsidiary office in San Francisco. Professional societies include the American Society of Swedish Engineers, New York, founded 1888, the purpose of which is the "promotion of the arts and sciences connected with engineering and mechanical construction." It awards biennially the John Ericsson medal, and for forty years has published a technical and news *Bulletin*. Since 1946 its President has been Arvid Lundquist. To commemorate the life of the best known Swedish engineer in America, the John Ericsson Society has been organized in New York City. Its President for 1948 was Vice Admiral C. E. Rosendahl and its all but perpetual secretary, E. T. Thygeson, an attorney at law. Societies of Swedish engineers are also to be found in Pittsburgh and Chicago.

Svenska Societeten (The Swedish Society), founded in 1836, was primarily charitable in its original purpose. It is the oldest Swedish society in New York, and probably in the United States. Since 1946 its President has been Birger Lagerlöf. The Swedish Beneficial Society, as it is called in English (*Svenska Föreningen*), of Philadelphia, of which Albin Pearson was President in 1948, has been in existence for over seventy years, and is also a social service club. In cities like Chicago and San Francisco the Swedes have impressive social clubs. In other cities, such as Hartford and New Haven, Connecticut, there are even Swedish Junior Leagues.

The American Swedes have, also, several societies that are primarily cultural. In addition to singers' and artists' organizations, gymnastic clubs and historical societies, there is, for example, an active Swedish Journalist Association of America (*Svenska Journalistförbundet i Amerika*), the President of which is E. Einar Andersson of Chicago, editor and publisher of Svenska Amerikanaren, the most widely read weekly. Institutes of Swedish culture are found in Rock Island, Illinois (Dr. Conrad Bergendoff, President), and Minneapolis, Minnesota (C. A. Anderson, President), both of which are national organizations, publishing valuable annuals. The *American Swedish Handbook,* issued biennially by the Augustana Institute of Swedish Culture, at Rock Island, is especially commendable. The Swedish Cultural Society of America (*Svenska Kulturförbundet*), organized in 1910, boasts of thirteen chapters and aims to "support and work for the preservation of the Swedish language and culture among the Swedes and their descendants in America." Its national President is Professor E. Gustav Johnson of North Park College, Chicago. Several of its officers, such as E. J. Vickner, Frans Ericsson, Joshua Larson, Erik Wahlgren, and Gösta Franzén have done splendid work in preserving some of their Swedish cultural heritage. The Society for the Advancement of Scandinavian Study, founded 1911, which publishes the *Scandinavian Studies and Notes,* is purely scholarly. Its Secretary-Treasurer for a generation was Professor Joseph Alexis of the University of Nebraska, an educator and linguist of Swedish parentage.

Most important of all organizations involving cultural exchange between Sweden and the United States is the American Scandinavian Foundation of New York, founded in 1911 by Niels Poulsen who was of Danish origin. The President in 1948 was Lithgow Osborne, former American Ambassador to Norway. Its first Secretary and later its President for many years was Henry Goddard Leach, who edits *The American Scandinavian Review* and other publications. By 1945 one hundred and eleven fellowships had been awarded to American graduate students for study in Sweden alone, and 392 Swedish Fellows had been sent by the corresponding Swedish Foundation in Stockholm for studies in America. Among the seventy volumes of literary classics, biographies, critical works, and travelogues published by the Foundation under the editorship of the late Hanna Astrup Larsen and others, a proportionate share have related to Sweden. The trustees of the Foundation who are of Swedish extraction were in September 1949, Conrad Bergendoff, Nils R. Johaneson, and G. Hilmer Lundbeck, Jr.

The keynote of all these activities organized by the former immigrants from Sweden is self-reliance. "Your best helper is yourself" (*själv är bästa dräng*) is an old Swedish proverb which for centuries has been drilled into the minds of the young. What effect the modern social welfare provisions will have on the people's character remains to be seen. Whatever it may be, the fact still persists that when a great majority of the immigrants left Sweden this system had not been started, and when they arrived in the United States social security legislation had not been thought of. "Root, hog, or die" was then the slogan. The notion that the Government should save anyone from starving was regarded as pure anarchism. Against the vicissitudes of illness, accidents, fire, floods and storms, as well as death and high funeral costs, the Swedish people in the United States as well as in Sweden itself continue to carry more and probably higher insurance per capita than any other group in the world.

XXXIV

SPORTS

The Swedish interest in gymnastics and other forms of physical exercise follows logically upon activities in sports that are centuries old. The ancient Scandinavians were taught early, in part because of necessity, to ski, hunt, shoot, row, swim, jump, wrestle, and ride horses. They had to be fleet of foot and dexterous in both martial and manual pursuits. They were trained to think fast in critical moments, to meet danger without fear, and to be ever ready for defense or attack. Their fighting instinct was strong, and games and athletic contests helped train their minds and bodies for possible war. The Vikings were said to have been able to catch a javelin in flight, and to keep pace with a horse in full gallop; we know they were experts with the sword as well as with the bow and arrow. Ball games were popular, particularly a game played on ice, which required great skill. Gradually the necessary development of hard muscles, self-control, precision, and dauntlessness, was obtained through mere voluntary exercise carried on for sheer pleasure and sportsmanship. And so, today, the Swedes take an enthusiastic interest in sports for the mere fun of the pastime. Sweden won the Olympic Games in Stockholm in 1912, and in 1948 ranked next to the United States in London. Per capita of population it scored the greatest number of points.

In America the Swedes "take part in the same sports as are enjoyed in their native land, and also new ones for which they are suited. They make excellent wrestlers, long-distance runners, and cross-country skiers. They take naturally to weight events (javelin, hammer, discus): they make sure marksmen, skilled equestrians, good bicyclists, fine soccer and rugby players. At swimming, sailing, and rowing, they are adept." To these sports the following have been added, in America: bowling, football, basketball and baseball. Most college teams in any sport have their share of players of Swedish descent if such students are enrolled at all; and when "Swede" So-and-So takes part in a contest the players on the other side have their hands full unless their team boasts a still bigger "Swede."

Sweden has produced some exceptionally strong men, and stories about their prowess border on the fantastic. Not only have they bent iron bars and lifted heavy weights, but they are alleged to have made corkscrews out of horseshoes and "driven long nails through wooden planks with bare hands." Swedes are very proud of such feats. There was for example, one Anders Anderson who exhibited his muscular stunts in America in the 'nineties, and who was so strong he literally had no idea how powerful he was. He couldn't be a brakeman, because he broke the brakes. "He handled big logs in the woods as though they were twigs, and he could hold three people suspended from each arm." Everywhere he performed stunts which no one could duplicate, one of which was to "lift five hundred pounds from the ground with one finger" wrote Gerhard T. Rooth in *Swedes in America*.

Probably the most outstanding among such Swedish mastodons in the United States was the wrestler Hjalmar Lundin who was for many years the undefeated champion of New York. He had started out as a professional "giant" in Ringling Brothers' circus, one of his exploits being to lift twenty men on a platform placed on his chest. But it was in wrestling that he achieved his greatest triumph. He was the only one who ever won a fall from the world champion, Frank Gotch. Rooth mentions twenty-two other Swedish American wrestlers, including Johan Richthoff who was a double Olympic champion.

Several Swedes have made good in boxing, but they have not as yet won any world's championships. The required speed and agility does not usually come with the Swedish temperament. An example was Harry Persson, a heavyweight, who reached the semi-finals in the first Dempsey-Tunney bout at Philadelphia in 1926. But take the sport of tug-of-war. Requiring brawn and staying power, the Swedes excel in it. A team of American Swedes was organized in 1888 and then took part in many contests in the old Madison Square Garden, New York. Teams were formed all over the country, "with the heavy, husky Swedes in greatest demand." One such team from New Britain, Connecticut, was champion of New England for several years. In 1897, to cite an outstanding example, the world championship tug-of-war contest was held in San Francisco, with ten nations competing. The finalists were Canada and Sweden, with Canada the favorite. But the Swedes won; they had as anchor-man, one "Power" Anderson from

Öland, who simply could not be moved by anyone under any circumstances. He could hold his own, it was said, against any three men.

A game suited to the Swedish disposition is soccer football, and the Swedes in America have helped popularize the sport. Some, also, have taken to the national game of baseball. Fred Lindstrom was one of the best third basemen in baseball history. The lanky Earl ("Swede") Johnson of the Red Sox is well known, and so is Johnny Lindell, left fielder of the New York Yankees. "Rube" Walberg was an all-time pitching star. In basketball we have, for example, Lieutenant Gus Broberg of Dartmouth, once an all-American star, who lost his right arm in the Second World War.

American football suits the Scandinavian physique and many Americans of Swedish parentage have done well in it. In former days, we heard about "Swede" Youngstrom from Dartmouth, "Pug" Lund from Minnesota, who may in fact have been of Norwegian ancestry, "Hank" Anderson from Notre Dame, and the late Captain Emery E. Larson, coach at Annapolis and later colonel in the United States Marine Corps. In 1948 his son and namesake played football at Yale. In 1946 Commander Oscar E. Hagberg, U.S.N., was head football coach at the Naval Academy at Annapolis. Republican ex-Congressman Frank L. Sundstrom of New Jersey was in 1923 an all-American tackle on the Cornell team.

Swedes have achieved even greater distinction in track and field athletics, especially in the long-distance events. There have been several good Swedish marathon runners, like John Svanberg, a first-class athlete, who finished second in the first Olympic Games at Athens in 1906, and who later came to America where he turned professional. Ernest Hjertberg, who had received his training in this country, won in New York "The First Race of the Century" at midnight, December 31, 1899, a widely heralded victory at the end of his running career. Later he became a celebrated coach. The Boston miler Oscar F. Hedlund represented the United States in the 1908 Olympics, as did also Frank Danielson and John Lindquist. Among other American Olympic athletes of Swedish descent was the discus thrower, Robert W. Edgren, who later became a famous cartoonist and a prominent New York sports writer. In jumping we find, among others, Egon R. Erickson, Olympic high jumper for the United States in 1908 and 1912; and Eric Almloef, another participant in Olympic field events, who won prizes in 1912 and 1920. In recent years middle distance runners from Sweden such as Gunder Hägg and Lennart Strand have made track history in the United States.

That Scandinavians should take to water sports was well nigh inevitable and here American girls of Swedish blood have especially come to the fore: Martha Norelius, Olympic swimming champion, and in her prime winner of several world records; Greta Johanson, another Olympic champion; and Marjorie Gestring, who at the age of thirteen won an Olympic title for the United States (1936), and several others. Hjalmar Johanson was an Olympic champion in diving, and Fred Spongberg, an Olympic prize winner in the same sport. In rowing, sailing, and yachting the Swedes have done very well. Many members of the university crews from the state of Washington, for example, have been of Swedish extraction. Paul Knapplund, six feet and three inches tall, was Captain of the 1948 Harvard Varsity crew. The sturdy yachts which for over eighty years have successfully defended America's cup have "in substantial part been manned by sailors of Swedish or Norwegian origin." The first mate on *Ranger,* the successful defender of the cup in 1937, for instance, was Vilhelm Karstens, a Swede from Norrköping.

Swedes, like the Norwegians, have been pioneers in winter sports. Among them has been Siegfrid Steinwall, who continues to give ski-jumping exhibitions though over fifty. Many outstanding skiers in the Northwest, the Middle West, and New England are of Swedish lineage, but the Swedish athletes are probably even better known on the ice. Gillis Grafström of Stockholm, three times Olympic winner in fancy skating, has several times exhibited his graceful talent in America. So has Vivi-Ann Hultén, who in the 1930s charmed thousands of Americans with her performances. And we need only mention that the producers and in many program numbers the principal performers in the *Ice Follies,* are three Americans of Swedish stock—Oscar Johnson and Roy and Eddie Shipstad. Many other skaters of Scandinavian blood have been associated with them in some of the most original, difficult, and delightful entertainment in America.

A popular sport in Sweden is bicycling, which the Swedish immigrants have continued in America. John S. Johnson was once the world's champion bicyclist and considered one of the best athletes of his day. In 1893, at Independence, Iowa, he rode a mile in 1:56, beating a competing horse. Among numerous other bicyclists of Swedish extraction was the colorful Tillie Anderson. She was an extremely fast and popular rider, who, at the end of the nineteenth century, often defeated competitors of the opposite sex.

Swedes also make good horsemen, especially the cavalry officers, and are keen supporters of equestrian sports. At the New York horse shows military teams from Sweden have won many prizes. Of the American-born Swedes, Captain C. Westlund of the American Army has made a name for himself in polo.

Other branches of sport in which the American Swedes have participated with more or less success are: archery, in which the leading figure has been the former brigadier general of the British Army, Ivar Thord-Gray, of Greenwich, Connecticut, who has formed clubs and helped to increase interest in this ancient sport; golf, represented by the well-known Patty Berg of Minneapolis; bowling; billiards; and rifle shooting. While Karl Schroeder of Stockholm has won two American championships in tennis, the authors cannot remember any high-ranking American-born Swedish tennis player. However, the Swedes are fond of tennis, including the world's oldest, most serious, and certainly most advertised player, "Mr. G." as King Gustaf is known the world over. The Swedes were tennis champions of Europe in 1946, but in competition for the Davis Cup lost to the United States.

Notable among the patrons of Swedish American sport have been Colonel Hans Lagerloef and the late Charles K. Johansen, both of New York City.

Lieutenant Commander Ralph Harold Colson, USNR, of Matapan, Massachusetts, who for fifteen years had followed the athletic performances of the American Swedes, had compiled by 1946 a list of about 1,800 Swedish American athletes. In 1943 in football alone, he had identified among over six hundred different college teams—sixty-five Johnsons, forty-four Andersons, twenty-five Petersons, twenty Nelsons, fifteen Pearsons, and so on. Charles Pearson, Dartmouth, '42, was captain of both the football and the basketball teams. The late John Murphy, star football end for Notre Dame, was half Swedish. So was Bill O'Laughlin. It is interesting to note that intermarriages between Swedes and Irish have produced many good athletes. As football coaches Swedes have been popular in the United States. Andy Gustafson, a former Pittsburgh star, once coached football at West Point (and later at Miami University). At the end of 1948 he coached the all-Southern team. Nils ("Swede") Nelson, Harvard, '20, played fullback on the Harvard team which then beat Oregon (7-6) in the Rose Bowl, and next coached the Harvard backfield for several years; Walter Holmes, all-American fullback for Northwestern (1929-30), was later football coach at Boston University.

Incidentally Mr. Colson himself is a former athlete of parts. Once a University of Pennsylvania star track man, he is now assistant supervisor of physical education in Massachusetts, and has acted as recreation and athletic officer at the South Boston Navy Yard. He once established a new world's record for the sixty-yard dash.

Among the sports writers, working for the Swedish American as well as the Swedish press, two men have especially distinguished themselves, Gerhard T. Rooth, already quoted, and Einar Thulin, the latter being a former all-round athlete himself, and now a full-time New York correspondent for *Aftonbladet* of Stockholm, Sweden's oldest popular newspaper, while Mr. Rooth is an editor of *Nordstjernan,* the New York Swedish-language weekly. On various occasions he has managed American track teams in Sweden and Swedish teams of different kinds in the United States.

Being as a rule physically sturdy, the Swedes in the United States have contributed considerably to the country's achievements in sports. They are fond of outdoor life and often take part in sailing, mountain climbing, fishing, hunting, and camping. As a rule they know how to take care of themselves in the open. Some of them have become highly skilled at billiards and other games requiring physical precision.

XXXV

THE CHARACTER OF AMERICANS FROM SWEDEN

On the basis of testimony from a variety of sources, foreign as well as domestic, Kendrick C. Babcock wrote in 1914 in *The Scandinavian Element in the United States:* "It is generally admitted that physically, morally and socially, no better class of immigrants than the Scandinavians enter the United States." Let us examine the foundation for this assertion, in so far as it applies to the Swedes.

First of all, like the Pilgrims, they had the true pioneer spirit, i.e., a readiness to bear all the toil and hardship involved in the settlement of a new and undeveloped land. In the early days they knowingly risked life itself. Since Viking times the Scandinavians have shown an unusual adaptability to new environments, and this was particularly true of the Swedes who settled in America. Furthermore, their Americanism is sincere; without mental reservations they have been loyal to the land which adopted them. Nor has Sweden itself ever laid any claim to their political allegiance.

Since everyone wants freedom, provided he can make his own interpretation of it, there is little real honor in cherishing it, but it should be emphasized that most Scandinavians, including the Swedes, associate freedom with a sense of responsibility and are willing to pay a high price for its privileges, whether social, religious or political.

With a love of liberty, and, conversely, with all forms of resistance to coercion, goes a degree of individualism and independence of thought, which in the case of the Swedes makes them both conservative and progressive. Nor are these qualities, in their case, necessarily contradictory. The northerners do make haste slowly.

While they are eager to invent and try new things and particularly alert to learn about new scientific discoveries, they are apt to question new theories and will not follow the first crackbrained innovator. As a rule, they try all new ideas with caution. Some of them will listen to strange religious doctrines, but the majority are conservative in such matters too. If in politics a so-called "idealistic" leader were to undertake to introduce some new system or philosophy under the label of "liberalism" or "progressive measures," or "new Americanism," he would not get very far with citizens of Swedish descent if his program seemed to them contrary to the basic tenets of the present political ideology. Like the man from Missouri, the Swede will have to be shown that the new scheme would be better than the *status quo*. This attitude may at times border on stubbornness, but it may also be a salutary mingling of stability with stolidity.

"It is very disconcerting," once said an American Army officer of Irish descent, who during the First World War had trained infantrymen at Camp Grant, in Illinois, "to face a squad of Swedish farm boys from Minnesota; you never can tell what they think. But that does not mean," he added, "that they don't think. I soon found that out."

Traditionally the Swedes are reputed to be less democratic in their ways than their fellow Scandinavians, but this difference has completely disappeared in America, if it ever existed there. Among the lower social classes from which most of the immigrants were recruited it probably never was found in Sweden either. Among the American Swedes who have become more than average well-to-do, some such slumbering ancestral traits may emerge on certain occasions, but if they do, they do not differ in essence or degree from the "airs" of the average American dollar magnate. The typical Swedish aloofness is principally due to their innate shyness, which on closer acquaintance soon melts away. "The Swedes are like fire logs," an American woman once remarked. "Outwardly rough, they have much warmth stored up inside." The late William Seabrook compared them in *These Foreigners* to electric stoves or violinists—"slow to heat up, but very hot when they do get warm."

In politics they are, as a rule, independent individualists, rather than loyal party members. No Swedish party boss has ever been able to deliver their vote. Their tendency is conservative, but they are not always rock-bound Republicans. On the slavery issue they supported Lincoln, but when Theodore Roosevelt split the Republican Party in 1912, they followed him too. In the Northwestern states they voted in large numbers for the Farmer-Labor candidates and to win them back the Republican Party needs to become more progressive. Conversely, if the Democratic Party should seem to them too dependent on the labor vote, the Midwestern farmers of Swedish descent would hesitate to support it until the labor leaders have proved more conclusively their sense of responsibility for the country as a whole, as they have in Sweden. In Minnesota the Swedish voters did support such Democratic governors as John Lind and John A. Johnson, irrespective of party affiliations, but, in retrospect, every one now admits both these men were good executives. As a rule the Swedes are less nationalistic than most other immigrant groups, much less so, for instance, than the Irish whose quick, emotional reactions they lack. Among the Swedes personal leadership or mass appeal is harder to achieve.

In 1948 Governor Dewey carried the thinly populated farm states of Kansas, Nebraska, South and North Dakota, while Truman won in Minnesota, Wisconsin, Iowa, and Illinois. In Minnesota, Hubert H. Humphrey, the young Democratic Mayor of Minneapolis, was elected United States Senator over Joseph Ball, but at the same time the Republican Governor, Luther W. Youngdahl, was re-elected without difficulty, as were the Republican governors, Frank Carlson in Kansas, and Val Peterson in Nebraska. In Colorado, Senator Edwin C. Johnson, a Democrat, was re-elected for a third term, but in Washington, the Democratic Governor, Mon C. Wallgren, was defeated, though his personal friend, President Truman, carried the state—all of which indicates that voters of Swedish origin are not party-bound.

Various writers have applied to the Swedes in America such terms as "reticent," "phlegmatic," and even "melancholy," but they have also called them "frank," "happy," and "vociferous," especially when under the influence of alcohol or religion. Their vitality and exuberance are reflected in Erskine Caldwell's famous Vermont Story, "A Country Full of Swedes." (Obviously, if that state did have more Swedes, it would be better off!) Undoubtedly they sometimes are solemn, stern, and stiff-necked and, when aroused, intemperate and profane. They are known to be kind, patient, polite, clean, both as to clothes and surroundings, but they can also be proud, sensitive, and introspective. As a rule they are rated as being honest and conscientious. Their sense of responsibility for their families, their jobs, and their property is very deep. In all things they have a perseverance that sometimes touches obstinacy. Like most immigrants, who almost invariably came from the so-called lower classes in every country, they at first appeared naive, or simple-minded, which was usually due to ignorance, but they were also shrewd and by degrees, as they felt more at home, they became more sociable. Ignorance of English was their greatest handicap. Neither the Irish nor the Scotch suffered from that.

They have at times been called "dumb," but the records of their children in the American public schools, colleges, and universities indicate the contrary. Their marks are usually among the highest. Their mental reactions sometimes may seem slow, but this is often due to a desire to be sure. A Swedish teacher of mathematics is quoted as having exclaimed when a pupil said that he *believed* he had the right solution to a problem, "Believe? Believe? That you can do in church, but here you must stake your immortal soul on it."

When a boy, one of the authors of this book worked in a Connecticut shop in which men of many nationalities were employed. From his observations there he is inclined to believe that the term "dumb" often meant that certain Swedish *greenhorns,* working by the hour, did not know enough to "kill time," that is, loaf on the job. They were just "dumb." But when later some of these "dumb Swedes" were made foremen, their scornful fellow workers couldn't understand why. The average Swede is likely to be honest when working for someone else, and even do a little more than he has to. In that respect he may be naive.

The physical sturdiness of the Swedes, like that of their fellow Scandinavians, has become proverbial. The legendary "big Swede" or "terrible Swede" type, probably stems from the physical size and strength of many of the pioneers, especially those working in the forests of the Northwest. Some of the mythical Paul Bunyan feats are supposed to have been first attributed to them. Their improvement in mental alertness after arriving in the United States has been credited to the sharper competition. As they remain in America they sometimes decline physically, but seldom mentally. Certainly, many lose their ruddy, facial color, though this may be due to the change in the climate or diet. In the early days many suffered severely from loneliness and homesickness and even today the incidence among them of tuberculosis and insanity is said to be relatively high. Undoubtedly the Swede's inborn sensitive, serious and sometimes brooding nature has helped produce this result.

The Swedes are also supposed to be deficient in a sense of humor. No doubt some of them are. But their inherited type of humor is more like the English than the American. It is apt to be quiet, dry and reserved, rather than exuberant or boisterous. Like the English and their own Norse forebears, they chuckle at the humor of understatement which seems to be unknown to many of the other national groups in the United States to whom only exaggerations seem funny. But to some people this characteristic seems a sign of a high mentality.

Generally a Swede is ambitious, eager to get ahead in his work or profession. His goal is to become his own boss. If he is a farmer he loves his soil and tries to improve it. Likewise he tries to own his home and then improve that. At his place of work he takes intense pride in the perfection of his output. In the machine shops of New England he is usually a pattern maker or employed at other tasks requiring precision. In such work he frequently becomes a foreman, a leader of labor in the literal sense. Usually he is industrious; in Sweden the corresponding word, *flitig,* is held in the highest regard, while, conversely, the word for lazy, *lat,* is the very nadir of disapproval. The average Swedish worker would not be happy leaning on a shovel. Even in times of depression he is seldom unemployed. But he also expects the employer to treat him fairly and do his part. If not, he does not hesitate to strike. At the same time, he is usually open to negotiation. In such matters few Swedes are unreasonable. They do not object to hard work if it brings them proper rewards—financial security for themselves and their families. Without work they are not happy.

Few Swedes have so far become millionaires, but the number with comfortable incomes is probably larger than commonly supposed. It is not a Swedish custom to display all wealth in the front window. When they die, the tax appraisals often bring surprises. Nor are many Swedes on the relief rolls. A Swedish tramp would seem a disgrace to the nation. Before asking for public relief those in unfortunate circumstances are likely to be aided first of all by their own Swedish friends and neighbors. To such appeals the latter seldom turn a deaf ear, that is unless the supplicants have only themselves to blame.

The Swedish cooks and housemaids who were once a boon to so many American households did not always come from humble homes in Sweden, nor did they always remain in domestic service. For a few years many of them were willing to do housework in a foreign country while they learned the language and American customs. In their native land some of them would have been too proud to do housework for others. In America they felt more independent. If they did not get married, they generally tried to qualify for better jobs. No longer are many such houseworkers to be had, and while Sweden remains an independent country, they probably never will be. In Sweden itself there is a similar shortage of domestic servants.

An American traveler, Laurence Longley, on returning from Sweden, once remarked that the Swedes were too "damnably sane." Their common sense and appreciation of relative values were disconcerting to a foreigner. His remark was intended, of course, to be a compliment. What he referred to was their practice of moderation, the Greek formula of "nothing to excess" or the French principle of *surtout pas de zèle*—the "Middle Way" of Marquis W. Childs. The Swedish word is *lagom,* or "just about right," or "neither too much nor too little," a word for which no exact equivalent is found in English.

The Swedes do not easily get excited or become boisterous, except when under the influence of liquor. They are not, as a rule, *temperamental,* but take things as they come. Their Viking ancestors were fatalists who believed certain things were bound to happen anyway; it was all in the hands of the gods, so why fret unduly? The Swedes are not only diligent physical workers, they are also apt to be dreamers, stargazers, mystics, and at times even believers in the occult.

Coming from a land that was once desperately poor, the Swede is thrifty, but without miserliness, and this quality he has brought to America. He does not like poverty, and so does something about it. Neither does he care inordinately for great wealth, but has no ethical objection to it. Usually he saves some of his earnings, but as soon as he has money available, he becomes a good spender, even at times a borrower, if he feels a strong desire for something. He has a decided liking for certain pleasant and generally laudable forms of extravagance, especially when it is a question of improving his home. He likes a high standard of living and is a good customer for all kinds of gadgets and machinery, such as radios, refrigerators, and washing machines. He must have as comfortable a home as possible, with good furniture, and as nice a lawn as possible. In most instances he spends less for books or works of art. Houses in which Swedes live usually look tidy, both inside and out. The Swede enjoys good food and likes to entertain friends, sometimes more generously than he can afford. He loves social gatherings, travel, motor cars, airplanes. It goes against his inherited instincts, for instance, to welcome a visitor without offering him something to smoke, eat or drink—a cigar, a cocktail, or at least a cup of coffee. If he serves a meal, it is apt to be a little more elaborate than really necessary. The abundance and variety of dishes in the Swedish *smörgåsbord* is an expression of this desire for display. Introduced in America by the more affluent of the former immigrants as well as by former American visitors to Sweden, it has become popular in wide circles. The word itself has recently been admitted to the *Unabridged* Webster's Dictionary.

Has the Swede any social graces or ambitions? Often he seems inordinately shy and retiring. In the past he has often failed to push himself forward socially as much as he might have done. But as a rule all Swedes, particularly those in urban communities, take part in club and lodge life, singing societies, sports events, and dances. They are, in fact, inveterate "joiners." In the rural districts their social activities are likely to be confined to church or lodge affairs. In the art of folk dancing the Swedes have made a delightful contribution to this country and ought to be encouraged to practice it more. Among the wealthier or "higher up" Swedes, sometimes labeled "cut glass" Swedes, a phrase that harks back to a past era, there is a penchant for formal dinners and receptions, a craving for such distinctions as titles, royal decorations, or honorary degrees, which usually have little or no academic justification. All such fripperies indicate, of course, a feeling of social insecurity, a craving for personal recognition. On the other hand, their adaptability is exemplified by frequent intermarriages with Americans of other ethnic groups, including members of the older stocks. In other words, the Swedes are not clannish.

Most Swedes are serious-minded. The adage that some people are happiest when sad, applies to them. They like music in the minor key— an inheritance from the traditional Swedish folk songs. The Lutheran form of worship, in which most were brought up, is noted for its almost medieval solemnity, ceremonial chants, stately hymns, long sermons, and dark vestments. In reaction to all this heaviness and pomposity, the Free churches have gone to the other extreme with their revivalism, pietism, and other forms of religious excesses, which are sometimes expressed in a well-nigh fanatic degree of missionary zeal. In America the Salvation Army has many members who are of Swedish origin. Others are Seventh Day Adventists, Pentecostalists, Latter Day Saints, or Jehovah's Witnesses, as the former Russellites now call themselves. In most of the older churches, on the other hand, a good deal of rationalism has crept in and the fire and brimstone sermons of a generation or so ago are now considered old-fashioned, though long, lugubrious, funeral sermons are still preached. In general, the average Swede is more light hearted than he appears on the surface.

Closely related to his religiosity, seriousness of purpose, and sense of personal responsibility, is his civic morality. Among all Scandinavian immigrants and their descendants the rate of criminality is low. The Swedish-sounding names sometimes adopted by professional criminals, such as the late "Baby Face" Nelson, are but disguises. Even Communist leaders of Slavic origin have been known to give themselves Scandinavian names. The most frequent petty offense of which the Swedish immigrants have been guilty has been drunkenness, but in general they have been peaceable and respectful of law and order.

Like their fellow Scandinavians, including the Finns, as well as the Germans and the Swiss, the Swedes are free from illiteracy. Only some of the very earliest pioneers of a hundred years ago were not able to write at least their own names, and practically all could read the Bible and religious works like the sermons by Luther and other German theologians. Carl Sandburg's father was not able to write, but he could read ordinary prose. The average Swede has a deep respect for culture, with the possible exception of certain successful businessmen and industrialists who have made their mark without much formal education. To get their children educated many Swedish parents have made heavy sacrifices and in most cases they feel they have been amply rewarded.

The besetting sin of the Swedes in America, as it is of those in Sweden, is a feeling of envy of the personal success of other Swedes, especially if they are old acquaintances or came from the same town in Sweden. If a distant Swede reaches true fame or public eminence such as a high office, or academic or literary distinction, they rejoice, but if he is a former neighbor and builds a better house, buys a more modern car, or wears finer clothes, or gets a slightly better job, they are apt to feel an irrational resentment. Perhaps this is a remnant of the often too marked class distinctions in Sweden based on inherited rank or wealth or other unfair privileges and not on personal merit or accomplishment. Unlike the lower classes in England, for instance, the Swedes do not "know their place." They do not "struggle against emancipation" to quote Emily Hahn. Their slogan is rather the French Revolutionary "liberty, fraternity and equality." By long tradition they have been taught to respect persons in authority, but they also want to have the right to remove them, if they so choose. The deep reverence they feel for the King is partly symbolic as long as he remains an emblem of the state, but, in reality, a purely personal tribute.

In the United States the younger generation has acquired more of the general American spirit of generosity. Here, they feel, is more room for talent, less crowding for place and preferment, less favoritism for sons or sons-in-law. Gradually the old tendency to jealousy will therefore be bred out. As a matter of fact, the feeling may basically be but the reverse of the intense interest the Swedes take in each other, so clearly shown by their willingness to help in times of misfortune. But let no man vaunt himself. Bang, goes a bash on his head! "He needs to be reminded of his mortality," is a frequent Swedish expression which corresponds to the American dislike for any one who begins to "throw his weight around."

On the whole, there is little cause to worry about the character of the future Americans who stem from Sweden. Like the other Scandinavians they have usually become more soundly and thoroughly Americanized than the descendants of any other immigrant group. Some of their forebears have been here a long time and as they themselves study more closely their own history they will see that their ancestors too have had a big share in the making of the country.

BIBLIOGRAPHY

PART 1—HISTORICAL BACKGROUND

CHAPTER I: COLONIZATION AND TRADE

History of Sweden by Carl Hallendorf and Adolf Schück. Stockholm, 1938.

A History of Sweden by Andrew A. Stomberg. New York, 1931.

A Short History of Sweden by Ragnar Svanström and Carl Fredrik Palmstierna. Oxford, 1934.

A History of Sweden by Carl Grimberg. Rock Island (Ill.), 1935. Popular.

The Adventures and Escapes of Gustavus Vasa by Hendrik Willem Van Loon. New York, 1945. Popular.

Gustaf Adolf, the Great by Nils Ahnlund. New York, 1940.

The Swedish Settlements on the Delaware by Amandus Johnson. 2 vols. Philadelphia, 1911. The authoritative work on the subject.

The Dutch and the Swedes on the Delaware by Christopher Ward. Philadelphia, 1930. Popular.

Documents Relating to the History of the Dutch and Swedish Settlements on the Delaware River. B. Fernow, compiler. Albany, 1877.

The Log Cabin Myth by Harold R. Shurtleff. Edited by Samuel Eliot Morison. Cambridge (Mass.), 1939.

"Colonial Landmarks" by George H. Ryden. Chapter in *Swedes in America.* New Haven (Conn.), 1938.

Geographia Americae, With an Account of the Delaware Indians, based on Surveys and Notes made in 1654–1656. By Peter Lindeström. Translated by Amandus Johnson. Philadelphia, 1925.

The Instructions for Johan Printz, Governor of New Sweden. Translated by Amandus Johnson. Philadelphia, 1930.

A Catalogue of Books & Manuscripts Relating to Swedish Colonization on the Delaware River. Compiled by Julian P. Boyd. Philadelphia, 1938.

Willem Usselinx, Founder of the Dutch and Swedish West India Companys by J. Franklin Jameson. Papers of the Am. Hist. Association, Vol. II, No. 3. New York, 1887.

CHAPTER II: EARLY CULTURAL RELATIONS

Annals of the Swedes on the Delaware by Jehu Curtis Clay (1792–1863). Fourth ed., with an Introduction by Henry S. Henschen. Chicago, 1938.

A Short Description of the Province of New Sweden by Thomas Campanius Holm. Translated by Peter S. du Ponceau. Philadelphia, 1834.

The Records of the Swedish Lutheran Churches at Raccoon and Penns Neck, 1713–1786. Translated and compiled by the Federal Writers Project. Introduction and notes by Amandus Johnson. Trenton (N. J.), 1938.

"The Swedish Language in America" by Axel Johan Uppvall. In *Swedes in America,* New Haven (Conn.), 1938.

"History of the Swedes in the Eastern States from the Earliest Times Until 1782" by Amandus Johnson. In *The Swedish Element in America*, Vol. II. Chicago, 1931.

The Journal and Biography of Nicholas Collin, 1746–1831 by Amandus Johnson. Philadelphia, 1936.

Martin Luther's Little Catechism. Translated into Algonquian Indian by Johannes Campanius. Facsimile of the edition printed in Stockholm in 1696, with some notes by Isak Collijn. Stockholm, 1938.

John Campanius' Delaware Translation of the Catechism by Nils Holmer. Uppsala, 1946.

New Sweden on the Delaware by Christopher Ward. Philadelphia, 1938.

Journal of Andreas Hesselius. Translated by Amandus Johnson. Philadelphia, 1947.

Peter Kalm's Travels in North America, 1748–51. English version of 1770, revised and edited by Adolph B. Benson. New York, 1937.

A History of New Sweden by Israel Acrelius. Translated by William M. Reynolds. Philadelphia, 1874.

Amerika i Svensk Litteratur av Harald Elovson. Lund, 1930.

"Representatives of the Intellect" by David F. Swenson. In *Swedes in America*. New Haven (Conn.), 1938.

Where Pennsylvania History Began by Henry D. Paxson. Philadelphia, 1926.

" 'Old Swedes' Churches" by George H. Ryden. *Am. Swed. Monthly* (New York), June, 1938.

Scandinavian Immigrants in New York, 1630–1674 by John O. Evjen. Minneapolis, 1916.

"President Roosevelt's Swedish Ancestry" by Vilhelm Berger. *Am. Swed. Monthly* (New York), April, 1934.

CHAPTER III: "A STATE CREATES ITSELF"

"John Morton" by M. Atherton Leach. *The Am. Scand. Review,* July–August, 1915.

John Hanson, Our First President by Seymour Wemyss Smith. New York, 1932.

John Hanson and the Inseparable Union by Jacob A. Nelson. Boston, 1939.

"President John Hanson, Father of American Unity" by Frank W. Melvin. in *The Will to Succeed, Stories of Swedish Pioneers*. New York, 1948.

Sweden and the American Revolution by Adolph B. Benson. New Haven (Conn.), 1926. Bibliography.

The Naval Campaigns of Count De Grasse During the American Revolution 1781–1783 by Karl Gustaf Tornquist. Translated with notes by Amandus Johnson. Philadelphia, 1942.

"Former Swedish Officer Directs Settlement in Colonial Louisiana" by Adolph B. Benson. *Year Book,* Am. Swed. Hist. Found. Philadelphia, 1944.

Longfellow and Scandinavia by Andrew Hilen. New Haven (Conn.), 1937.

"The Dawn of a New Day" by George M. Stephenson. In *The Religious Aspect of Swedish Immigration*. Minneapolis, 1932.

CHAPTER IV: THE EARLY SWEDISH PIONEERS

The Background of Swedish Emigration by Florence E. Janson. Chicago, 1931.

The Background of Swedish Emigration to the United States by John S. Lindberg. Minneapolis, 1930.

"John Lindmark, Versatile Swedish Immigrant in New York" by Adolph B. Benson. *Year Book,* Am. Swed. Hist. Found. Philadelphia, 1946.

"Texas, the Lone Star State, and Its Swedish Settlements" by Carl M. Bergquist. In *The Swedish Element in America*, Vol. I. Chicago, 1931.

"The Swedes of Texas" by Carl M. Rosenquist. *Year Book,* Am. Swed. Hist. Found. Philadelphia, 1945.

"Sven M. Swenson, The First Swede in Texas" by Margaret Barclay. In *The Will to Succeed, Stories of Swedish Pioneers*. New York, 1948.

"Sir Svante Palm's Legacy to Texas" by Mayme Evans. *Am. Scand. Review,* Spring, 1949.

"SMS Ranch" by Mary Whatley Clarke. *The Cattleman* (Fort Worth, Texas), March, 1948.

Minnen Från En Sjuttonårig Vistelse i Nordvestra Amerika. av Gustaf Unonius. Vols. I–II. Uppsala, 1861–1862.

New Upsala, The First Swedish Settlement in Wisconsin by Filip A. Forsbeck. Milwaukee, 1936.

"Pioneering in Wisconsin a Century Ago" by George M. Stephenson. *Am. Swed. Monthly* (New York), Nov., 1941.

"A Lieutenant and His Lady" by Victor M. Freeburg. *Am. Swed. Monthly* (New York), Nov., 1941. Polycarpus von Schneidau.

Summer on the Lakes in 1843 by Margaret Fuller. Boston, 1844.

Homes of the New World by Fredrika Bremer. New York, 1853.

America of the Fifties. Edited with Introduction by Adolph B. Benson. New York, 1924. Letters of Fredrika Bremer.

"The Early Swedish Settlements in Iowa." In *The Swedish Element in America,* Vol. I. Edited by Erik G. Westman. Chicago, 1931.

"Early Swedes in Iowa" by Eskil Carlson and Oval Quist. *Am. Swed. Monthly* (New York), June, 1948.

"Historik" (Jamestown, N.Y.) av Julius Lincoln. In *Minnes-Album.* Rock Island (Ill.), 1907.

"Chandlers Valley Pioneers" by Evald Benjamin Lawson. *Am. Swed. Monthly* (New York), July, 1941.

"The Swedish People in Jamestown, New York," by Jennie Vimmerstedt. In *The Swedish Element in America,* Vol. I. Chicago, 1931.

CHAPTER V: HOW THE SWEDES SETTLED IN ILLINOIS

The Swedish Element in Illinois by Ernst W. Olson. Chicago, 1917.

"The Story of Illinois and the Swedish People Within Its Borders" by Oliver A. Linder. In *The Swedish Element in America,* Vol. I. Chicago, 1931.

"Olof Gustaf Hedstrom, Pioneer Leader of Swedish Methodism" by Evald Benjamin Lawson. *Year Book,* Am. Swed. Hist. Found. Philadelphia, 1945.

"The Beginnings of Swedish Immigration Into Illinois 100 Years Ago" by Conrad Bergendoff. *Am. Swed. Monthly* (New York), June, 1948.

"Eric-Jansonism and the Bishop Hill Colony" by George M. Stephenson. In *The Religious Aspect of Swedish Immigration.* Minneapolis, 1932.

"Erik (*sic*) Janson and the Bishop Hill Colony" by Sivert Erdahl. In *Illinois State Historical Society Journal,* 1925.

The Bishop Hill Colony by M. A. Mikkelson. In Johns Hopkins University *Studies in Historical and Political Science.* Baltimore, 1892.

"The Bishop Hill Settlement" by David E. Lindstrom. *Year Book,* Am. Swed. Hist. Found. Philadelphia, 1945.

"The First Swedes in Chicago" by Nils William Olsson. *Am. Swed. Monthly* (New York), June, 1948.

"The City of Rockford and the Share of the Swedes in Its Development" by Carl Hjalmar Lundquist. In *Swedish Element in America,* Vol. I. Chicago, 1931.

CHAPTER VI: THE SWEDES IN THE CIVIL WAR

The Swedish Element in Illinois by Ernst W. Olson. Chicago, 1917.

Swedish Immigrants in Lincoln's Time by Nels Hokanson. Foreword by Carl Sandburg. New York, 1942.

"Soldiers and Sailors" by Nils G. Sahlin. In *Swedes in America.* New Haven (Conn.), 1938.

The Life of John Ericsson by William C. Church. New York, 1911.

Battle of the Ironclads by Louis A. Roe. New York, 1942.

Memoirs of Admiral John A. Dahlgren by M. V. Dahlgren. Boston, 1882.
"Dahlgren of the American Navy" by Gloria V. Cappola. In *The Will to Succeed, Stories of Swedish Pioneers*. New York, 1948.
"Swedish-born Graduates of West Point" by George T. Ness. *Am. Swed. Monthly* (New York), Dec., 1946.

CHAPTER VII: THE MASS MIGRATION OF THE SWEDES

"Swedish Immigrant Guide Books in the Early 1850's" by Märtha Ångström. *Year Book,* Am. Swed. Hist. Found. Philadelphia, 1947.
"Frontiersmen of Minnesota" by Roy Swanson. *Am. Swed. Monthly* (New York), June, 1948.
"Sweden in Fiction" by Edith Paine Benedict. *Am. Swed. Monthly* (New York), June, 1936.
"Amerikanskt Inflytande i Svenska Folkrörelser" av Gunnar Westin i *Nordisk Familjeboks Månadskrönika*, June, 1938.
A History of the Swedish Americans of Minnesota by Algot E. Strand. Vols. I–III. Chicago, 1910.
Reminiscences, The Story of an Immigrant by Colonel Hans Mattson. St. Paul (Minn.), 1891.
The Swedes and the Swedish Settlements in North America by Helge Nelson. Lund, 1943.
Decennial, 1870–1880, New Sweden, State of Maine by the Rev. A. A. Wirén. Republished by Marie Valborg Malmquist, Stoneham (Mass.), 1931.
"The New Sweden Settlement in the State of Maine." In *The Swedish Element in America*, Vol. I. Chicago, 1931.
"A Noble Experiment" (New Sweden, Maine) by Wallace E. Cedarleaf. In *The Will to Succeed, Stories of the Swedish Pioneers*. New York, 1948.
"Pioneers in Nebraska" by Joseph Alexis. *Am. Swed. Monthly* (New York), June, 1948.
O! Pioneers by Willa Cather. Boston, 1913. A novel.
Red Rust by Cornelia James Cannon. Boston, 1928. A novel.

PART 2—RELIGIOUS LIFE

CHAPTERS VIII–XIV

The Religious Aspect of Swedish Immigration by George M. Stephenson. Minneapolis, 1932. The authoritative work on the subject includes a comprehensive Bibliography.
"Religion" by George M. Stephenson. In *Swedes in America*, New Haven (Conn.), 1938.
"Churches" by Oscar N. Olson. In *American Swedish Handbook*. Rock Island (Ill.), 1948. Background and statistics.
Svenskarna i Amerika. Edited by Karl Hildebrand and Axel Fredenholm. Vols. I–II. Stockholm, 1924, 1925.
Minnen av Gustaf Unonius. Uppsala, 1861–1862.
"Swedish Methodism in America" by C. G. Wallenius and Ernst W. Olson. In *The Swedish Element in America*, Vol. II. Chicago, 1931.
De svenska lutherska församlingarnas och svenskarnes historia i Amerika av Erik Norelius. Vols. I–II. Rock Island (Ill.), 1890, 1914.
Early Life of Eric (sic) *Norelius*. Translated by Emory Johnson. Rock Island (Ill.), 1934.
"The Augustana Synod, Its History and Development" by Dr. Gustav Andreen. In *The Swedish Element in America*, Vol. II. Chicago, 1931.
A Century of [Lutheran] *Life and Growth* by Oscar N. Olson. Rock Island (Ill.), 1948.
Andreen of Augustana by Associates, Family, and Friends. Rock Island (Ill.), 1942.
"The Swedish People of Kansas and Adjoining States" by Ernst F. Pihlblad. In *The Swedish Element in America*, Vol. I. Chicago, 1931.

Olof Olsson, The Man, His Work, and His Thought by Ernst W. Olson. Rock Island (Ill.), 1941.

The Swedish Settlements in Kansas by Alfred Bergin. Rock Island (Ill.), 1909.

Swedish Baptists in America by J. O. Backlund. Chicago, 1933.

A Pioneer Trio, Fredrik Olaus Nilsson, Gustaf Palmquist, Anders Wiberg by Jonas Oscar Backlund. Chicago, N.D.

K. O. Broady, En levnadsteckning av N. J. Nordström. Stockholm, 1922.

"The Swedish People of Utah and in the Mormon Church" by Andrew Jenson. In *The Swedish Element in America*, Vol. I. Chicago, 1931.

"Ola Nilsson Liljenquist and His Cooperative City" by William Mulder. In *The Will to Succeed, Stories of Swedish Pioneers*. New York, 1948.

"History of the Swedish Mission Friends in America" by David Nyvall. In *The Swedish Element in America*, Vol. II. Chicago, 1931.

PART 3—DENOMINATIONAL EDUCATION

CHAPTERS XV–XXII

"Colleges" by Ernst W. Olson. In *Swedes in America*. New Haven (Conn.), 1938.

"Colleges" by Peter P. Person. In *American Swedish Handbook*. Rock Island (Ill.), 1948.

"When Upsala Moved to the Garden State, The Saga of a College" by Evald Benjamin Lawson. *Lutheran Companion*. (Rock Island, Ill.) October 20, 1948.

A History of North Park College by Leland H. Carlson. Chicago, 1941.

John Alexis Edgren, Soldier, Educator, Author, Journalist by L. J. Ahlstrom. Chicago, 1938.

Seventy-Five Years—Bethel Theological Seminary by Adolf Olson and Virgil A. Olson. Chicago, 1946.

PART 4—AMERICAN ACTIVITIES

CHAPTER XXIII: LAWYERS AND PUBLIC OFFICIALS

"Lawyers" by G. Aaron Youngquist. In *Swedes in America*. New Haven (Conn.), 1938.

John Lind of Minnesota by George M. Stephenson. Minneapolis, 1935.

"John Albert Johnson, Three Times Governor of Minnesota" by Harriet Bunn. In *The Will to Succeed, Stories of Swedish Pioneers*. New York, 1948.

"Governor Youngdahl and the Gamblers" by Rufus Jarman. *Sat. Ev. Post*, Dec. 3, 1947.

"Mike Holm, Ten Times Minnesota's Secretary of State" by Roy W. Swanson. *Am. Swed. Monthly* (New York), May, 1940.

The Lindberghs by Lynn and Dora B. Haines. New York, 1931.

"Father, Like Son" by Walter Eli Quigley. *Sat. Ev. Post*, June 21, 1941.

"Public Officials" by O. Fritiof Ander. In *Swedes in America*. New Haven (Conn.), 1938.

"Participation of the Swedes in American Politics." In *The Swedish Element in America*, Vol. I. Chicago, 1931.

Autobiography by Samuel A. Carlson, Mayor of Jamestown. Jamestown (N.Y.), 1943.

"Gotham's Guardian of Law and Order, a Sketch of the Life of Arthur William Wallander" by Cedric Larson. In *The Will to Succeed, Stories of Swedish Pioneers*. New York, 1948.

CHAPTER XXIV: ARCHITECTS AND BUILDERS

"Architects and Builders" by C. Theodore Larson. In *Swedes in America*. New Haven (Conn.), 1938.

"Swedish Architects in Illinois" by John A. Nyden. In *The Swedish Element in America*, Vol. II. Chicago, 1931.

"Some Swedish Business Pioneers in Washington" by Svante Lofgren. *Year Book*, Am. Swed. Hist. Found. Philadelphia, 1947.

CHAPTER XXV: SCIENTISTS AND EDUCATORS

"Professors" by Adolph B. Benson; "Public School Educators" by O. Fritiof Ander. In
Swedes in America. New Haven (Conn.), 1938.
"Physiologist Carlson, Scientist's Scientist." *Time,* Feb. 10, 1941. Cover story.
"The Man who Understands Your Stomach" (Anton J. Carlson) by R. M. Cunningham,
Jr. and Greer Williams. *Sat. Ev. Post,* Sept. 13, 1947.
"Granite in His Bread" (Anton J. Carlson) by Dorothy Gobelle; "A Questing Norseman"
(George Norlin) by Hulda Forsman; "And So Our Lord Created the Smålander"
(Blenda Olson) by Mrs. Earl A. Gulbrandsen. In *The Will to Succeed, Stories of
Swedish Pioneers.* New York, 1948.
"Gustavus A. Eisen, Scholar and Benefactor" by Edgar Swenson. *Am. Swed. Monthly*
(New York), Nov. 1935.
The Other Side of Main Street. History of a Swedish-born Teacher From Sauk Center by
Henry Johnson. New York, 1943.

CHAPTER XXVI: HEALTH SPECIALISTS

"Doctors" by Selma Giving and David L. Tilderquist; "Gymnastics" by Theodore Me-
lander. In *Swedes in America.* New Haven (Conn.), 1938.
"The Life of William W. Keen, M.D. LL.D." by Clare B. Bonnafon. In *The Will to
Succeed, Stories of Swedish Pioneers.* New York, 1948.
The Descendants of Göran Kyn of New Sweden by Gregory B. Keen, LL.D. Philadelphia,
1913.
"Plantation Babies Okay Now" (Dr. Nils P. Larsen) by Blake Clark. *The Reader's Digest,*
Jan. 1927.

CHAPTER XXVII: WRITERS

"Melting-Pot Literature" by Carl Wittke. *College English,* Jan., 1946.
Pennfäktare, Svensk-Amerikanska Författare och Tidningsmän av Ernst Skarstedt. Stock-
holm, 1930.
La Littérature suédoise d'Amérique par Joseph E. A. Alexis. Paris, 1930.
"Swedish American Literature" by Adolph B. Benson. In *The History of Scandinavian
Literatures* by Giovanni Bach. Edited by Frederika Blankner. New York, 1938.
"Swedish American Literature" by Jakob Bonggren. In *The Swedish Element in America,*
Vol. II. Chicago, 1931.
Carl Sandburg, A Study in Personality and Background by Karl Detzer. New York, 1941.
"Newspapers" by Oliver A. Linder. In *Swedes in America.* New Haven (Conn.), 1938.
"The Swedish-American Press. In *American Swedish Handbook.* Rock Island (Ill.), 1948.
"The Swedish-American Press Nears its Century Mark" by Edgar Swenson. *Am. Swed.
Monthly* (New York), Aug., 1948.

CHAPTER XXVIII: MUSICIANS AND ACTORS

"Swedish Song in America" by Hjalmar Nilsson. In *The Swedish Element in America,*
Vol. II. Chicago, 1931.
Jenny Lind by Edward Wagenknecht. Boston, 1931.
Enchanting Jenny Lind by Laura Benét. New York, 1939.
"Composers" by Victor Nilsson; "Opera Singers" by Marie Sundelius; "Stage and Radio
Performers" by Holger Lundbergh; "Moving Picture Actors" by Leonard Clairmont.
In *Swedes in America,* New Haven (Conn.), 1938.

CHAPTER XXIX: ARTISTS

"Scandinavian Contributions to Early American Art" by Willietta Goddard Ball. *Am.
Scand. Review,* Jan., 1915.

"Painters and Sculptors" by Oliver A. Linder. In *Swedes in America*. New Haven (Conn.), 1938.

"Swedish American Art and Artists" by Jacob Bonggren. In *The Swedish Element in America*, Vol. II. Chicago, 1931.

From Forecastle to Academy: Sailor and Artist, Autobiography by Lars Gustaf Sellstedt. Buffalo, 1904.

Lars Gustav (sic) *Sellstedt* by Henry Ware Sprague. Buffalo, 1913.

The Testament of Caliban by David Edstrom. New York, 1937.

Carl Milles, An Interpretation of His Work by Meyric R. Rogers. New Haven (Conn.), 1940.

CHAPTER XXX: INDUSTRIALISTS

"Farmers" by Eric Englund; "Inventors" by Johan Liljencrants; "Engineers" by Lawrence E. Widmark; and "Manufacturers" by Bernard Peterson. In *Swedes in America*, New Haven (Conn.), 1938.

Our Viking Industrialists by W. Elmer Ekblaw. Worcester (Mass.), 1946.

"Swedish American History in Lower Michigan" (Detroit) by C. E. Hoffsten; "Swedish American Life in Jamestown" by Lloyd L. Malmstrom. In *The Swedish Element in America*, Vol. IV. 1934.

"Rockford, in Illinois, Retains Its Swedish Flavor" by Herman G. Nelson. *Am. Swed. Monthly* (New York), June, 1948.

"Worcester, Mass. and Its Swedish American Population." In *The Swedish Element in America*, Vol. I. Chicago, 1931.

"Celluloid Jewelry—Berkander Got the Idea First" by Garrett D. Byrnes. *Am. Swed. Monthly* (New York), Jan., 1937.

"Ernst F. W. Alexanderson, Inventor Extraordinary" by Ruth Carlson Frankel; "Great-Hearted Genius, Emil Tyden, Inventor, Industrialist, Philanthropist" by Nancy R. Wait. In *The Will to Succeed, Stories of Swedish Pioneers*. New York, 1948.

CHAPTER XXXI: AVIATORS AND AIRPLANE BUILDERS

"Aviation" by John Goldstrom. In *Swedes in America*. New Haven (Conn.), 1938.

"Out of the Doghouse" (Philip Johnson) by W. L. White. *Sat. Ev. Post*, Nov. 15, 1941.

"Charles Augustus Lindbergh" by James Creese. *Am. Scand. Review* (New York), Aug., 1927.

"Army Flyer Pioneers at Labrador Base" (Bert R. J. Hassell) by Herman G. Nelson. *Am. Swed. Monthly* (New York), Feb., 1945.

CHAPTER XXXII: BUSINESSMEN

"History of the Swedes in the Eastern States, 1783–1841" by Amandus Johnson. In *The Swedish Element in America*, Vol. IV. Chicago, 1934.

"Big Butter and Egg Man" (Carl A. Swanson). *Fortune Magazine*, Oct., 1943.

"C. A. Swanson, the Turkey King" by Joseph A. Moore. *Am. Swed. Monthly* (New York), Dec., 1945.

"Businessmen" by Gustaf Sundelius; and "Imports and Importers" by Victor O. Freeburg. In *Swedes in America*. New Haven (Conn.), 1938.

"Publishing and Printing" by Ernst W. Olson. In *The Swedish Element in Illinois*. Chicago, 1917.

"Captain William Matson, a Modern Viking" by J. S. Schnell. In *The Will to Succeed, Stories of Swedish Pioneers*. New York, 1948.

"Ahoy, Australia; Ahoy, New Zealand" (Matson Line) by Peter B. Kyne. *Sat. Ev. Post*. Oct. 24, 1934.

"White Ships of the Viking Trail" (Swedish American Line) by Holger Lundbergh. *Am. Swed. Monthly* (New York), 1936.

"Map King of New York" (Andrew G. Hagstrom) by Cedric Larson. *Am. Swed. Monthly* (New York), July, 1948.

CHAPTER XXXIII: CHARITIES AND OTHER ORGANIZATIONS

"Histories of Fraternal Orders." In *The Swedish Element in America,* Vol. II. Chicago, 1931.

"Charities and Selfhelp" by Julius Lincoln. In *Swedes in America.* New Haven (Conn.), 1938.

"Welfare Institutions" by C. G. Carlfelt. In *American Swedish Handbook.* Rock Island (Ill.), 1948.

"Twenty Years of Service" (American Swedish Historical Museum) by Naboth Hedin. *Am. Swed. Monthly* (New York), Nov., 1946.

CHAPTER XXXIV: SPORTS

"Sports and Sportsmen" by Gerhard T. Rooth. In *Swedes in America.* New Haven (Conn.), 1938.

On the Mat and Off by Hjalmar Lundin. New York, 1937.

CHAPTER XXXV: THE CHARACTER OF SWEDES FROM AMERICA

The Scandinavian Element in the United States by Kendrick Charles Babcock. Urbana (Ill.), 1914.

"Our Foreigners." In *The Chronicles of America.* New Haven (Conn.), 1920.

These Foreigners by William B. Seabrook. New York, 1938.

Scandinavian Themes in American Fiction by George Leroy White, Jr. Philadelphia, 1937.

INDEX